SOCIETY

*The Social Life of the Teenager
and its Impact on Education*

By James S. Coleman

JOHNS HOPKINS UNIVERSITY

With the assistance of JOHN W. C. JOHNSTONE
and KURT JONASSOHN

GREENWOOD PRESS, PUBLISHERS
WESTPORT, CONNECTICUT

Library of Congress Cataloging in Publication Data

Coleman, James Samuel, 1926-
    The adolescent society.

    Reprint. Originally published: New York :
Free Press of Glencoe, 1961.
    Includes index.
    1. Adolescence. 2. Education, Secondary--United
States. 3. Education, Secondary--1945-
4. Social status. I. Johnstone, John Wallace Claire,
1931-   . II. Jonassohn, Kurt. III. Title.
HQ796.C64 1981   305.2'3   81-1737
ISBN 0-313-22934-1 (lib. bdg.) AACR2

Reprinted in 1981 by Greenwood Press
A division of Congressional Information Service, Inc.
88 Post Road West, Westport, Connecticut 06881

Printed in the United States of America

10 9 8 7 6 5 4 3 2 1

To my own high school
du Pont Manual Training High School
Louisville, Kentucky

Introduction

THIS STUDY WAS CONCEIVED IN THE spring of 1955, before the competition with Russia in science brought the current spate of interest in educational matters. It had its origins in two sources: first, a deep concern I have had, since my own high school days, with high schools and with ways to make possible their better functioning, ways to make an adolescent's experiences with learning more profitable and his whole adolescence a more satisfying period. Secondly, though not unrelated to this, was an interest in different kinds of status systems. What are the consequences, upon the people within them, of status systems which give rewards only for achievement in one particular activity, and how do they differ from the consequences of systems which equally reward many activities? Not only the consequences of status systems are of concern, but the sources as well: how does it happen that certain activities have status in a given society, and what changes will alter the distribution of status?

The conjunction of these two interests led naturally to research on high schools, schools which differed in the kinds and number of activities which brought to a boy or girl status among his fellows. One can imagine that the effect of such status systems is great, coming as they do at a time when boys and girls are in a kind of limbo, between childhood and adulthood, and thus highly responsive to the social constraints of their peers. The actual variations between adolescent status systems in high schools are of course far more complex than the single type of variation mentioned above. The research, as it has turned out, has been broadened to consider some of these other variations—such as, for example, the variation between systems where status is gained primarily by achievement and those where status is ascribed more nearly on the basis of some background characteristic, such as a family's position in the community.

The previous research in this area is not extensive, perhaps partly because of the difficulty of examining a social system, however small, in action. The two most closely related works, to which this research is indebted, are A. B. Hollingshead's *Elmtown's Youth*, and Wayne Gordon's *The Social System of the High School.*[1]

1. *Elmtown's Youth*, (New York: John Wiley, 1949), *The Social System of the High School*, (Glencoe: The Free Press, 1957).

vii

Research Design

A proposal for this research was initially written in the Spring of 1955 while I was at the Bureau of Applied Social Research at Columbia University; in the fall of 1957, when I came to the University of Chicago, a modified proposal was submitted to the U.S. Office of Education, under its Cooperative Research Program, and in January, 1957, funds were allocated for the research.

To indicate the general plan of the research and the questions it aimed to investigate, the proposal on the basis of which the funds were allocated is included in the appendix. Footnotes of two kinds are appended there: to indicate at what points in the report various hypotheses of the research are dealt with; and to indicate points at which the research design was modified. The general design of the research will be described briefly below.

a) Selection of ten schools in varying types of communities, of varying sizes, and with apparent differences in their status systems, in Spring, 1957.

b) Administration of a questionnaire by our field staff to all students in the Fall of 1957, after pretests in the Spring. (This and other questionnaires are reproduced in the appendix.)

c) Administration of a second questionnaire by our field staff to all students in the Spring of 1958.

d) Informal interviews with a number of students in each school in the Spring of 1957 and the Spring of 1958.

e) Collection of information (grades, I.Q., attendance, etc.) for every student, from school records, in Spring, 1958.

f) In addition, questionnaires were distributed to all teachers in the schools and questionnaires were mailed to all parents. However, the results of these questionnaires are used very little in the succeeding report.

The Ten Schools

In chapter 3 there will be a short description of the ten schools, and the communities in which they are located. The schools have been given fictitious names in the pages which follow, and these names give something of the flavor of the community. The schools, together with sizes of student bodies and communities are listed below.

	School	School size	Community Population
	0 Farmdale	150	1000
	1 Marketville	350	4000
small towns	2 Elmtown	500	7000
	3 Maple Grove	400	6000
	4 Green Junction	500	5000
large city (parochial)	5 St. John's High	750 (boys)	(Chicago)
suburb	6 Newlawn	1050	9000
small city	7 Millburg	1400	25,000
small city	8 Midcity	1950	100,000
suburb	9 Executive Heights	1850	17,000

The schools are all located in northern Illinois, but are not intended to be "representative" of this section. To the contrary, they were selected with diversity in mind. For example, it is likely that there are more similarities between Executive Heights, a well-to-do midwestern suburb, and Scarsdale, New York, and more similarity between Green Junction and a farm town of 5000 population in Oregon, than there are between Executive Heights and Green Junction. The results of the study, then, are not intended to apply to "schools in northern Illinois," but to all schools encompassed within the range of community composition exhibited by these schools. This range, roughly, is from prosperous farming or farming and industrial community (the five smallest schools) to working-class parochial boy's school in the center of a large city (St. John's), to new working class suburbs (Newlawn) to small cities (Millburg—heavy industry; Midcity—light industry) to well-to-do suburb (Executive Heights).

Some parts of the analysis will examine all schools together; other parts will examine each school separately. Thus the common characteristics of the adolescent culture will be examined, along with those which vary from one kind of school to another.

Acknowledgments

This research owes most of all to the ten schools who agreed to subject themselves to this research. I have come to feel that the task of a high school principal is one of the most difficult and complex of any in our society. The willingness of principals (and their school boards and teachers) to add to this difficulty and complexity by participating in research of this sort is an indication of their interest in finding ways to better carry out the task of educating adolescents.

To Roy Clark, Assistant Illinois State Superintendent of Public Instruction, and his colleagues, thanks are due for information which aided the selection of schools.

Kurt Jonassohn, John Johnstone, and I constituted the core personnel of the project throughout its whole period, from questionnaire design to analysis. Though the report thus represents the results of a cooperative effort, in particular that part of Chapter 8 dealing with mass media was analyzed and written by John Johnstone as part of his Ph.D. thesis which examines leisure use of these adolescents in general, as a function of their high school experience.[1] Kurt Jonassohn's Ph.D. thesis, parts of which were intended to be included here, will be an examination of the social structure of the communities in the study.

Of the other project personnel, those whose special efforts were particularly important to its success were Eugene Selmanoff, Thomas Long, Wayne Dockery and a two-man team who recorded grades and test scores for every student: Robert Behrens and Peter Vea. The coding staff included Robert Brown, Dorothy Chacarestos, Betty Fackler, Carolyn Huson, Nancy Johnstone, Ethan Kaplan, Claire Kuhne, and Andre Saumier.

Besides the project staff, the project received help from many persons during the research, including, among others, Jack Feldman, Clyde Hart, Everett Hughes, Paul Lazarsfeld, Martin Lipset, William McPhee, David Riesman, Albert Reiss, Natalie Rozoff, Peter Rossi, and Martin Trow. Arnold Anderson, Peter Blau, Jan Hajda, and Arthur Stinchcombe read an earlier draft of the research report and made extremely helpful comments, many of which are incorporated here. Kathy Blakeslee, a high school student in Baltimore, read the manuscript, and made valuable comments in the course of several interviews. Some of these comments have been incorporated as footnotes, suggesting similarities and differences between the schools under study and a large public girls' high school in Baltimore. To my wife, I am thankful for continued encouragement in this venture, despite the hardships it created for her.

I am grateful to Malle Lauritis, whose aid in the final stages of research was invaluable, and whose detailed editorial work on the manuscript greatly increased its readability. I am pleased also to acknowledge the aid of Martin Levin, who constructed the index, and Virginia Bonhage, who aided in general preparation of the manuscript.

1. John Johnstone, "Social Structure and Patterns of Mass Media Consumption," unpublished Ph.D. Dissertation. University of Chicago, 1961.

The National Opinion Research Center and the Operations Analysis Laboratory at the University of Chicago have been of great assistance in the use of their facilities.

Besides the grant from the U.S. Office of Education which made this research possible, financial support from three other sources made possible a far more comprehensive analysis than could otherwise have been carried out: a) a grant from the Ford Foundation to facilitate the basic research of the author; b) free time from teaching duties at the University of Chicago for the author; c) and free time from teaching duties at the Johns Hopkins University, to complete work on the manuscript.

Baltimore, Maryland JAMES S. COLEMAN

Contents

I The Emergence of an Adolescent Subculture in Industrial Society

EDUCATING ITS YOUNG IS PROBABLY A society's second most fundamental task—second only to the problem of organizing itself to carry out actions as a society. Once organized, if a society is to maintain itself, the young must be so shaped as to fit into the roles on which the society's survival depends.

It might seem that the problem of socializing the young would be handled similarly in every society, for the young, as they enter this world, are much the same everywhere. Yet the problem is faced in very different ways. A good example of this is the recent and continuing conflict between the Amish community in Ohio and the Ohio State Board of Education. The Amish, a small Protestant sect, attempting to maintain their small society as an enclave within the larger society, have views very different from those of the Ohio laws as to what constitutes a reasonable education for their young. To quote at length a news account:

Last week, by a vote of 19–2, the Ohio Board of Education ruled that two Amish high Schools—in Holmes and Tuscarawas counties—would have to measure up to state standards or close. The Amish schools, the board said, have no graded courses in geography, American and Ohio history, natural sciences, government, and other required subjects. Some teachers, the board added, have no more than an eighth-grade education.

With few textbooks, the children spend much of their school day copying phrases from their diaries into composition books. Examples: "I plowed and cleaned raspberry patch." "Ironed all day." "In the forenoon I went to church. In the afternoon I fed the turkey broilers."

Bearded Henry Hershberger, chairman of the Amish School Committee, admitted the schools didn't meet state standards, but he hoped for a compromise. "It seems that our way is quite different from what the public demands," he said. "Worldly wisdom taught in public schools conflicts with our way of life. Our religion is built around simplicity."[1]

One's first reaction to such an education might be one of sympathy for the children deprived of their birthright in a free society. Upon further consideration, however, the example illustrates not the depravity of the Amish parents, but the sharp difference in the educational task of a stable farming society and that of a rapidly changing, highly industrialized society. In a stable farming society—of which the Amish represent one of the few remaining examples within the United States—the problem of the society is simply to *reproduce* itself; to give its young members the values, habits, and skills of their parents. In such a stable, localized, and personalized society—which is not long past in our country as a whole—education is a simple task, and it is carried out as a part of the same "natural process" by which a parent teaches his child to walk or to talk. This is not to say that this process constitutes the "best of all educations in that best of all possible worlds." It is often far from it, for each child is at the mercy of his parents, and whether they are good citizens or ne'er-do-wells, the "natural processes" by which they socialize him makes him a replica of them. Nevertheless, the problem is handled as naturally within the family as is the problem of teaching a child to walk or talk.

By contrast, in an industrial society committed to equality of opportunity, there are two facts that make the task fundamentally different and more complex. The first is the fact of change itself. Our society is changing at an ever increasing rate; adults cannot afford to shape their children in their own image. Parents are often obsolescent in their skills, trained for jobs that are passing out of existence, and thus unable to transmit directly their accumulated knowledge. They come to be "out of touch with the times," and unable to understand, much less inculcate, the standards of a social order that has changed since they were young.

Second is the fact of economic specialization. In an industrial society, each father's skills are highly specialized, while his son, if he is to start on an equal footing with his fellows, must be trained through public schooling as a *generalist*, able to choose the role in society that he wants to fill. Furthermore, the father's activities are carried out far from home, often in a place where his son never sets foot. Neither the son of a steelworker nor the son of a business executive may become an apprentice at age thirteen or fourteen. While their fathers vanish into their respective worlds of work, the sons must prepare themselves for an uncertain future—neither for steelworker nor for business executive, but for a range of possibilities.

---

1. "Ironed All Day," *Newsweek*, January 26, 1959, p. 64.

The child can no longer help the family economically; in turn, the family has little to offer the child in the way of training for his place in the community. The family becomes less and less an economic unit in society, and the husband-wife pair sheds its appendages: the grandparents maintain a home of their own, often far away, and the children are ensconced more and more in institutions, from nursery school through college.

This age-segregation is only one consequence of specialization: another is that the child's training period is *longer*. With every decade, more of the jobs available in our society require a high level of training. As our industrial economy comes of age, it has less and less room for laborers and skilled workers, more and more room for engineers and managers. Thus not only do we relegate education to an institution outside the family, we must keep a child there longer before he is "processed" and fit to take his place as an adult in society.

This setting-apart of our children in schools—which take on ever more functions, ever more "extracurricular activities"—for an ever longer period of training has a singular impact on the child of high-school age. He is "cut off" from the rest of society, forced inward toward his own age group, made to carry out his whole social life with others his own age. With his fellows, he comes to constitute a small society, one that has most of its important interactions *within* itself, and maintains only a few threads of connection with the outside adult society. In our modern world of mass communication and rapid diffusion of ideas and knowledge, it is hard to realize that separate subcultures can exist right under the very noses of adults—subcultures with languages all their own, with special symbols, and, most importantly, with value systems that may differ from adults. Any parent who has tried to talk to his adolescent son or daughter recently knows this, as does anyone who has recently visited a high school for the first time since his own adolescence. To put it simply, these young people speak a different language. What is more relevant to the present point, the language they speak is becoming more and more different.[2]

---

2. Most students of adolescent behavior have agreed upon the existence of an adolescent subculture, a fact which is indisputable at the extreme of gang behavior. See Frederick Thrasher, *The Gang: A Study of 1,313 Gangs in Chicago* (Chicago: University of Chicago Press, 1936, 2nd ed.), and Albert Cohen, *Delinquent Boys: The Culture of the Gang*, (Glencoe: The Free Press, 1955). However, one study in a middle class suburb suggests that such a subculture can hardly be said to exist in modern upper-middle class suburbia. This is discussed in Frederick Elkin and William A. Westley, "The Myth of Adolescent Culture," *American Sociological Review*, XX, 1955, pp. 680-684. The results of the present study are in direct contradiction to Elkin and Westley's thesis, for these results indicate the adolescent society is becoming stronger rather than weaker in modern middle class suburbia.

As if it were not enough that such an institution as today's high school exists segregated from the rest of society, there are other things that reinforce this separateness. For example, adolescents have become an important market, and special kinds of entertainment cater almost exclusively to them. Popular music is the most important, and movies, since television took away their adult audience, have moved more and more toward becoming a special medium for adolescents.

To summarize: in a rapidly changing, highly rationalized society, the "natural processes" of education in the family are no longer adequate. They have been replaced by a more formalized institution that is set apart from the rest of society and that covers an ever longer span of time. As an unintended consequence, society is confronted no longer with a set of *individuals* to be trained toward adulthood, but with distinct *social systems*, which offer a united front to the overtures made by adult society.

Thus, the very changes that society is undergoing have spawned something more than was bargained for. They have taken not only job-training out of the parents' hands, but have quite effectively taken away the whole adolescent himself. The adolescent is dumped into a society of his peers, a society whose habitats are the halls and classrooms of the school, the teen-age canteens, the corner drugstore, the automobile, and numerous other gathering places. Consequently, the non-occupational training that parents once gave to their children via "natural processes" has been taken out of their hands as well, not by the school teachers—many of whom are dismayed at the thought of having to take over parental functions—but by those very social changes that segregated adolescents into a society of their own.

A good index of those changes is given by the number of teen-age youths in high school. We think of high school in our society as having been in existence for a long time. But in 1900, only 11 per cent of this country's high-school-age youth were *in* high school; as late as 1930, the proportion was only 51 per cent. Sometimes this is viewed as "progress" toward making our society more democratic, but there is considerable evidence to suggest that these changes are simply necessary consequences of industrialization. For example, a parallel trend, thirty years delayed in time, has occurred in the Soviet Union.[3] Fifty years ago, in an earlier stage of industrialization, comparatively few persons needed the lengthened training that high school represents. The rest were learning their work on the farms or in the stores or in the trades of their parents and neighbors.

---

3. This is not to say that the increasing level of education is not progress toward a democratic society. Rather, it is to say the cause of such changes is not democratic values, but the necessities of an industrial economy.

Perhaps it is self-evident that the institutional changes that have set apart the youth of our society in high schools should produce an "adolescent culture," with values of its own. These changes have been discussed speculatively by numerous authors.[4] Whether or not there is a separate adolescent subculture is partly a matter of definition as to what constitutes a separate subculture. However, there are several items from the present study that give a sense of the degree to which these adolescents are oriented to parents and peers. In one set of questions, they were asked whether they would join a club in school (1) if their parents disapproved, (2) if their favorite teacher disapproved, and (3) if it would mean breaking with their closest friend (I.134, 135, 136).[5] Then they were asked whose disapproval would be most difficult to accept—parents', teacher's, or friend's (see Table 1).[6]

Table 1—I.137. Which one of these things would be hardest for you to take—your parents' disapproval, your teacher's disapproval, or breaking with your friend?

	Boys	Girls
Parents' disapproval	53.8%	52.9%
Teacher's disapproval	3.5	2.7
Breaking with friend	42.7	43.4
Number of cases (excluding non-responses)	(3,621)	(3,894)

The responses indicate a rather even split between friend and parent, while the teacher's disapproval counts most for only a tiny minority. The balance between parents and friends indicates the extent of the state of transition that adolescents experience—leaving one family, but not yet in another, they consequently look both forward to their peers and backward to their parents.

Thus, teen-agers are not oriented solely to one another; yet the pulls are extremely strong, as the responses in Table 1 show. It seems reasonable, however, that those adolescents who are more oriented to their parents might "set the standard" in school, while those more oriented to their peers would tend toward delinquency or at least enjoy less esteem

---

4. An early statement of the general problem is that of Talcott Parsons, "Age and Sex in the Social Structure of the United States," reprinted in his *Essays in Sociological Theory, Pure and Applied* (Glencoe, Ill.: The Free Press, 1949).

5. These questions are in the fall questionnaire, which is included in the Appendix. In referring to questions, "I" or "II" preceding the question number will indicate the fall or spring questionnaire respectively. When both fall and spring responses are tabulated, the fall (I) question number will be used.

6. The results in Table 1 are based on responses from the students in the nine public schools. The nine-school totals will be used throughout the book rather than totals for all ten schools. This facilitates comparison between boys and girls, which would be confounded if the all-boys parochial school, St. Johns, were included.

than those who are parent-oriented. If this were so, then the adolescent cultures existing in the school would be oriented toward parents to a greater degree than the individual responses indicate, because the central persons in the schools were more oriented to parents. But this is not at all so; a slight reverse tendency exists.

This can be seen by looking at those students who are named most often (ten times or more) by their fellows in response to the following question: (I.51) "If a fellow came here to school and wanted to get in with the leading crowd, what fellows should he get to be friends with?" Quite reasonably, we can infer that the students named in response to this question include most of the "leaders" or the "elite" of the adolescent culture in the schools. For this group and for the students as a whole, the proportion who say parents' disapproval would be hardest for them to take is shown in Table 2.

Table 2—Proportion who say that "parents' disapproval would be hardest to take"

BOYS		GIRLS	
All boys	Leading crowd	All girls	Leading crowd
53.8%	50.2%	52.9%	48.9%
(5,621)	(167)	(3,894)	(264)

The elites in the school are not closer to their parents than are the students as a whole, but are pulled slightly farther from parents, closer to fellow-adolescents as a source of approval and disapproval. Thus, those who "set the standard" are more oriented than their followers to the adolescent culture itself. The consequences of this fact are important, for it means that those students who are highly regarded by others are themselves committed to the adolescent group, thus intensifying whatever inward forces the group already has.

Turning back to the suggestion that the existence of an adolescent culture is more pronounced than it once was, there is little the present research can do to document this possibility. However, our data does afford some insight into changes that have taken place. The present study includes five small-town or rural schools and five city and suburban ones, and it is possible to study the stable small-town schools so as to look back into the past a short distance. These small-town schools represent a segment of American society that was once far more important than it is now: They are located in small-town mid-American market centers for the surrounding farmland, with a few industries, but not highly industrialized. At the other extreme, in keeping with the times, are two homogeneous suburbs of Chicago: one a new working-class suburb with a school only seven years old (to be called Newlawn throughout the book);

the other an older, but similarly homogeneous, upper-middle-class suburb with a mushrooming population (to be called Executive Heights throughout the book).

Before examining the statistical data which can give some evidence of these changes, let us quote a passage of a letter from a particularly perceptive parent, a lawyer living in Executive Heights:

Mrs. —— and I do not believe we could give you much useful information about the teen-age culture as it exists in Executive Heights. We see this culture in a very limited aspect, through our sophomore daughter, and our limited familiarity with her contemporaries. It is truly surprising how little one person knows about the inner thinking of another, particularly when the other is an adolescent. I suspect that the interests and values current in the high school group are more independent of those of the adult community than we generally believe.

Most children of this age, at least in Executive Heights, I believe do not have serious responsibilities, such as helping to support a family or to prepare to pay their way through college, and therefore are not acquainted with people engaged in making a living, and do not understand the problems and responsibilities which parents have. As a result, they do not obtain the experience which goes with such responsibility, . . . and, in effect, live in a world separate from the adult community.

This letter indicates what may be a general feeling among many parents today: that their teen-age children are in "a world apart." An index of such "apartness" might be the degree to which boys want to follow in their father's occupation. They were asked: (I.101) "What kind of work do you plan to go into when you finish your schooling?" The answers were coded (except in some cases where it was not possible) as to whether the occupation named was the same as their father's or different. The results are tabulated in Table 3, for the five small-town or rural schools and for the four public high schools in larger towns, cities, and suburbs.

Table 3—Per cent of boys who want to go into their father's occupation

	Five small-town schools	Four city and Suburban schools
Same	23.0%	9.8%
Different	77.0	90.2
Total classifiable	100.0 (710)	100.0 (2,177)
(Unable to classify)	(66)	(173)
(No answer to own occupation)	(252)	(643)
Total	(1,028)	(2,993)

Twenty-three per cent of the boys in the small towns want to enter their father's occupation; only 9.8 per cent of the boys in the city and suburban schools want to do so.[7] This difference is even more impressive when one realizes that it is the small-town occupations that will be less numerous in the next generation, as an industrial society more nearly replaces a rural one.

In examining the school of Executive Heights, we can see more directly the greater orientation to peers on the part of boys and girls who are fully a part of modern society. One question asked all students to rank four items according to these items' importance for him. The items were: "pleasing my parents"; "learning as much as possible in school"; "living up to my religious ideals"; and "being accepted and liked by other students." The ranking of "being accepted and liked by other students" is considerably higher in this school than in the average of all schools, as Table 4 shows.

Table 4—Average rank of "being accepted and liked by other students" (I.29–32) for all schools and Executive Heights

(Rank 1 is high; 4 is low)

	BOYS		GIRLS	
	All schools	Executive heights	All schools	Executive heights
Average rank	2.63	2.34	2.53	2.17
Number of cases	(4,020)	(932)	(4,134)	(898)

This comparison and the comparison in Table 3 show differences suggesting a movement toward a separate adolescent culture. But it is likely that the attempt to "reach back into history" by examining these small towns or to "reach forward" by examining an upper-middle-class suburb is impeded by the very shifts that have occurred in small towns themselves. The general prosperity, rapid transportation, and the mass communication media have radically altered the style of life in small towns, bringing them into the general culture. In particular, small-town adolescents have far greater access to one implement of our modern culture than do teen-agers in a large city or even a suburb: the automobile.

Despite the many ways in which small towns are representative of an older, non-industrial society, in this one way—the prevalence of automobiles among teen-agers—they are very much a part of modern culture.

---

7. Although the schools are not shown separately, each of the small-town schools is higher than any of the others in this percentage, with one exception: Elmtown, the most industrialized of the five small towns, scores lower than the upper-middle-class suburb, Executive Heights. It is interesting to note in passing that in the two working-class schools (Newlawn and Millburg) the son's choice shifts *away* from his father's occupation over the four years from freshman to senior; in Executive Heights, the son's choice shifts *toward* the father's occupation.

(In Chapter II, Table 9 shows automobile ownership by seniors in each school.) It seems that only where there have been conscious efforts to maintain an older way of life—as with the Amish—or where there are physcial or economic barriers—as in the center of a large city—or in economically depressed areas have the implements and culture of modern society failed to penetrate deeply.

In sum, then, the general point is this: our adolescents today are cut off, probably more than ever before, from the adult society. They are still oriented toward fulfilling their parents' desires, but they look very much to their peers for approval as well. Consequently, our society has within its midst a set of small teen-age societies, which focus teen-age interests and attitudes on things far removed from adult responsibilities, and which may develop standards that lead away from those goals established by the larger society.[8]

Given this general condition, there are several directions in which educational efforts could turn. One is toward a channeling of the adolescent societies so that the influence they exert on a child is in the directions adults desire. Rather than attempting to motivate children one by one, each parent (with teachers' assistance) exhorting his own child in one direction while the adolescent culture as a whole pulls in other directions, efforts can be made to redirect the whole society of adolescents itself, so that *it* comes to motivate the child in directions sought by the adult society. This is not a new device; "playing by ear," perceptive principals and teachers have long attempted to do this. Yet it has never been the focus of any general philosophy of education, nor have any general means for redirecting the adolescent society been set forth in schools of education, perhaps because we know too little about the ways in which subsocieties, such as those of our teen-agers, can be guided and directed.

Before any such attempts are made in this direction, it is important to examine carefully the ways in which these subsocieties operate, the kinds of effects they have on the teen-agers within them, and the elements that shape them in one direction or another. This will be the intent of the succeeding chapters of this book.

The values, activities, and interests characterizing the "teen-age cul-

---

8. A teen-ager comments: As an adolescent, looking at our society from a distance, it seems to me to be merely an immature adult society. This immaturity is responsible for the "world of difference" between the culture of the teen-ager and the adult. Immaturity and lack of responsibility lower the goals and standards of an adolescent society. The adolescent borrows for his society the "glamorous and sophisticated" part of adult society. The high goals and worthwhile activities of the adult world are scorned because they involve responsibilities, which the adolescent is not ready to accept.

ture" as a whole will be examined first. But of primary importance will be the ways in which these adolescent societies differ from school to school, from community to community, so that some insight can be gained into the factors shaping them in one or another direction. Looking both at the separate schools and at the various "crowds" or groups within the schools, it will be possible to achieve some understanding of how the climate of education within a school may better implement the hopes and ideals of our society.

II The Adolescent Culture

THE SIMPLE FACT THAT ADOLESCENTS are looking to each other rather than to the adult community for their social rewards has a number of significant implications for educational theory and practice. To be sure, parents and parental desires are of great importance to children in a long-range sense, but it is their peers whose approval, admiration, and respect they attempt to win in their everyday activities, in school and out. As a result, the old "levers" by which children are motivated—approval or disapproval of parents and teachers—are less efficient.

As long as meaningful social rewards could be directly supplied by adults, there was little need to be explicit about them in educational theory, for they were naturally provided by the very process of interaction between parent and child, or student and teacher. To be sure, these rewards were often distributed in ways that reinforced the stratification system and took away the lower-class child's meager chance for equality; as some authors have shown very well, the middle-class backgrounds of teachers often made them unable to hold out reasonable rewards for reasonable achievement to lower-class children.[1] The situation, however, was fundamentally simpler than it is today, because teachers and parents had direct control over the levers they could apply to motivate children. Now the levers are other children themselves,

---

1. This is graphically illustrated by A. B. Hollingshead, *Elmtown's Youth* (New York: John Wiley & Sons, 1949), a study showing the various mechanisms by which the school reinforced the class structure. Because the present study includes "Elmtown" as one of its ten schools, it will be possible to show the greater cross-cutting of social-class lines that occurs in Elmtown today as compared to 1941.

acting as a small society, and adults must come to know either how to shape the directions this society takes, or else how to break down the adolescent society, thus re-establishing control by the old levers.

I suspect that this latter solution would be exceedingly difficult, for it flies in the face of large-scale social changes, and would seem to require a reorganization of work and community, which is hardly in the offing. The major thesis of this book is that it is possible to take the other tack, to learn how to control the adolescent community *as* a community, and to use it to further the ends of education.

The first step is to examine a number of adolescent communities themselves, in order to discover just what the value systems are. On what grounds do adolescents give approval to one another or withhold it? How does a boy or girl become a member of the "inner core" or "leading crowd"? What makes a boy or girl popular, admired, and imitated by his fellows? There are differences from community to community and from school to school, some of which will be examined in detail later; there are also similarities, which make it worthwhile investigating first the values of the general adolescent culture and the possible effects of these values on children. The similarities among different schools suggest there are some general elements in the role to which adolescents are relegated by the adult society. The differences indicate that it is not hopeless for adults to attempt to modify the adolescent cultures.

The General Interests and Activities of Teen-Agers

Because adolescents live so much in a world of their own, adults remain uninformed about the way teen-agers spend their time, the things that are important to them, and the things that friends have in common. Several questions were asked in the study that give a picture of these patterns of activities and interests. Every boy and girl was asked: (I.108) "What is your favorite way of spending your leisure time?"

The boys' responses (see Table 5) indicate that boys like to spend a great deal of their time in fairly active outdoor pursuits, such as sports, boating, and just going around with the fellows. They also spend time on hobbies—the most frequent of which is working on their car—and on such passive pursuits as movies, television, records, and the like. Being with girls does not, as adults sometimes think, constitute a large part of their leisure activities—although it comes to occupy more time as they go from the freshman year to the senior year.

Table 5—Leisure activities of boys and girls in the nine public high schools

	Boys	Girls
1. Organized outdoor sports—including football, basketball, tennis, etc.	22.0%	6.9%
2. Unorganized outdoor activities—including hunting, fishing, swimming, boating, horseback riding	14.7	11.3
3. "Being with the group," riding around, going up town, etc.	17.2	32.5
4. Attending movies and spectator events—athletic games, etc.	8.5	10.4
5. Dating or being out with opposite sex	13.6	11.6
6. Going dancing (girls only)		12.0
7. Hobby—working on cars, bicycles, radio, musical instruments, etc.	22.5	20.1
8. Indoor group activities—bowling, playing cards, roller skating, etc.	8.0	8.1
9. Watching television	19.4	23.6
10. Listening to records or radio	11.2	31.7
11. Reading	13.7	35.5
12. Other, e.g., talking on telephone	7.1	9.3
13. No answer	8.1	3.7
Number of cases	(4,020)	(4,134)

Girls' leisure-time activities show a sharp contrast in some categories. Girls' favorite leisure activities less often include the active outdoor pursuits of boys. More frequent are activities like "just being with their friends," watching television and movies, attending games, reading, and listening to records. Their more active pursuits include one that never exists for boys—dancing among themselves. Perhaps this is an activity that substitutes for the sports at which boys spend their time; in part, it is certainly preparation for dancing with boys. In any case, it suggests the oft-heard quip that boys are interested in sports and girls are interested in boys.

The general pattern of these leisure pursuits, showing considerably more activity among the boys, is indicative of a situation that seems to be quite general in the adolescent community: boys have far more to *do* than girls. Whether it is athletics, or cars, or hunting, or model-building, our society seems to provide a much fuller set of activities to engage the interests of boys. Thus, when girls are together, they are more often just "with the group" than are boys. A frequent afternoon activity is simply "going up town" to window shop and walk around.[2]

There is a point of particular interest in these responses, in relation to the school. Only one of the categories, organized sports, has any direct relation to school. Some of the hobbies and other activities may, of

2. A teen-age girl comments: This greater activity among boys is the reason that "being accepted" or being in the "right clique" means more to the girls, who have less to occupy their leisure time. Boys engaged in many activities have many different kinds of friends. They have different interests in common with different friends. Although they are friends they may have only one interest in common with a certain other boy and therefore could not be in a successful clique with all their friends. Because girls have fewer interests they form small cliques according to these interests.

course, have their genesis in school, but except for such hobbies and organized sports, school-related activities are missing. No one responds that doing homework in his favorite way of spending his leisure time. This is at least in part because homework is assigned work, and cannot be leisure. Yet athletics, which involves work during practice, manages to run over into leisure time, breaking the barrier that separates work from leisure. Perhaps it is not too much to expect that other in-school activities directly tied to learning could—if the right way were found— similarly spill over into leisure and be a favored way of spending free time.

Another glimpse of teen-age interests, and the way these interests differ for boys and girls, may be obtained from answers to the following question: (I.38a) "What do you and the fellows (girls) you go around with here at school have most in common—what are the things you do together?"

Table 6—Activities and interests that friends have in common, for boys and girls in the nine public schools*

	Boys	Girls
1. Organized outdoor sports—including football, basketball, tennis, etc.	34.5%	8.2%
2. Unorganized outdoor activities—including hunting, fishing, swimming, boating, horseback riding	11.7	6.6
3. In-school activities, interests, clubs	8.9	19.2
4. Attending spectator events		
a) School-related games and events	5.4	22.1
b) Out-of-school—movies, etc.	17.8	33.0
5. Eating together at lunch or taking classes together	9.1	13.7
6. Dating together or going to dances together	19.7	39.6
7. Having parties together (girls only)		10.6
8. "Hanging around together," "going uptown"	13.4	26.8
Number of cases	(4,020)	(4,134)

* Listed in the table are all the categories of activities or interests mentioned by at least 10 per cent of the boys or girls.

The activities and interests that friends share, as seen in Table 6, show similar patterns to the leisure interests expressed in Table 5. Missing, of course, are the activities carried on alone, such as watching television and reading. Again, there is the striking difference in outdoor activities; girls seldom engage in them, while they are the focus of common interests for a large proportion of the boys. This time, however, activities carried on in school show up in several ways: friends attend games and other events together; they engage in school clubs and activities together; and some of them merely eat together at lunch or see each other in the halls. All of these school-related activities are more nearly a basis of friendship among girls than they are among boys; for boys, the one activity within the school which overwhelms all others as a common interest of friends is athletics. This can be seen also by examining the activities of boys who name each other as friends. The one factor most related to boys' friendship was being out for football. The measure of similarity on this attribute was near 0.5 in every school (using an index where chance association is zero, and the maximum possible is 1.0), higher than any other interest or activity among either boys or girls—except being in the same grade.

Table 6 does show a greater amount of activity within school among friends than does Table 5. The fact that this is most true among girls (except for the one activity of athletics for boys) indicates a rather general characteristic: in all these schools, the clubs and activities were more the province of the girls than of the boys. For example, in almost every school of the more than fifty whose yearbooks were examined during this study, a girl was editor of the yearbook and a girl was editor of the school newspaper. Some activities, of course, are either solely for boys (such as the Hi-Y clubs) or are largely populated by boys (such as a chemistry club or photography club). However, in general, it seems that there is a kind of tacit division of labor in most schools: activities and clubs are for the girls, athletics are for the boys.

A note should be added for those who may have expected to find a whole range of delinquent activities in the responses to these two questions. Such an expectation is quite out of accord with the facts. Adolescents as a whole are *not* delinquent, and their activities, although quite different from adult activities and sometimes irresponsible, are not in general antisocial or delinquent. Some teen-agers feel strongly about this matter, as they see adults judge all adolescents by the delinquent activities of a few. Once again, this is evidence of the gulf that separates the adult culture from the adolescent community. The stereotypy and suspicion to which adults succumb in such circumstances is similar to that which generates prejudice and antagonism against other minority groups judged by the actions of their most visible members. Many whites know Negroes almost solely through what they read in the newspaper. If they think of Negroes as athletes, criminals, and dope addicts, it is in part because these are the only Negroes who make the news, who are "visible" to them. Similarly, many adults have little contact with teen-agers except through their newspapers. If they think of teen-agers as football players, members of delinquent gangs, and rock-and-roll addicts, it is in part because these are the only activities visible to them via the news.

This is not to say that delinquent and antisocial activities were never mentioned as common interests by these teen-agers, but rather that they constituted a tiny minority of the total responses. For boys, the following categories of response to question 38a in Table 6 are the only ones which suggest antisocial and delinquent behavior. The proportion of boys is very small in each category:

	Per cent
Stirring up trouble	0.7
Drinking or smoking together	1.5
Picking up girls	0.5
Number of cases	(4,020)

It is true that many boys would hesitate to mention the trouble they get into or their delinquent activities. Although they were assured that no teacher or other student would ever see their responses, adults administered the questionnaires, and this must have had an inhibiting effect. Yet, throughout the study—in interviews, in the questionnaires, and elsewhere—it became quickly evident that really delinquent behavior was confined to a small minority in all these schools.

In another set of questions, students were asked directly about activities prohibited in school: smoking, which is not illegal for high-school age children, and drinking, which is. The questions are listed below, and the answers tabulated separately for boys and girls.[3]

Table 7—Drinking and smoking by students in the nine public schools

		Boys	Girls
I.167.	Do you smoke?		
	Yes, regularly	15.2%	7.6%
	Yes, occasionally	17.0	15.5
	No	67.7	76.9
	Number of cases	(3,497)	(3,825)
I.168.	Do you drink beer?		
	Yes, regularly	3.4	0.5
	Yes, occasionally	26.8	12.6
	No	69.6	86.9
	Number of cases	(3,493)	(3,820)
I.169.	Do you drink liquor?		
	Yes, regularly	1.9	0.4
	Yes, occasionally	17.0	11.8
	No	81.0	87.8
	Number of cases	(3,492)	(3,821)

These responses indicate that a minority indulge in these habits, which can hardly be labeled delinquent since adults engage in them with high and increasing frequency.[4]

---

3. Students who failed to answer are excluded from the tabulation, since the question was near the end of the questionnaire, and most no-answers were nonfinishers.

4. It is quite likely that these responses were affected by the fact that an adult administered the questionnaire. A high-school junior distributed short questionnaires on drinking and smoking in a Baltimore girls' high school, and found that 58 per

TELEVISION AND HOMEWORK

Another perspective upon the activities of these teen-agers can be seen by examining the amount of time they spend watching television and the amount they spend doing homework. The questions were:[5]

I.17. How much time, on the average, do you spend doing homework outside school?

None, or almost none
Less than .5 hour a day
About .5 hour a day
About 1 hour a day
About 1.5 hours a day
About 2 hours a day
Three or more hours a day

I.28. About how much time, on the average, do you spend watching TV on a weekday?

None, or almost none
About .5 hour a day
About 1 hour a day
About 1.5 hours a day
About 2 hours a day
About 3 hours a day
Four or more hours a day

The results for the two questions are shown in Figure 2.1. This graph merely gives a quick view of the general level of studying and television-viewing. Any immediate comparisons between television habits and studying habits must be held in abeyance for two reasons: the schools under study cannot be considered a representative sample of American teen-agers; and, even more important, study habits (and to a lesser extent, television habits) vary radically among the ten schools in the

---

cent of the girls reported that they smoked (compared to 23% in the study), and 30 per cent reported that they drank, (compared to less than 15% in the study). There are several differences that could account for the discrepancy between these results and the ones in the schools of the study: this is a girls' public high school, while the others are coeducational; it is in Baltimore, while the others were in northern Illinois; it was distributed by a teen-ager, while the others were administered by adults; and the sample was not in any sense random, including fewer underclassmen, fewer non-social girls, than would a random sample of the school. The last difference certainly accounts for part of the discrepancy. However, the distribution by a teen-ager must have been in part responsible also.

5. The slight difference in categories in these two questions results from a pretest with open-ended questions, which showed that these categories would best subdivide the students. However, this unfortunately introduces a slight non-comparability of responses, because of the effect of the list of categories upon the response.

study. These variations will be discussed later; for now, it is sufficient to observe that:

a) There are greater individual differences in time spent watching television than in time spent on homework. There are more teen-agers who watch no television at all than there are who do no homework; but there are also far more teen-agers (over 20 per cent) who spend as much as three hours a day watching television, than there are who spend that much time on homework.

b) Boys spend more time watching television, and less doing home-work, than do girls.

c) The average amount of time girls spend watching television is about the same as that they spend on homework. Boys spend, on the average, more time on television than on homework.

The greater time reported by the boys watching television is not consistent with their reported leisure interests in Table 5, for they report *less* often than do the girls that television is their favorite leisure activity. This discrepancy is puzzling; apparently boys spend a little more time watching television, but it occupies less of their interest. This may be true. Boys tend to watch more sports on TV and less drama, and tend not to think of this activity so much as "watching television" as "watch-ing a ball game." And there is some evidence that men pay less attention to the content of television dramas than do women. In a recent study of TV-viewing, men were questioned about the television shows they

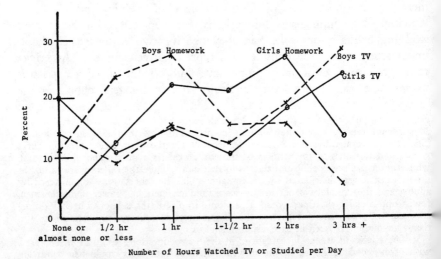

Figure 2.1—Hours spent watching television and hours spent studying per day by boys and girls.

watched with their wives. When asked why they watched these shows, they answered less often in terms of the program's content than did their wives, and more often in terms of sociability.[6]

The sharply different patterns of television-viewing, which shows a U-shaped distribution, with many persons at the extremes and few in the middle, and homework, which has the usual unimodal distribution, tailing off at the extremes, suggests the quite different sources of television-viewing and homework. A U-shaped distribution, with its wide individual differences, suggests a kind of contagion effect, in which some viewing leads to more for those whose interest is captured, so that they "can't stop," while others never have their interest captured, but instead go on to other things. The unimodal distribution for homework, however, suggests not an interest-capturing process, but a process of conforming to some standard. Few feel free to do none at all, and few have their interest captured so that they can't stop.

These two different patterns raise an important question for education. Is it best to have intellectual activity among adolescents compressed to a mean by setting "requirements" that call out energy enough to meet, but never greatly exceed, these requirements? Or is it better to have a distribution of energy more like that in television-viewing, with greater freedom to put it aside or carry it to extreme lengths? Our educational system through high school is predicated upon the former strategy; but the latter merits serious consideration as well. It would require, of course, a better educational system than does the first, for scholastic activity would have to compete for adolescent attention, without the present use of compulsion.

FREQUENCIES OF OTHER TEEN-AGE ACTIVITIES

Figures 2.2 and 2.3 tabulate the frequency of other teen-age activities, showing something of the way teen-agers spend their time, interest, and money. The relevant questions were as follows:

I.21. How many records have you bought in the last month? (Circle the number of records bought.)

0   1   2   3   4   5   6   7   8   9 or more

I.26. How often do you go to the movies?

Never, or almost never
About once a month or less
About once every two or three weeks
About once a week

---

6. See Charles W. Day, "The Television Adult Western: A Pilot Study." Master's thesis, (University of Chicago, 1958), Table 30.

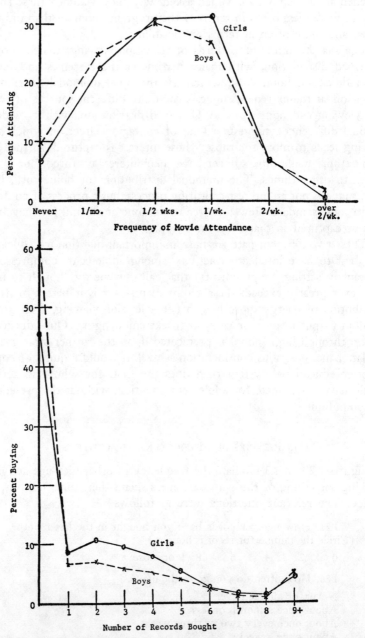

Figure 2.2—Frequency of movie attendance and purchase of records by boys and girls.

About twice a week
More than twice a week

I.19. About how many evenings a week do you spend out with other fellows (girls)? (Circle the number of evenings.)

0 1 2 3 4 5 6 7

I.20. About how many evenings a week do you spend at home? (Circle the number of evenings.)

0 1 2 3 4 5 6 7

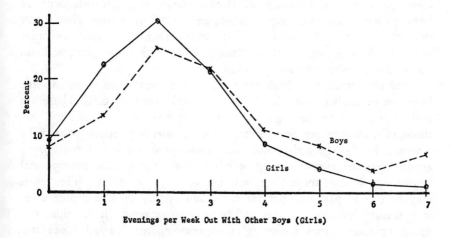

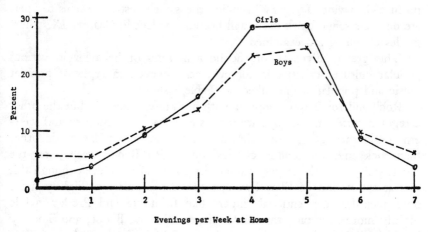

Figure 2.3—Evenings spent out with other boys (girls) and evenings at home by boys and girls.

As with homework and television-viewing, these results cannot be extrapolated to American teen-agers as a whole. However, the *differences* between boys and girls, and between other subgroups to be examined in later chapters, are undoubtedly more general. It is true also that in response to these last four items, the schools varied much less than they do in the amount of time spent on homework, so that there is some stability in these figures from school to school.

A comparison of the boys and girls in their movie attendance and locus of evening activity shows general differences that one might expect. Girls go to movies slightly more than do boys, although a majority of both go less often than once a week; and girls buy a somewhat larger number of records than do boys. Boys spend considerably more evenings out a week with other fellows than girls do with other girls, and, on the average, fewer evenings at home.

One phenomenon in both these charts is somewhat more surprising: boys are somewhat more *diverse* in these activities than girls. There are more boys at both the high and low frequencies in each activity. Although the *average* girl goes to more movies, more boys attend over twice a week; the average girl spends more evenings at home, but more boys report spending every evening at home; and although the average girl buys more records, more boys buy nine or more per month. This result may be due in part to a greater constraint felt by girls to report some intermediate level of activity, rather than an extreme. But if this constraint operates in their reporting on a questionnaire, it probably operates in their leisure behavior as well, so that they very likely *do* tend more to cluster about an intermediate level of activity, closer to some expected norm of behavior. The way in which this same constraint seems to operate on their schoolwork itself will become evident in Chapter IX, where grades in school are examined.

This greater diversity of the boys in *rates* of behavior in various popular culture activities is not evident, however, in *types* of popular music and popular singers liked, as Table 8 shows.

Rock and roll is most popular with both boys and girls, but the other categories differ: more boys are interested in jazz and country and western music than girls; more girls are interested in popular music other than rock and roll, and in classical music. Pat Boone was by far the favorite singer of the largest number of boys and girls, even though this was at the period of Elvis Presley's greatest popularity. Slightly more boys pick less conventional singers like Belafonte and Presley, while slightly more girls pick the milder singers, Sinatra, Boone, and Tommy Sands—a slightly watered-down version of Elvis Presley.[7] Again, these

7. These six singers were listed in the questionnaire after pretests showed that they were the six most popular at the time.

choices reflect a somewhat greater tendency of girls to conform to adult values. Their choices are no less diverse than those of boys, but they are somewhat more conventional.

Table 8—Favorite types of music and favorite singers among teen-agers

		Boys	Girls
I.25.	What kind of music do you enjoy most?		
	Rock and roll	51.6%	48.1%
	Calypso	7.1	5.5
	Other popular music	17.5	27.5
	Jazz	10.1	5.2
	Classical	6.5	9.4
	Country and western	6.3	3.8
	No answer	0.8	0.5
	Number of cases	(4,020)	(4,134)
I.24.	Among the following singers, which one do you like best?		
	Pat Boone	43.5	45.2
	Perry Como	10.5	10.1
	Elvis Presley	21.5	17.5
	Tommy Sands	7.8	10.7
	Harry Belafonte	10.3	9.0
	Frank Sinatra	5.1	7.1
	No answer	1.5	0.5
	Number of cases	(4,020)	(4,134)

Cars in the Adolescent Culture

Cars are an important matter to a teen-ager. Without a car, a boy must be chauffeured to movies, sports events, and—most embarrassing of all—to dates. As cars have become more important for adults, they have become more important for their adolescent children—as parents of adolescents will quickly attest. Consequently, as a boy reaches the age when he can possess a driver's license (sixteen in most states, including Illinois, in which all these schools are located), his pressure upon parents for permission to have a car of his own becomes extremely great. Parents find it hard not to give in, at least by letting him buy a car if he can pay for it. The great jump in car-owning in the sophomore and junior years is attested by Figure 2.4, which shows how car-owning changes from the freshman to the senior years.

The increasing importance of cars is partly due to the blossoming of the suburbs. Boys who would have lived in the heart of the city, where a car is not important for transportation, now live in the suburbs, where it is important. A comparison of increase in car ownership from freshmen to seniors in St. John's High, in the center of Chicago, with Newlawn, in a suburb, shows this well (Figure 2.5). These two schools contain boys with almost identical family backgrounds (first generation East European immigrants, working-class, predominantly Catholic); yet car ownership increases sharply over the four years in Newlawn, and remains at a low level among the boys of St. John's High. Ecological changes in society, however, cannot fully account for the great increase in car ownership among teen-agers. A boy can most use a car in a small town or in the country—and in the past these areas housed many more teen-agers than they presently do.[8]

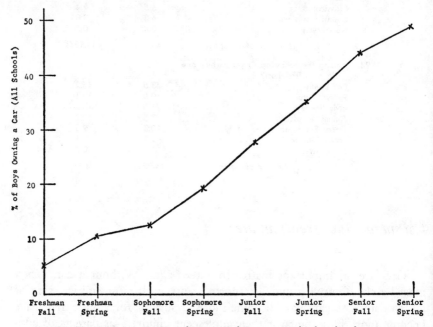

Figure 2.4—Boys' car ownership at eight points in high school career.

Table 9 shows that car ownership is far more prevalent among teen-agers in small towns than in cities and suburbs, and in small cities than in a very large one. One boy from the smallest school, Farmdale, when asked if most of the boys in his senior class had cars, replied that they did, because many of them lived in the country and it was a matter of necessity. This is certainly true, if they must have independence. However, necessity is not the whole answer; even the non-farmers' sons in the

8. Schools are examined separately in a few places in this chapter, as in Table 9. However, because differences between schools will not be discussed in detail until Chapter III, thumbnail sketches of each school will be reserved until the beginning of that chapter.

small towns more often have a car than do their city and suburban counterparts. And the school buses run for the farmers' sons, who ride them in earlier grades.

Table 9—Car ownership by senior boys in each school (spring)

Approx. town size	School	Per cent owning a car	Number
1,000	Farmdale	81.3	(16)
4,000	Marketville	56.4	(39)
7,000	Elmtown	42.2	(45)
6,000	Maple Grove	68.4	(38)
5,000	Green Junction	63.8	(58)
9,000 (suburb)	Newlawn	50.8	(59)
17,000 (suburb)	Executive Heights	42.2	(154)
25,000	Millburg	36.6	(93)
110,000	Midcity	46.2	(221)
3,600,000	St. John's High	17.5	(102)

The general level of economic prosperity accounts in part for the high ownership of cars among teen-agers. But this only provides the opportunity; the frequency and speed with which this opportunity is seized when a boy or girl comes of driving age indicates just how important a car is to most of these teen-agers. If a boy has a car, then there is no great

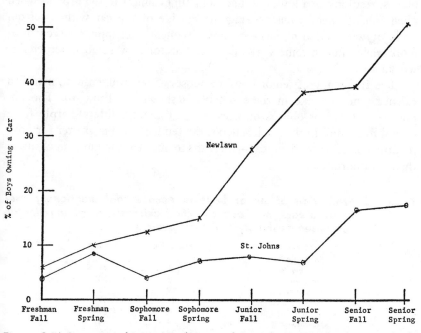

Figure 2.5—Car ownership in Newlawn and St. Johns, at eight points in high school career.

problem in dating and in going to the local hangout. If he does not, he is still a child, for he is able to date a girl only with difficulty—with public transportation poor or nonexistent in most suburbs and small towns, and becoming poorer in cities.

The place of the car in the culture of these schools differs considerably from school to school. That is, a car is more than a means of transportation. It occupies boys' attention in numerous ways. Each boy was asked, in the fall questionnaire:

> I.40a. Among the crowd you go around with, what are the styles or things that are popular right now—that is, in your group?
>
> Description of style
>
> Clothing ——————————————————————————
> Haircuts ——————————————————————————
> Cars and accessories ——————————————————
> Anything else? ——————————————————————

The responses to the "cars and accessories" part of this question varied widely, but centered around such things as dual exhausts; Hollywood mufflers, which give a loud, racing-type exhaust noise; lowering the blocks, resulting in a lower outline, sometimes almost to the ground when piled full of friends; customizing the outside of the car with a custom grille or with added chome—or, more frequently, stripping the chrome; more elaborate custom work; dual carburetors; or some other engine work.

The frequency of senior boys' responses of hot-rod, custom, modified exhaust, and the like in these schools is shown in Table 10. The importance of cars as objects of attention and interest differs sharply from school to school. In the small schools, the tendency is far greater for boys to do something to their cars—for cars to mean something much more than transportation.

Table 10—Proportion of senior boys in each school mentioning customized cars, hot rods, modified exhausts, or giving similar responses as the style of their groups

School	Proportion	Number
Farmdale	.56	(16)
Marketville	.29	(41)
Elmtown	.46	(50)
Maple Grove	.39	(39)
Green Junction	.39	(59)
St. John's High	.24	(121)
Newlawn	.28	(64)
Millburg	.22	(107)
Midcity	.25	(222)
Executive Heights	.19	(164)

Yet the extent to which this is true differs greatly from school to school, even among the small schools. It is greatest in the smallest school, Farmdale, where, as later analysis will show, academic values count for little among the boys. Among the small schools, it is least in Marketville, where, as will be evident later, the boys seem to stay longer under parental constraint. It is second highest in Elmtown, although, as the preceding table showed, fewer of these boys own cars than in the other small schools. This is consistent with other evidence, to be presented in the next chapter, that cars are a great focus of interest in Elmtown, although many boys cannot afford one. Attention to cars in the other two small schools, Maple Grove and Green Junction, is of roughly equal importance, though the first is considerably more white-collar. Among the large schools, it is Executive Heights whose boys show least focus of attention on fixing up cars, with the others somewhere between it and the small schools.

The question of what car-owning *does* to a boy in relation to his schoolwork has been speculated upon by parents and educators alike, usually with a less than optimistic conclusion. It is not possible here to examine car-owning in its effect on grades, on studying outside school, and on dating patterns. Its different role in the different leading crowds, however, will be examined in Chapter IV. The aim here is to show the incidence of car ownership by boys in school, its variation among schools in different ecological areas, and the different importance attached to cars in different communities of adolescents.

Values and Attitudes in the Adolescent Community

The next step toward examining the nature of the adolescent community will be to look at the attitudes expressed and values held by adolescents. For example, the boys were asked:

I.68. If you could be any of these things you wanted, which would you most want to be?

	Fall	Spring
Jet pilot	31.6%	31.3%
Nationally famous athlete	37.3	36.9
Missionary	5.7	5.9
Atomic scientist	25.6	25.9
Number of cases (no-answers excluded)	(3,892)	(3,746)

These results show strikingly the way in which the adolescent culture departs from the educational norm: the nationally famous athlete leads, the atomic scientist is a poor third after the jet pilot, and the missionary is almost neglected. The shifts over the period of the school year are little, if any.. This result, of course, differs from school to school, but it is striking that in *every school* the nationally famous athlete and the jet pilot were first and second in popularity. These adolescent attitudes seem to reflect the dominant themes and heroes in the mass media far more than the heroes their teachers would have them follow. It may be that the most impressive contacts adolescents have with the adult culture are through the distorted lens of the mass media and its "newsworthy" events, just as the most impressive contacts many adults have with adolescents are through the mass media, with their focus upon newsworthy behavior.

In response to the same question, with the following alternatives, the girls gave responses slightly more in line with traditional values of service:

	Fall	Spring
Actress or artist	18.4%	19.2%
Nurse	29.2	26.0
Model	32.0	33.5
Schoolteacher	20.6	20.6
Number of cases (no-answers excluded)	(4,057)	(3,922)

Yet the glamorous model was first in popularity, and schoolteachers third, with the nurse between. Over the period of the year, there was a slight *increase* for the glamorous model and "actress or artist," while the nurse *decreased* and the teacher remained constant. In Chapter X, a variation in these changes in Elmtown will give some insight into the processes by which these images, somewhat counter to educational ideals, develop.

Another attitude question focuses more sharply on the values current in the schools themselves. It asks a boy or girl how he or she would like most to be *remembered* in school, a matter that presumably in part reflects his own interests and in part the things important to his fellows. The question is:

I.131. If you could be remembered here at school for one of the three things below, which one would you want it to be?

Boys: Brilliant student
        Athletic star
        Most popular

Girls: Brilliant student
        Leader in activities
        Most popular

The responses for fall and the next spring are shown on Figure 2.6, for both boys and girls. The three corners of the graph indicate 100 per cent brilliant student, at the top; athletic star or activities leader, at

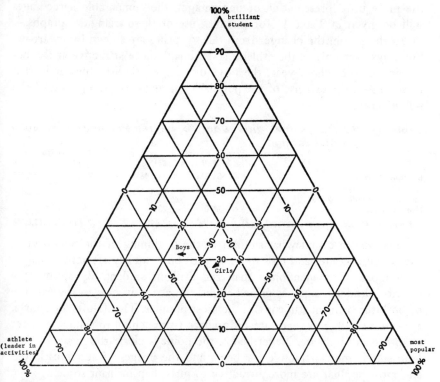

Figure 2.6—Relative choice of image of athletic star, (leader in activities for girls) brilliant student, and most popular, in fall and spring.*

* This graph, and others like it later in the book, will be unfamiliar to many readers. A particular group (e.g., boys in fall) is represented by a point within the triangle. The nearness of this point to a given vertex indicates how closely the group is to 100% response on that category. A point lying on the edge of the triangle opposite a given vertex represents zero per cent response on that category. Thus the center of the triangle represents 33⅓% response on each of the three categories. In this Figure, a line is drawn connecting the points representing fall and spring responses with an arrow pointing from fall to spring. On several subsequent graphs, a line will join the students as a whole to the leading crowd, with an arrow pointing toward the leading crowd.

the left; and most popular, at the right.[9] The more students giving a particular response, the closer the point is to that corner.

Graphs like this will be used at several points in succeeding chapters to "locate" different schools, and to trace their course over the period of the year. In order to give some sense of the relation of these graphs to

9. I am indebted to James Davis and Jacob Feldman, of the National Opinion Research Center at the University of Chicago, for suggesting the use of these triangular graphs for three-part items. Instructions to aid reading the graphs are given with Figure 2.6.

the more usual presentation of percentages, the comparable percentages will be given in Table 11 for this first use of these triangular graphs.

In the graph, the changes from fall to spring are shown by an arrow. For boys, not only is the athletic star's image more attractive at the beginning of the school year; the boys move even slightly further in that direction—at the expense of the popularity image—over the period of the school year.

Table 11—How boys and girls want to be remembered in school— fall and spring

	BOYS		GIRLS	
	Fall	Spring	Fall	Spring
Brilliant student	31.3%	31.5%	28.8%	27.9%
Athletic star (boys) Leader in activities (girls)	43.6	45.1	36.1	37.8
Most popular	25.0	23.4	35.2	34.2
Number of cases (no-answers excluded)	(3,696)	(3,690)	(3,955)	(3,876)

The girls are somewhat similar: at the beginning of the school year, the activities leader and most popular are about equally attractive images, both more often mentioned than the brilliant student. By spring, the activities-leader image has gained slightly in attractiveness, at the expense of both the brilliant student and the most popular. These shifts, of course, are quite small, and there are differences from school to school, as later chapters will indicate. Nevertheless, the point is clear: the image of athletic star is most attractive for boys, and the images of activities leader and most popular are more attractive to girls than brilliant student.

The importance of athletics in these cultures is striking, particularly when we realize that the school as an institution is designed to focus attention on studies and, presumably, upon the brilliant student. Some suggestion as to why the brilliant-student image is not more popular is given by a parallel question as to whom they would like to *date*:

I.129. Suppose you had a chance to go out with either a cheerleader, or a girl who is the best student in class, or the best looking girl in class. Which one would you rather go out with?

Cheerleader
Best student
Best looking

Suppose you had a chance to go out with either a star athlete, or a boy who is the best student in class, or the best looking boy in class. Which one would you rather go out with?

Star athlete
Best student
Best looking

The responses of the boys and those of the girls were as indicated in Figure 2.7. Perhaps the most striking result shown in the graph is the fact that the brilliant girl student fares so poorly as a date for boys. Less striking but still evident is the poor showing of the image of brilliant boy student as a date for girls. For both boys and girls, the movement over the school year is *away* from the brilliant student as someone to date. The "best looking" boy or girl gains at the expense of the best student.

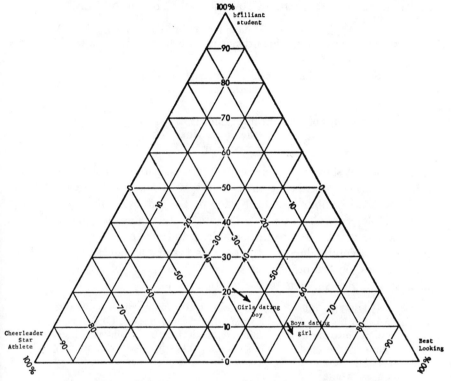

Figure 2.7—Relative attractiveness of cheerleader (star athlete for girls), brilliant student, and best looking, as a date in fall and spring.

These values held by the adolescent community are fairly well known, at least by adults who are in contact with teen-agers. They sometimes manifest themselves strikingly, however, as in the following query taken from an adolescent advice column in a church magazine:

Q. If a boy isn't an athlete he isn't anything. I've been dating a girl. Last night she stood me up and went out with a football player. I get good grades and I have brains. That athlete is dumb. Why should he rate higher than I do?—A.G.

A. Probably it isn't fair, but in high school athletes usually outrate non-athletes. Is there any sport in which you could excel? Or might you be elected to a student-body office? After graduation you'll find the really dumb athletes fade out of the scene. Among adults brains are more respected than brawn.[10]

10. *Together*, the Methodist Church Magazine, February, 1959, p. 45.

The impact that such values have upon the ways in which boys and girls expend their energies is not a light one. Many parents deplore these effects, as they see their sons caught up in athletics or their daughters pining to be cheerleaders or other "important" figures.[11] Parents' desires for their children are suggested by the parents' responses to a question similar to the "be remembered" question asked of the students:

> P.13–14. If your son or daughter could be outstanding in high school in one of the three things listed below, which one would you want it to be?
>
> For parents of boys: Brilliant student
> Athletic star
> Most popular
>
> For parents of girls: Brilliant student
> Leader in activities
> Most popular

The results are shown for parents of boys and parents of girls in Figure 2.8. The sharp contrast of these values with those expressed by the students again exhibits the divergence of the parental values and those of the adolescent subculture. To be sure, these values may not be those they express day by day to their children. Indeed, the disparity between professed parental values, on the one hand, and the values expressed by their actions, on the other, may be very great. A set of questions asked of boys and girls suggests such a discrepancy.

> II.110–112. Bill (Ann) was doing well in biology class, because he had a hobby of collecting and identifying insects. One day his biology instructor asked Bill (Ann) if he would act as the assistant in the class. . . . If something like this happened to you, would it be something that would make your parents proud of you, or wouldn't they care?

	Boys	Girls
Both would be very proud of me	60.2%	63.5%
They might feel a little proud		
Mother would be proud, father wouldn't care }	36.6	30.9
Father would be proud, mother wouldn't care }		
They wouldn't care	5.3	4.6
No answer	2.9	1.1
Number of cases	(3,831)	(3,956)

> II.113. What if a different situation occurred—you made the basketball team (cheerleader), much to your surprise. Would that make your parents proud of you, or wouldn't they care?

---

11. A Baltimore girl, junior in high school, comments: In our school being a cheerleader is not an important mark of popularity. Most of the cheerleaders are "neat" girls, but they are not "neat" because they are cheerleaders. A member of my sorority is the head of the cheerleading squad and she is very popular but it is not because she is a cheerleader. I believe this is because Eastern is an all girls' school.

	Boys	Girls
Both would be very proud of me	68.2%	77.0%
They might feel a little proud		
Mother would be proud, father wouldn't care	23.8	18.9
Father would be proud, mother wouldn't care		
They wouldn't care	5.6	3.4
No answer	2.5	0.8
Number of cases	(3,831)	(3,956)

According to the boys' responses, parents would more likely be proud of them for making the basketball team than for being chosen biology assistant. The girls' responses indicate even more strongly that their parents would more likely be proud of them for making cheerleader than for being chosen biology assistant.

These responses are at great variance with those the parents themselves gave—for the overwhelming majority of parents said they wanted their sons to be brilliant students in school, and a smaller majority, but

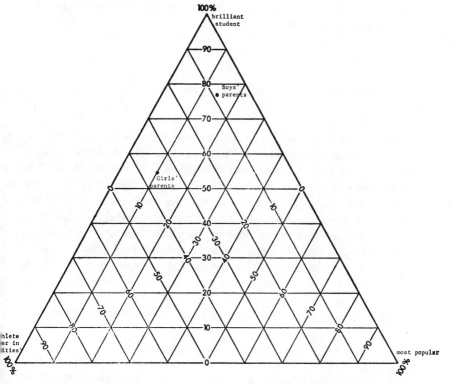

Figure 2.8—Relative desirability in parents' eyes of success as athletic star (leader in activities for girls' parents), brilliant student, and most popular.

still a majority, of parents said they wanted their daughters to be outstanding as brilliant students.

Why this discrepancy? Is someone not being honest? Are the parents'
professed values and expressed values as greatly at variance as they seem
—or do boys and girls see their parents' values as they want to see them?
Perhaps neither is the case. It may be that most parents hold academic
achievement as an ideal for their children in school, as their responses
indicate. But parents also want their children to be successful in the things
that "count" in the school, that is, the things that count in the eyes of
the other adolescents. And parents know what things count. Being a
biology assistant counts far less in the adolescent culture than does making the basketball team for boys, or making the cheerleading squad for
girls.

Thus, even the rewards a child gains from his parents may help reinforce the values of the adolescent culture—not because his parents hold
those same values, but because parents want their children to be successful and esteemed by their peers.

The Leading Crowds in the Schools

Returning to the boy who didn't "rate" because he wasn't an athlete,
let us examine what it takes to "rate" in these schools, both among one's
own sex, and with the other sex. What does it take to be in the "leading
crowd" in school? This question, of course, presumes that there *is* a leading crowd in the school. To be sure, when students were asked such a
question, some, particularly in the smallest school, did object to the idea
that there was a leading crowd. Yet this kind of objection is in large part
answered by one of the boys in another small school, Maple Grove, in a
group interview. A friend of his denied that there was any leading crowd
at all in the school, and he responded: "You don't see it because you're
in it."

Another boy in the same school had this to say in an interview:

(What are some of the groups in school?)
You mean like cliques? Well, there's about two cliques. There's one that's
these girls and boys—let's see, there's ——, ——, and ——. I'm in it, but as far
as I'm concerned, I'm not crazy about being in it. I tell you, it wasn't any of
my doing, because I'm always for the underdog myself. But I'd rather be with
a bunch like that, you know, than have them against me. So I just go along
with them.
(What's the other clique?)

Well, I don't know too much about it, it's just another clique.

(Kind of an underdog clique?)

Sort of.

(Who are some of the kids in it?)

Oh—I couldn't tell you. I know, but I just can't think of their names.

(How do you get in the top clique?)

Well, I'll tell you, like when I came over here, I had played football over at ———. I was pretty well known by all the kids before I came over. And when I came there was ——— always picking on kids. He hit this little kid one day, and I told him that if I ever saw him do anything to another little kid that I'd bust him. So one day down in the locker he slammed this kid against the locker, so I went over and hit him a couple times, knocked him down. And a lot of the kids liked me for doing that, and I got on the good side of two or three teachers.

(What are the differences between these two cliques?)

Well, I'll tell you, I don't like this top clique, myself. Just to be honest with you, they're all scared of me, because I won't take anything off of them, and they know it. I've had a run-in with this one girl, she really thinks she's big stuff. And I don't like her at all, we don't get along, and she knows it and I know it, and they don't say nothing. But a lot of them in the big clique, they're my friends. I get along with them real good, and then I try to be real nice to the underdogs, the kids that haven't got—not quite as lucky—they haven't got as much money, they have a hard time, maybe they don't look as sharp as some of the others.

(What are the main interests of the top clique?)

Just to run everything, to be the big deal.

(Are most of the boys in athletics?)

Yeah—you couldn't really say that in this town, though. The really good athletes, a couple of them may be in the clique—the clique's a funny thing, it's just who they want to be in it. They don't want to have anybody in there they think might give them trouble. They want to rule the roost.

(Do most of them have fathers that have good jobs, are well-to-do?)

Most of them. They come from families that have money.

(Would this be the main thing that divides the top clique from—)

Could be, very easily; it sure could.

(What does this underdog clique have in common?)

Well, you might say they just stick together, for self-protection. And they do things together.

(And there are both boys and girls in the cliques?)

Yeah.

(And they all go around together?)

Um-hm.

(In a party, would—)

Now there you go. The big deal clique, that's all that's there. None of the underdogs are there at all. They won't invite—I've got some graduation pictures now here, and we can get some names from that. Now she's not in the clique.

(What's her name?)

Now this girl here, she's Joyce. She's real sweet, not very sharp-looking or nothing, and I sat by her in home room. And I talked with her and stuff like that, and she really—I mean, I think she thinks a lot of me. And this is a girl who sort of sticks to herself, more or less. She's a very nice girl, but I don't think she's in the clique. And she's not in the clique and neither is ———.

(And they aren't in the other clique either?)

No. Well, yeah, they're probably—I'll tell you, some of them—see, the big clique rules the roost, and this underdog clique, you might say, is just there to give the other one a little competition, just to know there is another one. And a lot of them are not in it. I was just automatically put in it, you might say. I didn't ask to be in it or nothing. . . . I've junked the whole outfit once or twice about jumping on somebody—

(How do they go about jumping on somebody?)

Oh, just rub it in, you know, ignore them, not liking them—in class they ignore them when they walk by, laugh—there's a lot of ways you can agitate someone.

They'd want to break off with this certain— But this is a real nice town and that. There's just too much jealousy. Everybody's out—they can't stand to see prosperity, if you know what I mean. They can't stand to see anybody get away with anything. This girl moved in here from Michigan. This ———, —she's a real nice-looking girl, see—oh, I'd say she's above intelligence—she's average, anyway. And she's real nice, and—but these girls got it in their heads that they didn't want to have her around. So now she's completely left out. She's a nice kid.

——— wanted to ask her out, and his sister didn't want him to go with her, because he'd been going with ———,—he still goes around with her, but he just wanted to ask her out, no harm in it. But his sister couldn't see that, so his sister started making it hard for her. And then a couple other girls got it in for her about something, I don't know what it was. And then she was just dropped. That's the way it works.

This account of the leading crowd in one school gives a vivid picture of how such crowds function; not that the leading crowd in every school functions in just the same way. Most interviews in other schools suggested a somewhat less closed circle than in this school, yet one that is not greatly different.

In every school, most students saw a leading crowd, and were willing to say what it took to get in it. This should not be surprising, for every adult community has its leading crowd, although adults are less often in such close and compelling communities. Adults, however, are often blind to the fact that the teen-agers in a high school *do* constitute a community, which *does* have a leading crowd. Consequently, adult concern tends to be with questions of better ways to teach "the child," viewed as an isolated entity—whether it is the "gifted child" or the "backward child."

The major categories of response to the question, "What does it take to get into the leading crowd in this school?" are shown in Figure 2.9. Consider first the girls' responses. Most striking is the great importance of "having a good personality." Not only is this mentioned most often in the total responses, but it is mentioned most often in seven of the nine schools.

The importance of having a good personality, or, what is a little different, "being friendly" or "being nice to the other kids," in these adolescent cultures is something that adults often fail to realize. Adults often forget how "person-oriented" children are; they have not yet moved into the world of cold impersonality in which many adults live. This is probably due to their limited range of contacts. In the world of grade school, a boy or girl *can* respond to his classmates as persons, with a sincerity that becomes impossible as one's range of contacts grows. One of the major transitions for some children comes, in fact, as they enter high school and find that they move from classroom to classroom and have different classmates in each class.

After "a good personality" come a wide range of attributes and activities. The diversity of responses is indicated by the collection of remarks listed below—some respondents were hostile to the leading crowd, and, in their hostility, often thought it immoral; others were friendly to it, and, in their friendliness, attributed positive virtues to it.

(What does it take to get into the leading crowd in this school?)

Wear just the right things, nice hair, good grooming and have a wholesome personality.

Money, clothes, flashy appearance, date older boys, fairly good grades.

Be a sex fiend—dress real sharp—have own car and money—smoke and drink—go steady with a popular boy.

Have pleasant personality, good manners, dress nicely, be clean, don't swear, be loads of fun.

A nice personality, dress nice without overdoing it.

Hang out at ——'s. Don't be too smart. Flirt with boys. Be co-operative on dates.

Among these various attributes, the graph shows "good looks," phrased in some fashion, to be second to "personality" in frequency. Having nice clothes, or being well dressed, is the third most frequent item mentioned. What it means to be well dressed differs sharply in a well-to-do suburb and in a working-class school, of course. Nevertheless, whether it is the number of cashmere sweaters a girl owns or simply having clean and attractive dresses, the matter of "having good clothes" is important. The importance of clothes appears to derive partially from the fact that clothes symbolize family status. However, it also appears to stem from the same source that gives importance to "good looks"; these items are crucial in making a girl attractive to boys. Thus, in this respect, the values of the girls' culture are molded by the presence of boys—and by the fact that success with boys is of overriding importance.

Another attribute required if one is to be in the leading crowd is indicated by the class of responses labeled "having a good reputation," which was fourth in number of times mentioned. In all these schools, this item was often mentioned, although in each school, some saw the leading crowd as composed of girls with bad reputations and immoral habits.

A girl's "reputation" is crucial among adolescents. A girl is caught in a dilemma, posed by the importance of good looks, on the one hand, and a good reputation, on the other. A girl must be successful with the boys, says the culture, but in doing so she must maintain her reputation. In some schools, the limits defining a good reputation are stricter than in others, but in all the schools, the limits are there to define what is "good" and what is "bad." The definitions are partly based on behavior with boys, but they also include drinking, smoking, and other less tangible matters—something about the way a girl handles herself, quite apart from what she actually does.

It is not such an easy matter for a girl to acquire and keep a good reputation, particularly if her mother is permissive in letting her date whom she likes as a freshman or sophomore. Junior and senior boys often date freshman and sophomore girls, sometimes with good intentions and sometimes not. One senior boy in Green Junction, in commenting upon the "wildness" of the leading girls in his class, explained it by saying that when his class was in the eighth grade, it was forced to go to school in the high-school building because of a classroom shortage. A number of the girls in the class, he explained, had begun dating boys in the upper classes of high school. This, to him, was where the problem began.

Another criterion for membership in the leading crowd was expressed by a girl who said simply: "Money, fancy clothes, good house, new cars, etc.—the best." These qualities are all of a piece: they express the fact that being born into the right family is a great help to a girl in getting into the leading crowd. It is expressed differently in different schools and by different girls—sometimes as "parents having money," sometimes as "coming from the right neighborhood," sometimes as "expensive clothes." These qualities differ sharply from some of those discussed above, for they are not something a girl can *change*.[12] Her position in the system is ascribed according to her parents' social position, and there is nothing she can do about it. If criteria such as these dominate, then we would expect the system to have a very different effect on the people in it than if other criteria, which a girl or boy could hope to meet, were the basis of social comparison. Similarly, in the larger society a caste system has

---

12. To be sure, she sometimes has a hard time changing her looks or her personality; yet these are her own personal attributes, which she can do something about, except in extreme situations.

quite different effects on individuals than does a system with a great deal of mobility between social classes.

It is evident that these family-background criteria play some part in these schools, but—at least, according to these girls—not the major part. (It is true, however, that the girls who are *not* in the leading crowd more often see such criteria, which are glossed over or simply not seen by girls who are in the crowd.) Furthermore, these criteria vary sharply in their importance in different schools, as will be evident in the next chapter.

Another criterion for being in the leading crowd is scholastic success. According to these girls, good grades, or "being smart" or "intelligent," have something to do with membership in the leading crowd. Not much, to be sure: it is mentioned less than 12 per cent of the time, and far less often than the attributes of personality, good looks, clothes, and the like. Nevertheless, doing well in school apparently counts for something. It is surprising that it does not count for more, because in some situations, the "stars," heroes, and objects of adulation are those who best achieve the goals of the institution. For example, in the movie industry, the leading crowd is composed of those who have achieved the top roles—they are, by consensus, the "stars." Or in a graduate school, the "leading crowd" of students ordinarily consists of the bright students who excel in their work. Not so for these high school girls. The leading crowd seems to be defined primarily in terms of *social* success: their personality, clothes, desirability as dates, and—in communities where social success is tied closely to family background—their money and family.

Perhaps, however, achievement in other areas within the school is important in getting into the leading crowd. That is, participation in school activities of one sort or another may be the entree for a girl into the leading group.

A look at the frequency of responses in Figure 2.9 indicates that this is not true. Activities in school, such as cheerleading, and "being active in school affairs" were mentioned, but rather infrequently. The over-all frequency was 6.5 per cent, and in none of the schools were these things mentioned as much as 10 per cent of the time. It may very well be, of course, that activities help a girl's access to the leading crowd through an indirect path, bringing her to the center of attention, from whence access to the leading crowd is possible.

What about boys? What were their responses to this question about criteria for the leading crowd? Figure 2.9 shows the boys' responses, grouped as much as possible into the same categories used for the girls. The first difference between these and the girls' responses is the over-all lower frequency. The girls sometimes set down in great detail just what

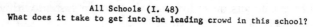

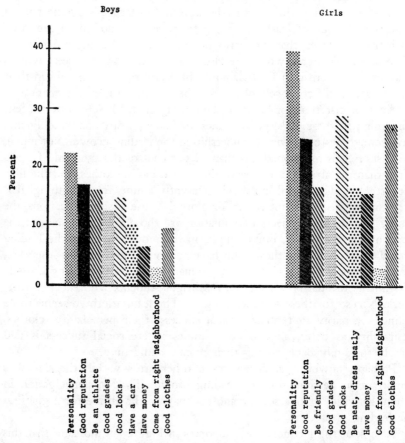

Figure 2.9—Attributes seen as important for a boy's or a girl's membership in the leading crowd.

is required to get in the leading crowd—but the matter seems somewhat less salient to the boys.

For the boys, a somewhat different set of attributes is important for membership in the leading crowd. The responses below give some idea of the things mentioned.

A good athlete, pretty good looking, common sense, sense of humor.

Money, cars and the right connections and a good personality.

Be a good athlete. Have a good personality. Be in everything you can. Don't drink or smoke. Don't go with bad girls.

Athletic ability sure helps.

Prove you rebel the police officers. Dress sharply. Go out with sharp Freshman girls. Ignore Senior girls.

Good in athletics; "wheel" type; not too intelligent.

By categories of response, Figure 2.9 shows that "a good personality" is important for the boys, but less strikingly so than it is for the girls. Being "good-looking," having good clothes, and having a good reputation are similarly of decreased importance. Good clothes, in particular, are less important for the boys than for the girls. Similarly, the items associated with parents' social position—having money, coming from the right neighborhood, and the like—are less frequently mentioned by boys.

What, then, are the criteria that are more important for boys than girls? The most obvious is athletics. Of the things that a boy can *do*, of the things he can *achieve*, athletic success seems the clearest and most direct path to membership in the leading crowd.

Academic success appears to be a less certain path to the leading crowd than athletics—and sometimes it is a path away, as the final quotation listed above suggests. It does, however, sometimes constitute a path, according to these responses. The path is apparently stronger for boys, where scholarly achievement is fifth in frequency, than for the girls, where it is eighth in frequency. This result is somewhat puzzling, for it is well known that girls work harder in school and get better grades than boys do. The ambivalence of the culture concerning high achievement among girls will be examined in some detail later. At this point, it is sufficient to note that academic achievement is apparently less useful for a girl as a stepping stone to social success in high school than it is for a boy.

An item of considerable importance for the boys, as indicated on the bar graph, is a *car*—just having a car, according to some boys, or having a *nice* car, according to others. Whichever it is, a car appears to be of considerable importance in being part of the "inner circle" in these schools. In four of the five small-town schools—but in none of the larger schools—a car was mentioned more often than academic achievement. When this is coupled with the fact that these responses include not only juniors and seniors but also freshmen and sophomores, who are too young to drive, the place of cars in these adolescent cultures looms even larger.

As a whole, how do the boys' membership criteria for the leading crowd differ from the criteria for girls? Several sharp differences are evident. Family background seems to matter less for boys—it is apparently considerably easier for a boy than for a girl from the wrong side of the tracks to break into the crowd. Clothes, money, and being from the right neighborhood hold a considerably higher place for the girls. Similarly with personal attributes, such as personality, reputation, good looks—all of which define what a person *is*. In contrast, the criteria for boys include a much larger component of what a person *does*, whether in athletics or in academic matters. Such a distinction can be overdrawn, for a girl's reputation and her personality are certainly determined by what she does. However, these are not clear-cut dimensions of achievement, they are far less tangible. Furthermore, they are pliable in the hands of the leading crowd itself, who can define what constitutes a good reputation or a good personality, but who cannot ignore football touchdowns or scholastic honors. Numerous examples of the way the leading crowd can shape reputations were evident in these schools. For example, a girl reported:

It is rumored that if you are in with either ——— or ——— that you've got it made. But they are both my friends. You've got to be popular, considerate, have a good reputation. One girl came this year with a rumor started about her. She was ruined in no time, by ——— especially.

The girl who had been "ruined" was a top student and a leader in school activities, but neither of these things were enough to give her a place in the leading crowd. At the end of the school year she was just as far out of things as she was at the beginning, despite her achievements in school.

The matter is different for boys. There are fewer solid barriers, such as family background, and fewer criteria that can be twisted at the whim of the in-group, than there are for girls. To be sure, achievement must be in the right area—chiefly athletics—but achievement *can* in most of these schools bring a boy into the leading crowd, which is more than it can do in many instances for girls.

There is the suggestion that the girls' culture derives in some fashion from the boys: the girl's role is to sit there and look pretty, waiting for the athletic star to come pick her. She must cultivate her looks, be vivacious and attractive, wear the right clothes, but then wait—until the football player, whose status is determined by his specific achievements, comes along to choose her. This is, of course, only part of the matter, for in a community where the leading crowd largely reflects the "right families" in town (as in Maple Grove, whose leading crowd was described in the earlier quotation from an interview), the girls have more independent power. Furthermore, the fact that girls give the parties and determine who's invited gives them a social lever that the boys don't have.

It is as if the adolescent culture is a Coney Island mirror, which throws back a reflecting adult society in a distorted but recognizable image. And, just as the adult society varies from place to place, so, too, the adolescent society varies from school to school. These variations will be dealt with in Chapter III, but their existence should be kept in mind here, in order to avoid the serious mistake of seeing the "adolescent culture" as all of a piece, as a single invariant entity.

What Does It Take to Be Popular?

Membership in the leading crowd is but one aspect of the values of these adolescent cultures. Only a minority can be members of the leading crowd, and sometimes the crowds are hard to break into. *Popularity*, however, is something anyone can aspire to. Anyone can be popular, if he exhibits the right qualities, and the "right qualities" are determined by the culture. In a farming culture, the farmer who helps his neighbor in time of need is popular; in a hunting culture, the bravest hunters are popular; among little girls playing dolls, the girl with a fancy doll house is popular. As these examples suggest, the "right qualities" for being popular depend on the activities important to the culture in question. In discovering the qualities essential for popularity in the adolescent culture, we learn something of the relative importance of various activities.

The dynamics of popularity is a complex matter, which can only be touched superficially by a questionnaire. Without pretending to investigate these dynamics deeply, it is possible to gain a further perspective by investigating what it takes to be popular. Every boy was asked the following pair of questions:

> I.143–8. Among the items below, what does it take to get to be important and looked up to by the *other fellows* here at school? (Rank from 1 to 6.)
>
> Coming from the right family
> Leader in activities
> Having a nice car
> High grades, honor roll
> Being an athletic star
> Being in the leading crowd
>
> I.149–54. Which of these items is most important in making a fellow *popular with the girls* around here? That is, among the girls who *really rate*, which of these things count most? (Rank from 1 to 6.)
>
> Coming from the right family
> Leader in activities

Having a nice car
High grades, honor roll
Being an athletic star
Being in the leading crowd

Figure 2.10 shows the average rankings given by the boys in answer to these two questions. The answers show the prime importance of athletics in making a boy popular. In answer to both questions, athletics ranks highest of all six items. Second to athletics is being in the leading crowd. That is, if a boy wants to be popular, either with boys or with girls, it helps most of all to be an athlete; but beyond this, being a member of the leading crowd helps greatly in being popular also. That this is true can be seen by the *actual* popularity of athletes and of members of the leading crowd. Each boy in school was asked: (I.38.) "What fel-

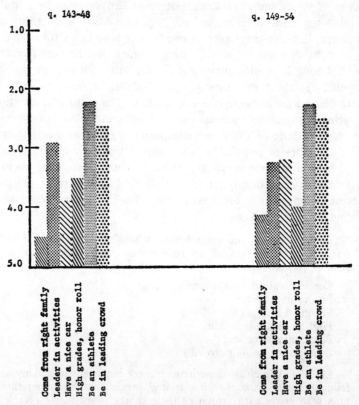

Figure 2.10—Average ranks given by boys to six criteria for popularity with other boys and popularity with girls.

lows here in school do you go around with most often? (Give both first
and last names.)" Each boy listed his friends, whose names were coded;
then each boy was scored by the number of choices he *received* from the
other boys. Since almost every boy in school filled out a questionnaire,[13]
this score was a true representation of the boy's popularity among his
fellows in school. Some boys were never mentioned, although they themselves usually mentioned several names; a few boys were mentioned by
more than fifteen other boys.

Using this score as a measure of a boy's popularity, it is easy to see
in Figure 2.11 that there are many football players among the most popular boys, few among the least popular. This relation is an extremely
strong one, as can be seen by a comparison with another: the popularity
of boys who report studying more than an hour and a half each night.
The graph shows that these boys are *not* much more popular than those
who don't study. Popularity apparently comes easily to an athlete. The
general importance of being an athlete is perhaps even obscured by this
graph, for it includes as "athletes" everyone who *went out* for football
in the fall, quite apart from their proficiency. Later, in Chapter V, the
popularity and the general status of those boys who not only went out
for athletics but were successful enough to be recognized as such by their
fellows will be evident.

When the same question is raised about the leading crowd—that is,
as to the actual popularity of the persons who say they are in the leading
crowd—the picture looks much the same as it does for athletics (Figure
2.11). Their general popularity is quite high, again in contrast to the
popularity of the studiers—those boys who studied more than one and
one-half hours at night on the average. Thus, no matter how one looks
at the question of popularity—whether in terms of the way the boys *see*
the system functioning, or in terms of the *actual* popularity of different
boys—being an athlete and being in the leading crowd are of great importance in making a boy popular.

Looking again at the way the other items are ranked in question
143–48 (Figure 2.10), there is a general consistency with the earlier
question of what it takes to get in the leading crowd. For general popularity, just as for being in the leading crowd, good grades count for much
less than athletics, standing fourth among the six items. Another attribute

---

13. Only 1 per cent of the boys did not fill out a questionnaire. The non-response
to this question was 10 per cent. This is an upper limit to the non-response, for
some of these apparent non-responses were legitimate statements that the boy went
around with no boys in the school. The non-response was highest by far in St.
John's High, the only school in the study where boys could easily have most of
their friends outside school.

shows its importance, however—being a leader in school activities. Although this was seldom mentioned by boys in question 48 as a criterion for membership in the leading crowd, it does rank high here—higher than good grades, and third among the group of six. Having a nice car stands fifth, with "coming from the right family" in sixth position.

The differences these boys perceive in what it takes to be popular with *girls* is striking: being an athlete and being in the leading crowd hold about the same importance, according to these boys' view; but being a leader in activities and, even more, getting good grades are seen as *less* important in making a boy popular with girls. Having a nice car moves up from fifth position to third, and coming from the right family becomes slightly more important than before.

In general, then, these boys feel that school-related activities other than athletics are of considerably less importance in being popular with girls than they are in being popular with other boys. Good grades and

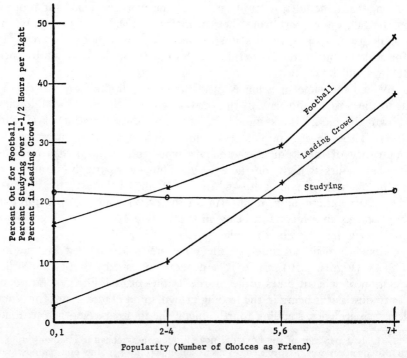

Figure 2.11—Relation between popularity and a) being out for football; b) membership in leading crowd; and c) studying more than one and one half hours per night.

leadership in school activities decrease, and two extra-school considerations arise—a car, which greatly facilitates dating, and family background, an accession to parental constraints or general social status.

The girls' responses to a parallel pair of questions shows a variation upon this pattern.

I.143–48. Among the items below, what does it take to get to be important and looked up to by the *other girls* here at school? (Rank from 1 to 6.)

Coming from the right family
Leader in activities
Clothes
High grades, honor roll
Being cheerleader
Being in the leading crowd

I.149–54. Which of these items is most important in making a girl *popular with the boys* around here? That is, among the boys who *really rate*, which of these things count most? (Rank from 1 to 6.)

Coming from the right family
Leader in activities
Clothes
High grades, honor roll
Being cheerleader
Being in the leading crowd

Figure 2.12 indicates that girls see "being in the leading crowd" as the most important of these attributes in achieving popularity. They rank it 2.25, higher than any other item. Being a leader in activities is second, followed by the other four items grouped closely together—clothes, family background, grades, and being a cheerleader. These responses present some puzzling differences from the responses to the question about what it takes to get into the leading crowd. In particular, activities were seldom mentioned as a criterion for the leading crowd, yet here they rank second, higher than several items that were mentioned more frequently there.

The significance of activities for popularity is shown also by the *actual* popularity of girls who went out for some activity as a freshman compared with those who did not. (See Figure 2.13.) Just as athletics for the boys shows a high relation to actual popularity, so does activities for the girls. Similarly, membership in the leading crowd is strongly related to popularity.

One result (shown in both halves of Figure 2.12), surprising to anyone unfamiliar with the high-school culture, is the relative importance

of being a cheerleader. As the counterpart of the athletic star, the cheerleader is not nearly so important as the athletic star, yet in many schools,
her role comes closer to paralleling that of the athlete than does any other
role that girls have. It is not our intention to examine the reasons why
this is so, but it might be suggested that, like the athletic star, the cheerleader focuses the attention of the school as a whole in a common activity,
and in a sense "leads them on toward victory." Thus she, and even more
the athletic star, are leaders of the school in a very active sense, for theirs
is one of the few activities in which the school as a whole is led into
action *as a school* rather than as a set of separate individuals.

The importance of high grades or being on the honor roll for popularity is evident in further examination of Figure 2.12. For girls, as for
boys, grades rank low. In fact, in relation to the other five items listed
for girls, good grades rank *lower* for girls than they do for boys.

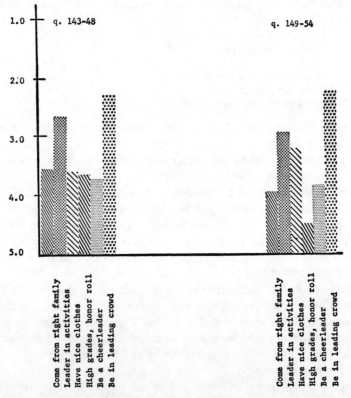

Figure 2.12—Average ranks given by girls to six criteria for popularity with
other girls and popularity with boys.

To be sure, the other items are not alike for the boys and the girls; however, casual inspection suggests that, if anything, the five other categories for the boys were more attractive than were the five other categories for girls. These data are not conclusive, but they are consistent with the earlier indicators that doing well in school is even less help for a girl's popularity than it is for a boy's.

What are the differences in the things it takes for a girl to be popular with *boys*? That is, how do the girls rank the importance of each of these items for a girl's being popular with boys? Figure 2.12 shows that the one most outstanding difference is in good grades—these girls feel that scholastic success counts for even less in being popular with boys than it does in being popular with other girls. In seven schools (all but Marketville and Midcity), it ranks lowest of the six items. In contrast, in

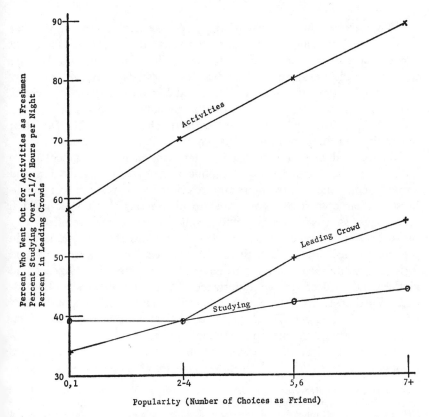

Figure 2.13—Relation between popularity and a) having gone out for some activity in school as a freshman; b) membership in leading crowd; and c) studying more than one and one half hours per night.

only three schools did the boys rank good grades lowest as a criterior for a boy's popularity with girls. A lesser decline is evident in the rank of "leader in activities"—along with an increase in having nice clothes. The parallel with the boys' pattern is interesting. For both boys and girls, popularity with one's own sex is believed to involve good grades and school activities more than does popularity with the opposite sex. For popularity with the opposite sex, cars are more important for boys; and clothes, for girls. These two attributes feature prominently in dating. while good grades and school activities do not.

Boy-Girl Relations and Their Impact on the Culture

What are the implications of these results? Let us suppose that the girls in a school valued good grades more than did the boys. One might expect that the presence of these girls would be an influence on the boys toward a higher evaluation of studies. Yet these data say *not*; they say that a boy's popularity with girls is based less on doing well in school. more on such attributes as a car, than is his popularity with other boys Similarly for girls—scholastic success is much less valuable for their popularity with boys than for their popularity with other girls.

We have always known that the standards men and women use to judge each other include a large component of physical attractiveness, and a smaller component of the more austere criteria they use in judging members of their own sex. Yet we seem to ignore that this is true in high schools just as it is in business offices, and that its cumulative effect may be to de-emphasize education in schools far more than we realize.[14] In the normal activities of a high school, the relations between boys and girls tend to increase the importance of physical attractiveness, cars, and clothes, and to decrease the importance of achievement in school activities. Whether this *must* be true is another question; it might be that schools themselves could so shape these relations to have a *positive* effect, rather than a negative one, on the school's goals.

The general research question is this: what kinds of interactions among boys and girls lead them to evaluate the opposite sex less on

14. One cannot infer from the above considerations that single-sex high schools would produce more attention to academic matters. One other matter, evident in later chapters at St. John's, is the tendency of some adolescents in a single-sex school to have few interests in school. The opposite sex in a school pulls interests toward the school, and then partly diverts it to non-scholastic matters.

grounds of physical attraction, more on grounds that are not so superficial? It seems likely, for example, that in some private schools (e.g., the Putney School) where adolescents engage in common work activities, bases develop for evaluating the opposite sex that are quite different from those generated by the usual activities surrounding a public high school. The question of practical policy, once such a research question has been answered, is even more difficult: what can a school do to foster the kinds of interactions that lead boys and girls to judge the opposite sex on grounds that implement the school's goals?

It is commonly assumed, both by educators and by laymen, that it is "better" for boys and girls to be in school together during adolescence, if not better for their academic performance, then at least better for their social development and adjustment. But this may not be so; it may depend wholly upon the kinds of activities within which their association takes place. Coeducation in some high schools may be inimical to *both* academic achievement *and* social adjustment. The dichotomy often forced between "life-adjustment" and "academic emphasis" is a false one, for it forgets that most of the teen-ager's energy is not directed toward either of these goals. Instead, the relevant dichotomy is cars and the cruel jungle of rating and dating versus school activities, whether of the academic or life-adjustment variety.

But perhaps, at least for girls, this is where the emphasis *should* be: on making themselves into desirable objects for boys. Perhaps physical beauty, nice clothes, and an enticing manner are the attributes that should be most important among adolescent girls. No one can say whether girls should be trained to be wives, citizens, mothers, or career women. Yet in none of these areas of adult life are physical beauty, an enticing manner, and nice clothes as important for performing successfully as they are in high school. Even receptionists and secretaries, for whom personal attractiveness is a valuable attribute, must carry out their jobs well, or they will not be able to keep them. Comparable performance is far less important in the status system of the high school, with its close tie to the rating and dating system. There, a girl can survive much longer on personal attractiveness, an enticing manner, and nice clothes.

The adult women in which such attributes *are* most important are of a different order from wives, citizens, mothers, career women, secretaries: they are chorus girls, models, movie and television actresses, and call girls. In all these activities, women serve as *objects of attention* for men and, even more, objects to *attract* men's attention. These are quite different from the attributes of a good wife, which involve less superficial qualities. If the adult society wants high schools to inculcate the attributes that make girls objects to attract men's attention, then these values of good looks and nice clothes, discussed above, are just right. If not, then the values are quite inappropriate.

A second answer to what's wrong with these values is this: nothing, so long as they do not completely pervade the atmosphere, so long as there are *other* ways a girl can become popular and successful in the eyes of her peers. And there are other ways, as indicated by the emphasis on "a nice personality" in the questions discussed above. Yet the over-all responses to these questions suggest that in adolescent cultures these superficial, external attributes of clothes and good looks do pervade the atmosphere to the extent that girls come to feel that this is the only basis or the *most important* basis on which to excel.

EFFECTS ON GIRLS OF THE EMPHASIS ON ATTRACTIVENESS

There are several sets of responses in the questionnaire indicating that girls do feel these attributes of attractiveness are most important. One is the responses to question 68 (see tabulation on p. 28), in which more girls checked "model" as the occupation they would like than any of the other three—"nurse," or "schoolteacher," or "actress or artist." As suggested above, a model is one of the occupations that most embodies these attributes of beauty and superficial attractiveness to men.

Further consequences of this emphasis on being attractive to boys are indicated by responses to a set of sentence-completion questions. Comparing the boys' responses and the girls' gives some indication of the degree to which the high school culture impresses these matters upon girls. The questions are listed in Table 12, together with the proportions responding in terms of popularity with the opposite sex or relations with the opposite sex.

To each one of these sentence-completion questions, girls gave far more responses involving popularity and relations with others than did boys. These responses suggest that the emphasis on popularity with boys has powerful consequences for these girls' attitudes toward life and themselves. A further indication that success with boys is tied to rather superficial external qualities is shown by the great proportion of girls who say that they worry most about some personal characteristic—most often an external attribute such as weight or figure or hair or skin, but also including such attributes as "shyness."

One might suggest, however, that the girls' concern with popularity and with the physical attributes that help make them popular would be just as strong in the absence of the adolescent culture. A simple comparison of these four sentence-completion questions suggests that this is

Table 12—Boys' and girls' sentence-completion responses related to popularity—totals for nine schools*

		Boys	Girls
s.11.	More than anything else, I'd like to		
	Responses involving popularity with opposite sex	5.4%	10.8%
	Responses involving popularity, unspecified	5.3	11.4
	Total codable responses	(2,343)	(2,776)
s.12	The best thing that could happen to me this year at school would be		
	Responses involving relations with opposite sex	4.5	20.7
	Responses involving relations with others, unspecified	3.2	9.0
	Total codable responses	(2,222)	(2,702)
s.13.	The most important thing in life is		
	Responses involving popularity with opposite sex	6.3	7.4
	Responses involving popularity, unspecified	4.6	7.9
	Total codable responses	(2,151)	(2,737)
s.14.	I worry most about		
	Responses involving popularity with opposite sex	9.2	13.9
	Responses involving personal attributes related to popularity (weight, hair, figure, etc.)	2.7	8.6
	Total codable responses	(2,201)	(2,803)

* These questions were asked in a supplementary questionnaire, filled out in the 9 schools by the 6,289 students who completed the basic fall questionnaire early.

not so. The question in which girls *most* often give responses involving relations with the opposite sex is the one referring directly to the school life: "The best thing that could happen to me this year at school would be. . . ." When the question refers to life in general ("The most important thing in life is. . . ."), then the boy-girl differential is sharply reduced. This suggests that it is within the adolescent social system itself that relations with boys and physical attractiveness are so important to girls.

The emphasis on popularity with the opposite sex has other effects on the girls, of which we have only the barest knowledge. One of the effects is on her feelings about herself. We may suppose that if a girl found herself in a situation where she was not successful in "the things that count," she would be less happy with herself, and would want to change, to be someone different. On the other hand, the more successful she was in the things that counted, the more she would be satisfied with herself as she was.

We have no measure of the objective beauty of girls, and we are not able to separate out those who are particularly unattractive in dress or beauty, to see the impact that these values have upon their conceptions of themselves. However, we can pick out those girls who are, in the eyes of their classmates, the best-dressed girls. This will allow an indirect test of the effect of the emphasis on clothes. On the questionnaire, we asked every girl: (I.40b.i.) "Of all the girls in your grade, who is the best dressed?" The girls named most often by their classmates are at one end of the continuum. Thus, if this is an important attribute to have, these girls should feel considerably better about themselves than do their classmates. Table 13 below shows that they do, and that those named most often felt best about themselves.

Table 13—I.156. If I could trade, I would be someone different from myself

	Per cent who agree	Number
All girls	21.2	(3,782)
Girls named 2–6 times as best dressed	17.0	(282)
Girls named 7 or more times as best dressed	11.2	(98)

The effect of being thought of as "best dressed" by her classmates is quite striking, reducing by nearly half the likelihood of her wanting to be someone different. Or, to put it differently, the effect of *not* being thought of as "best dressed" by her classmates nearly doubles a girl's likelihood of wanting to be someone different.

To see the strength of this effect, relative to the effect of competing values, it is possible to compare these responses with those of girls who were highly regarded by their classmates, but in other ways. The following questions were asked along with the "best-dressed" question: (I.40b.) "Of all the girls in your grade, who . . . is the best student? . . . do boys go for most?"

The girls who were named most often by their classmates on these two questions and the previous one can be thought of as "successful" in each of these areas—dress, studies, and relations with boys. Insofar as these things "count," they should make the girls feel happier about themselves—and conversely, make the girls who are not successful less happy about themselves.

Figure 2.14 indicates the relative effectiveness of these three values, the degree to which they "count" in making a girl happy or unhappy about herself. For each of the three values, the girl who is named as "best" seven times or more is least likely to want to be someone different. It is apparent that all three values have some effect. However, success with boys apparently has most effect; being thought of as best dressed—which seems to be important largely because it contributes to being successful with boys is somewhat less effective; and being thought of as best student is apparently least effective of the three. The results of the companion questions for boys are shown along with those for the girls, to indicate that this result is not simply due to the personality of those popular with the opposite sex. For boys, athletics is apparently most effective, more so than popularity with girls. (Further consequences of the value systems on the self-conception of various teen-agers will be examined at length in Chapter VIII.)

Altogether, then, it appears that the role of girls as objects of attention for boys is emphasized by the adolescent values in these schools. Its consequences are multifarious, and we have only touched upon them, but one point is clear: just "putting together" boys and girls in the same school is not necessarily the "normal, healthy" thing to do. It does not necessarily promote adjustment to life; it may promote, as is indicated by these data, adjustment to the life of a model or chorus girl or movie actress or call girl. It may, in other words, promote *mal*adjustment to the kind of life that these girls will lead after school.

Common sense is not enough in these matters. It is not enough to put boys and girls in a school and expect that they will be a "healthy influence" on one another. Serious research is necessary in order to discover the kinds of activities and the kinds of situations that will allow them to be such, rather than emphasizing the superficial values of a hedonistic culture.

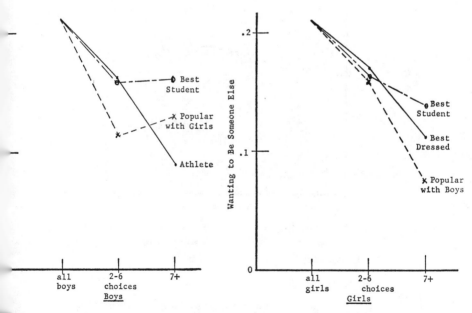

Figure 2.14—Relation between number of choices received as "best" on three criteria and proportion wanting to be someone else.

The way in which such interactions can affect the value system pervading a school is shown clearly by a comparison with one of the two supplementary schools in the study, school 10. This is a private school, with students of upper-middle-class backgrounds similar to those of the students in Executive Heights, but in a very scholastic university setting. Figure 2.15 shows the importance over the four years of "good looks" as an attribute for membership in its leading crowd, together with the over-all average for the nine schools of the study. The contrast is striking. They start out at almost the same point in the freshman year. But in school 10, the importance of good looks goes *down* sharply over the four years; in nine schools of the study, the average even *rises* slightly, as dating begins in earnest in the sophomore and junior years, before dropping off somewhat in the senior year. This graph gives only the faintest hint of the different experiences these two school situations would present for a girl.[15]

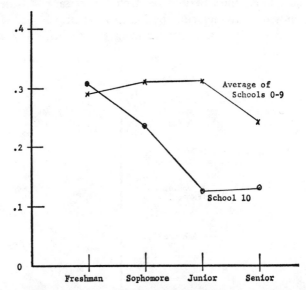

Figure 2.15—Proportion of girls mentioning popularity or good looks as important for membership in the leading crowd, in all schools and in a university laboratory school (#10).

15. One author who studied a group of adolescents says this: "In the adolescent culture itself girls encounter many changes in the conception as to what constitutes desirable behavior, changes and even reversals in the value system and in the relative ranking of traits which are important for popularity and prestige. Perhaps the principal single change which we have found in our California group is that at the beginning of adolescence the group standards for conduct among girls emphasize a quiet, demure, rather lady-like demeanor. By the age of fifteen this has altered,

This is not to suggest that all the schools of the nine in the study showed this same pattern; some did not. In particular, Marketville showed a continual decline similar to that of school 10, while several others showed a sharp rise in the sophomore and junior years, before decreasing among the seniors.

---

and we find that the girls who are now most popular in their set are active, talkative, and marked by a kind of 'aggressive good fellowship.' These traits, which may in part be adaptations to the hesistant and immature social approaches of boys, must again undergo considerable change in the later years of adolescence, if a girl is to maintain her status in the group."

Harold E. Jones, "Adolescence in Our Society," in *The Adolescent*, Jerome Seidman, ed. (New York: Dryden Press, 1953), p. 60.

Jones' results show changes which are in part due to maturation. It may be that the rise in importance of "good looks" among our sophomore girls, and the decline among seniors, are a result of this maturation. The example of school 10, however, shows that far more than maturation shapes the character of the culture from grade to grade.

III Value Climates of Each School

THE EFFECTS OF THE ADOLESCENT CUL-
ture in our society are difficult to discover, because of its very pervasiveness, among adolescents. There are few good "control groups" of
adolescents growing up in the absence of an adolescent society. Thus,
some of the comparisons must be implicit ones with the past, when adolescents constituted a less developed society of their own. But some of the
effects can be discovered through present-day variations from place to
place. That is, each school contains a somewhat distinct adolescent society,
and the structure and values may differ from one to the other.

It is this technique which the present study uses to examine the effects
of adolescent cultures. Schools were selected not for their similarities nor
their "representativeness" but for their differences. The aim was to find
schools whose adolescent cultures were various enough so that differing
effects could be studied. The preceding two chapters have neglected these
differences, for the sake of showing the most outstanding features that
these adolescent cultures share. Many of these features show strikingly the
differences between the adolescent and the adult worlds. But there are
variations within the adolescent society, and it necessary to identify these
variations if their effects are to be studied.

The Ten Schools

In this and succeeding chapters, the ten schools will often be examined
separately. To help establish an image of each school, the schools have
been given names roughly descriptive of the communities they serve. The

names along with numbers which will sometimes be used in graphs for convenience, are:

Small towns	0—Farmdale
	1—Marketville
	2—Elmtown
	3—Maple Grove
	4—Green Junction
Large-city, parochial	5—St. John's High
Suburb	6—Newlawn
Small city	7—Millburg
Small city	8—Midcity
Suburb	9—Executive Heights

All parents' questionnaires were coded by one person, who was otherwise unfamiliar with the communities, the schools, or the aims of the research. After finishing the parents' questionnaires for a given school, he made a page or two of notes on the community and school as seen through the parents' eyes and as reported by them in their comments.[1] These descriptions, of course, are not accurate, but they give a flavor of the community and school as seen by parents.

For two schools, Marketville and Elmtown, almost no notes were made; in place of that, a paragraph from the earlier study of Elmtown will be quoted, again to give a flavor of the communiity; for Marketville, a few comments are taken directly from the parents' questionnaires.

0—FARMDALE

Population 1,000; school, 169.

Farmdale seems to be one of these country communities where the teen-agers are expected to work hard for their parents during certain hours of the day, and are left free to roam as they please afterward. It is reported that there is much running around in cars at late hours, and wishes were expressed that the authorities should clamp down. The two or three taverns in the town evidently do a good deal of business and are open every day of the week.

One comment stated that there is not enough industry in Farmdale to keep graduates at home after high school. Most of the parents are farmers with rather nice-sized farms.

Ma and Pa —— claim that there is much division in town among the parents and that they can't work together. There seem to be a number of women's clubs in town, but they can't work together as far as education is concerned. Although it isn't evident from the way the people seem to live, there are one or two reports of there being very much money "about."

One would expect a small town like Farmdale to be a warm-hearted, friendly place. Judging from some comments, it is rather a cold place to outsiders, and new people find it hard to make friends there.

---

1. The project is indebted to Thomas Long for these notes.

The high-school band is Farmdale's pride and joy. Evidently, it is the top high-school band in the area. A Band Parents Association has been formed and seems to be popular among the parents. There are some, however, who think that too much attention is given to activities, such as a band, and they stress the need for returning to the three R's.

The two Baptist churches that dominate the religious scene also wield influence in the school. It is reported that because of the church, no dances are allowed to be held in the school or sponsored by the school.

Some parents hold that there aren't enough recreational facilities for their children; others are glad that they are living in Farmdale, for there is plenty of room for them to play. All in all, the importance of education seems to be little realized.

1—MARKETVILLE

Population 4,000; school, 364.

Parent A: This town is sharply divided into three sections. The South side looks down on the North and West side. The North side looks down on the West side. The West side has an almost impenetrable barrier social-wise upon entering High School. It is very difficult and is of long, long standing. The school is divided in just this way too. I know of no other school that equals this one in snobbery.

Parent B: We feel there is a high type of faculty members—morally sound and offering good influence for teen-agers. The past 2 years a specialist in counseling from the U. of I. spends one day at the High School each week and also helps with remedial reading and study habits. The town has good churches and supervision of youth groups. The new community swimming pool offers wonderful recreation during the summer and the nearby lagoon ice-skating in the winter. The High School sponsors "after game" dances and numerous skating parties at a nearby town.

Parent C: On the whole, our high school carries on a good extra curricular program for our children. However, there is very little the students can do, other than make their own private plans, such as house parties. There is a bowling alley which is outside the corporation and next to a tavern which isn't the most desirable location. There are no Y's, no skating rinks and not a particularly good sweet shop.

Parent D: When I graduated from 8th grade 35 years ago, my father did not think it necessary to go on to high school. So neither myself nor seven brothers and sisters had that opportunity. I have six children of my own and was left a widow 16 years ago just six weeks before my youngest son was born, it was my desire to do all I could to give them their schooling, four have high school diplomas, one quit in her junior year to be married, so I have one left in school. I am working in a low paid factory with no promotions or future except more work on a salary of $1.13 an hour which adds up to $39.90 a week (with all taxes and insurance taken out). We have no car or fancy clothes or furniture but we're making the best of what we have and are very thankful for it.

Parent E: Many of the teachers with good religious backgrounds have the patience necessary to cope with teen-agers. They also seem to have enough self-respect that the students in turn respect them. Many of the students in this school as well as other schools in this county who are honor roll students are from homes where religious principles are regarded rather highly. Religious freedom, yes, but let's not teach Darwin theories any more. True science and true religion agree.

2—ELMTOWN

Population 7,000; school, 513.[2]

Elmtown's institutions are typical of a Middle Western county-seat town which politically, religiously, educationally, professionally, economically, and socially dominates its tributary area. All types of basic businesses and services common to a town of 6,000 people in the Corn Belt are found here. In addition, it is proud of its locally owned and published daily newspaper and its hospital. Two banks serve the financial needs of the farms, industries, and stores, and a small-loan business caters to the "little people." Several national insurance companies have local agents here. Chain stores compete with those owned by merchants whose families have been in business for two or three generations. A dozen doctors, 5 dentists, 20 lawyers, 15 nurses, and several other independent professionals live and practice in Elmtown. Organized churches in Elmtown itself consist of one Catholic as well as nine Protestant, including one Norwegian Lutheran; there is another Norwegian Lutheran church in the county. There are no state institutions either in the community or in Home County; neither are there any colleges, health resorts, or other establishments which might give it a distinctive character.

In the twelve states comprising the Middle West, there were 215 towns in 1940 that ranged between 5,000 and 10,000 in population. One hundred and eight of the 215 were the largest towns in their counties; they were also county-seat towns. Moreover, they were classed as agricultural-industrial; that is, between 25 and 50 percent of their male workers were employed in agriculture, and more than 20 percent were engaged in industry. Elmtown was one of these towns. In terms of its location, size, economic base, population, and institutions, Elmtown may be characterized as a typical Middle Western town. If the communal area is included, the "typical town" can be called a "typical community." . . . Elmtown and its dependent institutional area may be said to be a "typical Middle Western community" functionally, structurally, culturally, and historically. Moreover, it may be assumed with some confidence that the knowledge gained about its social structure could be duplicated in any similar community in the Middle West with only minor changes in detail.[3]

3—MAPLE GROVE

Population 6,000; school, 421.

One respondent describes Maple Grove as a town of older retired people with relatively no factories or businesses until recent years. The majority of people living in the vicinity at present include well-to-do old families, farmers, and some factory workers employed in the few industries in or near the town.

---

2. The following passage is taken from A. B. Hollingshead, *Elmtown's Youth*, p. 64–5.

3. The results of the present study will suggest that this assumption is far from valid.

Most of the parents present positive aspects of the community. They say that they enjoy living in a town of this size, and believe it has a favorable effect on their children. It is almost unanimous that a small and friendly town such as Maple Grove is an ideal place to rear children. To back this statement up, some state that all one has to do is to look at their children, their attitudes, and the close friendships they can develop, to get an idea of the town.

There are a few, however, who aren't entirely satisfied with things as they stand. A Presbyterian minister says that a social caste feeling exists in the community, and is supported by another parent whose words are: "If your family tree dates far back in the town's history and there is culture associated with it, you're in; otherwise you're not."

Most parents hold a favorable view of the academic program of the high school. A few mention that the teachers do not give the students the urge to continue their educations. Most agree that athletics is carried too far in the school program. Those who disparage teachers usually have something derogatory to add about athletics.

The last point that seems characteristic of Maple Grove is that several of the families have lived there only a short time. A few state specifically, and I sense from the others, that they have left larger communities to come to Maple Grove and work in her recently acquired industries.

4—GREEN JUNCTION

Population 5,000, school, 538.

If one were asked to describe what he thought to be the ideal American town, the picture he would paint would be very similar to that given by parents on these questionnaires.

The town is small enough so that everyone knows each other. The residents seem to be able to work together very well. There is an effort to provide more recreational activities for the teen-agers, the current project being a swimming pool for the town.

Perhaps this is one of those towns which suffered a period of neglect of recreation facilities. Parents often say that in their youth Green Junction had many things for them to do in their spare time. The merchants get along well together, as do the various organizations. It is reported that there is one Negro family living in the community.

Green Junction High School has a number of students from outlying areas. At present, the school is overcrowded, but an expansion program is in progress which promises to remedy the situation. Religious education is given in the school on "released time." It is complained at present that there are not enough courses to choose from, although one parent stated that Green Junction graduates "do well in college."

There is no public transportation system in the area, which makes it rather difficult for the children in the outlying districts and, on some occasions, those in town. In one area, a car pool has been organized by the parents to help their children get about. It doesn't quite solve the problem, and creates more difficulties for the parents.

Many of the people living in the Green Junction area earn their livelihoods by farming. The others perform some type of skilled-unskilled labor in small businesses or in some of the nearby factories. The average number of children seems to be high.

5—ST. JOHN'S HIGH

Population 3,600,000; school, 733.

St. John's High School is a Catholic school whose faculty is composed primarily of "Brothers." As teachers, these brothers are looked up to by parents as the best there are. As Brothers, they are completely free to teach, not having to perform any of the functions of the priest, and not being involved in outside activities as some public-school teachers are. The attention they show to the students is greatly appreciated by parents. There appears to be close co-operation between teachers and parents in this respect. The teachers report to parents of the child's progress, especially if he is having difficulties.

Because the school is overcrowded, those students who get into trouble frequently or who don't appear to be trying to keep their grades up are asked to leave. Such cases must be rare, because most of the students like the school and the teachers.

The main reason given by parents for sending their sons to St. John's is the "fine moral teaching, discipline, and Catholic instruction," which they feel that the school has to offer. The majority of parents are Polish, and I would judge that they are foreign-born or had parents themselves who were. They are primarily of the lower-middle class and place more importance on religion than on any other phase of life.

There is no neighborhood common to all of the parents reporting. Students are sent to St. John's from a number of different areas. Some say that their communities need a larger police force and a curfew system to keep their children out of mischief. In some areas, there are many unlighted streets. A couple of parents condemned politics as being crooked and said that the politicians exert an evil influence on teen-agers.

The parents seem to recognize and fear the bad influences of a large city upon their children. They turn to neighborhood youth clubs to keep them out of mischief, and send their children to parochial schools, hoping that there they will receive the religious and moral instruction necessary to make them good Catholics and desirable citizens.

6—NEWLAWN

Population 9,000; school, 1,053.

"What this town needs is a patrolling police force. If there is trouble or our children get into trouble, we have to go to the Sheriff."

The above quotation makes Newlawn sound like Dodge City, Kansas. Perhaps there is something to that analogy. Like Dodge was, Newlawn is a rapidly growing community. Unlike Dodge City, it is a suburb in the shadows of a metropolis. As yet, its streets aren't paved, nor are there any sidewalks. In winter, the situation is especially bad, for the teen-agers are wet and mud-spattered by the time they arrive at school. The sewage system is bad and there is no public transportation.

Except for the school, which does an excellent job of providing activities for teen-agers, there is relatively little for them to do. Due to this, and perhaps because of the lack of social control and street lights, a lot of vandalism occurs in the town. "Teen-agers throw rocks at mailboxes and break streetlights."

Some parents feel that the town is run by a group of money-hungry politicians who are a bad influence on teen-agers. One informant said that they built some sort of center near the fire hall and that they serve drinks there. There were hints that a number of teen-agers drink.

The fact that there is no program for youth has been attributed by some to the lack of interest on the part of Newlawn parents. In many instances, both parents are working in the factories in or near the community and don't take time with their children. Many of the youngsters are permitted to drive before they are sixteen, and this is frowned upon by a number of people.

In spite of these negative aspects of the community, there is a spirit of satisfaction running through the majority of questionnaires. The town is new, and one can sense the hope its inhabitants have for it in the future by such comments as: "I would like to see a college established in Newlawn." People are glad that there is plenty of room around the town for their children to move about and play in. Very little class consciousness makes itself known in the questionnaires. There are no Negroes living in Newlawn—in fact, these families' exodus from Chicago was in part an escape from Negroes.

The chief positive aspect of the community is its school. Except for one or two parents, the majority of informants praised the school. The building is new and the facilities are all very modern. Parent-teacher relations are good, and the teachers are looked up to by both parents and students. School activities, especially band and sports, receive a great deal of credit for helping students to develop wholesome attitudes in their relations with other people. During the summers, the teachers sponsor what is called a "summer canteen." This provides the teen-agers with swimming, other activities, and refreshments. Through it, they also get to know some of their teachers well.

Although most parents are extremely proud of the education their children receive at Newlawn High School, little evidence was available in the questionnaires to show that many graduates attend college or that there is much inspiration to go. The teen-age boys seem to spend much of their time working on cars, and the school has a place and facilities for them to do this type of work conveniently.

7—MILLBURG

Population 25,000; school, 1,383.

Millburg High School seems to be the pride of the three main communities that send their children there.

Football is the most popular sport at Millburg. The same two men have coached the team for the past forty years. Facilities for this and other sports were donated primarily by some of the older, wealthy families in the area. Although some think that football is carried too far, the parents seem to enjoy going to the games themselves.

Some parents feel that the school policy is to favor the bright student and not care about the less intelligent ones. The policy is also continued with the more social-minded students in the activities. A few stated that the backward students haven't got a chance in the social activities.

Some parents mentioned the need for more manual training in the school. They didn't believe that their children were being prepared to go out and get jobs after graduation—that is, those who weren't going on to college. One such comment condemned the teaching of the writings of Shakespeare, Byron, and others because they "are dead and gone."

A new problem is forcing the three communities to present a united front to outsiders. This problem is the shortage of industry in the area. The idea now is to make the area look good in an effort to attract new industries.[4] Most of the parents are employed at the several factories located here. In the past, these factories have offered much to the communities. Miss ——— of the ——— Cement Mill donated a recreational center and supplied it with excellent facilities. At present, however, the factories are no longer able to provide employment for the students as they are graduated from school. The factories also cater to female employment, and some persons mentioned that such women are neglecting their children by going to work.

It may be interesting to note that while minority groups are said to be well accepted in the school, a Negro hasn't spent the night in the community for fifty years. One parent felt that this was bad if her children are ever going to grow up without being prejudiced.

The community is 85 per cent Catholic[5] and includes many second-generation eastern Europeans. Several comments hold the Catholic Church responsible for all the "drinking, gambling, and other vice" that goes on. One person, himself a Catholic, said that he thought it bad for one church to predominate so greatly in a community. A woman said "the community has excellent recreation facilities and is sports-minded, but everybody and his dog drink. They take babies and children to taverns which are open even on Sundays."

A skeptical parent said, "the town is lazy and can't get anything done. The sewer system is an example. Also, the city council, and not the town, voted for fluoridation, something any fool knows we are better off without." Comments such as "always quarreling" and "can't get along" dominated the general comments about the communities.

Many people say that the area is a good place to rear children. They say that there is relatively no "hoodlum" problem, as in other places where they have lived previously. The police force seems understanding when something goes wrong, says one.

One parent disapproved strongly of the teaching of evolution in the schools.

8—MIDCITY

Population 10,000; school, 1,935.

Many of the parents are discontent with the high school and educational system in general, but for few common reasons. The common reasons are uninterested teachers and a poor guidance system. Some think that courses that do not prepare students for manual occupations should be done away with. Others ask for more emphasis on college preparation. It was mentioned several times

---

4. These towns underwent a slight population decline in each of two decades from 1930–1950.

5. The school is 67 per cent Catholic, 32 per cent Protestant, and less than 1 per cent Jewish.

that the teachers cater to the wealthier students. Parents whose children are having difficulties in school said that teachers were very unwilling to help. When students would ask for further explanation, the teachers would tell them to go and sit down. Investigating parents were often received coldly by teachers and were given only curt replies to the questions they asked about their children.

Some parents think that the school is *too* well equipped. These people think that the money should have been used to obtain better teachers and recreation for the students. Several mentioned this, but only one of these said she was talking about the home economics department, which is known to be quite elaborate.

There appears to be some evidence that certain cliques, which are very difficult for outsiders to penetrate, run most of the activities in school. Those who can't get in the cliques apparently take out their revenge by forming undersirable groups of their own. Hot-rod gangs and a so-called sex-gang (located, however, mostly on the other side of town), have resulted from this sort of thing.

The majority of parents agree that, for a city of its size, Midcity possesses very little in the way of supervised recreation and that it has a high juvenile delinquency rate. Reports of there being too many taverns and too many teen-agers using liquor were given. Several parents were quite wary about the ———— Inn, saying that places having such bad reputations should not be allowed to operate.

Lately, many families have moved into Midcity from some of the southern states. Most of these are low classes of people who are lowering the standards of the city. One parent said that they live in old run-down houses, which they bought cheaply, are lazy, sleep as many as a dozen in one room, etc.

The extreme West side of town has many Negroes and Italians. Although there is plenty of industry in or near the city, Negroes find it difficult to get jobs.

Midcity appears very cold to newcomers. Although there appear to be many organizations in the city, they are apathetic in regard to the education and recreational needs of teen-agers. Some other things indicate the presence of internal conflicts, besides the Negro and Southern "hillbilly" problems: the fact that the North end of the city is inhabited by the upper class of people, and the mention that the town is dominated by a "narrow-minded religion."

On the whole, Midcity appears to be a city of many industries, which are run by the middle class and manned by lower classes of people. It is large enough to contain several areas, some of which are scenes of discontent, and others which are well satisfying to residents.

9—EXECUTIVE HEIGHTS

Population 17,000; school, 1,862.

"You can't build muscles by slamming Cadillac doors."—former athletic director.

Executive Heights High School prides itself on high scholastic achievement. The townspeople seem to recognize the importance of an education, mainly because they are almost all well educated themselves. As a result of the vast accumulation of wealth in the town, the people have given their support to build one of the finest high-school systems in the country.

The majority of informants point out the advantages to be obtained in the school. Along with this, however, are comments to the effect that the school places entirely too much stress on the brilliant and socially adept child, and strives for national recognition. There is too much pressure toward getting Executive Heights graduates into outstanding colleges. It is complained that the only thing that counts is "grades," and that this has an adverse effect on the students, making them feel tempted to cheat at times—which is easy to do because of the quasi-honor system—and not really interested in knowledge for its own sake.

Students attend from the outlying districts of ⸺ and ⸺, as well as from the Executive Heights area. The children from the outlying districts seem to be left out of the school activities. Several questionnaires report the existence of cliques in the school, and that a few persons control things socially, although others say that no such things exist.

The majority of students are Jewish.[6] Some hard feeling results from the holding of Jewish religious services during school hours, for which Jewish students are excused from class. Resentment is also felt around holiday seasons, because the Jewish children not only get off for the usual holidays, but are also excused for their own holidays.

There is some mention that teachers favor the wealthy students: "It isn't what you are but who you are that matters."

The school has an advisory system, whereby students receive an advisor who coaches them through their entire high-school career. Comments on advisors are both positive and negative. Along this line, parents most resent the elaborate testing system used to determine what a student is best suited for. If students receive low grades on certain aptitude tests, they are usually discouraged from taking certain subjects. There are a number of comments to the effect that the advisors talk the students out of what they really want to do, in favor of what *they* want them to do, or in favor of what their tests show them most capable of doing.

Executive Heights is said to rank among the first ten high schools in the country. At the same time, it has attempted to keep up with schools outstanding in athletics, but inferior scholastically. The result is that its athletic teams are often defeated. They seem to be far outclassed in their conference. Parents feel that this has a deleterious effect on the students, and think the school should be scheduled to meet smaller schools on the gridiron or basketball court.

The wealthy parents picture the community as being almost a Utopia. Everyone supports the common efforts, especially the school system. Many are drawn to Executive Heights, especially to send their children to the high school.

The community has changed very much in the last few years. Many of the informants have recently moved to the community from the East, or from Chicago, or other large cities.

A more descriptive picture of the community is given by the older residents and the people needed to carry on community life, i.e., the fireman, police, butchers, etc.

While the rich seem to think that everyone supports education, the poorer class greatly resents having to pay high taxes to support the school. They say that their children are hurt because they can't afford cars, high fidelity sets,

---

6. Only 31 per cent of students are in fact Jewish; 47 per cent are Protestant; 22 per cent are Catholic. Almost all of the Catholics are from a neighboring community.

and other such things. There does not seem to be any place, outside of school, where children can gather to have a social time among themselves. Everything they do is planned and overseen by parents. Some seem to think that this deprives their children of opportunities to use their own initiative.

No public transportation system exists in the community, and parents have to drive the children wherever they want to go. This increases the desire on the part of the students to want cars, and also brings the social pressures involved with having a car down on those who have them.

Amid the praise of the majority of parents for the peace and tranquility of the community, appear comments such as ". . . the police chief and his force are entirely too rough on our children and will force them into delinquency," or, ". . . there is too much hoodlumism and vandalism around the school."

Some parents have qualms about the effect of the materialistic values of the community on their children.

These vignettes of the ten schools and communities can serve as a starting point, to help keep in mind a general picture of each community. The sketches of the ten communities and schools are different enough to lead one to predict differences in value climates: Executive Heights, with a large majority of its graduates going to college, and containing the sons and daughters of professionals and business executives, would have the most academically oriented climate; St. John's High, Newlawn, and Millburg, with their large contingents of working-class students, would be the least so; and the more middle-class school in Midcity, somewhere in between. Athletics would be of most importance in the small towns, which in the midwest are infected with basketball fever; hot rods and customized cars would be at their zenith in the working-class suburb, Newlawn, or the heavy industry town, Millburg.

Such expectations are *not* supported by the data. The first indication comes from the responses to this question: (I.48.) "What does it take to get in with the leading crowd in this school?" The frequencies for the major categories of response to this question are graphed in Figures 3.1 and 3.2, for boys and girls respectively. The graphs are for general reference; in examining the value-climates, only one category will be examined at a time.

The Importance of Good Grades

"Good grades," "doing well in schoolwork," and "intelligence" constituted one kind of response as to what it takes to get in the leading crowd. It was only a minority response in any school, and it differed widely from one school to another. To make it easier to "locate" each school according to the importance of good grades among boys and girls, this one response is separated out in Figure 3.3. Each school's position is located as a point on a graph; the x-axis is the proportion of boys who mentioned "good grades" as a criterion for membership in the leading crowd, and the y-axis is the proportion of girls giving this response. The center line separates those schools in which good grades was more often mentioned by girls (above the line), and those in which it was more often mentioned by boys (below the line). It is perhaps surprising that there are as many schools below the line as above, particularly when the average girl mentioned many more items than did the average boy—as a glance at Figures 3.1 and 3.2 will indicate. This hints at something that is evident throughout this analysis: although girls in general get better grades than do boys, and although girls appear more motivated to conform to teachers' and parents' desires, the social rewards from her peers give less importance to good grades, relative to other matters, than is true for the boys.

It is apparent in Figure 3.3 that for both boys and girls good grades are of most importance as a criterion for membership in the leading crowd in Midcity; and that Marketville is second for both boys and girls—leaving aside St. John's High, which is second for the boys, but has no girls. Executive Heights and Millburg deviate in opposite directions, with grades of more importance among girls in Executive Heights, and among boys in Millburg. Elmtown, Maple Grove, and Green Junction are about the same, on the average, as Executive Heights and Millburg, but they are more nearly equal for girls and boys. Farmdale and Newlawn are low for both boys and girls.

Thus, things are not at all as one might predict. The schools with high per-pupil expenditure, those with a high proportion of students from well-educated backgrounds, are found intermingled with the schools with low per-pupil expenditures, and with students from more poorly educated backgrounds. Small-town schools are intermingled with city and suburban ones, large schools with small ones.

In order to get a more reliable picture of the relative importance of good grades in these adolescent societies, it is well to turn to other measures. The ranking of various attributes according to their value in making a boy or girl "important and looked up to" in the school provides another perspective for examining the importance of good grades. For there are very few boys and girls—or adults for that matter—who are not interested in being "important and looked up to" in the eyes of those they associate with. The question and list of items to be ranked is given below.

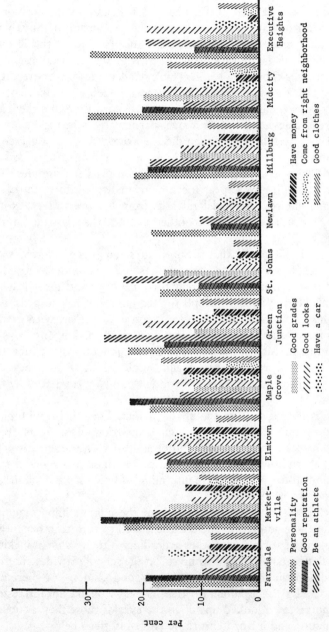

Figure 3.1—Attributes seen as important for a boy's membership in the leading crowd in each school.

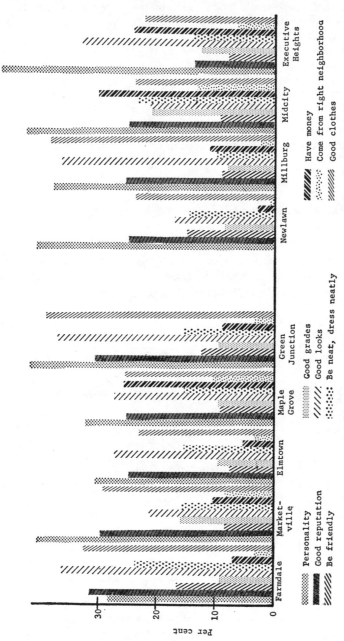

Figure 3.2—Attributes seen as important for a girl's membership in the leading crowd in each school.

I.143–48 (boys). Among the items below, what does it take to get to be important and looked up to by the *other fellows* here at school? (Rank from 1 to 6.)

Coming from the right family
Leader in activities
Having a nice car
High grades, honor roll
Being an athletic star
Being in the leading crowd

Girls were asked a similar question, and the items to be ranked were as follows (only the third and fifth were different from the boys' items):

Coming from the right family
Leader in activities
Clothes
High grades, honor roll
Being cheerleader
Being in the leading crowd

Our present concern is with the average rank of the item "good grades, honor roll," in each school. Chapter II showed that in all schools together, this item was not ranked high: it sood fourth out of the six items

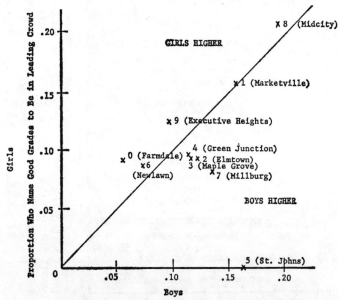

Figure 3.3—Perceived importance of "good grades" for a boy's and a girl's membership in the leading crowd in each school.

for boys, and fifth out of the six for girls. Regardless of this over-all low standing, its position differs considerably in the different schools. Figure 3.4 locates each school according to the average rank of "high grades, honor roll" among boys and among girls.

As with the question of what it takes to be in the leading crowd, Midcity and Marketville stand out. The relative positions of the two have shifted, because of the particularly high rank accorded to high grades by the Marketville girls. Among the Midcity girls, other items among the six, particularly being a cheerleader and being an activities leader, were more attractive, pulling down the relative importance of good grades. High grades among the Marketville boys has been similarly held down by the relative importance of two other items: "having a nice car," and "coming from the right family." Such constraints, of course, are not merely artificial ones stemming from the form of the question. If having a nice car is an important attribute for being important and looked up to

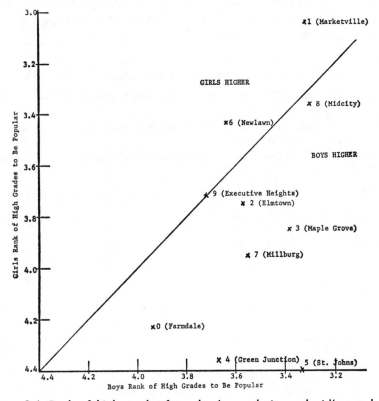

Figure 3.4—Rank of high grades for a boy's popularity and girl's popularity in each school.

by other boys, then it must crowd out, to some degree, other attributes, such as having good grades.

Among the other schools, those whose relative positions differ most from the leading-crowd question are Newlawn, in which the girls have jumped up from eighth place to third; Green Junction, in which the girls have dropped from fourth to ninth; and Maple Grove, in which the boys have moved up to a position close to Marketville, Midcity, and St. John's.

These differences make it difficult to pin down the valuation of good grades in certain schools, whose position differs sharply by the two different questions. A more definite indication of the differences in value climates in these schools comes by looking separately at the different classes in the school. Table 14 below gives for each class, freshman through senior, the ranks of each school relative to the others, in (a) the proportion of boys mentioning good grades as a criterion for membership in the leading crowd, and (b) the rank of "high grades, honor roll" in answer to the question about what it takes to get to be important and looked up to by other fellows in school.

Table 14—Position of each school relative to others, by class, in

      (a) Proportion of boys saying good grades necessary for leading crowd

      (b) Average rank of "high grades, honor roll" as a way to be looked up to

School	FRESHMAN (a)	(b)	SOPHOMORES (a)	(b)	JUNIORS (a)	(b)	SENIORS (a)	(b)
0 Farmdale	4	2	10	10	10	10	7	10
1 Marketville	7	1	1	2	1	2	8	9
2 Elmtown	8	6	2	3	5	7	4	5
3 Maple Grove	2	4	8	1	7	6	6	6
4 Green Junction	3	8	6	9	6	9	10	8
5 St. John's	1	3	5	5	4	4	1	1
6 Newlawn	9	7	9	8	9	3	3	3
7 Millburg	6	5	4	6	3	5	5	4
8 Midcity	—	—	3	4	2	1	2	2
9 Executive Heights	5	9	7	7	8	8	9	7
Rank correlation between (a) and (b)	.18		.60		.66		.88	

Comparing the rank positions of the school on the two items, for each class shows quite low correspondence among freshmen (the rank correlation is only .18), but closer correspondence among sophomores and juniors (rank correlations of .60 and .66), and even closer correspondence among seniors (rank correlation of .88). In other words, the freshmen seem to have no consistent estimation of the importance of good grades in the culture of their school, but such consistency develops over the four years of school.

It is understandable that the freshmen's perceptions would be inaccurate and inconsistent, for they had been in the school for only a few weeks when asked these questions. The fact that consistency does develop from the freshmen to the seniors indicates that there *is* a social system among the adolescents in the school, with its own distinctive norms.

This increasing correlation over the four years is only partly due to the seniors' better knowledge of the system and the fact that the social system becomes more completely a system as the four years of school go on; it is due also to the fact that the schools *diverge* in their value climates. If all 39 classes (4 classes × 9 schools + 3 classes for Midcity = 39) are ranked from 1 to 39 according to the average rank they give "high grades, honor roll," the standard deviation of the position of all 9 freshman classes is 8.4. The standard deviation for the ranks of the senior classes is 12.6. That is, the senior classes in the different schools are more dispersed than are the freshmen. The freshman classes, as they enter these schools, are more alike in the importance they attach to good grades than are the seniors. As these social systems develop, they diverge, going their own ways, depending on factors peculiar to the school itself.

Table 14 shows that these different ways depend not only on factors peculiar to the *school*, but also on factors peculiar to the *class* in school. Marketville provides the best example of this: all classes but the seniors are near the top of the list in the importance they attach to good grades; the seniors are near the bottom. The principal in this school and in others commented on the great variation among different classes. Each class gets a "reputation" according to its most salient characteristics, characteristics that make it far more than a random sample of teen-agers from the community.

Other schools besides Marketville show similar, though less dramatic, shifts: Elmtown goes from position 8 or 6 in the freshman year to 2 or 3 in the sophmore year, then back again to 5 or 7 in the junior year. Newlawn stays near the bottom through the freshman and sophomore years, but then by one measure in the junior year and both in the senior year, it jumps to third place. St. John's is high in the freshman and senior years, but only average in the sophomore and junior years. Other schools are more consistent: Green Junction and Farmdale, the two small-town schools with the highest portion of farm boys, are near the bottom every year after the first; Executive Heights, with the highest proportion of college graduates' sons, starts out in the middle, but by the last two years has joined those schools at the bottom. The school most consistently high is that of Midcity.

Perhaps it should have been expected at the beginning of the research that each of the different classes would have its own value system—for just as adolescents associate almost entirely within themselves, teen-agers in one class associate almost entirely within themselves. For instance, in the small-town schools of Marketville, Elmtown, Maple Grove, and Green Junction, only four cliques of four members or more—out of a total of 97—are not predominantly or entirely within one class.[7] Among pairs of friends, the one item that the two members had in common far more often than any other—including religion, father's occupation, father's education, common leisure interests, grades in schoolwork, and others— was class in school.

Although class-by-class variations in value climates confirm the notion that such value differences do in fact exist, they throw doubt on the very design of the research, that is, the study of the value climates and their effects in the school as a whole. If there is such a great variation from class to class, then it may be fruitless to look for similar effects through-out the four classes of the school. Fortunately, however, the majority of the schools stay within a fairly narrow range. One class may deviate, as, for example, do the seniors in Marketville, but the other classes remain fairly consistent.

Despite this fair consistency within the schools, it would be best if it were possible to carry out a class-by-class, rather than only a school-by-school, analysis. Unfortunately, such an analysis would present complexities that could not be overcome at present. The complexities arise in part because some of the effects of the prevailing value climate have to do with the elites—best athletes, best dressed, best students, most popular with opposite sex, leading crowd, etc.—who are few in number within each class. Thus, except in Chapter VII, which examines class-by-class the clique structures in the schools, the analysis will not consider the four classes separately. The boys' and the girls' value climates, however, will be characterized separately, in order to examine the differing relations between the sexes in different schools.

The Puzzle of Executive Heights and the Two Added Schools

Executive Heights is peculiarly low in the importance of academic achievement in its teen-age culture. Its position is not lowest among the schools; but it is almost lowest for the boys, and for the girls, far lower than might be expected. What is the source of this discrepancy? Does aca-

7. See Chapter VII where specific cliques are examined.

demic achievement really have so little currency in this school? It is something about the well-to-do comfort in which these teen-agers live? Is it the round of social activities in which some of their parents engage? Is it something about the suburban setting itself, which brings other values to the fore?

In an attempt to answer these questions, a questionnaire was administered to students in two private schools. School 11, although less than a tenth the size of Executive Heights High School, is in an almost identical suburban setting, with students whose backgrounds are very like those in Executive Heights. School 10, a high school of about five hundred (one-fourth the size of Executive Heights High School), also has students whose parents are very similar in education and occupation to those in Executive Heights. It is in the middle of the city, in the intellectual setting of a large university. These schools were added to help answer the puzzle of Executive Heights; however at this point we will turn to them merely to see whether, in fact, the ranking and the leading-crowd questions do measure the value climate. For if school 10, which by all external appearances has a very academically-oriented student body, does not appear to be so according to the responses to these two questions, there would arise

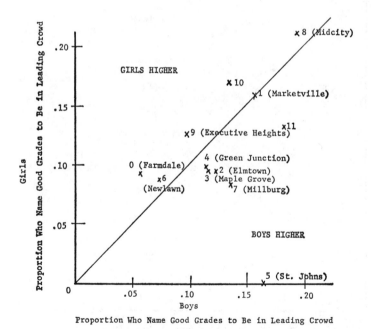

Proportion Who Name Good Grades to Be in Leading Crowd

Figure 3.5—Perceived importance of "good grades" for a boy's and a girl's membership in the leading crowd in each school, including schools 10 and 11.

serious doubts as to whether the questions actually measure the values of these adolescent cultures.

How *do* these schools compare to the others on these two questions? Figures 3.5 and 3.6 are replicas of the earlier Figures 3.3 and 3.4, except that schools 10 and 11 are added. Figure 3.5 locates the schools according to the frequency that good grades were mentioned as a criterion for membership in the leading crowd; Figure 3.6 shows the average rank that boys and girls in each school gave "high grades, honor roll."

In both graphs, schools 10 and 11 are at or near the top of the graph. In Figure 3.6 (the rank of "high grades, honor roll, as a requisite for being important and looked up to"), they are higher than any of the other schools. In Figure 3.5 (frequency of good grades mentioned as a criterion for the leading crowd), they are surpassed only by Midcity High School.

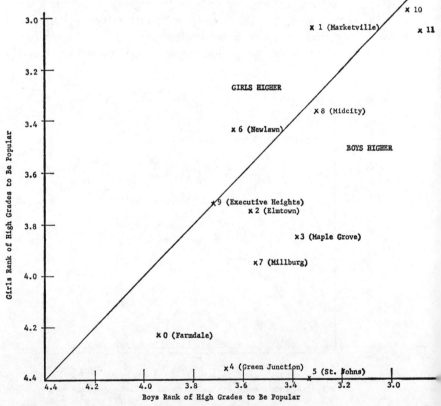

Figure 3.6—Rank of high grades for a boy's popularity and girl's popularity in each school, including schools 10 and 11.

According to both charts, academic values are slightly more important for the girls of school 10, and for the boys of school 11. The measures seem quite consistent in this respect, allaying any suspicions about whether the items measure what they are meant to. However, there is one slightly puzzling result: these two schools are *below* Midcity in the proportion mentioning good grades as a criterion for membership in the leading crowd; but they are far *above* Midcity in the average rank they give to other items.

Because there is less focus of attention upon the leading crowd in these two added schools than in the other ten, the total response to the leading-crowd question is lower for them. Consequently, although the absolute level of the "good grades" response to the question is lower than

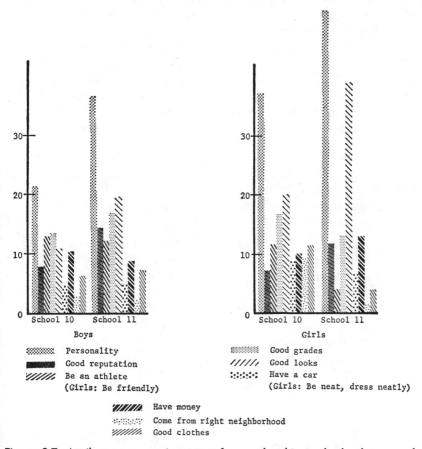

Figure 3.7—Attributes seen as important for membership in the leading crowd in schools 10 and 11.

in Midcity, the relative level is much higher. This can be seen by examining Figure 3.7 for these two schools, which shows all responses to the leading-crowd question, for both boys and girls. They mention far fewer things than do the students in the other schools. Consequently, among both the boys and the girls in these two schools, the category of "good grades" is the second or third most frequent response, higher than in any of the ten schools of the study. It is only seventh among the Midcity girls, for example, and fourth among the Midcity boys.

The position of the two added schools intensifies the puzzle of Executive Heights. Academic success clearly has little currency in its climate, not only relative to an observer's expectations, but also in comparison with diverse schools having students with similar as well as different backgrounds. This is not to say that the teen-agers in this school do not, as *individuals*, highly prize good grades. They do, because good grades are important for acceptance at the "right" college, and acceptance at the right college is of great importance to these adolescents and their well-educated parents. What these results *do* mean is that academic achievement counts for little in the culture, and does not give a boy or girl status in the eyes of his fellows. The effects of this devaluation of scholastic achievement will be evident in later chapters, particularly Chapter IX. The question of its causes will be reserved until Chapter X.

Classification of Schools According to Academic Orientation of the Adolescent Culture

In the later analysis (Chapters VIII and IX) of the effects of the different value systems, it will be necessary to have a definite classification of the ten schools in the study, according to the relative importance of academic success to the adolescent culture. The two questions studied in this section will be used to make the classification. Looking at Figures 3.3 and 3.4, the boys' climates are as follows: Midcity, Marketville, and St. John's show highest academic orientation on both questions; and Farmdale, Executive Heights, Green Junction, and Newlawn are lowest on both. Elmtown, Millburg, and Maple Grove are in the middle, although their order differs in the two questions. The classification, then, will be into three groups—high, intermediate, and low:

Boys:
High: Midcity, Marketville, St. John's
Intermediate: Millburg, Maple Grove, Elmtown
Low: Green Junction, Newlawn, Executive Heights, Farmdale

For the girls, Midcity and Marketville remain highest. According to one question, Executive Heights girls are next; according to the other, Newlawn girls are next, only slightly below the Midcity girls. Because of this inconsistency, Newlawn and Executive Heights girls will be classified as intermediate. Altogether, the classification for girls is:

Girls:
High: Midcity, Marketville
Intermediate: Executive Heights, Newlawn
Low: Elmtown, Maple Grove, Millburg, Green Junction, Farmdale

It is important to remember that these classifications show the position of each school relative to each other. Relative to other attributes, scholastic success is not most important in *any* school; nowhere, for example, does it surpass athletic achievement for boys; and for girls, its position relative to other attributes is even lower.

Grades of the Leading Crowd

It is difficult to say whether the grades of the leading crowd should be seen as a source, a consequence, or merely a confirmation of the status system and its rewards for scholastic achievement. This problem is like others in a study of this sort: when examining a complex system, it is not as easy to speak of cause and effect as it is of "consistency" of the parts with one another, especially when the system is viewed at only one point in time.

Whichever way the grades of the leading crowd are viewed—as a cause or consequence of the value system, or as both (a consequence of some other factor at one time, but a cause in future times by coming to constitute a value of the leading crowd)—there should be consistency between the leading crowd's grades and the character of the social climate.

The fall semester (1957–58) grades of all students in school were recorded on a scale of 8: $8 = A$; $6 = B$; $4 = C$; $2 = D$; $0 = F$. Some schools used different grading systems than others, so that the raw grades mean little. In a school like Midcity, for example, where the grading system was numerical, and translated into particularly low grades by our equivalences, the absolute position of the leading crowd is low by our measure. It is the leading crowd's position *relative* to the grades of others in school that is important. Therefore, listed next to each raw grade is the number of standard deviations by which this grade exceeds the average grade of all boys (or of all girls) in that school.

Table 15—Average grades of persons chosen ten times or more as a member of the leading crowd*

School	Leading crowd's Av. grade	#S.D. above girls' av.	Leading crowd's Av. grade	#S.D. above boys' av.
0 Farmdale	5.13	0.59	4.88	1.10
1 Marketville	6.28	1.76	5.17	1.87
2 Elmtown	5.32	0.64	5.68	1.76
3 Maple Grove	5.56	0.84	5.15	1.17
4 Green Junction	4.86	0.49	3.95	0.00
5 St. John's High	—	—	4.31	0.73
6 Newlawn	5.43	1.18	4.53	1.21
7 Millburg	4.83	0.31	4.40	0.89
8 Midcity	5.14	1.38	4.84	1.59
9 Executive Heights	5.42	1.12	5.05	1.23

* Given first as absolute grades, and then as number of standard deviations these grades exceed average grade for that sex in that school. The proportion of people mentioned ten times or more as being in the leading crowd differs somewhat from school to school, but is almost constant within the small schools and the large ones, for the two sex groups: 6 per cent for small-school boys, 11 per cent for small-school girls; 3 per cent for large-school boys, 4–6 per cent for large-school girls. Farmdale is an exception for the boys, being about 11 per cent, rather than 6 per cent, as in the other small schools. Thus, since these groups are a smaller part of the student body among the large schools than the small ones, and smaller among the boys than among the girls, this gives the large schools an advantage in the table, and it gives the boys an advantage, since these are more select groups. This should be kept in mind in interpreting the figures.

Among the girls, the grades are precisely consistent with the rewards given for good grades in the particular adolescent culture. The schools where good grades are most important are Midcity and Marketville, and these are the two schools where the leading crowd is highest above the average (1.34 and 1.76 standard deviations). Executive Heights and Newlawn girls were classified as intermediate, and the grades of their leading crowds are next highest above their averages (1.12 and 1.18 standard deviations). Finally, in the five schools that were classified as low in academic orientation, the grades of the leading crowds are much lower, ranging from 0.84 down to 0.31 standard deviations above the average.

Among the boys, there are some discrepancies from the classification of value climates, although the general character is consistent with the climates. Among the small schools, considered separately, the ordering of deviation from the average is in accordance with the classification: first Marketville, then Elmtown, then Maple Grove, then Farmdale, then Green Junction. In Farmdale, however, the leading crowd has higher grades than would be expected from the earlier examination of social rewards for good grades, far higher than Green Junction, whose leading crowd is exactly average.

The large-school boys' leading crowds are somewhat lower than those in the small schools, although they constitute a more select group, only half as large a segment of their student bodies. It is among those crowds that the only real inconsistency of grades with rewards comes about. Midcity is highest above the school average, consistent with the social rewards there; but St John's and Millburg are quite low in their deviations, while Newlawn and Executive Heights are not far below Midcity.

A partial explanation of this inconsistency is apparent, however, if one considers the "intermediate leading crowd," those boys chosen from two to nine times. Then Millburg comes up and Executive Heights goes down to a position consistent with the rewards. The intermediate leading crowds deviate from the mean as follows: St. John's, +.07 s.d.; Newlawn, +.48 s.d.; Millburg, +.92 s.d.; Midcity, +.47 s.d.; Executive Heights, −.08 s.d. Apparently, the grades of *top* leaders in Millburg, which include many athletes, are brought down by the athletes, while the less "central" part of the leading crowd has higher grades. As Chapter IX will show, the grades of the athletes are particularly low in this school, and those of the boys named as best students are particularly high. Correspondingly, the intermediate leaders in Executive Heights are *below* the average grade for the boys, in effect bringing the grades of the leading crowd down to a position consistent with the value system. The grades of Newlawn's and St. John's leading crowds, however, remain peculiarly out of position—Newlawn high and St. John's low, relative to the value climates.

Over all schools and both sexes, the general pattern of grades among the leading crowds is consistent with the social rewards for good grades. (It should be remembered that the absolute grades of most of these leading crowds are not especially high. Only among the girls in Marketville are they above 6.0, a straight B average.) Among the girls, the grades of the leading crowds are perfectly consistent with the value climates, as classified previously. Among the boys, there is a reasonable degree of consistency. Boys in Newlawn and St. John's present the only definite inconsistencies. Despite these minor inconsistencies, the schools will be classified, as indicated earlier, according to the way the boys *see* the value system. For it is the adolescents' ideas about what is important to their fellows which influences their behavior, and it is these influences upon behavior which concern us.

Ascriptive Criteria in the Adolescent Status Systems

Although there are various dimensions of achievement important for status in these adolescent cultures, one status element is purely ascriptive: family background. Communities differ in the importance of this element, and among the communities in this study, wide differences were found.

The importance of family background for actual membership in the leading crowd and for popularity will be examined in detail in Chapter IV; here, we can see how these different status systems *appear* to the adolescents within them.

The important attributes of family background differ from town to town. In only one school, Executive Heights, is religion mentioned with any frequency, and even then by only 5 per cent of the boys and 4 per cent of the girls. (This school contains Protestants, Catholics, and Jews, with no group constituting a majority. The Protestants constitute over 40 per cent; Jews, over 30 per cent; and Catholics, over 20 per cent.) Yet even in this school, "coming from the right neighborhood" was more often mentioned.

In all the other communities where background factors were seen to be important by some teen-agers, the matter of one's "neighborhood" was the only one mentioned frequently, except for coming "from an important family." In part, neighborhood has its effect through a boy's or girl's earlier associations in grade school. In Executive Heights, one family with a boy in grade school was contemplating moving back to the city, because they lived just out of the elementary school district where the nuclei of the high-school leading crowds formed. The mother was afraid her son would suffer, not because of any economic differences from that crowd (for there were none), but simply because his associations would not be within it. The same kind of concern was voiced by other parents as well, not only in Executive Heights, but also in others, particularly Marketville, Maple Grove, and Midcity.

Figure 3.8 shows how the teen-agers themselves see the importance of family background. Plotted on the chart are the frequencies with which boys and girls mentioned such ascriptive elements as neighborhood, family, and—in Executive Heights—religion, as a criterion for getting in the leading crowd. (Schools 10 [big city, attached to university] and 11 [suburban] are added to the graph for comparison, but they will not be treated in the subsequent analysis of the effects of these systems.)

The schools fall into two very distinct clusters: four schools in which background criteria are important among both boys and girls, and five in which they are not. The first four are Marketville and Maple Grove, two small-town schools; Midcity, a city school; and Executive Heights; a suburban school. In all the schools except Marketville, girls mention such criteria considerably more often than do boys.

Marketville and Maple Grove are both small-town schools, but they are quite different from the three other small-town schools—Farmdale, Elmtown, and Green Junction—in the importance of family background. In Marketville and Maple Grove, family background means much; in

Farmdale, Elmtown, and Green Junction, it is almost never mentioned as an aid to getting into the leading crowd.

The results of Hollingshead's earlier study of Elmtown would lead one to expect it to be far higher than any of the other schools in the importance of family background. The major point of Hollingshead's analysis was that a boy or girl was judged almost *solely* on background factors, by teachers and peers alike. This is not true for any of these schools, and family background is particularly unimportant in Elmtown, along with Farmdale and Green Junction. The great difference between the social structures within these schools and within Marketville and

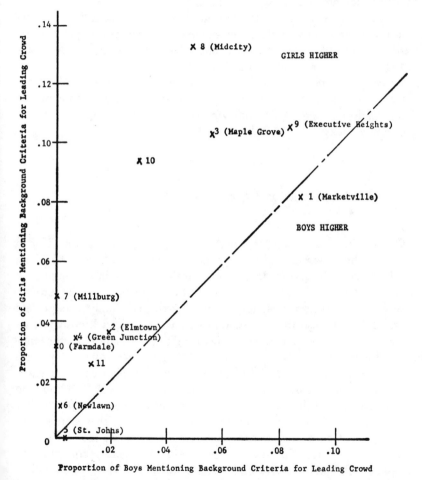

Figure 3.8—Perceived importance of a boy's or girl's background for membership in the leading crowd.

Maple Grove will be evident throughout the analysis, particularly in examining the cliques in Chapter VII.

Midcity and Millburg constitute another contrast. They are both in small cities, both fairly large schools, but they differ sharply in the importance family background plays in getting into the leading crowd. It plays an important part in the light-industry town, Midcity, and little part in Millburg, the heavy-industry town.

The final and greatest contrast is between Newlawn, the new working-class suburb, and Executive Heights, the older, upper-middle-class suburb. In Newlawn, family position, such as it is, counts for almost nothing; in Executive Heights, it counts very much.

This is the way it looks to the teen-agers in these schools. For the present, it is enough simply to characterize these schools according to the differences in perceived importance of family background. In the next chapter, the actual composition of the elites will be examined, as well as some of the causes of these differences. In Chapter VII, the way background relates to the association structures will be examined for some of the schools; and in Chapter VIII, some of the effects of the emphasis on "the right family background" will be studied.

Academic Orientation and Status Ascription

One of the great dilemmas a high-school principal faces is evident in comparing the importance of good grades and family background in these schools. Marketville and Midcity, which are the two definitely highest in the degree that "good grades" count for membership in the leading crowd, are also two of the four highest in the degree that family background counts. These are also the two schools that were criticized most by parents—and a few teachers in each—for favoring the children of "better families," at the expense of those from the wrong side of the town. This seems to be more than a coincidence. Because of the very high correlation between social background, on the one hand, and doing well in school and going to college, on the other, it is ordinarily the adolescents from "better families" who are most academically inclined. At least, this is true for a community having a fairly large proportion of children from low educational backgrounds. The special case of a predominantly college-background school, like Executive Heights, is different, in ways which will be discussed in Chapter X.

Thus, if an administration emphasizes academic excellence and finds ways to reward those who do well in school, then it is most often rewarding the few from "better families." Similarly, if the leading crowd of an adolescent culture is composed of these students most academically inclined, then the members of the leading crowd are predominantly those from the right side of the railroad tracks. These elements are often seen by adolescents as part of the same general cluster. When asked what it takes to get into the leading crowd of girls in Maple Grove, a girl replied: "You have to be smart; your folks have to have money; you have to have nice-looking clothes; and you have to join every activity in school."

The definition of the leading crowd comes to include both family background and doing well scholastically in such a school, primarily because these attributes reside in the same individuals, and because both attributes serve to set them apart from the others.

This presents a dilemma for the principal of such a school. If he finds ways to reward scholastic excellence and manages to make this important to the adolescent community, then he is charged—and not unfairly so— with favoring the "college-bound" children or those from "better families." Conversely, if he manages to break down the dominance of the students from the "better families," he may find that in doing so he has created a leading crowd that pays little attention to scholastic success. This is not to say, of course, that a principal has direct control over the composition of the leading crowd, for he can control it only through such indirect measures as focusing attention upon specific activities and individuals. Yet, even if he had, the high correlation between family background and interest in school would make it difficult to act. The question of how, in such socially heterogeneous communities as these, there can be an adolescent status system that rewards academic excellence, thereby motivating all students toward academic success, without heaping its rewards upon the few from good families, is not an easy one to answer. Some comments upon the problem will be made in Chapters X and XI.

The two elements are not, however, inextricably tied together in the status system. As Maple Grove and Executive Heights illustrate, background attributes are important there for membership in the leading crowd, but academic excellence is not. In both schools, family background is often mentioned as a criterion for membership in the leading crowd, but in neither are good grades mentioned any more often than for many of the other schools.

What is the difference between these schools and the other two, Marketville and Midcity? The leading crowds in Maple Grove and Executive Heights seem to have an extremely *social* character, more so than do Marketville and Midcity. It seems that a highly ascriptive system, with emphasis on family background, makes it *possible*, but not *necessary*, to have "good grades" as a criterion for membership in the leading crowd. The leading crowd may be more concerned with other matters besides schoolwork, for example social activities, which equally well distinguish it from the others in school.

Summary of Scholastic Achievement and Family Background

The analysis thus far allows a dual classification of schools—according to the importance of family background and according to the importance of scholastic achievement. The schools are located as follows on these two dimensions:

IMPORTANCE OF SCHOLASTIC SUCCESS

Boys	High	Intermediate	Low
Background important			
Yes	Marketville Midcity	Maple Grove	Executive Heights
No	St. John's High	Millburg Elmtown	Farmdale Green Junction Newlawn
Girls			
Background important			
Yes	Marketville Midcity	Executive Heights	Maple Grove
No		Newlawn	Farmdale Elmtown Green Junction Millburg

Athletics in the Status System

As has been evident earlier, athletic achievements are extremely important in adolescent status systems. In the schools of this research, the important sports are basketball and football, with only two variations: Farmdale has no football team; and Newlawn has excellent wrestling teams, which make wrestling an important means of gaining status. In the other eight schools, basketball is more important in some, football in others; but the dominance of athletics in these status systems is unequalled by any other activity.

In order, however, to examine the effects of this dominance, it is important to see the differences in its role in the ten schools. Figure 3.9 locates each school according to two measures: the frequency athletics was mentioned by boys as an attribute for membership in the leading crowd, and the rank of "being an athlete" as a way for a boy to be looked up to by other fellows. These items correlate somewhat less highly than one would hope, although some schools' positions are clear-cut. Farmdale, Maple Grove, and Midcity are low by both criteria; Green Junction is by far the highest according to both; and Millburg, Executive Heights, and St. John's are also high, although clearly below Green Junction.

Newlawn and Marketville show the greatest inconsistency, in the opposite directions. In Newlawn, athletics was not often mentioned as a way to get into the leading crowd, but it was ranked high as a way of being "important and looked up to." A glance at Figure 3.1 (p. 70), discussed earlier in the chapter, indicates the source of the discrepancy. In Newlawn, there was far less mention of *any* attributes for getting into the leading crowd. Relative to the other items mentioned, the athlete is about on a par with the athlete in Millburg and Executive Heights. (In Newlawn, athletics is the second most frequently mentioned category, as it is in Executive Heights. It is a close third in Millburg.) This would pull Newlawn up to the regression line, together with Executive Heights and Millburg. The discrepancy of Marketville is not so easily resolved. However, for the later analysis of effects of the systems, it will be grouped with

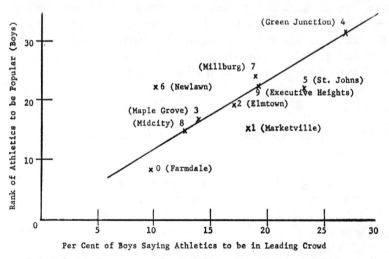

Figure 3.9—Relation between rank of athletics for a boy's popularity and perceived importance of athletics for membership in leading crowd.

Elmtown in a low intermediate position. The classification, then, is as follows:

IMPORTANCE OF ATHLETIC ACHIEVEMENT FOR LEADING CROWD

High	Medium High	Medium Low	Low
Green Junction	Newlawn	Marketville	Farmdale
St. John's	Millburg	Elmtown	Maple Grove
	Executive Heights		Midcity

Chapter V, which examines star athletes and star students, will show that the matter is far from as simple as this, for the culture of some schools seems to reward the athlete purely for his athletic ability. In others, being an athlete is only part of the general qualities of the "all-around boy," where without other attributes, social or scholastic, the athlete is not given special prominence.

There is more difficulty in classifying the schools according to the importance of athletics as an avenue for gaining status, than in classifying them in the ways examined earlier. There may be some structural sources for this difficulty, which compress the values in these schools closely together in the importance placed on athletics. In Chapter X, this apparent "compression" and its possible sources will be examined.

The classification above should not suggest that athletics is unimportant in Farmdale, Maple Grove, and Midcity. Basketball and football are extremely important in these schools generally. In particular, Midcity is by far the most successful in basketball, having recently won the state tournament, while Maple Grove probably fields the next best basketball teams among the ten schools. Yet, these two schools include several other avenues of gaining status, in part through family background and other school activities. Consequently, an athlete in these schools does not have the special status he has in Green Junction, for example, where the football player almost automatically has high status.

Popularity with Boys in the Status System of Girls

Among the girls in these schools, there is no clear-cut dimension in which they can "star" as can boys in athletics. The nearest equivalent for girls is social success—being sought after by boys. In some of the schools, a girl who is popular with the right boys has a special position, envied by other girls and fought over by boys. In a sense, this is a dimension of achievement just as is athletics. It contrasts sharply with a situation in which family background determines the leading crowd. For just as athletics is an activity in which all boys start on a fairly equal footing, regardless of background, so is a girl's popularity with boys. To be sure, this popularity depends partly on elements deriving from family position—clothes, social sophistication, ability to dance well, being well dressed, and so on, and in some schools the system is largely dominated by a ruling clique of girls which determines who shall be popular and who shall not (a situation suggested by the interview excerpt from a boy in Maple Grove in Chapter II, p. 34). Nevertheless, popularity with boys introduces into the status system an element of achievement in which all girls must compete regardless of family position.

Insofar, then, as dominance of a ruling clique does not control the competition for boys' attention, the girls can have an "open society," in which a girl's background need not prevent her from having status. The importance of family background and its variation in different schools was examined in an earlier section; it remains to be seen how important, in each of these cultures, is popularity with the opposite sex. Looking at both of these attributes together can tell just how much control a ruling clique can exert over the otherwise open competition.

As an attribute for gaining entry into the leading crowd, the category that most nearly reflects popularity with boys is the one we have labeled "good looks." Included here are all the responses involving attributes of popularity with boys. None of the items from the ranking question about what make a girl "important and looked up to by other girls," indicates exactly this. One, however, seems part of the same syndrome: being a cheerleader. Cheerleaders have different roles in different schools, but their status is always partly associated with dates, good times, and boys. At the same time, they have an "inside track" with the athletes, and are more likely to be dated by them. They are clearly a force in the direction of "open competition," and in a social rather than intellectual direction.

Taking the two attributes, then, cheerleader from this question and 'good looks, popularity with boys, etc." from the leading-crowd question, each of these schools can be characterized according to the prominence of this set of attributes.

Figure 3.10 shows that the schools fall roughly into two clusters. Farmdale, Green Junction, Millburg, and Executive Heights are in the 'popularity" group; while Marketville, Elmtown, Maple Grove, Newlawn, and Midcity are not. This classification has a negative relation to the scholastic-ascriptive pattern discussed earlier. Far at the non-popularity end are Marketville and Midcity, where scholastic achievement and family background were seen to be most important. Far at the popularity end are Farmdale, Green Junction, and Millburg, where scholastic achievement and family background were seen to be unimportant. Popularity with boys, however, is not just the opposite of the scholastic-ascriptive qualities, but is a somewhat independent dimension. This is evident in the positions of the other schools. This classification will help show, in Chapter VIII, the effects of the school's status system upon those who are "favored" by it and those who are not.

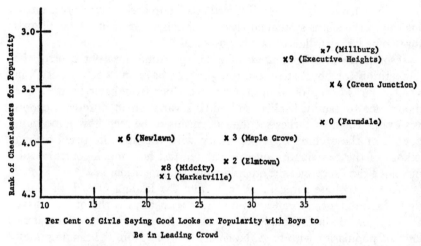

Figure 3.10—Relation between rank of cheerleader for a girl's popularity and perceived importance of good looks for membership in leading crowd.

Conclusion

The aim of this chapter has been almost the reverse of the preceding one. There, we attempted to look at the similarities in these adolescent cultures and to get a general picture of the processes operative in the adolescent culture. The task in this one has been to look at these schools separately—not, as yet, to study the effects of the different status systems, but only to *characterize* the status system—to look at several dimensions of status and to see how the status systems of the different schools differ in the importance they place on each of these.

A quick summary for each school will indicate its position on these various dimensions, relative to the other schools. It must be remembered, nevertheless, that these schools are more alike than they are different; that the relative positions of the various dimensions by which status is gained is somewhat similar in all of them. In our society, the adolescent subculture apparently gets its major characteristics from its general relation to the adult society; superimposed upon this basic mold are variations due to factors that differ from community to community or school to school.

0—FARMDALE

None of the status characteristics yet examined have special importance for the Farmdale boys. Neither athletics, grades, nor parental background are as important as they are in most of the other schools. The one item mentioned more frequently by these boys than by those in any other school is one that has not been examined here—cars. Cars, having a car, fixing it up, riding around, are of extreme importance to them. Motor scooters are a current fad among sophomores and freshmen in this school, who see these scooters as a way to gain independence of action and to recapture from the juniors and seniors the attentions of the freshman and sophomore girls.

The status system among the girls in Farmdale seems, at this point in the analysis, complementary to that just discussed for the boys. The only dimension on which this status system was not low is good looks and popularity with boys. A glance at Figure 3.2 (p. 71) will show that this is the only school in which such attributes are mentioned more than any other category—even more than the oft-mentioned attributes of "personality" and "reputation."

1—MARKETVILLE

The status system among the boys in Marketville presents a great contrast to that of Farmdale, although the populations from which the two schools draw their students are not greatly different. Despite the strange reversal among the seniors (see Table 14), as a whole, the boys have one of the two status systems most oriented to scholastic success. It is one of the highest in the ascriptive criteria of family position as well; it is in the low-intermediate group with respect to athletics—but athletic success is still more important than good grades. Cars are of less importance here than in any of the other small-town schools.

The girls' status system emphasizes good grades even more than that of the boys. This emphasis is not coupled with an "activities" orientation so much as it is in other schools; rather it places more insistence on purely academic success. Furthermore, ascriptive criteria of family background are also important here; but the cheerleader-popularity syndrome is not strong. In fact, the system is almost the lowest in the number of times good looks and popularity with boys are mentioned as a way into the leading crowd.

2—ELMTOWN

Somewhere between the status system of Farmdale and that of Marketville lies Elmtown's status system. It is not high, but not among the lowest, in the importance of grades; the ascriptive criteria of family background are unimportant. It is not high, but again not lowest, in the importance of athletic success. Cars, dates, and leisure pursuits are important although not so much as in Farmdale.

The position of this girls' status system is much like that of the boys: it is low, but not lowest, in the importance it attaches to scholastic success; ascriptive criteria are unimportant; and it is rather low—although not as low as Marketville—on the cheerleader-popularity dimension.

3—MAPLE GROVE

For the boys in Maple Grove, ascriptive criteria are important, as they are in Marketville, but the school is more like Elmtown in the lesser importance attached to scholastic achievement. Athletic success is not an important criterion for status, relative to its importance in other schools.

Like that of the boys, the status system of the girls here resembles that of Marketville in the significance of family position; but it is like Elmtown in the lesser importance it attaches to good grades. Like both Marketville and Elmtown, it is not one of the schools high on the popularity-cheerleader syndrome.

4—GREEN JUNCTION

The boys' system is distinctive in the emphasis it places on athletic success—unadulterated by family-background criteria or by scholastic achievement.

The girls' pattern complements that of the boys: low in the importance it attaches to good grades; low in the use of ascriptive criteria, and high on the cheerleader-popularity dimension.

5—ST. JOHN'S

On both the dimensions of scholastic and athletic achievement, this school stands high. Whether rewards are given for these achievements as separate avenues of success or as simultaneous ones is yet to be determined (in Chapter V), but it is among the schools high in both dimensions. Family status is unimportant.

6—NEWLAWN

Athletic success ranks fairly high in the status system of the boys at Newlawn. It is not, however, as important here as in some of the other schools. Family position is of no importance, and good grades are of little importance. Cars are more important, ranking Newlawn comparable to Farmdale and Elmtown in this respect.

The girls' status system is in an intermediate position in the importance it attaches to good grades. Good grades are more important for girls' status than they are for boys'. Ascriptive criteria are not important, and neither is the cheerleader-popularity dimension strong.

7—MILLBURG

For both athletic and scholastic achievement, the boys' status system in this school gives some rewards. It is not among the highest in either dimension, but it is in the second ranks for both. Family position is unimportant. Cars, and the activities they entail, give less status than in any of the schools so far mentioned, other than Marketville and St. John's.

Scholastic performance is of little importance for girls, less than it is for the boys; ascriptive criteria are not important; the cheerleader-popularity dimension is strong here.

8—MIDCITY

Ascriptive criteria and scholastic achievement are quite important for the boys of Midcity, relative to the other schools. This system is only approached by that of Marketville in the importance it places on both of these criteria. It is one of the lowest in the importance it attaches to athletic achievement as a means of gaining status.

Scholastic achievement and ascriptive criteria are more important for the girls of Midcity than for girls in any other school but Marketville. The cheerleader-popularity dimension is not important.

9—EXECUTIVE HEIGHTS

The combination for boys in Executive Heights is different from any yet examined. Although ascriptive criteria, such as neighborhood and elementary school are important, scholastic success is not. The system is high, although not highest, in the status it gives athletic achievement.

The combination for girls, too, is new: ascriptive criteria are important; it is in the second ranks in the status it gives scholastic success; but it is also one of the schools where the cheerleader-popularity dimension is strong. As Figure 3.2 (p. 71) indicates, extra-curricular activities are a more important means of status-achievement among these girls than in the other schools.

The foregoing locations of the separate subcultures are intended to serve two purposes: first, to serve as a guide in the developing picture of each of these social systems; and second, as classifications that will allow us to study the differential effects of the various systems and the differential sources. The position of each school on each of the dimensions examined above is given below:

Boys

Scholastic Achievement		HIGH		INTERMEDIATE		LOW	
Family Background		High	Low	High	Low	High	Low
Athletic Achievement	High		St. John's				Green Junction
	Medium high				Millburg	Executive Heights	
	Medium low	Market-ville			Elmtown		
	Low	Midcity		Maple Grove			Farmdale

Girls

Scholastic Achievement		HIGH		INTERMEDIATE		LOW	
Family Background		High	Low	High	Low	High	Low
Popularity with boys— cheerleader	High			Executive Heights			Farmdale Green Junction Millburg
	Low	Market-ville Midcity			Newlawn	Maple Grove	

IV Who Are the Popular Heroes and Leaders?

ANOTHER WAY OF GAINING UNDERSTAND-
ing of the adolescent societies, and the way they channel adolescent energies, is by considering those members that boys and girls most esteem—the
ones they most want to be like, the ones they would like to be friends
with, the ones they see as members of the leading crowd, the ones they
choose most often as friends. How are these people, who are held in
special positions of regard by their classmates, different from their less
distinguished fellows?[1]

Four questions were asked on the questionnaire to identify these informal elites:

---

1. A Baltimore girl, junior in high school and a sorority member, indicated the
role that sororities play in her school. (There were no sororities in the schools of
the study. Less formalized groups carried out most of the same functions as sorori-
tities.).

"At Eastern the sororities form the leading crowd. A combination of girls from
several different sororities run the school. (ΦΩ, ΔΑΦ, ΛΣ, ΦΔ, ΚΣΦ) Almost all of the
girls in the leading crowd at school are in sororities. Some girls come here from other
schools and get into the crowd first, but they are then taken in by some sorority.
They usually get into the crowd because they know of the people in it. It is interesting that almost every girl who comes to Eastern from a private school almost
immediately gets into the leading crowd. Being friends with three or four people in
each of these sororities would probably get you into the crowd. The parents of *most*
of the elite group have a good education or live in a respectable neighborhood. However, most ΛΣ girls come from Hamilton and I would not say their parents were too
well-educated. ΛΣ has recently become part of the leading crowd because of the
close friendships of some of the girls in that sorority with girls in other leading
sororities. ΛΣ girls are very friendly and dress neatly.

I.45. Thinking of all the boys (girls) in this school, who would you most want to be like?

I.40b.iv. Of all the boys (girls) in your grade, which boy (girl) would you most like to be friends with?

I.51. If a boy (girl) came here to school and wanted to get in with the leading crowd, what boys (girls) should he (she) get to be friends with? (Up to four names were coded.)

I.38. What boys (girls) here in school do you go around with most often? (Up to ten names were coded.)

Boys and girls named most often in answer to these questions may be viewed as persons with special status—persons who exemplify, more than their fellows, the values current in the culture. Each of these questions gives a somewhat different perspective on the culture—the persons whom others want to *be like* are not necessarily the members of the leading crowd. By examining the cultures from these several perspectives, it will be easier to see the kinds of things these students hold as important and why they hold certain things, rather than others, as important.

The Distribution of Elites

Almost everyone gave names of several friends in answer to question I.38: the average number of names given in the nine coeducational schools was 3.21 for the boys and 4.13 for the girls. In answer to the other questions, fewer names were given. Only 38 per cent of the boys and 57 per cent of the girls named a boy or girl they would like to be friends with (I.40b.iv.), and only 42 per cent of the boys and 57 per cent of the girls named a boy or girl they would want to be like (I.45). The average number of mentions of someone in the leading crowd was 1.44 for the boys and 2.54 for the girls. Part of the difference in response is due to the different form of the questions: the "be friends with" and "be like" questions asked for only one name, while the questions about whom they go around with most often and the leading-crowd questions asked for more than one.

The resulting distributions of these choices differed for the different elite criteria. On each criterion, some students were named by no one; and at the other extreme, some were named by a great many. However, on the friendship criterion of whom they go around with most often (question I.38), only a minority went unnamed, while on each of the other three questions—more truly indicative of elite status in the school as a whole—most students were never named, and a few students received most of the choices.

Figures 4.1 and 4.2 show the distribution, in Midcity, of each type of choice. Only Midcity is shown, but each school showed distributions similar to those of Figures 4.1 and 4.2. Most widely distributed is, of course, actual friendship; highest consensus exists on membership in the leading crowd. The consensus is less on those named as a person one would want to be like, but still quite great; and the consensus on those named as someone to be friends with is still less. In Table 16, measures of consensus are presented for each of these four criteria.

Table 16—Consensus in choices among boys and girls in Midcity High School on four choice criteria: actual friendship, someone to be friends with, someone to be like, and members of leading crowd*

	Boys	Girls
Friends	46.5	54.6
Be friends with	27.9	10.5
Be like	11.5	5.4
Leading crowd	4.3	1.8

* 100 = no consensus; 100 independent choices out of 100 choices.
1 = high consensus; 1 independent choice out of 100 choices.

This measure employed in Table 16 requires some explanation. It gives the equivalent number of *independent* choices for every one hundred actual choices. If choices were made at random, completely independently of everyone else's choice—that is, if every person had an equal chance of being chosen—then the measure would be 100, indicating 100 independent choices out of every hundred actual choices. If a hundred persons chose exactly alike—that is, if all hundred chose the same person—then the measure would be 1, indicating only 1 independent choice out of a hundred. If the measure is 50, this means that every hundred people chose as if they were 50 *independently* choosing people. Thus, as consensus upon one or a few people increases, the measure narrows down from a hundred independent choices to only a small number.[2]

The values of these measures of consensus in Table 16 indicate great differences between the different elite criteria. The least consensus, with about 50 independent choices out of one hundred, exists in naming one's friends. Second is someone to be friends with, which narrows for the boys to about twenty-eight independent choices, and for the girls to about ten independent choices. Next is someone to be like (which tends to be concentrated on upperclassmen) and which shows only about ten inde-

2. The calculation of this measure is given in Chapter X, p. 297, in examining varying degrees of consensus in different schools.

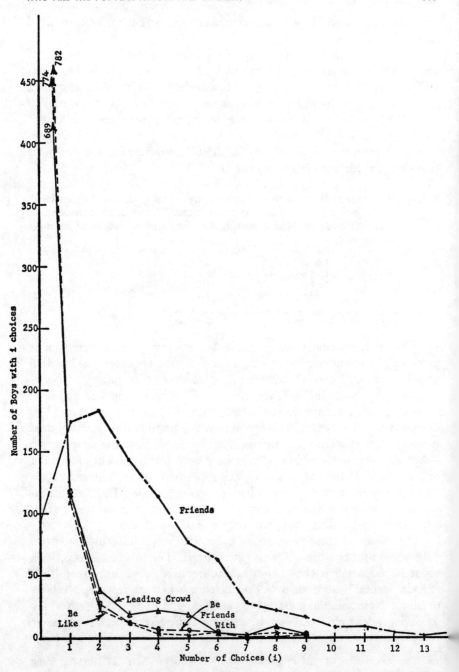

Figure 4.1—Distribution of choices among boys on four criteria in Midcity High.

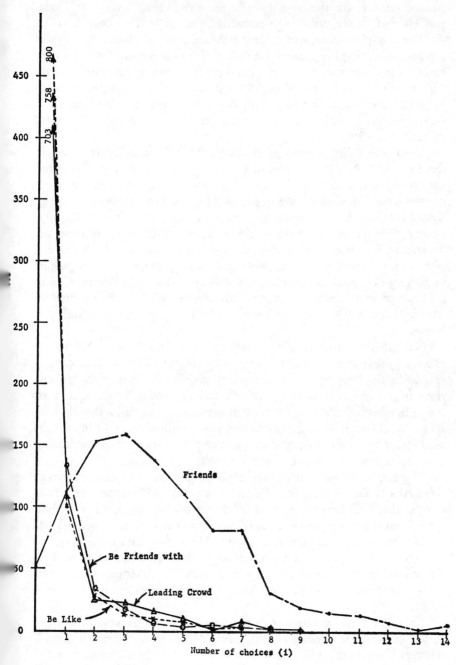

Figure 4.2—Distribution of choices among girls on four criteria in Midcity High.

pendent choices for the boys, five for the girls. There is very little independence of choice, very high consensus, for the leading crowd.

The boy-girl differences evident here are generally found in all these schools, indicating the greater strength of the social system for girls: they make more choices, and their choices show more interdependence or consensus with those of other girls. Although the girls' *friendship* choices are as widely distributed as those of the boys, the girls show more consensus on the leading crowd, persons they want to be like, and those they want to be friends with.

Given these distributions of choices, who shall be called the elites in these schools? At the extremes there is no question: those never named are obviously not elites, and those named most often are obviously elites (in the sense indicated by the questions). But the problem is not so easily solved for those in the middle who received some, but not a great many, choices. The answer seems to be that in such a situation of informal organization, people cannot be clearly divided into leaders and non-leaders, popular heroes and non-heroes. Instead, leadership resides in many people, in varying degrees. The distributions of choices shown in Figures 4.1 and 4.2 are a more accurate expression of the state of affairs than any division we might make between leaders and non-leaders, popular heroes and non-heroes.

Nevertheless, in some of the analyses below, it will be convenient to classify people as non-elites or elites, with respect to the various criteria of choice. For "top elites," the arbitrary division is seven or more mentions by other students—except for the leading crowd, where it is 10 or more; but because these are so few in number—particularly those whom others would want to be like or to be friends with—a group of intermediate elites who received from 2 to 6 choices, or in the case of the leading crowd, 2 to 9 will often be considered as well.

The notion of "elite" used here depends upon the specific questions in which the choices were given. There are important differences in the four criteria that will become evident in the succeeding pages. The leading crowd and those popular as actual friends appear to constitute active leaders in a sense that the other two do not. Those, in contrast, are *desirable* persons, either as someone to be friends with or as someone to be like. They may be thought of as "popular heroes," or "exemplars," or even "passive leaders," exerting their influence by example rather than by active effort.

There are other differences in the way the questions were posed: the person chosen as someone to be like was selected from the whole school, whereas the person chosen as someone to be friends with was selected from the chooser's own grade. The friendship and the leading-crowd choices were also made almost entirely within the same grade. Because students tend to look to the upper grades and because the "be like" choice was not restricted to their grade, the persons to "be like" were more concentrated in upper grades than in lower ones, while the other choices were evenly distributed among grades.

Finally, there is another difference between the "leading crowd" and the oft-chosen friends. The "leading crowd" is a leading crowd for the school as a whole—or for the grade as a whole, since each grade has its leading crowd. Those most often chosen as friends, in contrast, may only be leaders of a subgroup within the grade, perhaps even a subgroup antagonistic to the leading crowd. Thus, those often chosen as friends may be thought of as "local leaders," while those named as members of the leading crowd are leaders in the system as a whole.

Backgrounds of the Elites

How do the elites compare to the others in background? Do they all come from upper occupational and educational groups, or do they come from the community as a whole? Figure 4.3 shows the two ends of the educational continuum: those whose fathers had no more than a grade-school education, and those whose fathers had at least some college. The horizontal line from which the bars rise or descend is the level of the student body as a whole; the bars indicate how far below or above the student body each elite group is. (The leading crowd and friends consist of "top elites": 10+ and 7+ mentions respectively. The two exemplar criteria include the intermediate elites as well (2+) in order to make the sizes of the groups considered roughly the same.) For example, 23.8 per cent of all the girls have fathers with no more than a grade-school education (the base line for the girls in Figure 4.3a), but only 13.9 per cent of the girls who others want to be like have fathers with this little education.

These graphs show, for all four elite groups and for both boys and girls, that the elites have college-educated parents more often than do non-elites, and that they less often have parents with only a grade-school education. The effect appears to be greatest for the girls. That is, if a girl's father has had no more than a grade-school education, she is not at all likely to be looked up to as an exemplar or thought of as a member of the leading crowd—or even a "local" leader in her group of friends.

To look at it differently, a girl whose father went only to grade school is only .6 as frequently to be found among those who other girls would want

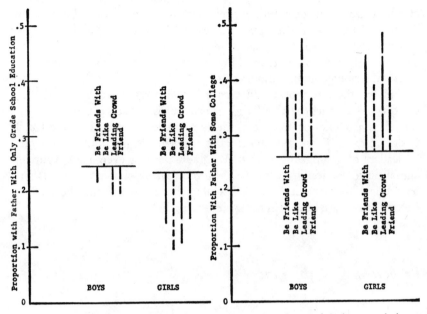

Figure 4.3—Representation of students with poorly-educated fathers and those with well-educated fathers in each of four elites.

to be like as she would be on the basis of chance. In contrast, the girl whose father had at least some college training is about 1.5 times as frequently among these exemplars as she would be on the basis of chance.[3] This is a rather great differential—an impact of parental background upon a girl's chances for status that is difficult to overcome. For boys, the differential is not so great—the boy from an uneducated family is represented among the elites only slightly less than in the student body as a whole and, at the other extreme, the boy from a college family is not quite so highly advantaged—an average differential for the four criteria of about .8 to 1.4.

The general effect of family background on a boy's or girl's position in the adolescent system has been well documented by other studies, particularly Hollingshead's study in the 1940's of one of the schools studied here, Elmtown. It is unnecessary to document the effect of other elements of family background—father's occupation, place of residence in town—on making a boy or girl looked up to or liked in school. It is enough to

3. These figures are derived by: $\dfrac{13.9\% \text{ low ed. in "be like" group}}{23.8\% \text{ low ed. in school}} \approx .6$;

and $\dfrac{38.9\% \text{ high ed. in "be like" group}}{26.9\% \text{ high ed. in school}} \approx 1.5.$

point out that the effect is greater for girls than boys, and greater for the leading crowd than the other three groups.[4]

Is this, then, all there is to the question of parental background and its influence on being a leader or exemplar in the school? Obviously not, for there are many ways in which the parents' position in the community influences the child's development in school, both intrinsically, in the kind of training the parent gives, and extrinsically, in the way the parent—and thus the child—is viewed by the rest of the community. Yet, in the preceding chapter, family background was seen by the students as an important criterion of status in only *some* schools. In others, it was almost never mentioned. Do the present results mean that students in some schools were blind to the effects of family background, or is the effect shown above confined to those schools where family background was seen as important?

Before turning to the separate schools to examine this question, it is useful to reflect briefly on two perspectives in research on leadership. The data examined in the discussion of the past paragraphs imply that boys and girls tend to look "upward" for their elites, to those among them whose backgrounds are more privileged than their own. This result accords with experience, as well as with research on leadership in other areas.

There is, however, another body of thought, also supported by research results, which suggests that people choose leaders who are *like* themselves, leaders with the dominant characteristics of the group they lead. This could be termed a "majority-group" theory of leadership in contrast to the previous "privileged-class" theory. If the "majority-group" theory were true for these schools, then the predominantly working-class schools would choose elites with working-class and lower-educational backgrounds, while the predominantly white-collar schools would choose elites with white-collar and high-educational backgrounds. In other words, the elites would exemplify in the extreme the characteristics of the dominant group in the population; the minority, whichever

---

4. Some authors emphasize the intrinsic effects of parents' status on the child himself and thus on his development in school, while others emphasize the extrinsic effects due to his position in the community. Louis Schneider and Sverre Lysgaard have discussed the "deferred gratification pattern" on the part of middle class children as a crucial intrinsic element in leading middle class adolescents to achieve. It it likely that much of the explanation of the effect of social class on educational achievement lies in the effects of social class on the development of such a pattern, rather than the more direct effects due to children's and teachers' social snobbishness, as Hollingshead implies in his study of Elmtown (*op. cit.*). See Schneider and Lysgaard, "The Deferred Gratification Pattern," *American Sociological Review*, XVIII, 1953, pp. 142-149, and Bernard Rosen, "The Achievement Syndrome: A Psychocultural Dimension of Social Stratification," *American Sociological Review*, XXI, 1956, pp. 203-211.

social class it was, would be underrepresented. Adolescents in the work-ing-class schools would less often turn to the minority of white-collar students as leaders and exemplars; adolescents in upper-middle-class schools would very seldom look to the minority of working-class boys and girls as leaders and as exemplars.[5]

Taking all schools together, these effects would cancel out; the elites would be roughly representative of the teen-agers as a whole. Figure 4.3 showed, however, that this was not so, that boys, and especially girls, from higher educational backgrounds are overrepresented among the elites. Yet what about the middle-class boy or girl in a lower-class school? Is he less likely to be among the elites, differing as he does from the population in the school? It is for such a situation that the "privileged-class" theory and the "majority-group" theory are in sharpest conflict. The former would predict that a middle-class boy or girl will be quite frequently in the leading crowd despite his small numbers; the latter would predict that his differences from the majority would lead them to neglect or exclude him from leadership.

Consider the two schools, both in fairly homogeneous suburbs, which are at the extremes in level of education—the working-class suburb, Newlawn, and the upper-middle-class suburb, Executive Heights. Are the teen-agers from highly educated families overrepresented among the leaders to the same degree in each? The data show that they are *not*. In Executive Heights, with more than 50 per cent of students whose fathers went to college, the proportion is still higher among the inter-mediate leading crowd, and extremely high—over 80 per cent for both boys and girls—among the top leading crowd. In contrast, in Newlawn, the proportion from college backgrounds is *less* among the intermediate and top leading crowd than among all boys or all girls.

In other words, in Newlawn, where students from well-educated families are very scarce, they are scarcer yet among the leading crowd; in Executive Heights, where students from poorly educated families are scarce, they are almost absent from the leading crowd. These results suggest that the "majority-group" theory does hold true, at least in these two schools. Matters are not so simple as implied by some earlier studies,

5. There has been some interesting experimental research with young children examining leadership, and showing the "majority-group" effects. Ferenc Merei in-troduced a new member into groups of nursery-school children who were already occupied with a given activity. Merei found that although the new members had been selected because of their previously-exhibited leadership and dominance of group activities, they seldom became leaders of the group into which they were introduced. When they did, it ordinarily occurred only through their giving up the activity which they had been carrying out in their old group, and compromising by leading the group in the activity it was already doing. See Ferenc Merei, "Group Leadership and Institutionalization," in E. E. Maccoby, T. Newcomb, and E. Hartley, eds., *Readings in Social Psychology*, 3rd edition (New York: Henry Holt, 1958), pp. 522–532.

which saw widespread middle-class domination of the adolescent social system. In particular, Hollingshead's study of Elmtown focused almost solely on this one matter, suggesting that a working-class child had almost no opportunity in this school system.

What about Elmtown, and the other schools besides the extreme cases of Executive Heights and Newlawn? Figures 4.4 and 4.5 show the level of education in each school as a whole, for the intermediate leading crowd and for the top leaders. In general, there is overrepresentation of boys and girls with college-educated fathers in all schools but New-lawn. This is consistent with the "privileged-class" theory of leadership. Yet the overrepresentation varies strikingly. In some, it is quite small. For example, among the Elmtown girls, only 25 per cent of the inter-mediate leaders and 32 per cent of the top leaders have fathers who have attended college, compared with 16 per cent among all girls. This

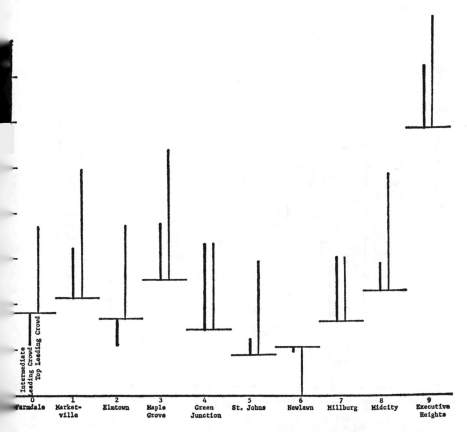

Figure 4.4—Representation of boys with college-educated fathers in intermediate and top leading crowd, for each school separately.

hardly suggests middle-class domination. In nearby Marketville, by comparison, among the intermediate and top leaders, 36 per cent and 59 per cent, respectively, have college backgrounds, compared to 24 per cent in the student body as a whole.

The way this overrepresentation varies from school to school is almost precisely consistent with the "majority-group" theory. In the schools with lowest educational levels—Farmdale, Elmtown, Green Junction, St. John's, Newlawn, and Millburg—the leading crowds show least overrepresentation of college backgrounds. In the schools with highest educational levels—Marketville, Maple Grove, Midcity, and Executive Heights—the leading crowds show most overrepresentation of college backgrounds. The pattern is most apparent among the girls. In *none* of

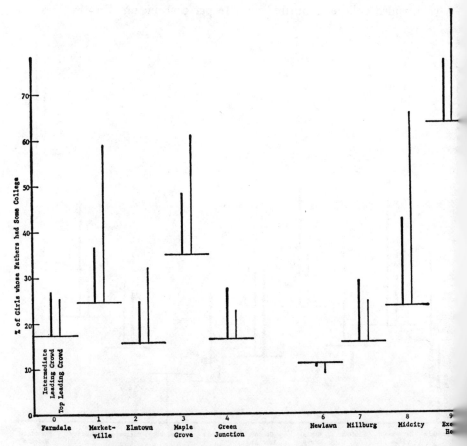

Figure 4.5—Representation of girls with college-educated fathers in intermediate and top leading crowd, for each school separately.

the first group of schools named above is the overrepresentation of college backgrounds as great as that in *any* of the latter schools.

In general, then, we can say this about the leading crowds in these schools: there is a tendency toward control by the higher-educated, more middle-class students in the school, but this tendency is sharply diminished when such students become a small minority in the system. The boys and girls from lower-class backgrounds tend to "take over"; at the extreme (in Newlawn), they even reverse the tendency toward middle-class control, leaving those few middle-class students outside the leading crowd.

The implications of this result are important. The leading crowd of a school, and thus the norms which that crowd sets, is more than merely a reflection of the student body, with extra middle-class students thrown in. The leading crowd tends to accentuate those very background characteristics already dominant, whether they be upper- or lower-class. A boy or girl in such a system, then, finds it governed by an elite whose backgrounds exemplify, in the extreme, those of the dominant population group. In particular, a working-class boy or girl will be most left out in an upper-middle-class school, least so in a school with few middle-class students.

Another implication of this dual effect has to do with changes over time. In 1900, only 11 per cent of high-school-age children were in school. As late as 1930, the proportion was as low as 51 per cent. Now it is over 90 per cent. Nearly all the added students are children of working-class and farm parents. Thus in the earlier years, the proportion of working-class adolescents in *school* was much lower than at present, even if the population composition of the community were the same. Consequently, a school where boys and girls with non-college backgrounds have taken over, such as Elmtown or Green Junction, may have once been dominated by a middle-class leading crowd. This may, in fact, be the explanation for the very different social structure in Elmtown's high school today from that found in the same town by Hollingshead in 1940. As Chapter VII will demonstrate, the working-class teen-agers have taken over the social system in Elmtown high school even more than the data of the present chapter suggest.

More generally, it is likely that the impact of "high school for all" has had an effect on the social system of the school beyond the direct effect of changing the population composition: the elites of the system have changed, and, with them, the norms that govern it.

This is not to say that the norms of the adolescent system derive directly from the population composition. Marketville has far fewer college-background students than either Executive Heights or Maple

Grove, yet good grades bring more status there than in either of the other two. One of the difficult and elusive tasks of a school principal is to shape the norms of the adolescent system in the direction of educational goals, without allowing all the elite status to accrue to students from the best backgrounds.

It should be noted that those schools where college backgrounds are most overrepresented in the leading crowd are also the schools—Marketville, Maple Grove, Midcity, and Executive Heights—where the teenagers themselves *saw* "a good family" or "coming from the right neighborhood" as an important attribute for popularity and status, both among the girls and the boys. These data on the composition of the leading crowds are in full accord with the way the teen-agers see their system, as a glance again at Figure 3.8 (p. 85) will show.

BACKGROUNDS OF "LOCAL LEADERS" AND "SYSTEM LEADERS"

Membership in the leading crowd, discussed above, is leadership in the system as a whole. What about the "local leaders"—those who received many friendship choices? These boys and girls are not necessarily leaders in their cultural system as a whole; some are leaders of subgroups that may even be at odds with the dominant culture. It is reasonable, then, to expect that these local informal leaders will be more like their constituencies than are the members of the leading crowd, just as a Congressional Representative is more like his constituents than is a Senator or the President. The "majority-group" theory of leadership should be more true for these local leaders, the "privileged-class" theory less true.

Results for the local leaders do in fact confirm this notion. In none of the schools are those with college backgrounds as highly represented among the oft-chosen friends as they are among the leading crowds. The data (not presented here) show similarities to those for the leading crowd in Figures 4.4 and 4.5, but in all cases, the "majority-group" effects weigh more strongly, and the "privileged-class" effects less so.

The data for the exemplars—those whom others want to be friends with or to be like—are more like those for the leading crowds than for the "local leaders." That is, they exemplify both the majority-group effects and the privileged-class effects, in roughly the same proportions as do the leading crowds. This fact is important, because it indicates that the composition of the leading crowds is not simply imposed from without by the adult community. When boys and girls choose those they most want to be like or to be friends with, they choose persons with backgrounds very like those of the leading crowd.

THE COMPOSITION OF ELITES—FROM TWO PERSPECTIVES

The composition of these "elite" groups may be viewed from two perspectives: that of the school as a whole, in which case the absolute composition of the leader groups and their composition relative to the student body are important; and that of the individual, in which case the individual's chances of being in these elite groups is important. In the previous discussion, the perspective was that of the system, for we were interested in the composition of these adolescent cultures. But even from this perspective, the leaders have been viewed *relative to* the school's composition only, not in absolute terms.

Considering only the top leading crowd—those named ten times or more—the different perspectives can be seen for the girls in the large schools in Table 17. In absolute composition, in Executive Heights there is the greatest majority of college-background fathers among the top leading crowd. Thus, in absolute terms, this leading crowd has highest educational background. Yet, the overrepresentation is greatest in Midcity —that is, the leaders differ most in educational background from the student body as a whole. In Newlawn, the leading crowd has the least educated background, and is closest to the student body in its educational background.

Table 17—Girls in large schools in the top leading crowd: absolute composition, representativeness, and individual chances as a function of father's education

		Newlawn	Millburg	Midcity	Executive Heights
In school: per cent with college background		10.9	15.6	23.2	63.5
		(470)	(696)	(907)	(873)
COMPOSITION OF THE CROWD					
Absolute composition: per cent with college background		8.7	24.3	65.5	88.5
		(23)	(33)	(58)	(52)
Relative composition: per cent over- or under-representation of college background		− 1.2	+ 8.7	+42.3	+25.0
A GIRL'S CHANCES					
A girl's absolute chances: By virtue of her father's education, she has x chances out of a hundred of being in the leading crowd	College: x = Non-college: x =	3.9 5.0	7.4 4.3	18.1 2.9	8.3 1.8
A girl's relative chances: by virtue of her father's education, she has x times as likely to be in the leading crowd as would be expected on basis of school composition	College: x = Non-college: x =	0.80 1.02	1.56 0.90	2.82 0.45	1.40 0.31

Turning to the perspective of the girl herself, the matter is somewhat different. The college-background girl's absolute chances are greatest by far in Midcity: she has eighteen chances out of a hundred to be in the leading crowd. Her relative chances are greatest as well, for she is 2.82 times as likely to be in the leading crowd as would be expected by her numbers in the student body. Executive Heights, however, is far worse for the girl with no college background. She has only 1.8 chances out of a hundred of being a member of the leading crowd, or only .31 of what they should be, compared with .45 in Midcity. Because such girls are few in number in Executive Heights, an underrepresentation which is only 25 per cent puts her at a greater disadvantage than does an underrepresentation of 42 per cent in Midcity. Conversely, the small number of college-background girls in Millburg, together with their slight overrepresentation, puts them at a relatively great advantage. Their chances are 7.4 out of 100, almost as great as in Executive Heights, although their overrepresentation is only 8.7 per cent, and in absolute composition of the leading crowd, they are outnumbered 75.7 per cent to 24.3 per cent.

Altogether, then, the matter is not so simple as any one set of statistics would suggest. For some purposes, such as comparing the behavior, attitudes, or aspirations of the leaders in two schools, *absolute* composition of the leading crowd is important. For other purposes, such as comparing the behavior, attitudes, or aspirations of the leaders to that of the student body as a whole, their composition *relative* to that of the student body is important. Finally, for seeing just how a boy's or girl's chances are affected by his father's education, other statistics, taking into account not only the overrepresentation but also the prevalence or rarity of college backgrounds in the school, are important.

OTHER BACKGROUND CHARACTERISTICS

Father's education is only one attribute of a boy's or girl's background. It is a rough indication of family status in the community, as well as a measure of educational level. As might be expected, father's occupation, another indicator of family status, shows nearly the same results as shown above—a "privileged-class" effect and a "majority-group" effect.

Religion does not show such results. In all schools but Executive Heights, religion was almost unrelated to membership in the leading crowd, although religion varied markedly from school to school—in Marketville, Catholics constituted only 13 per cent of the student body, while they were in a majority in Newlawn and Millburg. Despite this variation, the proportions of Catholics in the leading crowds accurately reflect their numbers in the student body, in these extreme schools as well as in the others. A number of factors suggest that religion plays a far smaller part in structuring these adolescent communities than does family social status in the community. For example, there was almost no tendency, except in Executive Heights, for boys and girls to name their friends from their own religious group.

In Executive Heights, religion plays a more important role. The Catholics are almost all Italian working-class from a neighboring service community. The Protestants, who have a plurality, live both in Executive Heights, the central suburb served by the school, and in the slightly lower-income surrounding areas. Nevertheless, they are almost exclusively upper-middle-class. The Jews live almost exclusively in Executive Heights and are almost all upper-middle-class. They live in neighborhoods somewhat separate from the Protestants.

In Executive Heights, Jews are overrepresented in the leading crowd and other elites, and Catholics severely underrepresented. The latter is certainly in part due to social-class differences, but the predominance of Jews in the leading crowds over the more numerous Protestants is not what one would expect. (This is discussed further in Chapter X.)[6]

The remainder of this chapter will examine the elites' behavior and attitudes toward the non-elites in each school. It is important to keep in mind the variations in absolute composition of these elite groups from school to school; despite these wide variations, there will be some striking similarities from school to school in the attitudes of the leaders. Also, there will be similarities from school to school in the way the elites differ from the non-elites. When such similarities among elites occur, it will be in spite of the background differences just examined, forcing us to ask just what it is in the adolescent culture that makes for elite similarity.

Post-High School Intentions

As the preceding sections have indicated, there are more boys and girls from well-educated families among the elites of these adolescent cultures. This overrepresentation is greatest in the most middle-class

---

6. The matter is different in one Baltimore high school. A junior girl reports: At Eastern there are relatively few Jewish girls. However we would not let a Jewish girl in our sorority and it would be very hard if at all possible for one to get in any sorority. I know of only one half-Jewish girl (in a sorority). There are a few Catholics in our sorority and I don't know of any sorority which wouldn't let them in. No colored girls would ever be let into one of our sororities. They have at least one sorority of their own. I know of one Japanese girl in a sorority. At Eastern I would say that there is little religious prejudice. The only prejudice is against Jewish girls, who are in a very small minority.

schools, that is, in Marketville, Maple Grove, Midcity, and Executive
Heights; and it vanishes in the working-class suburban school, Newlawn.
However, given these absolute and relative differences in educational
background among the elites, what is the educational *future* of the
elites in each school? Are the background differences between elites and
student body reflected in college intentions? Is the Newlawn leading
crowd below the school as a whole in its college intentions, as it is below
in college background? Are the elites in Marketville and Maple Grove
especially college-bound, compared with those of Farmdale, Elmtown,
and Green Junction?

Figures 4.6 and 4.7 show for each school the college intentions of
boys and girls in the leading crowd. Only the leading crowd is shown,
not the other elites. The various other elite groups within each school

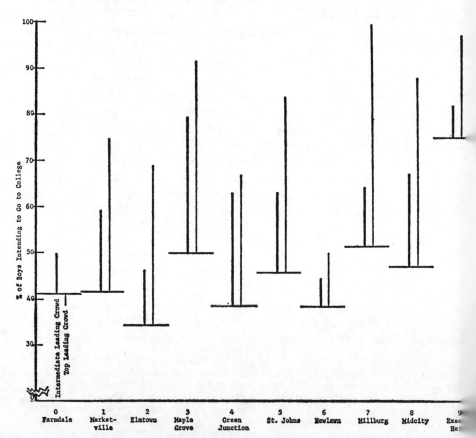

Figure 4.6—Representation of boys with plans for college in intermediate and
top leading crowd, for each school separately.

are similar, and will not be discussed. For each school, the intermediate leading crowd and the top members of the leading crowd (10+ choices) are shown, similar to Figures 4.4 and 4.5.

In general, the elites more often intend to go to college than do the students as a whole. In only three cases is this not so—the girls in the intermediate leading crowd in Elmtown, the top leaders among the girls in Newlawn, and the top leaders among the boys in Farmdale. In all the other schools, members of the leading crowd far more often intend to go to college than does the rest of the student body. The difference between elite and student body is greater in this respect than it was in educational background.

Thus, although the elites tend to include those from higher educational backgrounds more often than would be expected by chance, a

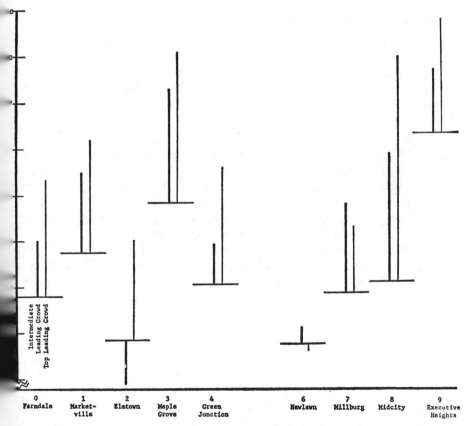

Figure 4.7—Representation of girls with plans for college in intermediate and top leading crowd, for each school separately.

comparison of Figures 4.4 and 4.5 with 4.6 and 4.7 shows that the background difference is not sufficient to account for their higher college-going intentions. Evidently something over and above background differences leads elites to be more college-bound. And whatever these factors are, they do not act to the same degree in all schools, nor to the same degree for boys and girls.

For the boys, the leading crowds deviate from the student body to nearly the same degree in every school. Only in Farmdale and Newlawn are their college intentions not much higher than those of the student body as a whole. The deviation of the leading crowd from the other boys, in their college plans, is generally more than the deviation of the girls' leading crowd, and there is less variation among the boys' leading crowds from school to school than among girls'. The girls' leading crowds in Newlawn, Elmtown, and Millburg are very close to their student bodies in college intentions, while those in Midcity and Maple Grove are much higher. The absolute variation among girls' intermediate leading crowds is from a low of 19 per cent in Elmtown to a high of 83 per cent in nearby Maple Grove, a difference of 64 per cent; the variation for boys' intermediate leaders is from a low of 44 per cent in Newlawn (46 per cent in Elmtown, the second lowest) to 79 per cent in Maple Grove, a difference of only 35 per cent.[7]

The greater variation among the girls' leading crowd is paralleled by a variation in the total student bodies. Excluding Executive Heights, where the proportion going to college is far above any of the other schools, the college intentions of the total student bodies of girls range from a low of 27 per cent in Newlawn to a high of 58 per cent in Maple Grove. The boys' student bodies range from a low of 34 per cent in Elmtown to a high of 51 per cent in Millburg.[8] This variation is only 17 per cent—just a little over half of that for the girls.

It appears, then, that the factors that make these schools different have much more impact on girls' college-going intentions than on boys', both in the leading crowds and in the student body as a whole. At this point, two hypotheses seem most reasonable: (1) girls' college-intentions are more a function of class background than boys', with a greater difference between white-collar-background girls and those from work-

7. These comparisons excluded Executive Heights, in which the total student body is much higher than the others in college-going. The boy-girl contrasts would be even slightly greater than stated if Executive Heights were included.

8. The high proportion in Millburg is explained by the existence of a free-tuition junior college in the same building with the high school, facilitating college attendance for Millburg boys. The existence of this junior college has much less impact on the college intentions of the Millburg girls, both in the student body as a whole and in the leading crowd (see again Figures 4.6 and 4.7, pp. 114 and 115).

ing-class backgrounds; or (2) the social climate of the school has greater effects on girls than on boys, in some schools encouraging college attendance among them—whether they come from working-class or white-collar backgrounds—or discouraging it. The practical implications of these two hypotheses differ greatly. If the first is true, then it provides no basis for action, since the backgrounds of adolescents cannot be changed. If the second is true, then by changing the climate of the school, college intentions of bright girls, from whatever background, can be increased.

The data of Figure 4.5 and Figure 4.7 suggest that backgrounds are important; two schools, Newlawn and Maple Grove, are at the extremes in girls' college intentions (excluding Executive Heights), not only in their student bodies, but in their leading crowds as well. These schools also differ most in social-class background, consistent with the differences in intention—although backgrounds are not so sharply different as intentions. However, Chapter III showed that the importance of good grades as means for status was higher among Newlawn girls than among Maple Grove girls, and that in fact the girls in the Newlawn leading crowd had better grades relative to the student body than did the girls in Maple Grove's leading crowd. This suggests that college intentions may be more a function of a student's background than of the status of scholastic effort in the system.

Yet the matter is not so simple as this. If a student's background were the sole or primary influence on college intentions, then differences between schools in college intentions should simply parallel differences in educational backgrounds. This is not the case: the schools tend to diverge *more* in college intentions of the girls than in college backgrounds. Two of the schools which were lowest in college backgrounds, Elmtown and Newlawn, are far more separated from the others in college intentions—both in their total student bodies and in their leading crowds. This divergence of schools suggests that the girls' college intentions may be highly influenced by the high-school climate—not the status of scholastic effort, but the status of college-going. That is, in some schools, college-going has high prestige, while in others, it has little. The divergence of girls' college intentions in different schools, beyond that of their educational backgrounds, suggests that this prestige influences girls to go or stay away from college. (This research did not obtain a measure of the prestige which college going had in each school, so this inference cannot be directly tested.) In contrast, the level of boys' college intentions in each school (Figure 4.6) more nearly parallels the level of college background (Figure 4.4).

This question will be examined again in Chapter IX, where college intentions of girls and boys with different backgrounds will be examined. At that point, the problem, with its important implications for educational policy, will be discussed further.

The Norms and Values of the Elite Groups

The differences in background and college intentions give only a glimpse at the kinds of informal elites that arise in these cultures. The values held by the groups in which these elites travel give a richer view of what they are like.

All students were asked:

> I.40. Among the crowd you go around with, which of the things below are important in order to be popular in the group?
>
> Be a good dancer
> Have sharp clothes
> Have a good reputation
> Stirring up a little excitement
> Have money
> Smoking
> Being up on cars (girls: know how to dress properly)
> Know what's going on in the world of popular singers and movie stars

Among these items (which were selected after a free-response pretest), the most frequently checked item by both boys and girls was "have a good reputation." About 70 per cent of the boys and almost 90 per cent of the girls checked this response. "A good reputation" is evidently of considerably greater concern to girls than to boys; this is consistent with the great frequency with which girls mentioned a good reputation as a criterion for getting into the leading crowd.

The members of the leading crowd and those whom others want to be like checked a good reputation even more often than the student body as a whole, as Figures 4.8 and 4.9 indicate. The importance of "a good reputation" among the boys and among the boys' elites varies from school to school, although the elites are above the school averages in every school except Elmtown. In St. John's and Newlawn, the student bodies themselves are quite low in the importance they place on this item. "A good reputation" seems, for the boys, something that the culture may or may not emphasize.

On the other hand, a *girls'* reputation seems a crucial and invariant element in the culture. For the girl exemplars (someone to "be like" or to "be friends with"), there was almost complete consistency in men-

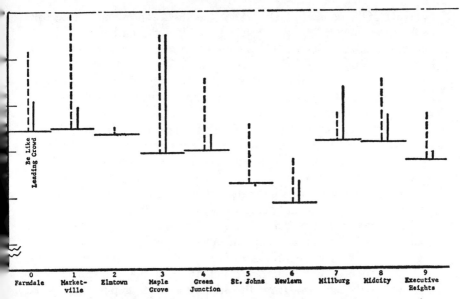

Figure 4.8—The importance of a good reputation among all boys in each school, and in two elites in each school.

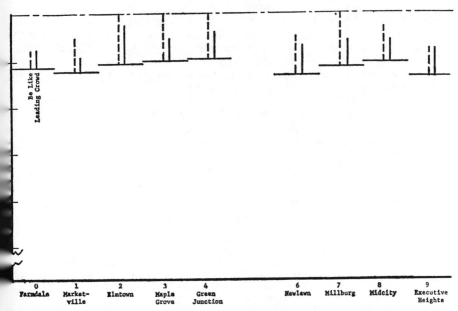

Figure 4.9—The importance of a good reputation among all girls in each school, and in two elites in each school.

tioning a good reputation. Of 111 girls in the 2 top exemplar categories (not represented in Figure 4.9, which includes the intermediates), only *one* girl in all nine schools failed to indicate that a good reputation was important among the girls in her group.[9] The norms of the *acting* leaders, named as friends or members of the leading crowd, are somewhat nearer to those of the student body, but still emphasize a good reputation with high frequency.[10]

In all the schools, having a good reputation was extremely important for the girls' elite groups. Figure 4.9 shows that although the *backgrounds* and *future plans* of the elites relative to the others differed from school to school, the norm of "a good reputation" among the girls' elites was always stronger than among the non-elites. Why is this so—not only among the exemplars, but among the active leaders as well?

The question is particularly relevant, because the importance of a good reputation is not as consistent among the boys. Yet for the girls, a good reputation seems crucial in every school for being in the elites. A boy in one school indicated at length how this functioned for a girl who was excluded from the leading crowd despite intelligence, activities in school, a family with money, and a vivacious personality.

(Tell me, what about ——?)
—— is sort of a black spot.
(Why is that?)
I don't know. I like her, myself; I haven't got a thing in the world against her. If I did, I'd tell you, because I haven't got anything to lose. A lot of the kids think she talks too much. She's just always running off at the mouth, talking about what she did or what her folks have got, or something like that.
(Well, how come she isn't in the clique?)
They just didn't accept her, is all I can tell you. I don't know how they work. I don't even try and pay any attention to it.
(Is she snobbish?)
No, she's not. But she's a little wild, I'll tell you that.
(How do you mean?)
Well—sex. She's wild as far as that's concerned.
(The clique is very much against this?)
Yeah, that's about it. Maybe for the boys it's pretty free. For the girls, boy, you've got to stay straight.

---

9. Only the "be like" exemplars and the leading crowd are included in the graphs; the other two elites manifest the pattern indicated in the text.

10. A Baltimore junior comments concerning her high school: At Eastern a good reputation is important. A girl was blackballed from our sorority because she did not have a good reputation. She drinks too much and is wild. She lives in the fringe of a good neighborhood, but in a very poor house. It's almost a shack. We took all this into consideration. Neat dressing is taken into consideration too, but a girl would not be blackballed unless she were a really impossible dresser. I think neatness is stressed the most. In a way this means all-aroundness. If a girl is a lot of fun, dresses fairly neatly, has a good reputation, wants to get in, she can get into a sorority, provided no girl in the sorority has a personal grudge against her.

(How come —— . . . ?)
She's a real intelligent girl. I know you know that from her records.
(But how come she's wild about sex?)
I don't know, because she fixed—this is just between you and I—because she fixed me up with one of her girl friends from ——. Now this is not my girl, this is a girl from ——. All this is on the sly, you might say. But this —— turned out to be—well, I'll tell you what we did. We went to the drive-in . . .
(Was this a double date?)
Yeah, double date. And we stopped and got half a case of beer. Then we went to the drive-in, and then we came back from the drive-in. So we went to her house. I was in one room and —— was in another. And you could just hear by the sounds—I know what happened. And I know what happened in mine. That would probably be one of the things—because I think the girls probably have a pretty good idea that she's like that.

The girl who is too free with herself, whatever her social background, is excluded—evidently first by the girls, with the boys concurring. It may be that such a girl is excluded because she "debases the currency" —just as a man of unlimited wealth who threw money away would be looked at askance by his fellows, because he was debasing the currency. It is evident that in adolescent dating patterns, a girl's favors— at the level of kisses when dating starts, at the level of sex play of greater or lesser degree in later adolescence—and her hints of favors, in coquettish talk and gesture, are something to be *used* in exchange for dates, and in order to keep the boy at least partly at her bidding. This has probably long been so; witness the wise mother's admonition: "Do not sell thyself too cheaply, child." Some girls fail to learn this; their reputations are ruined or tarnished; and they can no longer use these favors in return for control. The favors are no longer "worth so much" as they were, and a girl must dispense more and more of them if she is to receive the attention she wants.

In very early adolescence, before courtship has begun in earnest, kisses flow freely at party games. They have not yet become currency in the competition for status and control. Later, the girls who once played post office with abandon now dispense their kisses much more strategically.

The crucial importance of the girl's reputation is indicated by the following incident, which involved one of the girls in the same school whose reputation was untarnished, one of the girls who excluded the first girl from the "clique." A boy reports:

She's a pretty big wheel. It's been backfiring on her lately. She's losing out fast. A lot of kids don't like her. See, she's supposed to be a real nice girl. Well, I had her out about six months ago. . . . And she proved to be not a very nice girl at all. See, she went with this kid, ——; when he was a senior, she was a freshman—he graduated. And she'd been stepping out on him with different guys. So I took her out, and she didn't turn out to be so nice at all. She's pretty free with herself.

And so I guess the next day, she thought, "Well, here I went ahead and did that with him, and everything, and I shouldn't have done that, because I'm a big wheel." So she wouldn't speak to me the next day. So this kid came up to me, and she must have said something to him, because he said, "Say, I see you were out with ———." And I said, "That's right," and he said, "Well, how'd you do with her?" And I said, "Well, I did pretty good," I says, "I'm not going to say." So he runs right to her and tells her just what I said. She thought that I just wouldn't tell anybody. And the only thing I said was that I did all right with her, I didn't imply that I did anything to her, or anything like that.

And so she come back and she got real mad at me. But I didn't say nothing to her, and I said, "Well, I didn't say one thing about you. They asked me about that, I said I was out with her, and I did all right, I had a good time. And you can take that any way you want." And so I told her, "If you can find anybody that wants to go back on that. . . ." Oh, she got mad. So she was mad about that for a while. Boy, I'm telling you, she sure surprised me; I thought she would be a girl that was really on the ball, and that was really something. And when I got her out, I was so disappointed, because it was just—very simple.

And I come home that night, and I went in to wash my face and brush my teeth, And you know that makeup they wear, that pancake makeup? I had that makeup in the corner of my mouth, and everything. That did it with me—I've never had any interest in her ever since then. But like I said, she is slowly fading out of the picture, because they are really starting to catch up with her.

When this girl's reputation was put in jeopardy by her freedom with this boy, she did everything she could to maintain it: first, not speaking to him the next day, in an attempt to re-establish over him the power she had before being too free the night before; and then reacting angrily when this was made public. His reaction was one of lessened interest, because the fruits that he had seen as inaccessible were too easily obtained.

This is an example of the double standard at work in clear-cut terms. The boy is the pursuer, the girl is the pursued. If she fails to withhold anything he seeks, the cause for pursuit is gone. Thus, it becomes crucial for her status personally and for the maintenance of the system itself for her to be selective and dispense favors with extreme care. If not, the culture is threatened by her philanthropy, and punishes her by "ruining her reputation" and taking away her status.

A boy's sexual behavior, however, is not threatening to the culture, because he is the pursuer. His sexual exploits are conquests, and thus actions that *gain* him status rather than lose it. It is this pursuer-pursued asymmetry of the relationship between the sexes that seems, more than anything else, to maintain the double standard. If this were reversed, we might expect the double standard to be reversed as well:

males would have a desired commodity, and it would be important to the courtship system that they used this commodity to gain them the girl they wanted, and did not give it away with no strings attached. Thus, the maintenance of the system would depend more on boys keeping "a good reputation." So long as the pursuer-pursued relationship stands as it is, the present double standard will very likely remain as well.[11]

Perhaps this is a cynical view of courtship and marriage, but it nevertheless seems true that those girls who have best learned how to use their attractiveness at the great bargaining table of courtship are those who are most successful in getting the man they want. Whether learning such skills is the best way for an adolescent girl to use her time in view of her later life is a different question. It seems unfortunate that so much of adolescents' energies must be spent in cultivating skills that serve them only at one point in life—in playing the courtship game. These skills and habits may be impediments to happiness in later life. The "love of the chase" may linger after marriage for both male and female, making married life less content.

Or it may not. This is a matter about which we know little or nothing systematically.[12] It is safe to say, however, that the norms of adolescent groups—particularly those groups with high status in the system—are strongly oriented to the boy-girl relations in school and reflect the great energy expended on these relationships. Whether this expenditure of energy is beneficial to the individual and the society cannot be assessed here; but some of the consequences of this emphasis on social matters in the adolescent culture will be examined in succeeding chapters, particularly Chapters VIII and IX.

There are numerous consequences of these dating systems and the strong norms which are part of them. One fact, which may be a consequence of the norms which bear down upon girls, has to do with their attitudes toward their own town. Casual observation of differences

---

11. A reduction in role-differentiation between boys and girls in the modern middle class may reduce this asymmetry. Yet the school in which the above incident occurred is one of the most middle-class of the schools studied. Thus, the pursuer-pursued relation is a long way from gone, even in middle-class cultures. See Chapter IX for an examination of the role-differentiation in different schools.

12. Skillfully designed research could answer this question. It would help, for example, to be able to compare marriage and divorce rates among men and women who had gone to coeducational schools (in which more energy is expended on the relation between sexes) with those from comparable backgrounds who had gone to single-sex schools. It would also help to compare the divorce rates among men and women who had dated very much in high school with those who had dated little. Alumni records from coeducational and single-sex colleges could begin to give an indication of effects of coeducation. Or divorce records in cities that have had single-sex high schools could give some indications, lacking systematic research.

between boys and girls suggests that boys, less attached to the home, would be more eager than girls to leave the local community for another town or for the big city. But it is not so, as responses to two questions in the questionnaire show. The questions, and the responses by boys and girls, are shown below:

I.78. If you had a chance for two similar jobs, one in this town, and one in another town the same size but in another state, which would you choose?

	Boys	Girls
Other town	24.5	38.1
Number of cases	(4,020)	(4,134)

I.79. If one of the jobs were in this town and the other in a larger city, which would you take?

	Boys	Girls
Larger City	28.8	46.0
Number of cases	(4,020)	(4,134)

In response to both questions, the girls show a greater desire to get away from their home town. The difference is greatest when the alternative is a large city; and although the results are not shown for separate schools, the difference is much greater between boys and girls in the small towns than between boys and girls in the suburbs or cities. These results, so out of accord with naive expectations, suggest that the girls' desires to get away may be a reaction against a set of community constraints which are far more oppressive upon them than upon the boys.

OTHER NORMS OF THE ELITE GROUPS

For the students as a whole, 36.6 per cent of the boys and 24.1 per cent of the girls checked the item "stirring up a little excitement," as something important in their crowd. The boys in the leading crowd, those often named as friends, and those named as someone to be like, check this item considerably *more* often than do the other boys. In other words, not only is "a good reputation" more important among these informal elites than among the boys as a whole, but stirring up excitement, which would seem to be at the opposite extreme, is also. This apparent paradox was evident in responses to the question of what it takes to get into the leading crowd. Some of the responses indicate how the students themselves see it:

A good personality and reputation. Good appearance. And a little excitement but not too much. In other words not too loud.

A good reputation, good sense of humor, good discretion, sincerity, care for others, interest in what's going on, and not be a follower.

A good reputation, then, is required for being in the leading group, but it takes far more than a good reputation. Starting some excitement, or stirring things up a little, are ways to capture the energy and imagination of the group and become, in effect, its leader or the focus of its attention. Schools are filled with boys and girls with excellent reputations who are just "filling up space," as one boy put it, who never become the center of attention. These adolescent cultures differ, of course, from school to school, as well as from grade to grade; it would be incorrect to suggest that the same mixture of hedonism and propriety is found in all. Yet in each of the schools the mixture exists. Table 18 shows that the importance that "stirring up a little excitement" has for the boy elites exists in both the small schools and in the large schools. All sets of elites among the boys are higher than the student body as a whole. This reflects something that is apparently common to adolescent boys in all these schools, from the upper-middle-class suburb to the working-class suburb, from the city school to the small town school.

Table 18—The frequency of checking "stirring up excitement" (I.40), by members of the elites in large and small schools

Boys	All students	Be friends with	Be like	Leading crowd	Frequently-named friend
Small schools (0–4)					
Per cent	40.7	40.9	50.6	49.3	49.2
Number	(1,028)	(93)	(91)	(67)	(136)
Large schools (6–9)					
Per cent	35.2	38.0	43.0	38.3	43.2
Number	(2,992)	(189)	(172)	(106)	(308)
Girls					
Small schools (0–4)					
Per cent	24.9	16.0	16.4	26.9	29.1
Number	(972)	(144)	(104)	(104)	(172)
Large schools (6–9)					
Per cent	24.0	30.9	28.8	30.6	31.1
Number	(3,162)	(278)	(215)	(169)	(541)

Among the girls, the pattern is a little different (Table 18). In the small schools, the importance of stirring up a little excitement is above the student body for members of the leading crowd and for the highly chosen friends, again the *active* leaders. It is below, however, for the *exemplars*, the desired friends and the girls that others want to be like. The mixture of excitement and propriety, then, is a little more weighted on the side of propriety for the small-school girls than for the boys. Yet for the girls, the active leaders embody more excitement and love of fun than the exemplars, who embody more propriety.

The large-school elites among the girls are more uniformly directed toward stirring up excitement. This is most true for the active leaders—the leading crowd and the frequently-named friends—but it is true in lesser degree for the exemplars as well. This suggests that among the girls, the elites in the large schools are more liberated from the home, more focused upon the group itself in their interests and attitudes, than are the followers. In the large schools, the girls' elites are further removed from parental constraints, freer to "have fun," while in the small schools this is less true.

Why do the boys' leadership structures seem to be more nearly alike in the small and large towns? Why are elites among the small-school boys more independent from adults, oriented to "stirring up excitement," approximately like the large-school elites, while the small-school leading girls are less free from the adult community? The answer may lie in a difference in the ways a boy gets to be popular and the ways a girl gets to be popular. Because the boys gain popularity and attention more nearly through specific achievements, the boys' elites can remain more independent of the attempts of parents—attempts that seem to be more successful in small schools—to fix the composition and behavior of the leading groups in school.

In some ways, the mixture of hedonism and propriety in these elites characterizes the whole adolescent culture. The hedonism of popular music, for example, is found nowhere to such a degree as among adolescents. One might suppose, then, that the leaders of the adolescent culture would be most oriented to popular music, most attuned to the mass-produced popular culture, which provides for adolescents popular heroes like Elvis Presley and a special form of music, rock and roll. But this is not true, as Table 19 indicates. The table includes all of the schools, but in none of them do the elites, more often than the other students, check that it is important in their crowd to "know what's going on in the world of popular music and movie stars." The importance of this item is less for all elites—the leading crowd, those named as friends, those named as someone to be like, and those named as someone to be friends with.

The lesser importance of popular music in general, and rock and roll in particular, among these elites is evident in other ways. The proportion favoring rock and roll is lower than for the student body, and the proportion liking Elvis Presley most among the singers listed in the questionnaire is lower, for all the elites.[13] The difference between student

---

13. A Baltimore teen age girl comments: "Among the elites at Eastern there is no swooning over rock and roll singers. It is the drapettes and the unaccepted girls who are in fan clubs and swoon over these singers. The elites like the music, but not the singers."

body and elites is greatest for girls—and it is for girls that the whole phenomenon of popular music and mass-media stars is of most importance. (The great importance of popular music for girls is indicated by the fact that 33.2 per cent of the boys, but only 15.3 per cent of the girls, had no favorite song.[14] For adolescent girls, popular songs are consistent with and reinforce the "romantic" role which they are expected to play, while songs have no such function for boys.)

Table 19—The frequency of checking "know what's going on in the world of popular music and movie stars" (1.40), by members of the elites in large and small schools

	All students	Be friends with	Be like	Leading crowd	Frequently-named friend
Boys checking "popular music and movie stars"					
Per cent	19.2	11.4	10.7	6.9	14.6
Number	(4,020)	(282)	(263)	(173)	(444)
Girls checking "popular music and movie stars"					
Per cent	26.3	19.0	16.3	11.7	18.5
Number	(4,134)	(422)	(319)	(274)	(713)

There is a peculiar difference in the behavior of elites in the two matters we have labeled hedonistic, that is, "stirring up a little excitement," which they mention *more* often than the non-elites, and "keeping up with the world of popular music and movie stars," which they mention *less* often than the non-elites. What accounts for this difference in response? It is difficult to say from these data alone; but there is a fundamental difference between the two activities. Attention toward popular music and movie stars is directed *externally*, away from the group of adolescents itself. Stirring up excitement among the group, however, is a matter of *internal* significance—it does something for, or to, the group itself. Thus, it might be that attention to the mass media acts in some part as an alternative to, or perhaps a withdrawal from, performance upon the real-life stage of these adolescent societies. Later evidence will show this more clearly; the girls, and groups of girls, who pay most attention to the external popular culture are on the fringes of the social system of teen-agers, while those in the center of things are apparently busier *doing* things that keep them in the center. Popular music, of course, is not so externally directed as are movies and television; it serves as a medium for group activities, that is, parties and

_____

14. This is one bit of evidence on a matter that is discussed in detail by John Johnstone, *op. cit.*—the odd role that popular music seems to play for some teen-agers, serving, for the least popular among them, as a substitute for the social interaction with their fellows which they lack.

dancing. For the real *fans*, however, popular music is less an instrument than it is an object of attention in itself, drawing them away from the activities of the crowd.[15]

Cars among the Elites

There is no question of the impact of cars on the strength and character of today's adolescent culture. Without cars, teen-agers would be much more nearly children, much more subject to parental dictates. Does the importance of cars in the culture mean that the elites are especially interested in cars? Table 20 compares car-ownership of elites with non-elites, in large and small schools separately.

Table 20—Car-ownership of boys' elites in large and small schools (all grades)*

	All students	2+ Be friends	2+ Be like	10+ Leading crowd
Small schools (0–4)				
Per cent	23.7	23.2	32.5	42.7
Number	(944)	(86)	(83)	(61)
Large schools (6–9)				
Per cent	19.7	24.2	24.3	27.4
Number	(2,501)	(106)	(151)	(95)

* No-answers have been subtracted.
Results are not tabulated for those chosen seven or more times as a friend.

This table includes all four years in school, and therefore far understates the car ownership by both the elites and non-elites among those who can legally drive. But except for the "be like" criterion, which overrepresents upperclassmen, the choices are quite evenly distributed over the four grades, so that the figures are comparable for the other elite groups.

As Table 20 shows, in general the elites own cars somewhat more often than the non-elites. This is especially true for the active leaders— boys who are members of the leading crowd. It appears that being an active leader, which involves activity with others and not just being an example, is aided considerably by owning a car, while being looked up to is only slightly so. Among the active leaders, then, cars play a larger part than among the non-leaders. Before concluding this, however, it is instructive to examine, in Table 21, the leaders' responses to the item, "being up on cars," as something important in their crowd. This is different from *owning* a car; it indicates the degree to which cars are an object of attention and the degree to which a boy's knowledge about cars increases his status among his friends.

15. See John Johnstone, *op. cit.*, for a detailed examination of the role of popular music and television in the lives of these adolescents.

Table 21—"Being up on cars" as an item of importance among all boys and elites

	All students	2+ Be friends	2+ Be like	10+ Leading crowd	7+ Friends
Small schools (0–4)					
Per cent	29.2	26.9	23.1	26.9	30.9
Number	(1,028)	(93)	(91)	(67)	(136)
Large schools (6–9)					
Per cent	25.6	18.5	14.5	16.0	21.8
Number	(2,992)	(189)	(172)	(106)	(308)

Paradoxically, the elites are generally *below* the rest of the school in the importance of "being up on cars" in their crowds, not only in the large schools, where cars are less frequently owned, but in the small ones as well (although the differences are less in the small schools). This seems oddly inconsistent with the fact that the elites own cars more often than do the non-elites. Why should the elites own cars as often or more often than the others, yet say less often that being up on cars is important in their groups?

Boys' involvement with cars is similar to girls' involvement with popular music: boys in the elites use cars, and girls in the elites use popular music, in their participation in the adolescent culture; but the strange phenomenon of extraordinary attachment to cars or to popular music and its stars appears less often among the elites than among the others. Possibly extreme attachment to popular music and to cars may in some respects be a substitute for status and for activity within the adolescent group itself. Both popular music and cars are important elements in the culture; but when they become all-absorbing they are either an individual matter between the girl and her singing star or the boy and his car, or else a matter that engages the attention of a small, tightly knit clique—the fan clubs and the hot-rod clubs. Whether it is purely individual or in the context of a small clique, fixation on cars or popular music has no articulation with the students as a whole, nor with school activities; thus, it tends to segregate its devotees into small, closely knit groups, whose attention is directed away from the school and, ordinarily, away from the larger community of adolescents.[16]

Nevertheless, there are three schools in which the elites are not less attached to cars than are the non-elites. The elites in Farmdale, Elmtown, and Newlawn report, slightly more often than do the non-elites, that being up on cars is important in their crowd. This seems somewhat con-

---

16. A Baltimore teen-ager comments: In Baltimore this is very true. It is the drapes and unaccepted teen-agers who drive around and show off in cars and seem almost addicted to their cars. The elites use cars for activities, dating, etc., but they do not just use them to show off. I believe that cars *are* a substitute for status among unaccepted teen-agers.

tradictory to the ideas expressed above, that an extraordinary devotion to cars focuses a boy's attention away from the larger crowd, and in this way removes him from leadership activity. The apparent explanation is that some adolescent cultures are *themselves* focused around cars. In Farmdale, for example, over 42 per cent of all boys indicate that being up on cars is an important matter in their crowd. More generally, in Farmdale, Elmtown, and Newlawn, the boys as a whole frequently mention this item. In other words, it appears that in these schools, cars themselves are a fairly prominent part of the adolescent culture, as suggested in Chapter III.

These schools are three of the least middle-class schools in the study, and three of the schools in which the composition of the elites is least middle-class, both relative to the school and in absolute terms. Fascination with cars seems more prevalent among working-class boys, and in working-class cultures, than in the middle class.

Even in Farmdale, Elmtown, and Newlawn, however, it is not the *most* car-oriented who are the elites. One question asked: "What boy here in school knows most about cars?" Of the 178 boys in these three schools who named someone, only 10 named the same boy they had named earlier in the questionnaire as someone they would like to be friends with. This compares with 84 cases out of a possible 208 in these same schools, in which the boy named as the best *athlete* was also named as someone they would like to be friends with. This clearly indicates that even in these three schools, the boys really fascinated with cars were not often among the elites.

Thus, some adolescent cultures are more oriented to cars than others; consequently, their elites show interest in, and knowledge about, cars. In all schools, however, the elites are not the boys most fascinated with cars, just as the girl elites are not the girls most fascinated with popular music and movie stars.

Athletics among the Elites

Those who show an uncommon interest in cars or popular music are not often among the elites. Is the same thing true with boys who show an uncommon interest in athletics?

There are a number of ways to find out. First, all students were asked if they went out for football in the fall—only a single one of several sports in each school, but an important sport in each (except in Farmdale, which had no football team), and a crude indicator of whether the boy was regarded as an athlete or not in the school. Figure 4.10 shows the responses for each school separately. The relationship is striking. Going out for football is related to being a member of the various elites more than any other variable in this study. None of the background variables examined earlier, combined in whatever way, relate so strongly and consistently with membership in the elites. The overrepresentation of football players among the elites is about as great in Maple Grove and Midcity, where athletics was least often mentioned as an attribute for membership in the leading crowd (Chapter III), as in Green Junction and St. John's, where it was most often mentioned. There seems to be little difference among those schools where athletics was seen as a very important attribute for social success and those schools where it was less important. In all, the elite groups contain a high proportion of athletes.

In Newlawn or in Executive Heights, in Elmtown or in Millburg across the diversity of social class, school size, and community size, football players are highly overrepresented in the elites. In the small towns, where

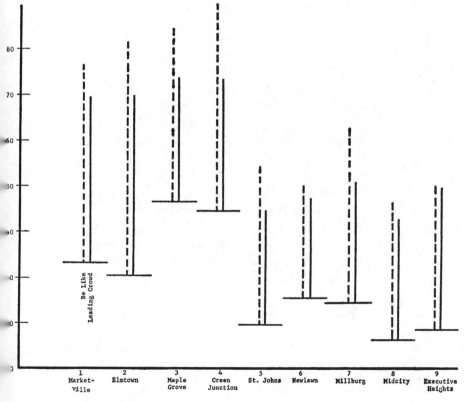

Figure 4.10—Boys out for football, in each school and in two elites in each school.

more boys go out for football (between 30 and 50 per cent in these schools), the elites contain a higher proportion of football players (around 70 to 90 per cent) than in the large schools, where 15 to 25 per cent of the student body, and 40 to 60 per cent of the elites, turn out for football. But in both large and small, there are about two or three times as high a proportion of the elites out for football as in the school as a whole. The pervasiveness of athletics throughout widely varying types of schools presents a puzzle, for the difference in backgrounds among the student bodies is enormous.

The pervasiveness can be seen not only in the activities of the elites, but in their attitudes. When boys are asked which they would most want to be—jet pilot, nationally famous athlete, missionary, or atomic scientist —the most frequent over-all response was "nationally famous athlete," checked by 37 per cent of the boys (see p. 27). Among the elites, however, this response was far greater. In Figure 4.11, the responses by boys in

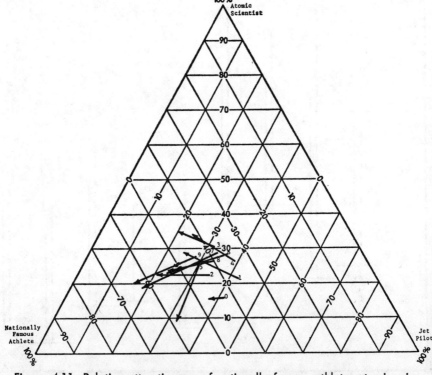

Figure 4.11—Relative attractiveness of nationally famous athlete, atomic scientist, and jet pilot, by boys in each school and leading crowd of boys in each school.

each school and their leading crowds are presented. (The relative proportions responding "nationally famous athlete," "atomic scientist," and "jet pilot" are plotted, subtracting out the proportion responding "missionary," which was small in all schools. The point representing elites is joined to that representing the school as a whole by an arrow directed toward the elites. See Figure 2.6, p. 29, for an explanation of this type of graph.) In every school, the leading crowd tends further in the direction of "nationally famous athlete" than do the boys in the school as a whole. In Millburg and Executive Heights, working-class town and well-to-do suburb, this athletic pull of the elites is greatest. It is puzzling to see all these cultures so similar, despite radical differences in the composition of the schools.

In contrast, in only three of the schools—Marketville, Maple Grove, and Green Junction—do the leading crowds tend more toward "atomic scientist" than the boys as a whole. In all the large schools, the pull is *away* from atomic scientist.

Considering all schools together, the leading crowds answer "nationally famous athlete" about twice as often as they do "atomic scientist." This is just as true for the upper-middle-class schools as the others; the leading crowds show the same absolute level of response and the same direction of deviation from the student body. The indication is that despite any background differences in these schools, there is something about the high school itself, rather invariant from school to school, which creates a strong bias toward athletes and athletics. As a result, in every school, elites include a high proportion of athletes, and both elites and student bodies hold nationally famous athletes as a personal ideal more than atomic scientists.[17]

Another question shows the strength of competing images in adoles-

17. Boys were asked the same question in the spring of 1958, after the advent of the first sputnik, and the proportion responding "nationally famous athlete" was 36.0, compared with 36.1 in the fall; the proportion responding "atomic scientist" was 25.3, compared with 24.6 in the fall. The advent of sputnik may have had an immediate impact on parents, but not an immediate impact on the ideals and popular heroes of their sons. It is likely, however, that the indirect impact, as the continuing news about missiles and scientific competition filters into the adolescent culture, may be greater than on adults.
There is little "adventure" in space activities to capture the imagination of most boys (except the phantasy of very young boys). In contrast to athletics, or the Old West, or aviation, or a gold rush, there is no room for adventurous *people* in the exploration of space, except those willing to subject themselves to the long discipline of scientific training. There is no counterpart today of the physical or economic frontier that could absorb the undisciplined energy of those adolescents who otherwise can see only a bleak, passive, frustrating future. Probably the nearest to a counterpart in popular images is the athletic star for the boys and the movie star for the girls. Although both these activities require training and discipline, they excite the imagination of the adolescent, who can easily imagine himself in their place.

cent life itself, as the above question does for future adult life. Boys were asked:

> I.131. If you could be remembered here at school for one of the three things below, which one would you want it to be?
>
> | | All boys (9 schools) |
> | --- | --- |
> | Brilliant student | 31.3% |
> | Athletic star | 43.6 |
> | Most popular | 25.0 |
> | Number of cases | (3,696) |

The over-all responses indicate the prominence of the athletic star. Figure 4.12 shows the responses in each school, as well as in each leading crowd.[18] In every case, the star athlete is overchosen by the elites, relative to the rest of the students. This reinforces the notion that there is something about the structure of activities in the high-school that consistently leads the elites to be even more oriented to the athlete and to athletics than the school as a whole. There is some variation among schools, but in all, the image of the athletic star fares better among the elites than among the student body as a whole—where he nevertheless fares very well indeed.

This would be understandable, since athletics is one of the activities of the school, were it not for the fact that in this last question the choice was between athletic star and brilliant student. Scholastic effort is a part of school activities just as is athletics, and it is not unreasonable to expect that the elites—in some of the schools, if not all—would be more oriented to the image of the brilliant student than to the athletic star, and would be above the rest of the students in this orientation. Yet this is not so.

Thus, the elites are selective in their overchoice of school-related activities. They overchoose athletics and the star athlete, but they underchoose the brilliant student. Again, the paradox is that in spite of different parental backgrounds and in spite of far different educational backgrounds, the value structure of these adolescent communities—that is, the values of the elites relative to the non-elites—shows a marked similarity from school to school. There are variations, to be sure, but these are variations within the general structure of values—in which fascination with cars, popular music, and school work are not characteristic of the elites, but fascination with athletics is. The emphasis upon athletics is true, not only of the active leaders—we might have expected this from the earlier

---

18. In this figure, as in the preceding one, each school is located according to the proportion of boys who chose each image: that of the brilliant student, that of the athletic star, and that of most popular. The leading crowds are located relative to the students as a whole by an arrow leading from the school to its leading crowd, indicating the direction in which the leading crowd of boys is "pulling." The other elites, not included on the graph because of overcrowding, show the same tendency.

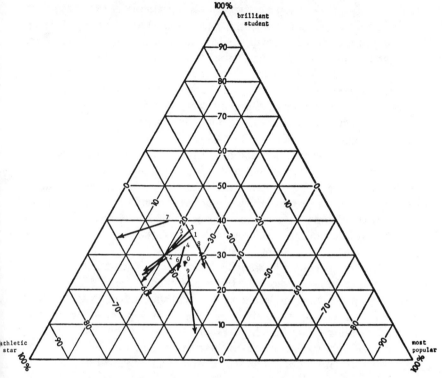

Figure 4.12—Relative choice of image of athletic star, brilliant student, and most popular, by boys in each school and leading crowd of boys in each school.

examination in Chapter II of what students said it takes to get into the leading crowd and to get to be popular—but of the exemplars as well, those adolescents who others would most like to be friends with, and those they would most want to be like.

Activities among the Girl Elites

Somewhat comparable to athletics for the boys, in its relation to the adolescent elites, are school activities for the girls. Each girl was asked: (I.11) "Did you go out for any clubs or activities in school as a freshman?" The elites are considerably more likely to have done so; very few had failed to go out for some activity. This is particularly so for the active leaders of the system as a whole, the "leading crowd." Of 274 girls named 10 or more times as members of the leading crowd, 268, or 97.8 per cent, went out for some activity as a freshman, while only 74.2 per cent of the girls as a whole did so. It appears that participation in some school activity is a *sine qua non* for membership in the leading crowd among girls, just as it was apparent earlier than a good reputation is a *sine qua non*. This excess of participation in activities among elite girls is found in all schools, and at roughly the same level.

The level of participation among all girls in the student body, however, varied greatly from school to school. In all the small schools, more girls had gone out for an activity as a freshman (over 80 per cent in all) than in any of the large ones. Even though extracurricular activities played a larger part in some large schools—particularly Executive Heights—participation is higher in the smaller schools, just as the participation of boys in athletics is higher in the smaller schools.

Not only do girl elites *participate* in activities. When forced to choose between being remembered as a brilliant student, a leader in activities, and most popular, they underchoose the brilliant-student image in every school. They overchoose the image of being most popular or leader in activities, depending upon the school. Figure 4.13 shows this "pulling" away from the brilliant-student image on the part of the elites. In Green Junction, a small-town school composed of predominantly working-class and farm children, and in Executive Heights, composed of the sons and daughters of executives and professionals in a well-to-do suburb, almost *none* of the elite girls want to be remembered as a brilliant student. Moreover, data not presented here show that almost none want to date a boy who is a brilliant student, and in Executive Heights, almost none of the elite boys want to date a girl who is a brilliant student. This, of course, does not mean that the orientations of these upper-middle-class suburban adolescents in Executive Heights are identical to those of the working-class and farm adolescents in Green Junction. One difference is shown in Figure 4.13, which shows that in Green Junction it is the "most popular" image that attracts both the girls as a whole and, even more, their elites. In Executive Heights, it is the activities leader, the clubwoman of the adolescent society. Nevertheless, the relative strength of the image of "brilliant student," when pitted against that of activities leader and most popular, is very much the same in these two schools—and, if anything, lower among the girls of Executive Heights.

The schools differ far more from one another in the orientation of the girls and their elites than they do in the orientations of the boys (compare Figures 4.12, and 4.13). Girls in four schools are over toward the "most popular" image, and their elites tend even more that way. These

are from predominantly working-class communities—Elmtown, Green
Junction, Newlawn, and Millburg. Five schools are toward the "leader-
in-activities" pole—Farmdale, Marketville, Maple Grove, Midcity, and
Executive Heights. This division is almost identical to the classification of
schools according to whether ascriptive qualities of family background
are important (Chapter III). In all the schools tending toward "most popular," these ascriptive qualities are of little importance for membership in
the leading crowd; in all those schools tending toward "leader in activities," except Farmdale, these criteria are important.

Activities may help maintain the importance of family background in
a school, by giving the girls from "good families" a chance to hold office
and lead in formal activities, while the other girls find it hard to "break
in." When these formal activities are less important, then the competition
is more open, freer from the residues of family background, and popularity, beauty or attractiveness to boys comes to take their place.

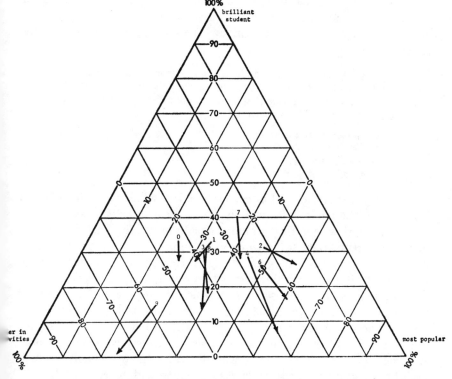

Figure 4.13—Relative choice of image of leader in activities, brilliant student,
and most popular, by girls in each school and leading crowd of
girls in each school.

To Whom Are They Oriented?

Adolescence is unique period of transition, a period of transition from childhood to adulthood. As part of that transition comes a shift of orientation, away from the preceding generation, toward one's own generation. This transition has been taking place since early childhood; even a young child often responds more to the pressures of his fellows than to the desires of his parents. But adolescence is a period in which parental control is in its waning days, a period in which a few teen-agers have already broken away from parental control for good.

In this peculiarly ambivalent period of life exists the teen-age culture. What kind of elites, then, do they look up to during this period—elites that are *more* oriented to parents than they themselves, or elites that are *less* oriented to parental demands, more oriented to the group of teen-agers themselves? Several questions in the questionnaire gave the boy or girl a choice between these two alternatives. The most appropriate here is the following question:

> I.134. Let's say that you had always wanted to belong to a particular club in school, and then finally you were asked to join. But then you found out that your parents didn't approve of the group. Do you think you would
>
> definitely join anyway?
> probably join?
> probably not join?
> definitely not join?

Looking first at the level of each school as a whole in Figure 4.14 and Figure 4.15, the range is from about 80 per cent of the boys and 85 per cent of the girls saying they would probably or definitely not join a club upon the parents' request, down to about 50 per cent for the boys and 60 per cent for the girls. The greatest regard for parents' demands is in the smallest school, Farmdale, the least regard is in Executive Heights, one of the two largest. The four schools in which the boys are 70 per cent or higher in adherence to parents—Farmdale, Marketville, Millburg, and Green Junction—and the three in which girls are 80 per cent or higher (the first three of these four), are schools outside any large metropolitan area, still somewhat in the traditions of the past. The two schools in which both boys and girls are least willing to go along with parents are the suburban schools—Newlawn, a working-class suburb, and Executive Heights, and upper-middle-class suburb.

This variation among schools accords with other indications of differences in these schools. Marketville, the second smallest, seemed at times to hold a quite different kind of adolescent from some of the others—an obedient child who had still not come into the freedoms and teen-age self-assurance of, say, the adolescents in Executive Heights. There, in an upper-middle-class suburb, the boys and girls seem to become adult sooner, to look more to each other for guidance, less to parents.

These differences between, at one extreme, a small farm community, and at the other, an upper-middle-class suburb of a large city, give an indication of the increasing strength of the adolescent community. For Executive Heights is an example of a style of life that is becoming more and more prevalent; Marketville or Farmdale exemplifies a style of life that is fast becoming extinct.

What are the orientations of the elites in these cultures? Are they more or less oriented to parental demands than the rest? Figures 4.14 and 4.15 show that at the two extremes—Farmdale vs. Executive Heights for the boys, Farmdale and Marketville vs. Executive Heights for the girls—the elites tend to diverge even more than the school as a whole: to be *more* parent-oriented than the student body in the most parent-oriented

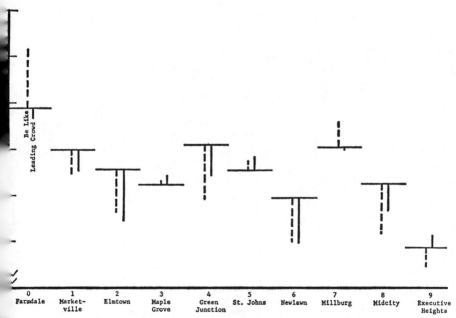

Figure 4.14—The refusal of boys to join a club in school upon parents' disapproval, among all boys in each school, and in two elites in each school.

schools, to be *less* parent-oriented than the student body in the less parent-oriented school, Executive Heights. In the various schools, there are some differences between the boys and the girls. In Maple Grove and St. John's, the boys' elites are more parent-oriented than the non-elites. Among the girls, there is greater parent-orientation of the elites in Marketville and Maple Grove and to a slight degree, Farmdale; there is *less* in Elmtown and Green Junction, and in all the large schools. This difference between the elites in Maple Grove and Marketville, on the one hand, and those in Elmtown and Green Junction, on the other, parallels the greater importance of family background in the former two; and it parallels as well the actual friendship structures in these schools, as will be evident in Chapter VII. Besides these differences between schools, it is relevant to note a difference between different elites within a school: the active leaders among the girls tend to be less parent-oriented than the exemplars (data not presented here), an indication of the active leaders' greater participation in the world of adolescents.

In general, the adolescent elites tend to be less oriented to parental demands than are their followers, particularly in those schools where liberation from parental constraint has progressed farthest. But there are several

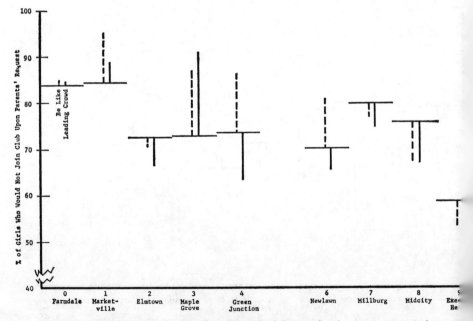

Figure 4.15—The refusal of girls to join a club in school upon parents' disapproval, among all girls in each school, and in two elites in each school.

directions in which their orientation could turn—to teachers, to immediate friends, to the larger adolescent community. Where *do* they turn?

In answer to a question similar to the one for parents above, less than 30 per cent of the boys in any school, and less than 40 per cent of the girls, indicated that they would comply with the teachers wishes. Only in one school, Marketville, are there nearly 40 per cent of the girls (but only 23 per cent of the boys) who would probably or definitely not join if the teacher said no.[19] The general level of compliance among all students with the favorite teacher's desires is quite low, both for boys and girls. The elites are even lower, even less likely to follow their favorite teachers' wishes by not joining the club.

These data indicate clearly that the teachers are not an intermediate step between a child's orientation to his parents and his orientation to peers. Neither the elites nor their followers indicate that they would pay much attention to a teacher's wishes outside the classroom—even if it is their favorite teacher. In fact, in a question following these, which forced a choice between best friend, favorite teacher, and parents, almost no one chose teacher, while the choices were about equally split between friend and parents.

Where then does the elite's allegiance lie? With friends? With the school, somehow apart from teachers? The following question gives some insight into this:

> I.133. Suppose school was dismissed an hour early one day for a pep rally down at the athletic field, and the principal urged everyone to go to the rally, although it wasn't compulsory. On the way some of your friends asked you to go riding instead of to the pep rally. What do you think you would do?
>
> Definitely go to the rally
> Probably go to the rally
> Probably go with friends
> Definitely go with friends

The responses of the student bodies, and of their elites, tended to be in the direction of the rally. There were interesting differences, however, as Table 22 indicates. The boys were in general less oriented to the rally than the girls, in both small and large schools, among both the elites and the student body. Least oriented to the rally were the large-school boys, with only slightly more than half choosing to attend. But the *elites* among

---

19. It is interesting that in Marketville the difference between boys and girls is greatest in their teacher-orientation, a difference of 16 per cent. Among the persons chosen two or more times in the leading crowd, this difference is magnified to 31 per cent—by far the largest boy-girl differences in any school's leading crowd. This seems related to the fact that several of the most outstanding teachers in this school are women, who pay most attention to the girls.

the boys in these large schools were far more likely to attend than the followers, and more likely to attend than the elites among the small-school boys. The small-school elite boys, in contrast, were hardly more oriented to the rally than the student body as a whole.

Table 22—Going to a rally vs. going riding with friends, for all students and elite groups in small and large schools*

	All students	Be friends	Be like	Leading crowd	7+ Friends
Boys who would attend rally					
Small schools (0–4)					
Per cent	61.2	62.2	65.5	65.6	59.1
Number	(987)	(90)	(87)	(64)	(132)
Large schools (6–9)					
Per cent	53.7	77.1	77.3	83.5	64.0
Number	(2,756)	(179)	(163)	(103)	(294)
Girls who would attend rally					
Small schools (0–4)					
Per cent	71.5	81.8	86.5	79.8	71.3
Number	(962)	(143)	(104)	(104)	(171)
Large schools (6–9)					
Per cent	73.6	84.6	85.3	88.9	80.8
Number	(3,031)	(267)	(211)	(162)	(514)

* Because this item was late in the questionnaire, and a few did not finish the questionnaire, the no-answers have been subtracted to give the totals.

Two inferences may be drawn from these data: First, the elites are in general more oriented to such school activities as rallies for athletic events than are the non-elites—except among the boys in small schools. Secondly, among the large-school boys this orientation to school activities most sharply differentiates the elites from the non-elites. For boys in the large schools, orientation to school activities is at its lowest ebb for those who are not in the center of things, and most clearly distinguishes them from those who are in the center of things.

In general, then, we can say this about the orientations of the elites. The elites are oriented slightly less to parents than are the non-elites—except among the girl elites in two small schools. Yet they do not turn in the direction of teachers. Little as the student body as a whole is oriented toward doing what teachers want, the elites are even less so. Nor do they turn toward close friends, when faced with the problem of going with friends or attending a rally. They turn to the teen-age society as a whole, to the pep rally, a ritual of the adolescent social system surrounding the high school.

V Sports and Studies as
Paths to Success

Introduction

IN ANY SOCIAL SYSTEM, STATUS BY ITS
very definition is in scarce supply. This is as true in a high school as in
society at large. The fundamental competition in a high school is neither
for grades, nor for athletic achievements, nor any other such activity. It
is a competition for recognition and respect—the elements of which status
is composed—in the eyes of one's fellows and the opposite sex. Competition for scholastic or athletic honors, as well as competition in other activities, is important to the competitors, not on its own account, but
because it helps win status in the eyes of other teen-agers. To be sure,
winning recognition and respect in the eyes of parents is important, too,
to most teen-agers; but preceding chapters have indicated its decreasing
importance, and its increasing replacement, in the adolescent's scheme of
things, by recognition and respect from his peers.

Status is partly gained from activities carried on within a social system,
and partly ascribed from without. If status were completely ascribed in a
high school, then a girl's or boy's position in the teen-age culture would
derive completely from his parents' position in the community. As Chapter III has shown, this external ascription of status occurs to varying ex-
tents in these schools, and it occurs more for girls than for boys.

But status in these systems is far from completely determined by the
social position of an adolescent's family. Other matters, some of them correlated with family position, but some not, are far more important. These

include athletic achievement, good looks and dressing well, doing well in school, maintaining a good reputation while still being willing to have fun, having a car but not being a fanatic about cars, knowing popular songs without being addicted to popular music, and having other less important attributes. Some of these are simply styles of behavior that distinguish the elites from the student body; others are attributes of *achievement*, something a boy or girl can *do* to gain recognition, respect, and attention from his peers. Most important to examine for boys are athletic achievement and scholastic achievement: athletic achievement because it is so pervasive in gaining status for boys in high schools; scholastic achievement because it has an ambiguous position in the status structure, and because it is *the* activity for which schools were created.

Because of the importance of athletic and scholastic achievement, it is useful to examine extensively those boys who were seen by their fellows to be the best students in their grade and those who were seen to be the best athletes. How much status is conferred upon these athletes and scholars? We will consider those boys mentioned two or more times by their classmates in answer to the questions: (I.40b.) "Of all the boys in your grade, which boy is the best athlete? . . . the best student?"

Whether these boys are in fact the best athletes and best scholars is irrelevant here, for these are the boys *seen by their contemporaries* to be the best athletes and the best scholars. We want to investigate how such a reputation affects a boy's status in the system—how it affects the tendency of other boys to want to be like him or to be friends with him, how it affects his chances to be in the leading crowd, how it affects the number of friends he has—in other words, how it affects his membership in the various elites.

THE EXEMPLARS

Each of the elites in these schools is important for somewhat different reasons. Other boys' wanting to be friends with a boy or wanting to be like him indicates who the "models" in the system are—who are the exemplars or popular heroes whose success leads other boys to work and strive in the same direction. They indicate, in a sense, the direction in which the *energy* of the system is flowing.

In any society in which achievement in some fields yields recognition and respect, the important question is, *what* fields? In 1942, a revealing study was made of popular biographies in mass-circulation magazines at two time periods, 1901–14 and 1940–41. The object of the study was to examine the characteristics of the "popular heroes" who were the subjects of biographies at these two periods.[1] In 1901–14, the popular heroes were

---

1. Leo Lowenthal, "Biographies in Popular Magazines," P. F. Lazarsfeld and Frank Stanton (eds.), in *Radio Research, 1942–43* (New York. Duell, Sloan and Pierce, 1944), pp. 507–48.

predominantly "heroes of production," that is, men who were leaders in industry, men who were the industrial giants of the period. In 1940–41, the popular heroes were "heroes of consumption," primarily men whose success was achieved in the entertainment world, in the movies, radio, and other media. This result suggested that different "models for success" were dominant in the two periods.

Just as the adult society has models of success, so does the adolescent culture, perhaps to an even greater extent, since the adolescent culture is in greater flux. Its models of immediate success are other boys within the culture, and may include boys who have achieved success in various fields. This, then, is the importance of examining athletes and scholars. It indicates the models for the less successful, and the directions in which energy will be exerted by the not-yet-successful freshmen and sophomores.

THE LEADING CROWD

Membership in the "leading crowd" shows somewhat different aspects of the system. Insofar as the leading crowd has gained its position by achievement, thus being open to all who can achieve in the right directions, it stands as a concrete reward for such achievement. In exactly the same way, a man's membership in the local Kiwanis Club or the town's most exclusive country club stands as a reward for achievement in directions approved by the adult community. Just as the values of the community determine the efficacy of various kinds of achievement in gaining a man entry into the country club, the values placed upon athletic and scholastic achievement determine their efficacy in gaining a boy entry into the leading crowd in the school.

Sometimes, however, a school's leading crowd is partly determined according to parents' position in the community. Chapters III and IV have shown that this occurs in quite varying degrees in the different schools. Parents' position is particularly important in Marketville, Maple Grove, Midcity, and Executive Heights. The first three of these are stable communities composed of all social strata, but fairly well dominated by middle-class or upper-middle-class members. Parents' position is least important, in fact almost negligible, in St. John's and Newlawn.

Because of such ascriptive criteria, membership in the leading crowd is only in part an indicator of rewards for achievement. Thus, the athlete's or scholar's being in the leading crowd may be due to his parental background rather than his achievements. This is particularly likely to happen for those named as best scholars, for they often come from higher social strata.

The leading crowd differs further from those whom others want to be like or be friends with, as an indicator of the direction a system's energy takes. Because the leading crowd is in fact a crowd that behaves in a particular way and because it is exclusive, negative as well as positive attitudes develop toward it. In all schools as a whole, 19.8 per cent of the boys and 28.9 per cent of the girls said they did not want to be a member of the leading crowd (spring questionnaire). Consequently, the leading crowd represents an effective reward, and thus a measure of how the energy of the system is being channeled, *only* insofar as it is not purely ascribed and insofar as its behavior leads many people to want to be members.

THE LOCAL LEADERS

The final elite, the "local leaders" who are often named as friends, is important as a different sort of indicator. By looking at the number of boys who name a boy as someone they go around with, we see the degree to which the system centers around him socially—or, in contrast, isolates him. As long as a boy or girl has his own circle of friends, he is not totally deprived of recognition and respect from his peers. To be sure, not many may look up to him or emulate him, but at least he is secure in his own group of friends. But if he is devoid of even this, his problem is more serious; the system not only fails to reward him with status and membership in the elite as a result of his achievement, it even deprives him of a circle of friends from which he can gain his rewards. These different adolescent systems vary considerably in the degree to which they do or do not surround a best athlete or best scholar with friends.

Social Rewards for Athletes and Scholars

The athletes and scholars, defined as such by the nominations of their peers, fared as indicated in Table 23. This table lists the *average number of times* the "best scholar" and "best athlete" and the student body as a whole was mentioned on each of the elite criteria above. Also included in this chart is the average number of times each was mentioned as someone the girls "go for most" (see I.40b,iii).

Table 23—Average number of choices received by athletes, scholars, and all boys, as members of the various elites

	Be friends with and be like	Leading crowd	Number of friends	Popular with girls	Number of cases
Athletes	5.6	7.8	6.1	3.0	(272)
Scholars	3.4	4.9	5.0	1.3	(278)
All boys	0.8	1.4	3.2	0.4	(4,094)

There is no ambiguity about these results. The athlete in every case outdistances the scholar, as the scholar outdistances the student body as a whole. But there are differences between the different criteria. The athletes most outdistance the others in being named as most popular with girls. They do so least in the number of friends they have—a matter which reaches practical upper limits, since it implies some degree of association. Overall, it appears that athletic stardom stands highest as a symbol of success, as an achievement to channel the energies of the naive freshman, as a means of entry into the leading crowd, as a way to gain popularity with girls, and as the man with the most friends. Being the best scholar also apparently stands somewhat as a desired achievement, for the scholar is above average on all criteria. Most important for the psychological equilibrium of the boy so named, he apparently has a full share of friends, although fewer than does the athlete.

ATHLETES, SCHOLARS, AND ATHLETE-SCHOLARS

Some good students are also good athletes. These achievements are not mutually exclusive; in some high schools they show a high coincidence. Consequently, to learn the effect of athletics and scholarship in bringing a boy recognition and respect from his peers, the two achievements must be separated. The question becomes, not "What is the relative status of athletes and scholars?" but, rather, "What is the relative status of the boy who is *only* an athlete, the one who is *only* a scholar, and the one who is *both?*"

Some schools, and some educational philosophies, emphasize the "well-rounded" boy. Does the adolescent status system concur in this, giving such a boy even greater status than those who are only scholars or only athletes? If so, what about the residual status of the boy who is only one or the other? For example, is the status of the scholars largely due to those among them who are also athletes, or is it independently gained, as a consequence of their being scholars? What about those who are neither scholars nor athletes? How likely are their classmates to want to be like them, to be friends with them, and how likely are they to be considered most popular with girls?

First of all, it is useful to see just how much overlap there is between athletes and scholars. In the small schools, 98 out of 1,032 boys, or 9.5 per cent, were named as athletes; 91, or 8.8 per cent were named as scholars. Of these, 21 boys were named as *both*. This constitutes 21 per cent of the athletes and 23 per cent of the scholars, or 2 per cent of the total students.

In the large schools, there is somewhat more centralization: 175 athletes and 187 scholars were named out of a total of 3,062 boys, constituting 5.7 per cent and 6.1 per cent of the student body, respectively. Of these, 34 were named as both athlete *and* scholar, constituting 19 per cent and 18 per cent of the total of athletes and scholars, respectively, or 1.1 per cent of the total students.

Thus, in the large schools, those boys thought of as both athlete and scholar were a smaller segment of the student body—as one might expect, since each grade is larger in the large schools, and thus any given boy has a smaller chance of being the "best athlete" or "best scholar" in his grade.

There are striking differences in the recognition and respect given these athletes, scholars, and athlete-scholars by their peers. The average number of choices received on each criterion by the athlete-scholar, the athlete-only, the scholar-only, and the neither-athlete-nor-scholar are given in Table 24.

Table 24—Average number of choices received by athletes, scholars, athlete-scholars, and other boys, in the various elites

	Be Friends with and be like	Leading crowd	Number of friends	Total	Popular with girls	Number of cases
Athlete-scholar	9.9	12.5	7.1	29.5	4.9	(54)
Athlete	4.6	6.6	5.9	17.1	2.5	(218)
Scholar	1.9	3.1	4.4	9.4	0.5	(224)
All other boys	0.4	0.8	2.9	4.1	0.2	(3,598)

The athlete-scholar far outdistances all the others. In total choices as a friend, as someone to be friends with or be like, and as a member of the leading crowd, the average athlete-scholar receives over three times as many choices as the average scholar who is not an athlete, and over one and one-half times as many as the average athlete who is not a scholar. The boy who is neither athlete nor scholar receives little recognition and respect, an average of only one-seventh the number of choices received by the athlete-scholar.

Thus, there is special attention to the "all-round" boy who is both athlete and scholar. He receives more social rewards from his peers than the boy who achieves in only one area. The athlete-scholars tend to be the focus of attention of the adolescent system. Although they constitute only 1.3 per cent of the total student body, they pre-empt 16.9 per cent of all the "be friends with" and "be like" choices, and 11.7 per cent of all the leading crowd choices (see Table 25). In number of persons who name them as friends they associate with, they stand out least. Yet even here, they stand above the others.

However, there are only a few athlete-scholars, and some attention goes elsewhere. What about the boy who is only an athlete or only a scholar, who does not try to excel in everything? Table 24 showed that the pure scholar fares far worse than does the pure athlete. He is mentioned as someone to be friends with or to be like only about a third as often as is the athlete, and he is mentioned less than half as often as a member of the leading crowd. He is seen as popular with the girls only about one-fifth as often as is the star athlete. In short, he fares far worse than he appeared to before the athlete-scholar was considered separately. Scholarship alone receives, in these schools, less than half the recognition and respect from peers than does athletic achievement alone.

From the point of view of the distribution of elites in the system, matters are as follows for the pure athlete and the pure scholar: The pure athlete constitutes 5.3 per cent of the boys' student body, but gets 30.5 per cent of the be-friends-with and be-like choices, and 24.8 per cent of the leading-crowd choices. The pure scholar constitutes 5.5 per cent of the student body, receives 12.7 per cent of the be-friends-with and be-like choices, and 11.9 per cent of the leading-crowd choices. These figures, together with those for the athlete-scholar and the boy who is neither, are shown in Table 25.

Table 25—Distribution of elite choices among athlete-scholars, athletes, scholars, and other boys

	Part of total population	Be friends with and be like	Leading crowd	Friends
Athlete-scholar	1.3%	16.9%	11.7%	2.9%
Athlete	5.3	30.5	24.8	9.8
Scholar	5.5	12.7	11.9	7.5
All others	87.9	40.1	51.6	79.7
Total	100.0	100.2	100.0	99.9
Number of cases (or choices)	(4,094)	(3,257)	(5,778)	(13,155)

The concentration of choices upon the athlete-scholars and the athletes is quite high; even the scholars get more than their share of the choices. Taking athletes and athlete-scholars together, 6.6 per cent of the population receives almost half the be-friends-with and be-like choices, and 37 per cent of the leading-crowd choices. Including the pure scholars, 12 per cent of the population pre-empts 60 per cent of the be-friends-with and be-like choices, and 48 per cent of the leading-crowd choices. The "left-overs," boys who are neither athletes nor scholars, constituting 88 per cent of the population, receive only 40 per cent of the be-friends-with and be-like choices, and only 52 per cent of the leading-crowd choices.

These results show in a striking fashion the large proportion of elite status that goes to the athlete-scholars and athletes, and the small amount left over for the boy who is neither athlete nor scholar. The pure scholars account for somewhat more recognition and respect than their numbers in the population, but they are completely outdistanced by the athlete or the all-around boy who is both athlete and scholar.

These results differ, of course, from school to school, as subsequent sections will indicate, but there are almost no differences due to size of student body, nor to small-town vs. city or suburb. When the five small schools are compared with the five large ones, only a few differences emerge. The differences *within* these groups are far more striking.

ATHLETE, SCHOLAR, AND LADIES' MAN

Before examining the structure of elites in the separate schools, another type of achievement warrants examination—being named by other boys as most popular with the girls, a "ladies' man." We have so far looked at such popularity as a *dependent* phenomenon, a possible consequence of achieving highly in athletics or in studies. So it appears to be, at least for the best athletes, but it is also in part independent. It is an attribute that, however acquired, in turn may give him entry into the leading crowd, and make others want to be friends with him, or to be like him.

Table 26 shows the average number of choices received by the boy who is neither athlete nor scholar, but is most popular with the girls. The pure athlete and pure scholar are repeated for comparison. In every criterion the ladies' man stands between the pure athlete and the pure scholar. He has more friends than the scholar, is more often in the school's leading crowd, and others would more often like to be like him or to be friends with him. He surpasses the scholar most in membership in the leading crowd, least as a person to be friends with or to be like. This reflects the fact that the leading crowd is a crowd of boys *and* girls, an actual crowd that goes around together.

Table 26—Average number of choices received by pure athlete, scholar, and ladies' man, as members of the various elites

	Be friends with and be like	Leading crowd	Number of friends	Total	Number of cases
Athlete (but not scholar)	4.6	6.6	5.9	17.1	(218)
Scholar (but not athlete)	1.9	3.1	4.4	9.4	(224)
Ladies' man (but neither athlete nor scholar)	2.4	6.4	5.8	14.6	(138)

A boy who is popular with the opposite sex seems to gain recognition and respect among his fellows, not as much as an outstanding athlete,

ut considerably more than an outstanding scholar. An alternative inter-
retation, however, is equally reasonable: that the same elements that
ring a boy popularity with the opposite sex bring him popularity among
ther boys. This is undoubtedly true and must account for a part of the
tatus shown by these boys. How much a part is a difficult question,
which cannot be answered satisfactorily by these data. However, even
his tells us something, for it indicates that a boys' status among other
oys is dependent on many of the same criteria that make him popular
with girls—a strong suggestion that the boy-girl relationship is important
1 shaping the status system among the boys.

Athletes, Scholars, and Ladies' Men in Each School

There are, of course, differences in the distribution of social rewards
1 the different schools. A formidable problem arises in comparing the
istribution, due to small sample sizes. The athlete-scholars, particularly,
re few in number. In Farmdale, there is only one. Maple Grove has the
argest number among the small schools, but even here there are only
even. There are more pure athletes and pure scholars (never less than
en), but the numbers are still small. Consequently, the problem of just
what differences in social rewards should be taken seriously is a difficult
ne. This is a sampling problem of a peculiar sort. Each class in school
a sample of children from the community, and in a small school, this
ample may be quite unlike the one before it or the next. The class comes
) be seen as a particularly athletic class or as a particularly studious
ne, or a nondescript one, because it is a small sample, different from
thers. This was evident at one point in Chapter III, where the impor-
ance of "good grades" was examined for each year in each school
parately.

The data to be presented shortly on number of choices received by
ach group may be seen in two ways: first, as purely descriptive of the
chool in the fall of 1957, in which case all differences should be con-
dered as true differences, their importance in proportion to their size;
r second, as descriptive of the school in a more abstract sense, that is,
ne school apart from the attributes of the particular teen-agers who
1ade it up in the fall of 1957.

Both interpretations are of interest. The purely descriptive one is important because we are interested in examining the consequences of these status systems for the teen-agers within them. The second, more general, interpretation is of interest because we are concerned with the attributes of the school and community that may have helped produce these status systems. In the second case, it is important to know whether the differences found are a stable characteristic of the school, or would likely disappear when another sample of teen-agers from the same community moves into the school a few years hence. For example, in Maple Grove, pure athletes have an average of 6.9 friends, while pure scholars have an average of only 3.7. Is it generally the case that pure athletes in this school have more friends than pure scholars, or is the difference between 6.9 friends for the athletes and 3.7 for the scholars due only to the particular student body in 1957–58?

To answer such a question, a statistical test of the difference is a useful guide. For all these schools, a boy's average number of friends is something between 3 and 4, and the standard deviation is around 2.45.[2] While the distribution of choices is not normal, the distribution of their average for subgroups such as those shown here will tend to be, so that one can use the normal distribution as a rough rule of thumb for comparing two groups. Using this, the standard deviation of a sample of 10 is about 0.8, so that if one is familiar with thinking in terms of "standard error," the number 3.7 would be "3.7 ±0.8."

A standard error is surpassed only about three times in ten; this would mean that only in about three out of ten "samples of this school" taken in different years would we find that the ten boys named most often as scholars would receive an average of more than 4.5 choices (3.7 + 0.8) or less than 2.9 choices (3.7 − 0.8). (This assumes, of course, that nothing changes about the administration of the school, the teachers, or the community.) Thus, a difference of 6.9 − 3.7 = 3.2 would be hardly likely to occur by chance when the sample sizes are 15 and 10 respectively. In fact, we find it would occur only about two times in a thousand such "samples of this school."

It is well to keep in mind that the data, interpreted directly, measure what *these* particular teen-agers are like in the school. The only differences from school to school for which an explanation should be sought in the community or school are those, like the example above, likely to recur when a new crop of teen-agers comes into the school.

The standard errors for the average number of friends have been calculated, and are nearly the same from school to school. They are

2. It would be preferable to compute the standard deviation for each subgroup separately, but the labor involved in this task would outweigh its contribution. The standard deviations in each school as a whole were computed, and are all very close to 2.45.

approximately as indicated in the footnote below.[3] Data in the tables below will include, however, not only number of friends, but number of times mentioned as a member of the leading crowd, and number of times chosen as someone to be friends with or be like. For this composite result, standard errors are unknown, and some caution should be used in attaching significance to differences. Only the large differences that are consistent from one criterion of choice to another will be considered in the discussion below.

SOCIAL REWARDS IN THE FIVE SMALL SCHOOLS

The social rewards received by athletes, scholars, and ladies' men differed somewhat among the small schools. In considering the differences, all elite criteria are shown together, for simplicity—leading crowd, someone to be friends with, someone to be like, and number of friends. Table 27 gives the average number of choices received on *all* these criteria taken together. The most reliable comparisons are among the pure athletes and pure scholars, for the numbers of cases are largest in these groups.

Table 27—Average number of choices received on all elite criteria by athlete-scholars, athletes, scholars, ladies' men, and all boys, in the five small schools*

	Farmdale	Marketville	Elmtown	Maple Grove	Green Junction
Athlete-scholar	18.0	17.0	27.5	28.1	33.6
	(1)	(3)	(4)	(7)	(5)
Athlete	12.3	22.1	18.2	18.7	23.3
	(13)	(15)	(18)	(15)	(16)
Scholar	7.5	14.1	8.7	9.0	8.9
	(10)	(11)	(17)	(10)	(22)
Ladies' man	13.2	17.8	9.1	16.2	16.6
	(5)	(5)	(7)	(5)	(13)
All boys	7.5	6.4	6.2	6.4	6.6
	(70)	(198)	(266)	(217)	(281)

* The number of cases is given in parentheses below each relevant category.

For the scholars, Marketville stands out sharply above the others. The social rewards received by a Marketville scholar are far above

3. Standard errors for number of friends:

Sample size 5 ± 1.1	Sample size 20 ± 0.55
Sample size 10 ± 0.8	Sample size 30 ± 0.45
Sample size 15 ± 0.6	Sample size 40 ± 0.4

Roughly, then, differences similar to that between the seven athlete-scholars and the fifteen athletes in Maple Grove (6.6 ± 1.0 and 6.9 ± 0.6) do not warrant seeking an explanation in the school or community, while differences between either of these groups and the scholars (3.7 ± 0.8) do. (The data for this example are taken from the tabulations on which Table 27 is based.)

those in other schools: they are almost twice those received by a Farm-dale scholar, and considerably higher than in Elmtown, Maple Grove, and Green Junction. This confirms the differences shown in Chapter III, where Marketville boys most often saw "good grades" or "being on the honor roll" as an aid to membership in the leading crowd or to being popular. Just as the boys in this school stood out over the other small schools in the frequency with which they mentioned academic achieve-ment, they stand out here, in the social rewards they actually give to the good student.

Elmtown, Maple Grove, and Green Junction seem to be quite similar in the rewards they give to the pure scholar; Farmdale is somewhat lower. This is not fully consistent with Chapter III, where the boys of Green Junction gave "good grades" no higher a position than did Farm-dale boys in the status system. The discrepancy would be somewhat reduced if the various elite criteria were shown separately. It is only his number of friends that brings the Green Junction scholar up to the position shown in Table 27. As someone to be like, or to be friends with, or in the leading crowd, he receives only 4.7 choices, less than in Elmtown (5.1) or Maple Grove (5.3), despite the fact that more choices were *given* on these criteria in Green Junction than in either of these schools (an average of 3.2 per person, compared to 2.8 and 2.9 in Elm-town and Maple Grove).

In general, then, the status of the pure scholar shows Marketville in front, Elmtown and Maple Grove in the middle, and Green Junction and Farmdale at the bottom. Thus, the rewards these scholars actually receive, in the form of recognition and respect from their peers, are consistent with the picture of the value climates seen in Chapter III.

The pure athlete receives most rewards in Green Junction and least in Farmdale. This again is consistent with the value climate expressed in Chapter III, where Green Junction was at the top, and Farmdale at the bottom in the importance of athletics. The other schools give less con-sistent results: Marketville and Elmtown were in the "intermediate-low" group in the importance attached to athletic success, and Maple Grove was in the "low" group. Yet, there is little difference between the social rewards received by Elmtown athletes and those received by Maple Grove athletes, while Marketville's pure athletes approach those of Green Junction in the rewards they receive.

These discrepancies notwithstanding, the general pattern is roughly consistent with the data of Chapter III, where Green Junction stood out —with St. John's—above the rest. Here it does as well, particularly when the athlete-scholars are included—for the athlete-scholars receive higher social rewards in Green Junction than anywhere else.

STRUCTURAL VARIATIONS IN THE SMALL SCHOOLS

In Elmtown, Maple Grove, and Green Junction, the "all-around boy," the athlete-scholar, receives special recognition and respect—far more than in Farmdale and Marketville. This is easily seen in Table 27—although the numbers of cases are small enough to make inferences only tentative. In Marketville, the athlete and scholar *separately* receive social rewards—with the athlete, as usual, receiving more—but the athlete-scholar receives no extra rewards, and in fact is less rewarded than the athlete. In Farmdale, the pattern is similar, except that the pure scholar gets few rewards—no more than the average boy with 7.5 choices. Here, too, the athlete-scholar receives fewer social rewards than in Elmtown, Maple Grove, and Green Junction.

In other words, the social systems in Elmtown, Maple Grove, and Green Junction seem to encourage athletic success and scholastic success, not as *alternative* paths to prestige, but as simultaneous paths. In Marketville, athletic success and scholastic success seem to be separately rewarded, with no special rewards for the "all-around boy" who is both an outstanding athlete and an outstanding scholar. In Farmdale as well, there are no special rewards for the "all-around boy," but none for the scholar either.

If there is this difference in the reward systems of these schools, then we would expect it to produce another result: in Marketville, boys would not attempt to be both athlete and scholar, but would "specialize," so to speak; while in Elmtown, Maple Grove, and Green Junction, many boys would strive for success in both fields. As a consequence, in these latter schools, many boys would be named as *both* athlete and scholar.

This is in fact the case, with great differences between the schools. Table 28 shows the average number of choices as scholar received by the athletes, plus the average number of choices as athlete received by the scholars, divided by the total number of athletes and scholars. The numbers in Table 28 are, therefore, crude measures of the covariation of athletic achievement and scholastic achievement in each school. The differences are striking, and generally accord with the results of Table 27.

Table 28—Average number of choices received by scholars as athletes and athletes as scholars in five small schools

	Farmdale	Marketville	Elmtown	Maple Grove	Green Junction
Average number of choices	0.59	0.78	2.32	3.13	1.50
Total athletes and scholars	(27)	(32)	(44)	(39)	(48)

Farmdale and Marketville are at one extreme, with very little overlap between the athletes and scholars. At the other is Maple Grove, followed by Elmtown and then Green Junction.

This difference in structure is not necessarily related to the *amount* of social rewards received by athletes and students in the school. It is quite evident from other data in the study, such as that presented in Chapter III, that scholars are most strongly rewarded in Marketville, followed at some distance by Elmtown and Maple Grove, then by Green Junction, and finally by Farmdale; and that athletes are most highly rewarded in Green Junction, followed at a distance by Marketville and Elmtown, then Maple Grove, and finally Farmdale. There is no relation—or very little—between these *amounts* of reward and the *structure* of reward, overlapping at the one extreme, virtually exclusive at the other.

What accounts for this difference in structure of rewards? There are several alternative explanations:

a) In some schools, like Elmtown, Maple Grove, and Green Junction, the determination of the scholar is not at all clear, so that the outstanding athletes who are reasonably good in their schoolwork are also seen as best scholars.

b) There is an actual norm in some schools, like Maple Grove and Elmtown, to be an "all-around" boy, not to be outstanding as *only* an athlete or *only* a student.

c) In schools like Marketville, there are two distinct systems of evaluation, that of the teachers, which strongly encourages and rewards scholastic success, and that of the students, which encourages and rewards athletic success. Different students are responsive to one or the other of these systems of evaluation, and thus achieve in one or the other area, but not both. In other schools, like Maple Grove, Elmtown, and Green Junction, these systems of evaluation are merged, with the teachers and students holding similar criteria. These criteria include *both* athletic success *and* scholastic success, combining the dimensions that are distinct in Marketville.

d) The difference is not due to a real structural difference in the school, but to the presence of particular boys in some schools, who happen to combine athletic ability and scholastic ability. A few years hence, when different boys are in the schools, they might reverse positions.

We will defer the question of which of these possible explanations accounts for the difference, until after examining the large schools in the same fashion as the small ones.

SOCIAL REWARDS IN THE FIVE LARGE SCHOOLS

Just as the patterns of social rewards differ among the small schools, they differ among the large ones. Because the number of cases is larger here, the over-all pattern in each school, including the athlete-scholar, may be examined with some confidence. Table 29 shows these patterns.

Table 29—Average number of choices received on all elite criteria by athlete-scholars, athletes, scholars, ladies' men, and all boys, in the five large schools*

	St. John's	Newlawn	Millburg	Midcity	Executive Heights
Athlete-scholar	32.7	20.2	22.2	33.5	44.5
	(14)	(7)	(9)	(8)	(10)
Athlete	15.1	16.2	17.2	15.5	15.2
	(37)	(29)	(26)	(45)	(41)
Scholar	7.4	6.9	10.2	11.3	7.5
	(29)	(23)	(27)	(53)	(51)
Ladies' man	12.3	11.1	11.0	12.9	21.7
	(21)	(15)	(25)	(41)	(21)
All boys	4.8	4.5	4.9	5.2	5.4
	(732)	(513)	(603)	(954)	(930)

* The number of cases is given in parentheses below each relevant category.

Executive Heights shows the greatest range of social rewards for the different kinds of achievement. The athlete-scholar is the object of the greatest amount of attention by far, pre-empting over twice as much as the next highest—which is, surprisingly enough, the boy who is neither athlete nor scholar, but ladies' man. The pure athlete fares more poorly, while the pure scholar gets just about a *sixth* as many choices as does the athlete-scholar, about a *third* as many as does the ladies' man, and is only slightly above the average for all boys.

The pattern in this school, then, seems to be one of the "all-around" boy receiving most attention, and the "social lion," the boy whose claim to status is his ability to get along with the opposite sex, following next. These two types are not seen as distinct and different types in the culture of this school, but both seem set apart from the pure athlete and the pure scholar. This is evidenced by the fact that the average athlete-scholar in Executive Heights received 10.3 mentions as the boy that girls go for most, while the pure athletes received less than one-fifth as many, 2.0, and the pure scholars received only *one thirty-eighth* as many, 0.27, an average only slightly higher than the boys who were named neither as best scholar nor as best athlete.

Thus, in Executive Heights, the athlete–scholar–ladies' man receives an extremely large amount of adulation. The pure scholar, on the other hand, receives very little recognition and respect from his peers. Nearly all the fathers in this community are engaged in pursuits where their primary tool is a trained mind—lawyers, doctors, business executives. In the high school, however, the boy who devotes his attention to scholarship alone is given few social rewards for his achievements, both in relation to others in his own school and in relation to the pure scholar in other schools. Meanwhile, this school literally falls at the feet of the all-around boy, the boy who is an athletic star, gets good grades, and romances the girls.

The pattern is similar—but far more pronounced—to that in Maple Grove, also a school heavily weighted with upper-middle-class, white-collar backgrounds. In that school as well, the athlete-scholar received far more choices as the boy girls go for most (an average of 6.0) than did the athlete-scholar in any other small school, more than the pure athletes in the same school received (an average of 3.1) and far more than the pure scholars in the same school (an average of 0.5).

Looking at a second large school in Table 29, Midcity, the pattern is quite different. Attention is distributed much more among the different groups, concentrated less on the athlete-scholars. In addition, it is distributed considerably more in the direction of the pure scholar. The pure scholar in Midcity receives more recognition from his peers—as measured by the total number of choices he received—than in any other of the large schools, and more than in any small school except Marketville. Midcity and Marketville have been consistently at the top in the evaluation of academic success in their boys' culture. It is worth noting that Midcity had among the seniors the closest thing found to an intellectual subgroup with high status in school. This was a group of boys and girls centered around the debate team, a group which "likes to discuss politics and such things," as one girl put it.

In Midcity there is some tendency for the athlete–scholar–ladies' man syndrome to emerge (athlete-scholars receive an average of 6.8 mentions as the boy most attractive to girls, while the pure athletes receive 2.0, and the pure scholars only 0.53), but the tendency is not nearly so pronounced as in Executive Heights. Furthermore, the pure athlete has higher over-all recognition than the pure ladies' man (15.5 vs. 12.9).

Millburg and Newlawn show little of this special attention for the athlete-scholar. The rewards for the athlete-scholar are much more nearly approached by those of the pure athlete than in Executive Heights. In Millburg, the boys give more attention to the pure scholar, close to that he receives in Midcity. In Newlawn, by contrast, the scholar's social rewards are very meager. In absolute quantity, his prestige is lower than in any other school; but relative to the average number of choices received by all boys, i.e., the average number of choices given, it is about at the level of St. John's and Executive Heights. The low position of the scholar in Newlawn coincides with the general picture of the values of this adolescent subculture, discussed in Chapter III.

The pure athlete in Newlawn and Millburg is not extremely highly rewarded in absolute numbers of choices received, but relative to the average number of choices in these schools (bottom row of Table 29), there is more focus on the pure athlete in these two schools than in any of the other large schools, equalled only by Green Junction among the small ones.

To summarize for Millburg and Newlawn: both give high rewards to the pure athlete, and neither heaps much extra attention on the athlete-scholar. The ladies' man receives some attention, but nothing comparable to what he receives in Executive Heights. In Newlawn, the pure scholar receives few rewards; in Millburg, he receives considerably more, approaching the rewards his counterpart in Midcity receives.

In St. John's, the athlete-scholar is especially prominent, as in Executive Heights, and, to a lesser extent, Midcity. The pure athlete gets more recognition than does the ladies' man, and both get more recognition than the pure scholar. The pattern is much like that in Midcity, with one exception—the pure scholar gets few rewards in St. John's. The position of the pure scholar in this school is similar to that in Newlawn and Executive Heights—quite low.

Considering the five schools together, the rewards show some consistency with the climates, as seen by the boys themselves, but not perfect consistency. The analysis in Chapter III indicated that Midcity and St. John's were high in rewards for scholarship; Millburg, in the middle; and Newlawn and Executive Heights, low. The one school in which the social rewards are inconsistent with this is St. John's. According to the data just examined, St. John's falls at the bottom, alongside Newlawn and Executive Heights.

What is the source of this sharp discrepancy between what the boys at St. John's *report* about the status of "good grades," and the *actual rewards* they give to those who are scholars? It may be a structural matter: more boys are *both* athlete and scholar here than in any other large school, and these athlete-scholars receive high rewards. Perhaps there is a strong constraint on the scholars to become all-around boys, by going out for athletics. Observation in the school in part confirms this. It appears that the sharp distinction among boys in this school is between those who are interested in school, both its athletics and its scholastics, and those whose interests lie wholly outside school. Although such a pattern exists among boys in all the schools (far more than among the girls, for example), it seems most pronounced at St. John's. The school has less to capture the attention of its teen-agers than do most of the others, making the gap greater between those interested in it, on the one hand, and those not interested, on the other.

The rewards given to athletes in the large schools show little variation. The pure athlete gets slightly higher rewards in Newlawn and Millburg, but in these two schools, the athlete-scholar receives fewer. In Chapter III, the schools were grouped closely together in the status they accorded athletics, and this clustering is evident here as well. Despite the clustering, it was possible to classify St. John's high, Midcity low, and the other three large schools medium high. No such pattern appears here in the data of Table 29; little can be said beyond the fact that the schools seem very much alike in the degree of recognition they provide for athletic achievement. In all the schools, athletic achievement, relative to other achievement, maintains the high position it has exhibited in earlier chapters.

One striking addition to the earlier pictures of the large schools in Chapter III is the recognition accorded the ladies' man in Executive Heights. When combined with the athlete-scholar, he forms the complete all-round boy in the eyes of these teen-agers, the boy on whom they heap attention. Even without the added attractions of athletic or scholastic achievement, he is a boy much admired by his fellows, with plenty of friends, and solidly in the leading crowd—more solidly than the pure athlete, and beyond comparison with the pure scholar.

STRUCTURAL VARIATIONS IN THE LARGE SCHOOLS

The large schools exhibit structural variations in the way in which they provide rewards, as was the case for the small schools. At the opposite extremes are Executive Heights and Millburg. In Executive Heights, the pure athlete and pure scholar receive only 22.7 choices combined, just *half* of what the average athlete-scholar receives. In Millburg, the pure athlete and pure scholar receive 27.4 choices combined, *more* than does the athlete-scholar. The other schools also show variations. St. John's shows high rewards for the athlete-scholar, and so does Midcity. Newlawn, on the other hand, is much like Millburg in not giving special rewards to the athlete-scholar.

Does this mean that in St. John's, Midcity, and especially Executive Heights, there is strong pressure to be *both* athlete and scholar, to be an all-around boy? If so, in these three schools—with Executive Heights in the lead—many boys should achieve in both areas, in contrast to Newlawn and Millburg. Thus, the first three schools should be like Maple

Grove, with choices overlapping between athlete and scholar. The latter two should be like Marketville and Farmdale, with little overlap.

The data shown in Table 30 show no such result. There is far less variation in overlap than existed in the small schools—Maple Grove showed *more* overlap than any of the large schools, while Marketville and Farmdale showed *less*. Millburg, which provides few social rewards for the athlete-scholar, shows as much overlap as does Executive Heights; Midcity, where the athlete-scholar does receive extra rewards, shows least overlap of roles.

Table 30—Average number of choices received by scholars as athletes and athletes as scholars in five large schools

	St. John's	Newlawn	Millburg	Midcity	Executive Heights
Average number of choices	2.37	1.83	2.10	1.28	2.05
Total athletes and scholars	(94)	(66)	(71)	(114)	(112)

Evidently other factors are operative here to affect the amount of overlap. The composition of the school, for example, must have an important effect in these large schools whose student bodies differ so radically. In Millburg, for example, the *average* boy has a background similar to the Newlawn boy, but the *distribution* is far broader than in this school.

Thus the amount of role overlap does not follow the special rewards given to athlete-scholars in these schools. Despite this, the differences in rewards shown in Table 29 indicates that there are definite differences in the degree to which the roles of athlete and scholar are encouraged separately by the adolescent culture, or combined into a single all-around boy. In Executive Heights and, to a lesser extent, Midcity and St. John's, there are rewards for the combined achievements (although the Midcity culture gives more rewards to the pure scholar than in any other large school); in Millburg and Newlawn, there are no special rewards for the combined achievements (although these schools differ in that the pure scholar is rewarded more in the Millburg culture than in the Newlawn culture).

Sources of the Structural Differences

In examining the small schools, we suggested several possible sources of the role-specialization in Marketville and the combination in Elmtown and Maple Grove. Some of these may be disposed of briefly; the final question of what *is* the source of the differences will remain unanswered.

First, it is evident that the difference is not due to particular persons or one particular class in school. In every class, freshman, sophomore, junior, and senior, in Maple Grove, there is more overlap between athlete and scholar than in Marketville; the high overlap in Elmtown also is distributed over the four classes.

A second possible explanation suggested earlier is that in a school like Marketville, there are two distinct systems of evaluation, provided by teachers, on the one hand, and other boys, on the other. Some boys respond to the first and strive for high scholarship; others respond to the second, thus acquiring athletic prowess. This explanation, however, is not consistent with the facts. The teachers were asked, in a question-naire, what kind of boy they would like to see as class president: brilliant student, athletic star, or activities leader. The Marketville teachers men-tion "brilliant student" no more often than do the teachers in the other small schools. The boys themselves were asked, both in fall and spring, to choose how they would like to be remembered. There was just as much shifting from fall to spring between "brilliant student" and "ath-letic star" in Marketville as in Maple Grove—indicating that there are no more boys in Marketville than in Maple Grove who have fixed perma-nently on the image of brilliant student or athletic star. There is just as much fluctuating between these images in Marketville as in Maple Grove.

Thus, the source of these structural differences lies neither in genetic chance nor in two separate systems of evaluation. It seems likely that the difference has to do with the *independent* status that scholastic achievement has in a school. Boys in some high schools—including some of the boys in this study—feel that good grades and doing well in school helps gain recognition and respect from others, but *only* if he is also good in other things. If he is also an athlete and a good social companion, then good grades help his cause. If not, then he's a grind, and his good grades merely confirm that he works too hard. In such a school, scholastic achievement has no independent status at all—and in such a school social rewards accrue to the scholar only if he is an all-around boy.

Maple Grove, the most middle-class of the small-town schools, and Executive Heights, the most upper-middle-class of the large schools, are at the extremes in the social rewards they provide for the all-around boy. At the same time, the pure scholar who is not an athlete receives few rewards in Maple Grove, and even fewer in Executive Heights. It may be that in a middle-class community, where most of the adolescents are college-bound, giving rewards to the all-around boy for his good grades together with his other activities is the adolescent culture's compromise with reality—the reality that parents want to see good grades, and the reality that good grades will be important for college. This kind of recognition is very different from the status accorded scholastic achievement in Marketville or Midcity or, to a lesser extent, Millburg, where the pure scholar receives social rewards on his own, *as* a scholar.

VI Beauty and Brains as Paths to Success

THERE IS NOT, AMONG GIRLS IN HIGH school, an activity comparable to athletics among boys, an activity in which a girl may achieve highly and thereby gain recognition and respect from her peers. Extracurricular "activities" serve as such an avenue to some degree, but their effects on a girl's status are not comparable to the effects of athletic stardom on a boy's status. There is one path, however, that girls have traditionally been able to take toward social prestige, a path that, in these high schools, is still often used: success with boys. Girls were asked:

II.11. Is it easier for a girl to get to be important and well known among the students in this school by making friends with a very popular girl or by dating a very popular boy?

Making friends with a popular girl	55.1%
Dating a popular boy	44.9%
Number of cases	(3,956)

Although a minority replied that dating a popular boy was the way to success, it was not a small minority. In these high schools, as traditionally, an important way for a girl to "get ahead" is through her success with boys. At the same time, scholastic achievement is very important to girls in high school. Motivated as they are to conform to the demands of parents and teachers, they work harder in school (as will be evidenced in Chapter IX by their better grades), and are, on the whole, more oriented to "doing well' in scholastic matters than are the boys. Thus, scholastic achievement is important to some girls, just as is social success with the opposite sex.

Table 31 shows just how much status, in all schools together, accrued to girls who were named as best scholars, those who were named as most successful to boys, and all girls together.

Table 31—Average number of choices received in various elite criteria by girls who were chosen as best scholars (2+ times), those named as most successful with boys (2+ times), and all girls in school

Choices received by:	Be friends with and be like	Leading crowd	Number of friends	Total	Number of cases
Beauty	5.6	9.3	6.6	21.5	(278)
Brains	4.8	4.6	5.7	15.1	(380)
All girls	1.2	2.5	4.1	7.8	(4,135)

Just as the athletes outdistanced the scholars in recognition and respect from other boys, the girls successful with boys outdistance the scholars in recognition and respect from other girls. The difference is greatest for the girl whom others want to be like and as a member of the leading crowd. At the same time, the girl named as best scholar is ahead of the student body as a whole in these criteria.

The immediate question, then, is how does this differ among schools? Is it alike in all, or do brains mean more than beauty in some?

Beauty and Brains in the Small Schools

Considering the small schools first, Table 32 below compares in each school, the girls who are most popular with boys with the scholars (in both cases, all those named two time or more) on the same elite criteria of status used above in Table 31.

Looking first at the totals on the right, it is apparent that brains does best in Marketville, both in absolute terms and relative to beauty. Even in Marketville, however, it does slightly less well than does beauty. In only one of the fifteen specific comparisons in the five schools does brains win out—in the number of girl friends she has in Marketville. However, in this school she is close to beauty both as an exemplar and as a member of the leading crowd.

It is in Green Junction that beauty most surpasses brains, having over twice as many choices altogether. Not only is the difference greatest,

Table 32—Average number of choices received in various elite criteria by girls chosen as best scholars (2+ times) and those named as most successful with boys (2+ times), in schools 0-4

	Be friends with and be like	Leading crowd	Number of friends	Total	Number of cases
Farmdale					
Beauty	5.4	10.3	3.6	19.3	(20)
Brains	3.7	5.2	3.4	12.3	(16)
Marketville					
Beauty	6.9	13.9	6.1	26.9	(25)
Brains	6.0	11.2	7.5	24.7	(18)
Elmtown					
Beauty	5.6	11.8	5.9	23.3	(29)
Brains	4.0	8.9	5.3	18.2	(23)
Maple Grove					
Beauty	7.3	13.7	7.7	28.7	(27)
Brains	5.6	8.5	5.9	20.0	(23)
Green Junction					
Beauty	7.3	15.9	7.7	30.9	(28)
Brains	3.8	5.1	5.4	14.3	(25)

but beauty receives more choices in that school, and brains receives fewer, than in any other of these schools (with the exception of brains in Farmdale, which is lower than Green Junction, but which cannot be directly compared, since the concentration of choices is so much less in Farmdale). Green Junction is the school in which athletics is dominant for the boys, and the girls give good grades a very low position as an attribute for popularity and status, as Chapter III indicated.

Elmtown is closest to Marketville in the status accorded to brains relative to beauty, but in absolute terms, brains receive more choices in Maple Grove. Farmdale is somewhere between these two schools and Green Junction, although it is harder to compare with the others because of its lower concentration of choices.

The positions of girls seen by their classmates to have "brains" accord completely with the perceived importance of scholastic achievement in the status system of these schools. In Marketville, the scholar gains most status among her fellows; Elmtown and Maple Grove follow at a distance; and, finally, Farmdale and Green Junction. Green Junction is definitely lowest of the five schools.

Beauty and Brains in the Large Schools

The same comparison between beauty and brains is given in Table 33 for the large schools.

As in each small school, beauty outdistances brains in each of these

Table 33—Average number of choices received in various elite criteria by girls chosen as best scholars (2+ times) and those named as most successful with boys (2+ times), in schools 6–9

	Be friends with and be like	Leading crowd	Number of friends	Total	Number of cases
Newlawn					
Beauty	5.8	8.8	5.8	20.4	(42)
Brains	3.8	4.0	4.9	12.7	(57)
Millburg					
Beauty	6.2	10.4	6.4	23.0	(59)
Brains	4.0	4.2	5.2	13.4	(81)
Midcity					
Beauty	10.0	12.2	6.9	29.1	(57)
Brains	7.3	9.0	6.5	22.8	(81)
Executive Heights					
Beauty	5.2	12.4	7.2	24.8	(58)
Brains	4.0	4.5	6.2	14.7	(61)

large ones. Consistent with the perceived status system, brains does far better in Midcity than in any of the other schools; the total number of choices she receives is far more than she receives in the other schools. The other schools are very similar to one another, both in the absolute position of brains and in its position relative to that of beauty. Yet in Chapter III, it was quite evident that the social rewards for scholastic achievement were higher for the girls in Newlawn and Executive Heights than for those in Millburg. Because of this discrepancy, it is useful to look at the girls named seven times or more as "best students" in these schools—the extremes of "brains" as perceived by the other girls. Table 34 shows how the top beauty and brains fared in each of these four schools.

Table 34—Average number of choices received in various elite criteria by girls chosen as best scholars (7+ times) and those named as most successful with boys (7+ times), in schools 6–9

	Be friends with and be like	Leading crowd	Number of friends	Total	Number of cases
Newlawn					
Beauty	15.2	18.7	7.5	41.4	(12)
Brains	9.4	7.4	6.5	23.3	(12)
Millburg					
Beauty	14.5	22.2	8.7	45.4	(15)
Brains	6.8	5.5	4.9	17.2	(22)
Midcity					
Beauty	14.3	16.2	6.3	36.8	(22)
Brains	12.9	11.6	6.2	30.7	(23)
Executive Heights					
Beauty	10.9	21.2	9.1	41.2	(17)
Brains	8.9	7.5	6.6	23.0	(16)

When these "top brains" and "top beauty" are examined by themselves, there is a clear-cut difference between, on the one hand, Newlawn and Executive Heights and, on the other, Millburg. In Millburg, the top brains get hardly more choices than do the total group chosen two or more times shown in Table 33: 17.2 total choices compared to 13.4. Among the top brains of the other schools, the increase is much larger, an increase of eight to ten choices. In this table, Midcity still stands far above the others, separating the schools clearly into three levels of rewards for brains: Midcity is high; Newlawn and Executive Heights are intermediate; and Millburg is low. Again, as with the small schools, the differences coincide with those found in Chapter III, where the perceived status system was examined. Midcity and Marketville, among the large and small schools respectively, are clearly those where brains stands out most—or suffers least in comparison with beauty. Millburg, among the large schools, and Green Junction, among the small ones, are clearly the places where brains stands out least—or suffers most in comparison with beauty.

Changes over the Four Years

There is a definite shift in the way "brains" are viewed by other girls over the course of four years in school. The one girl in the small schools who in each class is named most often as the best scholar, and the two girls so named in the large schools, experience a double shift over the course of their school career. Figure 6.1 shows (with the analogous boys charted at the left) the average number of choices received by this one (or two) most outstanding girl(s) in each of the four years in school. The small schools are represented by one line, the large schools by another. (Midcity is omitted from this grade-by-grade analysis, for it includes only grades ten through twelve.) The freshman best scholar receives an average of 23.6 choices on all the criteria in the small schools, but by the junior year, this has decreased to little over *four* choices— including those who name her as friend, as a member of the leading crowd, and as someone to be friends with or to be like. In every one of these small schools but Marketville, the junior best scholar has only two persons who mention her as friends, and not a single mention as a member of the leading crowd, or as a person to be friends with or to be like, except one lone mention in Farmdale. That is, in four small schools— Farmdale, Elmtown, Maple Grove, and Green Junction—the junior best scholar is a girl almost completely isolated and out of things. This is not at all true among the seniors or the freshmen, but is beginning to be true by the sophomore year.

Among the large schools, the effect is similar, although not so pronounced, possibly beginning and ending earlier. That is, there seems to be an end to this isolation, just as there was a beginning. Among the seniors in the large schools, the two best scholars received an average of forty-seven choices; and in *each* of the schools, they received more choices in the senior year than in any of the other three years.

Apparently, there is a period in the sophomore and junior years when good grades among girls is particularly devalued. It seems likely that this is related to the beginning of regular dating and the consequent importance of attractiveness. Figure 2.15 (p. 56) showed the importance of good looks and popularity with boys for membership in the leading crowd over the four years of school. It is the sophomore and

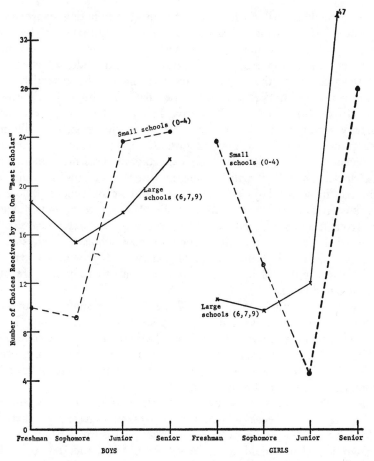

Figure 6.1—Number of choices received by the one best scholar in each grade, in large and small schools, boys and girls separately.

junior years when these criteria are most important, and the senior year that they are least important.

One point has been omitted throughout this examination: the degree to which beauty and brains coincide in a given school. Or, less colloquially and more accurately, how much coincidence is there between the girls who are seen as most successful with boys, and those seen as most successful academically?

The Coincidence of Beauty and Brains

The preceding analysis leads to two quite conflicting expectations about the degree to which girls who are seen as "best student" by their classmates will also be most popular with boys in school. The results immediately above suggest that in Marketville and Midcity, where the social rewards from other girls are greatest, she will be generally more "in the center of things," thus more popular with boys. In Elmtown, Maple Grove, Newlawn, and Executive Heights, she should have some popularity with boys. Finally, in Farmdale, Green Junction, and Millburg, where grades count for little in the girls' status system, she should have little success at all with boys. These expectations seem most reasonable.

Yet in Chapter IX, it will become evident that "brains" in a girl are discounted most by boys in the most middle-class schools: most in Executive Heights, but also in Marketville, Maple Grove, and Midcity. Thus, from those results, one would expect a quite different pattern of success with boys by the girls who are best scholars. Such success should be lowest in Executive Heights, somewhat higher in Marketville, Maple Grove, and Midcity, and highest in the others, which are uniformly less middle-class.

How does it actually turn out? Table 35 below shows the overlap between success with boys and scholastic success in each school. These figures are calculated as was the athlete-scholar overlap of the preceding chapter, in which the total number of choices received on the other criterion, by those chosen two times or more on one, were divided by the total chosen two times or more on either criterion.

The results coincide with neither of the above two expectations— but they coincide precisely with the two taken together. Marketville and Midcity are highest in overlap, although they surpass Elmtown and Newlawn less than would be expected from the earlier tables in this chapter. Social-class expectation operates most strongly among the

Table 35—Average number of choices received by "most popular" as "best scholar" and by "best scholar" as "most popular"

	Average number of choices	Number of cases
Small Schools		
Farmdale	0.93	(30)
Marketville	2.18	(33)
Elmtown	2.06	(48)
Maple Grove	0.82	(44)
Green Junction	1.08	(50)
Large Schools		
Newlawn	2.02	(106)
Millburg	1.92	(140)
Midcity	2.79	(138)
Executive Heights	0.92	(119)

schools where brains receive intermediate rewards from other girls. In the two middle-class schools, Maple Grove and Executive Heights, the best scholars do most poorly with boys; while in the more nearly working-class schools in this same intermediate category, Elmtown and Newlawn, they receive over *twice* as many mentions as most successful with boys—almost as many as in Marketville and Midcity. Even in Millburg, where the best scholars received least rewards among the large-school girls, they do over twice as well in popularity with the boys as do the best scholars in Executive Heights. Among the more working-class schools, only in Farmdale and Green Junction does the girl with brains do especially poorly with boys, and even in these schools she does better than in middle-class Maple Grove and Executive Heights.

These results, consistent with the middle-class boys' devaluation of brains in a girl (to be examined in Chapter IX), are certainly not in accord with naive expectations. Yet they are consistent throughout this research, most evident in the upper-middle-class suburb, Executive Heights, but evident as well in other schools. They seem to be related to fairly general changes occurring in society. Some of these are discussed in Chapter X, which compares traditional middle-class constraint of daughters with modern middle-class pressures toward social maturity —and, as a by-product, liberation from parental constraints.

Data to be presented in Chapter IX will suggest a greater role-differentiation between the sexes in working-class cultures than in middle-class ones. In the middle class, girls—and wives—are expected to be companions far more than in the working class. The combination of this lesser role-differentiation with one other factor seems to be the source of this middle-class male devaluation of brains in a girl. The other factor is the increasing "adulthood" of adolescents, the increasing liberation from adult control. This greater liberation means that they are no longer children, and the girl who is admired and sought after by boys is the *active* girl, not the girl who is still conforming to adult standards by her concern with studies and good grades.

"Good grades" and concentration upon studies are seen by the adolescent community, and rightly so, as acquiescence and conformity to adult constraints. Social affairs, extracurricular activities, and athletics are activities of their "own," activities in which they can carry out positive actions on their own, in contrast to schoolwork, where they carry out "assignments" from teachers. Such demands are galling to any community that feels itself at all autonomous. It is no wonder that the acquiescent girls, who are still conforming to parental and school "assignments," and getting high grades, are not more popular with boys. Middle-class boys, feeling their liberation from parental control, want partners in liberation, not girls still responding to the controls of childhood.

This is not to say that they want girls who have shed moral constraints, for it is not these girls who dominate the culture. They want to date girls who have constraints, but not girls who are still subject to parental demands. Their interest is in the *active* girl. More traditionally in adolescence, and still so among working-class boys, the relevant dichotomy is the *good* girl vs. the *bad* girl—the first to respect and admire, the second to exploit or have fun with. It appears that this dichotomy is being replaced, in the modern middle class, with that of the *active* girl vs. the *passive* girl—the first to respect and have fun with, the second to ignore. The girls who strive for good grades are among the passive group, for they are merely acquiescing to external demands.

It needn't be this way, of course; academic achievement is inherently no more passive than is any extracurricular activity. It is only that academic matters in school are still largely presented to adolescents as something to be received, as prescribed "exercises," as "assignments," that is, as matters requiring more receptivity than positive action. The results of this research strongly indicate that this structuring of scholastic activity for adolescents is incompatible with the goals of secondary education in modern society. Chapters X and XI make some suggestions in the direction of possible changes in the structure.[1]

---

1. The matter is discussed more fully in "Academic Achievement and the Structure of Competition," *Harvard Educational Review*, Vol. XXIX (Fall, 1959), and in a paper in a symposium on citizenship education, *The Adolescent Citizen*, Franklin Patterson, ed. (Glencoe: The Free Press, 1960).

VII Structures of Association and Their Relation to the Value-Systems

ANY SOCIAL SYSTEM HAS SEVERAL RE-
ated components. Its values, norms, customs—that is, its "culture"—is
one component. Its elites and popular heroes constitute another. Its status
system, which accords prestige to certain people and certain activities,
is a third. All these components have been studied in preceding chapters.
One important component has not yet been examined: the association
patterns which compose the system.[1]

These associations help reinforce certain values, undercut others; pull
energies in the direction of some activities and away from others;
strengthen the prestige of some persons, weaken that of others. They
are, in part, a source of the culture, and in part are determined by it.

---

1. Such association patterns have been studied only infrequently. The best example
in a high school is Wayne Gordon, *op. cit.*, who studied all grades in one midwest-
rn high school about the size of Newlawn. Another excellent study in this area is
H. J. Hallworth, "Sociometric Relationships among Grammar School Boys and Girls
between the Ages of Eleven and Sixteen Years," *Sociometry*, XVI, 1953. There have
been many sociometric studies in the classroom, but these have largely been done
as social therapy. See J. M. Moreno, H. Jennings, and Stockton, "Sociometry in the
Classroom," *Sociometry*, VI, 1943, p. 428. Research along these lines is reported in
C. M. Fleming, *Studies in the Social Psychology of Adolescence*, (London: Rout-
edge, Kegan, and Paul, 1951), Mary L. Northway, "Outsiders: A Study of the Per-
onality Factors of Children Least Acceptable to their Age-mates," *Sociometry*, VII,
944, pp. 10–25, and George A. Lundberg and Lenore Dickson, "Selective Association among Ethnic Groups in a High School Population," *American Sociological
Review*, XVII, 1952, pp 23–35.

Thus, the clusters of girls who dance together at one another's house provide an association pattern that "resonates" to popular music an singing stars, strengthening the importance of popular music in th culture, and even providing the base for fan clubs. Yet these clusters ar not only a *source* of interest in popular music; they are in part *create* by such interest.

There are few periods in life in which associations are so strong intimate, and all-encompassing as those that develop during adolescenc Because adolescence is a unique transitional period, when a boy or gi is no longer fully within the parental family, but has not yet formed family of his own, close ties with friends replace the family ties that ar so strong during most of the rest of his life. During adolescence, he i moving out of the family he was part of in childhood, not yet withi the family he will be part of as an adult.[2]

The high schools are partly responsible for these strong association: By gathering adolescents together for six hours each day, they constitut the locus for associations that expand into the rest of the day. Thi chapter will examine the association structures among these adolescent to see just how the values of the culture are held in place through reinforcement by association patterns, and to get some idea of how th association structures develop in the various schools.[3]

The association structures in each school are pictured in the socio grams of Figures 7.1.1-7.2.4 (pp. 175-182). A boy or girl is represente by a small circle, and associations are represented by lines connectin the circles. Only mutual associations, that is, those reported by bot members, are charted. Thus, non-reciprocated choices do not appear o the diagram, nor do persons appear who were not involved in at leas one mutual choice. The smallest unit to appear on these sociograms is pair of small circles joined by a line, indicating that both persons chos one another, but neither was involved in another mutual choice.

The size of the boy's or girl's number within his small circle indicate

---

2. A number of authors have discussed the transition from parental family to ow family and the social-psychological strains it induces. See Kingsley Davis, "Th Sociology of Parent-Youth Conflict," *American Sociological Review*, V, 1940, p 523–535; Mirra Komarovsky, "Functional Analysis of Sex Roles," *American Socic logical Review*, XV, 1950, pp. 508–516. The relation of this to the development c a deviant subculture is discussed in Albert Cohen, *op. cit.* For cross-cultural com parisons, see Margaret Mead, *From the South Seas: Studies of Adolescence and Se in Primitive Societies*, (New York: William Morrow and Co., 1939).

3. We will restrict our examination to the association structures of the small schools—Marketville, Elmtown, Maple Grove, and Green Junction. The associatio structure of Farmdale is not examined because there are so few people in each grad that there are no well-formed cliques other than the dominant one in each grad The association structures of the large schools could not be examined here withou gross oversimplification. It is hoped that they may be reported in a later publicatio

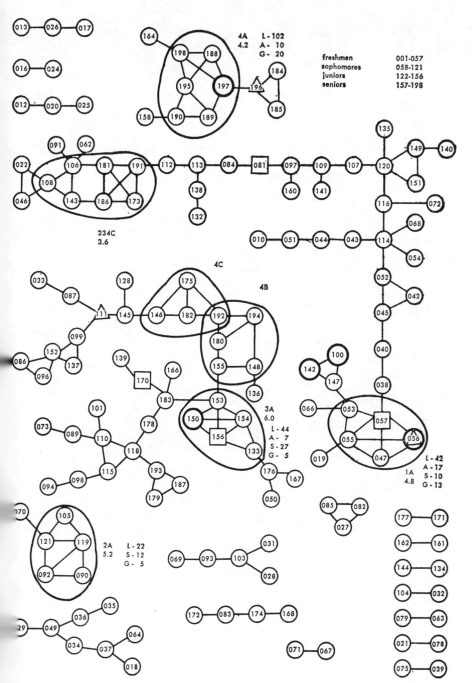

Figure 7.1.1—Network of reciprocated friendships among Marketville Boys.

175

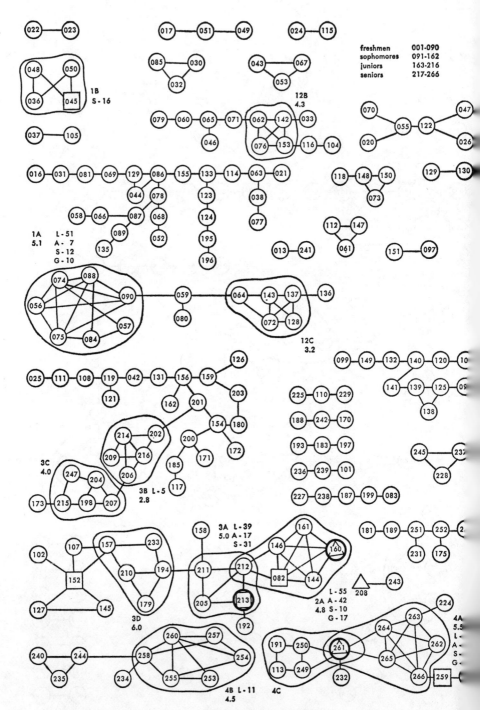

Figure 7.1.2—Network of reciprocated friendships among Elmtown boys.

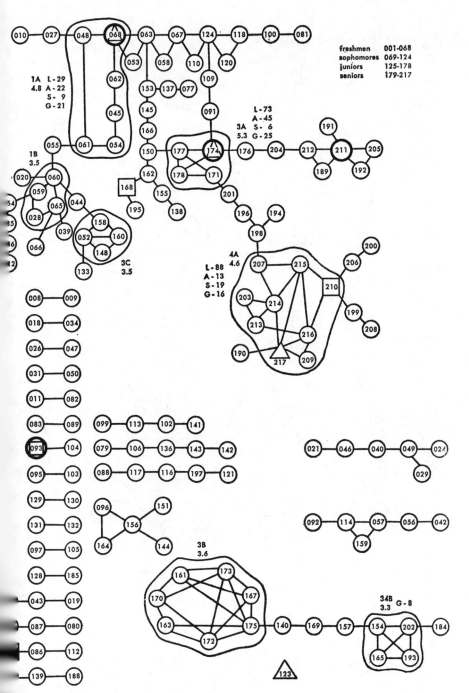

Figure 7.1.3—Network of reciprocated friendships among Maple Grove boys.

177

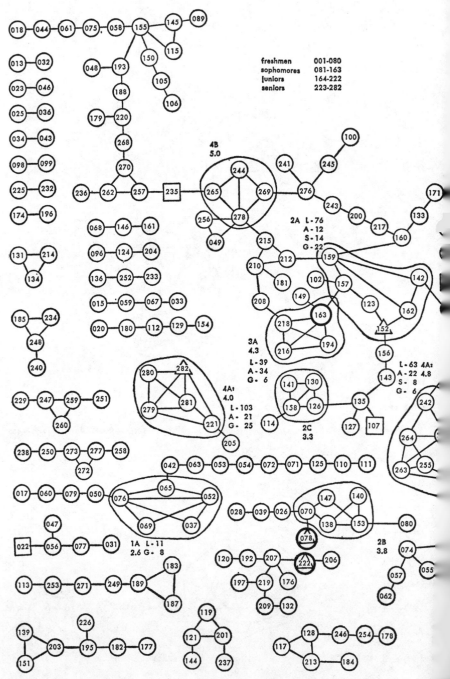

Figure 7.1.4—Network of reciprocated friendships among Green Junction boys

178

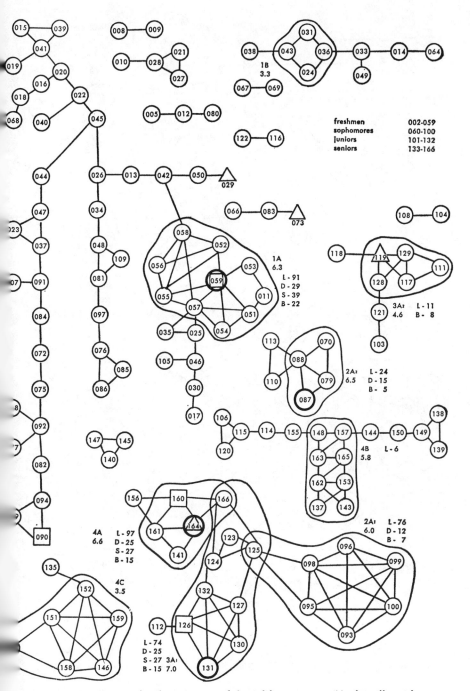

Figure 7.2.1—Network of reciprocated friendships among Marketville girls.

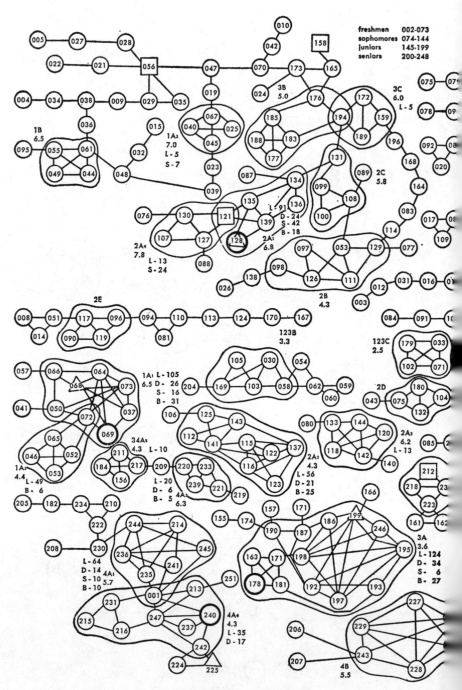

Figure 7.2.2—Network of reciprocated friendships among Elmtown girls.

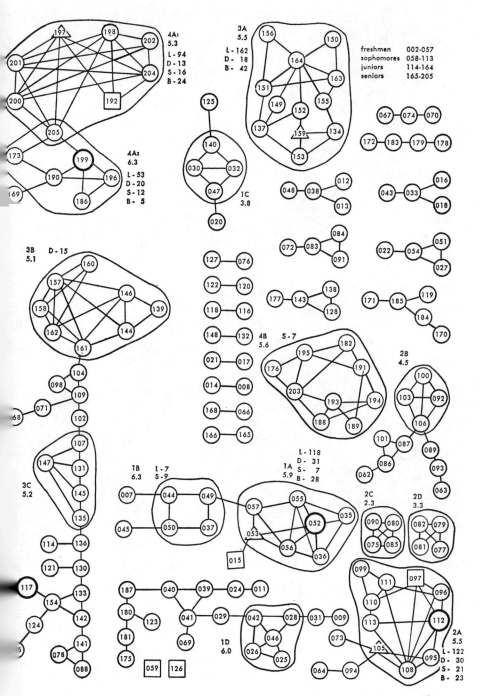

Figure 7.2.3—Network of reciprocated friendships among Maple Grove girls.

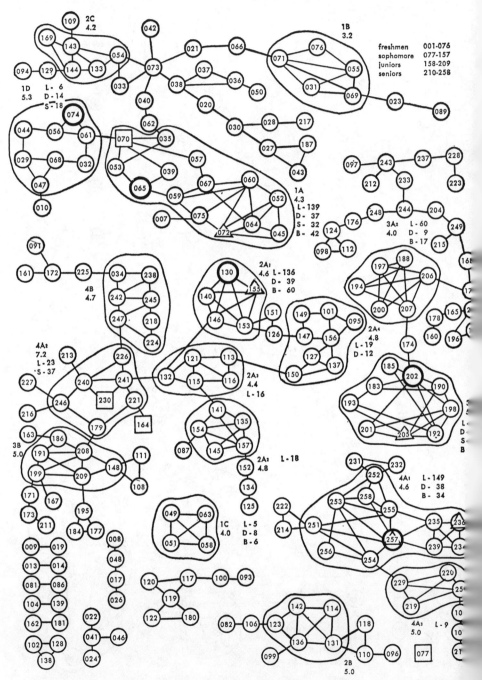

Figure 7.2.4—Network of reciprocated friendships among Green Junction girls.

his grade in school and the number of choices he received from others. If there are 57 boys among the freshmen, as in Marketville (Figure 7.1.1), then the least-chosen is numbered 001, and the most-chosen is numbered 057. The least-chosen sophomore is then numbered 058, and so on.

In each grade, the boy who was most often mentioned as best athlete and the girl who was most mentioned as best dressed are represented by a heavy circle; the boy or girl mentioned most often as best scholar is represented by a square; and the boy or girl mentioned most often as most attractive to the opposite sex is represented by a triangle. "Cliques" have been delineated and circled in the sociograms on the basis of the reciprocated choices.[4] These delineations are necessarily somewhat arbitrary, for they break apart into discrete units what is, in fact, a complex interconnected network.[5] Despite this necessary arbitrariness, the cliques and what they have in common can tell much about how the system functions.

The senior clique whose members received most total mentions as being in the leading crowd is labeled "4A"—"4" for senior, "A" for being the leading clique. If more than one clique in a class received an average of more than two mentions per person as being in the leading crowd, the cliques are labeled "$4A_1$," "$4A_2$," etc., $4A_1$ being the senior clique whose members received most mentions. Other senior cliques are labeled "4B," "4C," etc., according to the class of all or most of their members, and the average number of friendship choices received by the clique members. Any clique that does not have a majority of its members from one grade is labeled with the numbers of all grades it includes. Thus, in Marketville, there is a clique of not-very-popular boys in the upper three classes, labeled 234C.

If the members of a clique received a total of five or more mentions as being in the leading crowd, best athlete (or for girls, best dressed),

---

4. The definition of a clique was a group built around a nucleus of four or five, each member of which chose and was chosen by at least two others in the nucleus. The group was extended from the basic nucleus of four or five until the new person to be added was not in a mutual choice relation with at least two members of the group. If he was in a mutual choice relation with someone whose membership in the group was contingent upon his own, both were brought in. This was continued so long as the cycle of persons being simultaneously brought in was not larger than five.

5. In carrying out this study, a technique was developed for working with such a complex network using electronic computers, but it has not yet been perfected. The technique is described in James S. Coleman and Duncan MacRae, Jr., "Electronic Processing of Sociometric Data for Groups up to 1,000 in Size," *American Sociological Review*, 25, 1960, pp. 722–27. A computer, Univac I, was used for locating all the mutual choices, from which these diagrams were drawn. The development of methods for quantitatively studying such structures as more than aggregates of individuals seems one of the most promising, and yet most difficult, methodological and theoretical tasks awaiting sociologists.

best scholar, or most attractive to the opposite sex, this is indicated beside the clique. A letter indicating the criterion of choice, and opposite it the number of choices received, is used, as follows:

Boys = L-n (leading crowd)   Girls = L-n (leading crowd)
       A-n (athlete)   D-n (best dressed)
       S-n (scholar)   S-n (scholar)
       G-n (attractive to girls)   B-n (attractive to boys)

In Marketville, the members of the leading junior boys' clique, 3A, received 44 mentions as being in the leading crowd, 7 as being best athlete, 27 as being best scholar, 5 as being most attractive to girls. This is indicated by:

L-44
A- 7
S-27
G- 5

These indications will show not only the relative status of the various cliques, but also the general "personality" of the clique—whether it is made up of athletic stars, bright students, or teen-agers successful in the world of dating. A glance at the cliques in almost any of the schools shows that most such choices are highly concentrated in one or a few cliques in each grade.

Finally, average grades of the members of each clique, in the fall semester 1957–58 (the semester during which the questionnaire was administered), are listed below the clique identification number. Grades range from 8 to 0 (8 = A, 6 = B, 4 = C, 2 = D, 0 = F).

There is one important defect in these sociograms: the boys and girls are charted separately. Each boy was asked what *boys* he associated with, while each girl was asked what *girls* she associated with. Thus, the social structure was arbitrarily split along sex lines. At another point in the questionnaire, boys and girls were asked whom they *dated*, a question that could serve to partially rejoin the two separate structures. The technical difficulties involved, however, are great, and so it was not done. Techniques for analyzing such data are in their infancy, and until they are better developed, large-scale analyses like this one will continue to have serious omissions.

Structural Differences at a Glance

Before examining each school's association structures, a glance through the charts reveal striking differences. One must be careful in making visual comparisons, for there is no standard way of drawing such diagrams; nevertheless, some visible differences in these charts are obviously related to actual differences in the structures. Perhaps the most striking is the difference between boys and girls in each school. Anyone familiar with teen-agers knows the extreme importance of friends, cliques, groups, and crowds for girls. Nevertheless, the complexity of the clique structures among girls in these schools, compared to the relative simplicity of the boys' associations, is startling. The networks of girls, shown in Figures 7.2.1-7.2.4 are extraordinarily elaborated compared to those of the boys. Table 36 below shows this well, listing the number of boys' and girls' cliques in each of these four schools.

Table 36—Number of boys' and girls' cliques

School	Boys	Girls
Marketville	7	9
Elmtown	12	23
Maple Grove	7	14
Green Junction	8	17

Beyond this comparison, it is easy to see differences within the cliques in the elaboration of choices. For example, for Marketville, Figure 7.2.1 shows two sets of five girls and one set of six that form perfect stars, all possible choices made among them. For a group of six, this constitutes a total of thirty choices, all made among the six girls. For the boys in the same school, there is not a single such perfect group larger than four in size.

There are also obvious variations in the structures from school to school. In some schools, the association patterns are particularly intense. In the small schools, a higher proportion of boys and girls are part of definite cliques than in the larger schools,[6] where there seem to be many more simple pair relationships.[7] But even among the large schools, there are large differences among the structures. For example, the structure in Executive Heights is far more complete, more fully-developed than that in Newlawn, although both are suburban schools. At the time of this study, Newlawn's school was only seven years old. At least partly because of the difference in community solidarity in these two suburbs (and probably also partly due to the social-class differences and the greater interest of upper-middle-class parents in the school), a great many more community functions are carried out in school and after school hours in Executive Heights. Such clustering of social activities in and around the school strengthens the social system. The strength of the resulting social

---

6. Large schools are not shown here, although the sociograms for them have been constructed, and appear in the original report to the U. S. Office of Education.

7. The pair relations are not so distinct as these diagrams would suggest, since these include only reciprocated choices, which probably constitute less than half of the total choices.

system is suggested by the fact that the average number of choices made in Executive Heights is more than in any of the other large schools.

The Association Structures of Small-School Boys

BOYS IN MARKETVILLE: SIMPLE IN STRUCTURE, VARIABLE IN CONTENT

In Marketville, the structure among the boys is relatively simple, as Figure 7.1.1 indicates. In each grade, there is a separate leading clique, which includes no one outside that grade. The sizes of the identification numbers indicate that each of these cliques constitutes not only the leading crowd in school but also includes the persons most frequently named as friends. There are a few exceptions, boys who are not in one of these A-cliques but are more popular than some of those who are, but the general tendency remains.

Besides the leading cliques, there is little else: two interconnected senior cliques, labeled 4B and 4C, and one clique, labeled 234C, cutting across all grades except freshman. Beyond this, the remaining boys are either "hangers-on," extending in chains from the cliques, or in triads, pairs, or isolates. In this school, then, the boys outside the leading crowd are fragmented, and hardly offer a challenge to the dominant group.

In *content* of things they have in common and excel in, the leading cliques differ widely from grade to grade. The members of the senior A-clique are never named as best scholar, but often as athlete and ladies' man. The juniors contrast sharply with this: they contain the best junior scholar, but not the best athlete, and are seldom named as best athlete or ladies' man. Their grades are a grade-level above that of the senior leading clique—a straight B average (6.0), compared to a C among the seniors.

The sophomore A-clique is similar to that of the juniors, although the best scholar is outside it; and the freshman clique has an athletic complexion similar to that of the seniors, except that its members *are* sometimes named as best scholar. Its grades, too, reflect a position somewhere between the high concern with studies of the junior boys, and the much lower concern of the senior boys. The variation in content of the cliques' activities does not mean that they come from different backgrounds, or that they are headed in different directions. The fathers of the non-scholastic senior leading crowd are white-collar or farmers with some college education, just as are the fathers of the scholastically oriented juniors.[8] All, or almost all, of the members of each clique plan to attend college.

---

8. Of these four leading cliques, the freshmen do come from a predominantly working-class background.

Thus, the association structure of the Marketville boys shows the same variation between grades that was indicated in Chapter III (see Table 14). The leading cliques seem to show quite different complexions from year to year, although there is never a cohesive subordinate clique to challenge their position.

BOYS IN ELMTOWN: COMPLEX IN STRUCTURE, STABLE IN CONTENT

The structure of association among Elmtown's boys exhibits much greater complexity than that of Marketville, as a comparison of Figures 7.1.1 and 7.1.2 (pp. 175, 176) shows. This is partly due to the larger size of Elmtown (266 boys, in comparison to 198 in Marketville), but the increased complexity is more than can be accounted for by the size difference. There are 12 cliques in Elmtown, involving 60 boys, while there are only 7 in Marketville, involving 36 boys. Furthermore, the cliques in Elmtown are more cohesive. There are four cliques in Elmtown with six or seven members and a nearly perfect pattern of mutual choices; no such cliques exist in Marketville. Yet this greater complexity of Elmtown's structure occurs with an almost identical number of choices per person (3.4 in both schools).

Despite the greater complexity in Elmtown, there is a definite leading clique in each grade. The difference lies in the existence of strong and cohesive out-cliques in each grade in Elmtown, cliques that are missing in Marketville.

The leading cliques of the four grades are very similar in content. The top athlete in each grade is in the leading clique, although the freshman is in with the sophomore leaders. The leading cliques tend to be "all-around" cliques, for their members receive choices as athletes, scholars, and ladies' men—although the juniors are weak as ladies' men and the seniors are weak as scholars. The leading cliques all have reasonably good grades (B− or C+ averages) and a majority of their members are going to college. Their focus, however, is not especially scholarly; the top scholar is outside the top clique in three of the four grades.

These boys' questionnaires show leisure patterns considerably more directed to adult pleasures than do those of the Marketville leading cliques. Cars are a preoccupation of the 4A clique and the 3A clique, and the members of each enjoy drinking and dating together. Their general orientation is less toward the adult-approved virtues of school activities, more toward commercial entertainment and "riding around." They combine reasonably good grades with strong out-of-school interests. However, their younger counterparts, the 2A and 1A cliques, show more nearly the same adult-approved leisure activities—hobbies, sports, and other games—as the leading crowds in Marketville. This may be due to the fact that they are too young for cars.

The other cliques in the school vary widely in their orientations. This is best illustrated by a comparison between junior "out-cliques," 3D on the one hand, 3B and 3C on the other. The 3D clique, which includes sophomores, juniors, and seniors, is religiously oriented; it is the most studious and has highest grades of any boys' clique in school. The 3B and 3C groups are quite different. These boys are low studiers, they are not going to college, and they are involved neither in athletics nor in other school activities. (Of the ten, only two, in 3B, are out for either football or basketball.) Their out-of-school activities are not religious, though they follow them religiously: The activities of the 3C boys include hanging out at the skating rink; the 3B boys prefer the pool hall. Both groups spend a good deal of time going around with the same girls. Their attire is levis, their hair is in ducktails, and those in 3B smoke regularly and drink beer. They all come from working-class backgrounds in town.

In sum, the association structure of Elmtown's boys is complex for its size, and shows a large number of well-formed cliques. The leading cliques are quite similar from grade to grade in their focus on athletics, dating, and, to some degree, scholastic matters. They get good grades, although not the highest. They show little of the grade-to-grade variability of the leading cliques in Marketville.

BOYS IN MAPLE GROVE: SIMPLE IN STRUCTURE, STABLE IN CONTENT

Maple Grove boys show an association structure (Figure 7.1.3), that visually is far more like that of Marketville than that of Elmtown. It contains only seven cliques, and only two of these, 3B and 4A, are large, cohesive cliques. Only 38 boys of the 217 in school are involved in cliques—a pattern very similar to Marketville. The freshman, junior, and senior A-cliques (there is no sophomore A-clique) are similar in background and orientation. They all include the top ladies' man in the grade and all include boys named as athletes and as scholars—although only one top scholar is included in a top clique, the 4A clique. The average grades are similar (ranging from B— to C+) and their college plans are similar—the majority intend to go to college, a minority are undecided. Their leisure habits are much alike from grade to grade, and more like those of Marketville's top cliques than those of Elmtown's.

The one large and cohesive out-clique in Maple Grove, 3B among the juniors, is similar to the skating-rink crowd in Elmtown. Cars are the primary interest, and ducktail haircuts are the style. They are heavy laters, and only two of seven are out for football. Their parents include farmers, blue-collar workers, and white-collar workers; and their educational backgrounds are mixed as well. Most of them smoke, although only one indicates that he drinks. Only two of them work, in contrast to the 3B and 3C groups in Elmtown. In general, their activities indicate somewhat more of a middle-class orientation—but nevertheless an away-from-school orientation—than that of the 3B and 3C groups in Elmtown. In other words, the members of 3B don't hang out in the skating rink or the pool hall, but they work on their cars together, ride around, stir up some excitement, and go out with girls together. There are two hangouts in town, one where the leading crowd and its hangers-on congregate. This group hangs out at the other place, clearly setting it apart from the leading crowd, orienting it away from school-related events and activities.

In sum, the association pattern of Maple Grove constitutes a cross between Elmtown and Marketville. It exhibits a structural similarity to Marketville, with little organization beyond the leading clique in each grade. But like Elmtown, and unlike Marketville, the cliques are not highly variable from grade to grade in the content of their activities. They all include some scholastic activity, some athletic activity, and some social activity, containing, in every grade, the top ladies' man. The structure may be termed "simple in structure, stable in content."

BOYS IN GREEN JUNCTION: VARIABLE IN STRUCTURE, SIMPLE IN CONTENT

The association pattern in Green Junction is somewhat different from the others examined so far. Its difference has two dimensions: in content, its leading cliques are uniformly athletic; in structure, it exhibits not one, but two leading cliques in the senior class. This description over-simplifies matters, but it indicates the general pattern shown by Figure 7.1.4.

The sophomore, junior, and senior leading cliques are characterized by their high number of choices as best athletes.[9] A member of the sophomore leading clique receives some mentions as best scholar, but otherwise the cliques are solidly athletic. They may not always contain the *top* athlete, but every member is out for football, and each of the cliques receive a number of mentions as best athlete.

Among the seniors, there is a second leading clique, fully distinct from

---

9. The clique labeled 1A, as the freshman leading clique, is in fact not the leading crowd, for it receives only 11 total choices as such. The top athlete and ladies' man in this grade, who is not in this clique, receives alone more leading-crowd mentions than this. This difficulty arises because those named as the leading crowd among the freshmen did not name one another enough as friends to constitute a clique by our definition.

the first. This group is labeled 4A$_2$, since its members were also mentione —less often than the members of 4A$_1$—as members of the leading crow This clique is fully distinct from the top senior clique, with no mutu; choices joining them. This "second" group is composed of boys activ in school, and its members receive their full share of friendship choice. It studies far more than the top clique does—1.3 hours, compared wit 0.1 for the 4A$_1$ clique. Its grades are higher, although not greatly so. Th members of 4A$_2$ all plan on going to college, in contrast to complet indecision among the members of the top clique; and they come fror high-status backgrounds—all managers' or professionals' sons. They ar more oriented to other adult-opposed values than are the members of th top cliques. For instance, all the boys in the 4A$_1$ clique in Green Junctio drink beer, but in the 4A$_2$ clique, only two of six drink beer.

The division is not that of athletes vs. non-athletes. The boy who is b consensus the best athlete is in the second clique; but he is a relativel high studier, and he's going to college.

This peculiar bifurcation in the senior leading crowd presents a differ ent pattern than in any of the schools. It may be merely a function o size, but the evidence suggests not—for these cliques are fully distinct with no choices joining them. The single case does not allow a stron inference, but a possible source of the cleavage is suggested below.

Non-Scholastic Orientation, and the Emergence of a Second Leading Crowd

The senior leading crowd in Green Junction seems to have branche into two groups along the lines of scholastic orientation—high-studier vs. low-studiers, those interested in learning vs. those not, those going to college vs. those not. In Green Junction, the latter have more statu in the adolescent system, and the former conform more to the desire of teachers.[10]

Whether the bifurcation existed throughout the four years or formec only in the senior year with the divergence of post–high-school paths i impossible to tell here. The question may not even be meaningful, fo

---

10. The two groups differ in response to a question of what the teachers in thi school are like I. 142, with the second clique checking an average of 2 out of possible positive items concerning teachers, and the top clique checking an averag of only 0.8.

the junior-class A-cliques are less highly structured, since some high-status juniors are drawn off by the leaders among the seniors. Perhaps one or two junior boys, who were in a high-status senior clique that was not oriented to learning (like the one junior, No. 221, in clique 4A₁) become, in their senior year, the nucleus of the new non-scholastic clique, composed of part of the leading crowd, leaving others to re-form and constitute a second leading clique.

Why, then, does such a bifurcation not occur in the other schools? The answer is most clearly seen in Maple Grove. There, all but one of the 4A clique members are going to college, all study a reasonable amount, have a postive orientation to learning, and are positively oriented to teachers (an average of over 2.3 positive items checked). They include the boy named as best scholar, although their orientation is primarily social and athletic. They are not a highly academically oriented group, and some show a high interest in customized cars, but they do not represent a non-academic extreme as does the 4A₁ group in Green Junction. They are enough scholastically oriented to gain the support of those boys in the student body who are interested in studies, and the implicit support of teachers, but they never lose the attention of the school by relaxing their athletic and social activities. The boys who were forced to form a second group in Green Junction would have been in this 4A clique in Maple Grove. There, membership in the A-clique is consistent with studying enough to get into college, and with the fairly mild and middle-class good times not found in the 4A₁ clique in Green Junction.

The situation is similar in Marketville, although it seems to come about less naturally there. The community is intermediate between Maple Grove, on the one hand, and Elmtown and Green Junction, on the other, in the proportion of white-collar families it contains. Thus, the leading crowds naturally include fewer boys with a high educational or occupational background. Nevertheless, the leading crowds are a small fraction of the school, and thus have much room for flexibility. Consequently, the 4A group in Marketville is like that in Maple Grove in background and orientation, but even *more* oriented to adult standards. It is not interested in customized cars; it ranks "pleasing my parents" extremely high (a rank of 1.8, compared to 2.3 in the 4A clique of Maple Grove, 2.5 in that of Elmstown, and 2.2 in that of Green Junction); and checks an average of 2.5 out of 3 positive items concerning teachers.

Partly due to the population composition of the community, partly due to school policy, which focuses attention on good students, Marketville has a dominant senior clique that is relatively adult-oriented. It is primarily athletic in orientation, does not include the best scholar, nor are any of its members mentioned as the best scholar; but it "has room" for the popular boy whose concerns are relatively serious. Its interests center more around relatively mild and middle-class fancies; its norms do not pull a boy away from studies.

In part, the configuration in Green Junction is the result of chance combinations of personalities, and factors specific to that particular senior class; the junior class may structure itself in very different ways when it comes to be the senior class. Nevertheless, it suggests a pattern that may be more general in schools where athletics is important: the very high-status group among the boys themselves will be a group that gains its status and is held together largely by its athletic achievements; in a predominantly working-class community, many of the boys in this group will be uninterested in learning, and thus "too far to the left" to gain the full support of teachers. At the same time, this clique cannot encompass all the popular and high-status boys, whose status may have been gained through athletics, but who are also oriented toward scholastic matters. These boys, then, with the implicit or explicit support of the teachers, will have a group of their own, more adult-oriented than the top group. The top group expresses the interests and values of the majority of boys, but those who are oriented to educational goals look toward the second group that embodies these goals.

This is not to say that the second group is devoid of status, or that the top group is rebellious toward school activities. The $4A_2$ group in Green Junction *does* have some student status, and the $4A_1$ group is very much at the center of things in the school. The rebellious, anti-school groups are still a different set of boys, with little status in either the adolescent system or in the eyes of teachers.

It would be incorrect also to view the 4A cliques in Marketville and Maple Grove as strongly oriented to academic matters. Their primary focus of interest remains athletics, social activities, and similar pursuits. In each of these cliques, athletics is most often mentioned as the activity they "have most in common," and their interest in scholastic matters is never intense. Academic effort, as it occurs in American high schools, is highly individual, and thus offers little basis either for group formation or for support by the student body as a whole. Because of its very individualism, it pulls a boy *away* from the center of school activities.

The 4A cliques in Marketville, Elmtown, and Maple Grove represent a middle ground between concern with extracurricular activities, such as football, which generate group cohesion and student-body support, and concern with studies, the abstract ideal of teachers. The teachers must compromise, in a sense, in giving their support to a "leading group" far from this abstract ideal, because that ideal constitutes neither a cohesive group nor gains student support.[11] This is indicated well by the response of teachers in these schools to a question:

T.17–18. If you could see any of three boys elected president of the senior class, which would you rather it would be?

Brilliant student	19.0%
Athletic star	3.7
Leader in extracurricular activities	72.3
Number of teachers	(401)

The teachers want to see the brilliant student as senior-class president far less often than they do the activities leader. When asked why they named the boy they did, the largest number (32.7 per cent) mentioned his leadership ability and his responsibility. Next most frequently mentioned as a reason for naming the leaders in activities (and most frequently mentioned for naming the athlete) was because "he gets along better with the students." In other words, the brilliant student is not seen as the appropriate background for class president, partly because he is not seen as having administrative ability, and partly because he is not "close to" the other students and is not a focal point of attention for them. Again, this suggests that the organization of activities in these high schools acts to dampen enthusiasm for concentrating one's energy on scholarly matters. Teachers as well as students see the brilliant student as a boy whose interests pull him away from the center of school activities and make of him too much an individualist.

Athletics as the "Organizer" of Freshman Leading Cliques

The general focus of common interests of the A-cliques goes through a transition as the four years of school progress. Their initial focus is around athletics in each of these four schools. In the four schools, each

11. There is also evidence that teachers do not like students who are especially creative or original because these students will not sit passively still and be taught. Especially interesting results in this direction have been found by Jacob Getzels, who compared two groups of students in a university laboratory school: those with especially high IQ's but relatively low creativity, and those with high creativity (and equal achievement on standardized achievement tests), but lower IQ. Teachers liked the creative group less because they conformed less to the teachers' plans. See J. W. Getzels and P. W. Jackson, "The Study of Giftedness: A Multidimensional Approach," in *The Gifted Student*, Cooperative Research Monograph No. 2, U.S. Department of Health, Education, and Welfare (Washington: United States Government Printing Office, 1960) pp. 1–18.

of the twenty-three members of freshman A-cliques played either basket-ball or football. Most played both. In the upper grades, however, these cliques change their character, apparently as a function of the climate of the school. In Green Junction, the school in which football is the primary ladder for status, every single member of the top A-clique in every grade is out for football. Only nine of these nineteen boys, how-ever, are out for basketball. In Marketville, where scholastic success is relevant to status along with athletic success, one out of five sophomores, three out of five juniors, and two out of six seniors are not out for *either* football or basketball. Similarly, in Elmtown and Maple Grove, the leading cliques in later years become less uniformly athletic.

Athletics, then, seems to provide the initial focal point around which the freshman class centers its attention. Chapter X will examine the greater "visibility" of the star athlete then of the star scholar among the freshmen, a visibility which derives from the very nature of athletic activity in high schools. It is the one activity that creates strong association patterns at the very beginning of school, providing a tightly knit unit that commands the attention of the school.

Thus, the athletic team seems to provide the "starting point" for the boys' leading crowd in the school. Whether the crowd continues to be wholly athletic through the four years of school evidently depends on the existence of other status dimensions.

MINORITY INTEREST AND CLIQUES CROSS-CUTTING GRADES

Most cliques in these schools are wholly within one grade. About 85 per cent of friendship choices, in fact, are confined to the same grade. But there are a few cliques that cut across grades. The 234C clique in Marketville, and the 3D clique in Elmtown—which includes sophomores and seniors along with its majority of juniors—are the two cliques that cut across three grades. Why does this happen?

The interests of the 234C clique in Marketville lie not in athletics, nor in school activities, nor in dating, nor in cars. The members have one thing in common—religious interests. They all attend church every Sunday; five out of seven report that religion is the thing they have most in common; and five out of seven say they would most like to be a mis-sionary (question I.68). The members of this group are never mentioned as being in the leading crowd, nor are they interested in being in the leading crowd. None want to be remembered in school as most popular; only one would like to be remembered as an athletic star; and five as a brilliant student (one did not answer). The orientations of this group depart radically from the athletically-centered adolescent culture, focus-ing very specifically on religion.

The 3D clique of Elmtown has an almost identical religious orientation: all go to church every Sunday; three of the five members mention religion as their common activity; all but one rank "living up to religious ideals" first; two want to be missionaries. It too is scholastically oriented, and away from the adolescent culture: all five members want to be remembered as a brilliant student, and none want to be in the leading crowd. It makes higher grades than any other clique in Elmtown.

The distinctive interest of these two cliques suggests the answer to the cross-class choices. The intensity of the religious interest and the small number of people who share it force these boys outside their class to fill their needs. If this intense interest were focused on football, they would have no difficulty in finding around them fellows to share the interest. But because they are interested in matters that concern the majority of adolescents very little, they must either forsake the interest —as some certainly do—or look beyond the confines of their grade for friends.

THE CONSOLIDATION OF STATUS OVER TIME

In the first three years of high school, the A-cliques whose members are named as being in the leading crowd often fail to contain the boys most often named as friends. Among the seniors, however, the consolidation of these two kinds of status (being named as a friend and being in the leading clique) occurs. In Marketville, where it is least pronounced, the six-man 4A clique contains six of the eleven seniors most often named as friends; in Elmtown, the six-man 4A clique includes all the six seniors most often named as friends; in Maple Grove, the nine-man 4A clique includes nine of the eleven most-named seniors; in Green Junction, the five-man 4A clique includes the four most-named seniors. Nothing approaching this consistency occurs in the lower grades, in part because their most popular boys are sometimes pulled upward into a group in the next higher grade. For example, in Green Junction the second most popular junior is the fifth member of the $4A_1$ clique, while in Elmtown, the most-named sophomore is mixed up in a network consisting mostly of juniors, while the tightly knit leading crowd in his grade must get along without him. Hence, the leading crowds among the lower grades are sometimes undercut by the siphoning-off of their most popular members into upper grades. This sort of thing occurs generally in societies where there is movement between social classes: the potential leaders of the lower classes are drawn off by the opportunities for individual advancement, and cannot serve as leaders for the lower classes. The process seems quite similar to that exhibited in these schools.

Thus, one reason for the consolidation of leading-crowd status and personal popularity among the seniors is that they are the "upper class," and none of their leaders can be drawn away from the senior leading crowd as they draw away popular juniors. A second reason for the very great coincidence among seniors between popularity and being in the leading clique is that these boys are in effect the leaders of the *total* system. They have come into their full power, while their counterparts in earlier grades are standing-in-waiting and thus do not garner so many choices from others in their grade.

THE FOUR SCHOOLS: RELATION OF VALUES TO STRUCTURE

The association structures in these four schools are closely related to the values discussed earlier. The structures clearly show the *absence* of scholastic activity among most of the Green Junction leading cliques, the *combination* of scholastic interest with other more dominant concerns in Elmtown and Maple Grove leading cliques, and the year-to-year *variation* in scholastic concern among Marketville's leading cliques. These differences correspond to the results of Chapter V: a focus on the "all-around boy," who is athlete, ladies' man, and, to some extent, scholar in Elmtown and Maple Grove; a focus on the athlete in Green Junction; and in Marketville, *independent* status for the athlete and the scholar, not combined, but seen as two separate roles. The analysis of association patterns in Marketville shows how this independent status occurs— through sharp year-to-year shifts in the dominant interests of the leading clique. Some consequences of this structural peculiarity, which Marketville shares with no other schools in this study, will be discussed in Chapter IX.

The Association Structures of Small-School Girls

The proliferation and complexity of the girls' networks of association demands a more detailed analysis than that of the boys. This is necessary both because of the complexity of the structures and because of the greater variability in these different structures. The simplest structure is the smallest of the four, Marketville.

GIRLS IN MARKETVILLE: SIMPLE DOMINANCE, INTERLOCKING ELITES

Considering first the structure alone, the top cliques in each of the three upper grades are connected by common members—a senior joining the 4A and $3A_1$ cliques, and a junior joining the $3A_1$ and $2A_1$ cliques. The diagram of Figure 7.3 will simplify the picture. Each clique is drawn as a unit; the vertical dimension indicates the relative status of the clique, in terms of the number of mentions its members received as members of the leading crowd. The horizontal dimension is year in school. A connection between two cliques by a mutual member is indicated by a double line. (Other connections, through a direct choice and through three or fewer intervening persons, will be represented in later diagrams in this chapter by a single solid line and a broken line respectively. If there are more than three intervening persons, the cliques are not connected in the diagrams of Figures 7.3 to 7.6.)

As this diagram indicates, the A or A_1 cliques of each grade are practically unchallenged. There is, to be sure, a second clique in the sophomore and junior classes, the members of which get more than an average of two mentions as being in the leading crowd, but only among the sophomores does the A_2 group have a status at all comparable to that of the leading clique.

In Table 37 several features of the structure stand out. First, consider the proportion in each clique whose fathers had at least some college education and the proportion whose fathers hold white-collar occupations. In every grade but sophomore, the leading clique has a higher-status background than the others in that grade. In each A_1 clique except $2A_1$, white-collar backgrounds predominate; and in $1A_1$, $2A_1$, and $4A$, at least half have had some college. Compared to the other cliques in

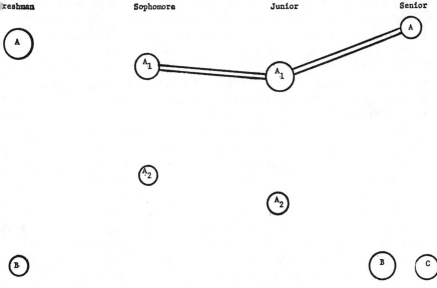

Figure 7.3—Status and connections among girls' cliques in Marketville.

these grades, the top cliques are of considerably higher educational and occupational backgrounds. This does not mean that they are exclusively middle-class; in every leading clique, there are girls from working-class families and farm families—although farm families, particularly in this area of rich farmlands, may be well-to-do.

Table 37—Characteristics of girls' cliques in Marketville*

Clique	Size	Educ.	Occ.	Study hrs/day	Date No. wk	Smoke, drink	Be re-membered S–A–P	College plans Y–U–N	Grades
4A	5	.8	3–1–1	2.8	1.2	0	2–3–0	4–0–1	6.6
4B	8	0	1–3–3	1.9	1.1	0	3–2–3	2–3–3	5.8
4C	6	0	0–3–2	1.9	2.0	.1	2–4–0	0–0–6	3.5
3A₁	9	.2	6–2–1	1.3	.6	.3	2–3–4	8–1–0	7.0
3A₂	5	.2	3–0–2	1.5	2.9	.6	1–2–2	1–2–2	4.6
2A₁	7	.5	3–3–1	1.6	.7	.1	2–2–3	3–4–0	6.0
2A₂	4	.5	4–0–0	1.1	2.8	.4	2–1–1	2–0–2	6.5
1A	10	.6	7–3–0	1.4	.3	0	3–1–6	5–1–2	6.3
1B	4	.4	0–1–1	2.3	.2	.3	0–2–2	0–4–0	3.3

* Listed in the "Educ." column is the proportion with some college (I, q.58/7, 8, 9). Under "Occ." is father's occupation, with white-collar, worker, farmer listed in that order. Under "Smoke, drink" is a score determined by adding the total number of smokers and the number of drinkers (I, q.167, 168) (counting 1 for occasional, 2 for regular) and dividing by twice the total number of people. Thus, if everyone smoked and drank occasionally, the index would be 1.0; if all smoked occasionally, but none drank, it would be 0.5. In the column "Be remembered," are listed the number saying "brilliant Student," "leader in Activities" and "most Popular" in answer to I, q.131. In the "College plans" column are listed the number saying Yes, Undecided, and No to the question about attending college (I, q.115). In the "Grades" column are listed average grades in the present semester, on an 8-point scale (8 = A, 6 = B, . . . 0 = F). In all the listings of absolute numbers, the total may be smaller than the clique size because of failures to answer.

Other attributes, of course, besides family background are important for membership in a leading clique. However, there is no activity for girls that plays the kind of role that athletics does for membership in the top cliques of freshman boys. Almost all members of *all* cliques, not just the top one, report participation in some school activity in their freshman year. The lack of any distinguishing activity among girls' leading cliques is another reflection of the absence of such means of achieving status for girls. Family background and previous associations create much stronger barriers to mobility for girls.

Yet the top cliques do differ in their activities. The two A cliques among sophomores, especially because of their background similarity, illustrate this well. Their differences in orientation are shown most easily by their dating frequency: the 2A₁ group has an average of only .7 dates per week, compared to 2.8 dates per week for the 2A₂ clique. Moreover, the 2A₁ clique studies an average of 1.6 hours a night, compared to 1.1 hours for the 2A₂ clique; all the 2A₁ girls are contemplating attending college, while half the 2A₂ girls say they are not going; and the smoking-drinking index is only .1 for 2A₁ (one girl of the seven reported smoking occasionally), compared to .4 for the 2A₂ group (two girls of the four reported smoking occasionally, and one reported drinking beer occasionally). In short, the $2A_2$ girls are considerably more interested in a good time, in dating, and a social life, than are the $2A_1$ girls. They *are* good students, however; their grade average is 6.5 (B+), slightly higher than that of the A_1 clique. The difference between the two cliques apparently lies almost wholly in their social life; the top clique hardly dates, while the second dates a great deal.

The division between these two cliques, and a similar division among the juniors, illustrates the two components of the leading crowd discussed in Chapter III: the concern, on the one hand, with propriety, a good reputation, conformity to adult demands and, on the other, with keeping out in front of the crowd, "stirring up a little excitement," and staying in the center of things. Some quantity of each of this seems necessary (in Marketville) for membership in the leading crowd, but associational cleavages occur within the larger crowd depending on the relative emphasis on the two components. It is probably true that the cleavage is greatest at the point where dating begins: some girls begin before others, and the crowd splits into two.

Recalling earlier information about the scholastically oriented climate of Marketville, it is characteristic of the girls in this school that the sophomore clique with greater emphasis on propriety, less on social activities and a good time, has higher status among the other girls. This is not to say that the top clique is seriously scholastic, for neither it nor the smaller second clique receive more than a few mentions for the best scholar. The girl most often so named is off to the side with two friends, not mentioned as a member of the leading crowd nor in either of the leading cliques.

The senior girls in the 4A clique exemplify propriety, conformity to adult standards, and involvement in school activities more than do any of the other A cliques in the school. They report that their common interests center around school activities; they study very diligently; none smoke or drink; all want to be remembered as a leader in activities or as a brilliant student. This clique includes, as does the $3A_1$ clique and the $1A_1$ clique, the girl most often named as best scholar. It also includes the girl named as best dressed, and the girl most attractive to boys. However, in contrast to the other three schools to be examined shortly, the girl who is most attractive to boys is *not* in the top clique in the other three grades, while the top scholar *is* in the top clique in all grades except sophomore.

It should be mentioned that while Marketville is predominantly Protestant (and religion is taken more seriously here than in any of the other communities), 16 per cent of the students are Catholic. They come from both white-collar and working-class families, and there is very little, if any, tendency for cliques to be restricted to one religious group. For example, the 1A clique and the $3A_1$ clique each have three Catholic members.[12]

The girls in the 1B, 4B, and 4C cliques in Marketville have quite different backgrounds from the girls in the A-cliques discussed above. They are made up of predominantly workers and farmers daughters. The members of the two senior cliques date a lot, and their activities together include dancing and double dating. Yet even they conform closely to adult standards. Some members emphasized in their questionnaires that their group had *quiet* good times. Their social backgrounds could lead in a very different, antischool and hedonistic direction, yet they do not. They are positively oriented to the school and its teachers, and girls in all three cliques devote more time to homework than any other clique except the 4A clique. Their behavior, along with that of the A-cliques, is consistent with the general impression this school leaves upon the observer: a student body largely controlled by the school and community, kept more nearly as children, less as semi-adult "teen-agers" than in any of the other communities.

The lower-class backgrounds of these "out-cliques," together with the unchallenged dominance of the A-cliques in the school's status system, show the other half of the coin—the importance of "family background" for being in the leading clique in the school.

Before turning to the girls in Elmtown, it may be noted that the variations between the four classes among *girls'* top cliques in Marketville shows little relation to the variation among *boys'* top cliques. The senior boys were least scholastically oriented, and the juniors most so; the senior girls show most devotion to studies and get high grades, topped only by the junior A_1 clique.

GIRLS IN ELMTOWN: FLUID, COMPLEX STRUCTURE

Because Elmtown's high school was studied some years ago, its clique structure is of particular interest. *Elmtown's Youth* indicates the powerful effect of family status upon the child's status and chances for success in the school.[13] The results of the present research indicate no such effect, but a very different state of affairs.

---

12. This lack of religious lines in association is not universal among these schools. Among the large schools, religious lines are very important in friendship in suburban Executive Heights, which has a sizeable number of Protestants, Catholics, and Jews.

13. Hollingshead, *Elmtown's Youth*. Other research on this community carried out at the same time is published in W. Lloyd Warner, *Democracy in Jonesville* (New York: Harper, 1949).

Although Elmtown includes only one and a half times as many girls as does Marketville, the association structure is far more complex, as a glance at the two sociograms, Figures 7.2.1 and 7.2.2, will quickly show. The number of cliques in this school (Table 36) is over twice that among the girls in Marketville, and more than in any other of these small schools.

The number of cliques indicates only faintly the complexity of the structure. Each grade except the juniors has real competition for status among several A-cliques. Figure 7.4, showing the status positions of the various cliques and the structural connections, contrasts dramatically with the pure dominance of Marketville. In every grade except the juniors, an A_2 clique is extremely close in status to the A_1 clique. In the sophomore and senior years, these "second" cliques are completely separate from the A_1 cliques, and have quite different orientations from theirs.

Table 38 summarizes some of the characteristics of these cliques. There are far fewer college backgrounds and fewer white-collar backgrounds here than in Marketville. This is only partly due to difference in the population characteristics of the schools, for as Figure 4.5 (p. 108) indicated, the backgrounds of the student bodies are not very different (16 to 25 per cent fathers with some college). The difference seems to

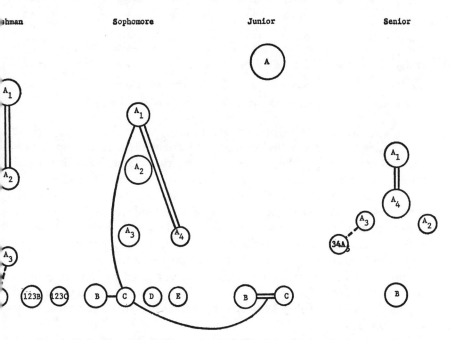

Figure 7.4—Status and connections among girls' cliques in Elmtown.

be due more to a different pattern of dominance in the two schools. In Marketville, the middle-class, college-oriented girls, traveling in fairly large groups, "rule the roost." In Elmtown, many of the working-class girls, whose counterparts in Marketville recede into two- or three-girl friendships, come out in full force.

Table 38—Characteristics of girls' cliques in Elmtown*

Clique	Size	Educ.	Occ.	Study hrs/day	Date No. wk	Smoke, drink	Be re- membered S–A–P	College plans Y–U–N	Grades
4A₁	7	.1	3–1–2	1.5	2.6	.1	2–2–3	2–1–4	5.7
4A₂	4	.3	1–1–1	0.1	2.8	1.1	0–0–4	0–0–4	5.3
4A₃	4	.3	2–0–1	1.3	2.0	.2	0–1–3	1–1–2	6.3
4A₄	9	0	2–5–1	0.8	1.1	.6	1–1–7	1–1–7	4.3
4B	6	0	0–6–0	1.7	1.5	.1	4–1–1	1–0–5	5.5
3A	14	.1	5–8–0	1.3	2.3	.4	3–2–9	1–3–10	3.6
3B	6	.3	2–2–2	1.8	0.7	0	1–4–1	3–1–2	5.0
3C	4	.3	1–2–0	1.8	2.0	0	1–2–1	2–1–1	6.0
2A₁	6	.8	5–0–1	1.9	0.2	0	3–2–1	6–0–0	6.8
2A₂	9	.2	1–1–6	1.0	0.5	.3	0–0–9	1–2–7	4.3
2A₃	5	0	0–4–1	2.0	0.9	0	1–0–4	1–0–3	6.2
2A₄	4	—	—	—	—	—	—	—	—
2B	6	.2	2–3–0	1.8	0.2	0	2–4–0	0–0–6	4.3
2C	4	.5	1–3–0	1.5	0.3	0	2–1–1	3–1–0	5.8
2D	4	0	2–1–0	1.0	3.2	1.3	1–0–2	1–1–2	—
2E	4	0	3–0–1	1.6	0.2	0	0–1–3	1–0–3	—
1A₁	8	.7	7–1–0	1.5	1.8	0	1–3–4	5–0–3	6.5
1A₂	5	0	1–3–0	0.8	0.6	0	2–0–3	1–0–3	4.4
1A₃	4	.7	0–0–4	1.2	0.1	0	0–0–3	1–3–0	7.0
1B	4	0	2–1–0	2.3	0.0	0	2–4–0	1–3–0	6.5
123B	5	0	0–1–1	0.5	2.8	.6	0–1–4	0–1–4	3.3
123C	4	.3	0–4–0	0.9	0.7	.5	2–1–1	0–0–4	2.5
34A₅	4	.3	3–1–0	1.0	2.8	1.1	1–0–3	0–1–3	4.5

* Explanation of each column of the table is provided in a footnote to Table 37.

Just as the structure of association in Elmtown is different from that of Marketville girls, the backgrounds and orientations of the top cliques are different: Among the seniors, there are two cliques of almost equal status, 4A₁ and 4A₂. The first is the only predominantly Catholic clique in the school, containing five Catholics and two Protestants. (In this school, as in Marketville, the cliques show little tendency to be religiously homogenous.) The contrast in orientations between the two cliques is extreme. The 4A₂ clique studies hardly at all; its members smoke regularly, drink occasionally or regularly; and they date more than any other group in school. By any criterion, they are oriented to "having a good time." All but one, for example, rank "having a good time" above a good reputation, and as Table 38 shows, all would like to be remembered as most popular.

This group appears to be somewhat puzzling, especially since it contains the girl most often named as the best student in the senior class, and its grades are reasonably good. Yet this seeming discrepancy is no accident, nor it it an isolated incident. The preceding year, the same phenomenon occurred: the girl who was recognized as the best scholar in the senior class had joined a different crowd in her sophomore year. She had decided, she said in an interview, that she wanted to "have a little fun," so she shifted to a "fast" crowd with characteristics similar to those of this year's $4A_2$ group. The contrast with Marketville is great, for there the "fast" crowds of girls have little status with their peers, and would be far less attractive to a girl faced with such a choice. In Marketville, moreover, there were no really cohesive "fast" cliques; all seemed to follow the general pattern set by the adult-oriented leading cliques. The "fast" girls were more nearly atomized, less organized into cohesive cliques.

The $4A_1$ clique, although not predominantly college-going, is far more oriented to school activities than the $4A_2$ clique. Yet compared to the A-cliques in Marketville, it is oriented to good times rather than studies. Its members date more, are more interested in being remembered as most popular, are mostly not going to college. They are closely associated with clique $4A_4$, which is explicitly out for a good time. In short, only relative to the given adolescent community in Elmtown are they "good" girls.

Of the activities mentioned by the girls in Elmtown's top senior cliques, "riding around" comes up frequently. This is a common activity in Elmtown, where customized cars are prevalent among the leading groups of boys, among whom a frequent pastime is simply cruising around looking for something to do, someone to "drag with." Such activities are common throughout the country; what is striking is that here, in contrast to Marketville, it is the activity of the *leading* cliques.

The other strongly cohesive group of some size in the senior class is 4B. Composed of girls described in every school as the "rest of the school," the "girls who don't count," they are neither looked up to nor looked down on; they simply attract no attention of any kind. Content to merge with the background, they are not "stirring up excitement," either as the center of school activities or as a free-wheeling pleasure-ent crowd. Characteristic of such groups, they study a lot and are positively (though not *actively*) oriented to school. Also characteristic of these groups, they choose nurse above model, actress or artist, or schoolteacher; and they are oriented to being remembered as a brilliant student, rather than either a leader in activities (which tends to be chosen by the elites in most schools, as Figure 4.13 showed) or most popular which tends to be chosen by the fast and loose crowd like $4A_2$ and $4A_4$).

In the junior class, there is no real competition for the leading crowd. The 3A group gets almost all choices, and it includes the girl named as best dressed and the girl most attractive to boys. It contrasts with 3B in both background and orientation. In background, it is more working-class and lower-education than 3B and 3C. Its members smoke and drink (while the 3B and 3C members don't); they date about three times as often as the 3B group; they study somewhat less; they are more interested in the "most-popular" image; and they are oriented away from college, while the 3B and 3C complex is predominantly oriented to college. The grades of the 3A girls average 3.6 (C—); those of the other two cliques average 5.0 and 6.0 (B— and B).

The over-all picture of the junior class is one of a status "upset"; those girls who by background and orientation would, in Marketville, be the leading crowd (and would, incidentally, have the cohesive strength and size that the 3A group here has), have little status among their peers. Not only are they unnamed as members of the leading crowd, but they are also mentioned an average of only 1.6 times per person as someone to be liked or be friends with by their classmates, compared to an average of 3.1 times for the 3A crowd (some of whose members mention the skating rink as a frequent hangout). In other words, in the junior class, and to some extent in the senior class, the girls whom other girls aspire to know and be like are those whose activities are considerably less in accord with adult standards than those of most girls in the school.

In the sophomore class, the status situation is just the opposite. Here the "good" girls of $2A_1$ are more often mentioned as the leading crowd. The $2A_2$ girls, a completely distinct group, are mentioned quite frequently, but they acknowledge the dominance of the $2A_1$ group by saying (with two exceptions) that they are not in the leading crowd. The backgrounds and orientation of the $2A_1$ group are the white-collar backgrounds found in Marketville A-groups. This group has the highest educational and occupational background of any clique of girls in the school, it has quite high grades, contains the girls who are best scholar, best dressed, and most attractive to boys. It is a completely college-going group; its members study about two hours a night and date seldom. It and its satellite, the $2A_4$ group, epitomize the general characteristics of the whole complex of cliques in the upper part of the Elmtown sociogram (Figure 7.2.2), characteristics that differ radically from the more tightly knit cliques found in the lower half of the sociogram. This difference between the sophomores and the other grades in Elmtown is quite evident in responses to the question regarding "what it takes" to get into the leading crowd. Among the sophomores, 21 per cent of the girls mentioned that it took "good grades" or "intelligence," while only 6 per cent of the freshmen and three juniors and seniors considered grades to be important.

Also striking is the relatively conformist behavior of the remaining cliques among the sophomores. The $2A_2$ and $2A_3$ cliques, predominantly farm and working-class, are oriented to adult-approved goals, and much less concerned with "a good time" than are their counterparts in other grades. The whole set of cliques in the sophomore class follows a similar pattern. Whether or not this is because of the norms established by the top clique among the sophomores can only be conjectured here. What is evident is that all the cliques in this class follow far more the pattern of Marketville than that of other grades in Elmtown.

The freshman class is in still a different situation. In background, in general orientation to school, in grades, and in college plans, the top clique conforms to the middle-class value system best exemplified by the A-cliques in Marketville and by the $2A_1$ and $2A_4$ cliques in Elmtown. However, its members date far more than any other freshman group, and are oriented to social matters generally. The other white-collar-background clique, 1B, on the fringes of the upper complex of cliques, conforms to the more usual freshman pattern of little dating.

In sum, then, the status systems in the four grades of this school are radically different. In the junior class, the fast crowd holds sway; in the sophomore, a very proper crowd. The seniors have counterparts of these two extremes—but both of them shifted in a hedonistic direction—in nearly equal status positions. The freshmen top crowd seems to combine within itself most of the middle-class values, together with heavy dating. These are attributes that may become incompatible, forcing girls to choose between them, as did the above-mentioned best student, who chose a good time.

The Cross-class Groups and Deviant Minorities among Elmtown Girls. Three cliques of Elmtown do not have a majority in any single grade. Two of these, 123B and 123C, cut across the three early grades, while one, $34A_5$, includes juniors and seniors. These cliques constitute, in varying degrees, the "rough crowd." Their black "rock and roll" jackets are a symbol in this school of orientation to a good time, cars, music, the skating rink, and unconcern with school.

When the choice is forced between friends and parents, or friends and school, these groups are all oriented to friends. Almost all smoke or drink, or do both. Their favorite singer is Elvis Presley, while that of most of the adolescent culture is Pat Boone, who dispenses rock and roll without the implicit deviance and rebellion in Presley's image. In short, these girls are extremely hedonistic, antischool, and rebellious. Their deviance is beyond that of the groups examined earlier (excepting $4A_2$) which are in serious contention for status and attention from their peers. Yet they are not "part of the background" as is 4B. They count in the system, but they are so oriented to out-of-school activities that even in this culture, where adult values have little currency, they do not have status among the adolescents as a whole.

It may be no accident that these groups cut across grades, as did the two religiously oriented boys' cliques. Almost the only cliques in these schools without a majority of members in one grade, or cutting across three grades, are the two boys' cliques in Marketville (234C) and Elmtown (3D), interested in religion, and these three girls' cliques, interested in rock and roll and a good time. Perhaps the deviance of these interests from those of the majority requires crossing grade lines to find friends who share them; perhaps it is the intensity of these deviant interests which *allows* grade lines to be broken down in clique formation. That these two interests, religion and rock and roll, are at opposite poles on a continuum of hedonism is not so important as that they set off a boy or girl from his fellows and lead him to look beyond the confines of his own grade for fellow-devotees. "Fans" and "fanatics" have an interest that pervades their behavior, including their selection of friends.

The same pressure to look for friends beyond the confines of one's grade is probably evident among boys or girls intensely interested in studies, since a strong interest like this is shared by only a small minority. But here grade boundaries present a barrier, because common problems and concerns in schoolwork exist only within one grade. Such activities may, as a consequence, be confined to two- or three-man cliques, for the lack of a larger number of interested fellows in the same grade.

A final note before turning to Maple Grove girls: In Elmtown as in Marketville, there is no relation apparent between the values and interests of the top cliques among boys and girls. The sophomore top clique of boys does not stand out from the junior and senior top cliques, as is true among the girls. Without knowledge of dating patterns, the way in which this separation of values occurs is not evident.

GIRLS IN MAPLE GROVE: SIMPLE MIDDLE-CLASS DOMINANCE, SOCIAL IN ORIENTATION

The sociogram of the girls in Maple Grove (Figure 7.2.3) is far more reminiscent, in its general configuration, of the Marketville sociogram than that of Elmtown. The structure is simple, with a pattern of unchallenged dominance in every grade (See also Figure 7.5). Only among the seniors are there two A-cliques, and they are closely connected, even having a member in common.

The general characteristics of the cliques are shown in Table 39 The difference in background between the dominant cliques here and in Elmtown is great. Here, in every grade, the A-cliques are primarily

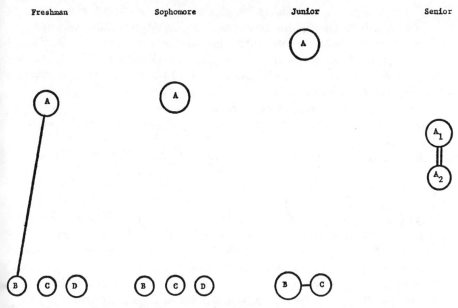

Freshman   Sophomore   Junior   Senior

Figure 7.5—Status and connections among girls' cliques in Maple Grove.

white-collar, containing only four girls of working-class backgrounds, out of forty-three members. Had Hollingshead's earlier study been of Maple Grove rather than Elmtown, these results would truly agree with his. For Hollingshead reported an unchallenged middle-class dominance, and this is what exists in Maple Grove. In every grade, the most white-collar clique is the dominant one.

Table 39—Characteristics of girls' cliques in Maple Grove*

Clique	Size	Educ.	Occ.	Study hrs/day	Date No. wk	Smoke, drink	Be re-membered S–A–P	College plans Y–U–N	Grades
4A₁	8	.4	7–1–0	1.2	1.5	.2	3–3–2	8–0–0	5.3
4A₂	6	.5	3–1–2	1.5	0.7	.3	0–4–2	5–1–0	6.3
4B	9	.3	3–2–3	1.4	1.8	0	4–4–0	4–1–4	5.6
3A	12	.4	7–0–5	1.0	1.4	.1	2–7–3	10–2–0	5.5
3B	8	.3	4–1–2	1.2	0.8	0	1–3–4	6–0–2	5.1
3C	5	0	3–2–0	2.4	0.3	0	3–2–0	2–1–2	5.2
2A	10	.9	10–0–0	1.4	1.2	.1	1–4–5	10–0–0	5.5
2B	4	0	1–1–2	0.7	1.8	.1	0–4–0	0–1–3	4.5
2C	4	0	1–2–0	1.5	1.3	.3	1–1–2	0–2–2	2.3
2D	4	0	1–3–0	1.4	0.3	0	1–3–0	2–0–2	3.3
1A	7	.6	5–2–0	1.8	.4	0	1–4–2	6–1–0	5.9
1B	4	.3	1–2–1	1.1	.1	0	3–0–1	3–1–0	6.3
1C	4	.3	2–2–0	0.5	.6	0	1–1–2	1–1–2	3.8
1D	5	.5	1–2–2	1.3	1.0	0	0–1–4	2–3–0	6.0

* Explanation of each column in the table is provided in a footnote to Table 37.

The girls in the top cliques are almost all college-going, and do not smoke or drink. They differ, however, from the Marketville top cliques: their grades are not especially high; they date more; they want more to be remembered as an activities leader, less as a brilliant student; they contain in every class the girl most attractive to boys, but *never* contain the top scholar—almost the reverse of Marketville.

In short, although these top cliques are even more middle-class in background than those in Marketville, their orientation is highly social, rather than academic. They are going to college, to be sure, but their present concerns are with dating, with extracurricular activities, and with maintaining their social position in the school. (It was a boy in this school whose descriptions of the machinations of the top cliques of girls were reported in Chapter II, p. 34.)

Since the dominance pattern in Maple Grove is so much the same in each grade, and since the leading cliques are so similar in background, it is useful to compare them from freshmen to seniors and to infer changes from the trends. One change, not indicated in the table, is the increasing involvement of these girls with school activities—the chorus, the yearbook, the newspaper, etc.—as a common focus of group activity. None of the girls in the freshman A-clique mentions some extracurricular activity as a common focus of interest with her friends; three of the ten sophomores do mention it; and half of each of the junior and senior A-clique members mention it. A similar trend occurs in Marketville, but there is no such trend evident in Elmtown. (In Elmtown, only two A-clique girls, both in the school-oriented sophomore A-clique, mention school activities as a focus of group interest, though the school sponsors more clubs and formal activities than any of the other small schools. The source of this paradoxical situation will be examined in Chapter X.)

One important change from the freshman to senior A-cliques in Maple Grove, a change also evident in the leading cliques of Marketville, is the shift in dating frequency, from almost none to about one and a half times a week. It is signicant, however, of the fact that the adolescents in Marketville are under tighter adult control and remain more nearly as children, that the real increase in dating among the A_1 cliques in Marketville comes between the junior and senior years, while the increase here in Maple Grove comes between the freshman and sophomore years. This is not to say that there is not an increase in dating at the sophomore year among some girls in Marketville, for the $2A_2$ and $3A_2$ girls date frequently. But these cliques are not the *top* cliques, and in fact, seem to have split away from the top cliques primarily through differences in dating frequency.

Corresponding to the increase in dating over the four years among

Maple Grove's A-cliques is a slight—but very slight—tendency to begin smoking and a decline in the hours devoted to studying. The decline in studying is symptomatic of their general social orientation. Another symptom is the existence of two senior A-cliques, with the A_2 group interested more in studying and in school activities, less in dating and partying, than the A_1 clique. All six of the A_2 girls say they would take another course in school if they had a choice between a course and an activity, study hall, or athletics; only three of the eight A_1 girls say this. Although the A_1 clique contains the top scholar, the other seven A_1 girls receive only three mentions altogether as top scholar, while the A_2 girls are mentioned an average of two times a piece. The average grades of the A_1 girls is only 5.3 (B−), while that of the A_2 clique is 6.3 (B+). Quite simply, the more social clique is the top clique; among the Marketville sophomores and juniors, where a similar bifurcation occurred, the more serious clique was the top clique.

A number of the non-leading cliques in Maple Grove are of the general "background" variety—girls who are around without anyone really being aware of it, girls who are never in the limelight for any reason. Cliques 4B, 3C, 2C, and 2D are of this variety. The only clique that shows the essentially out-of-school, antischool, and hedonistic orientation characteristic of so many cliques in Elmtown, is the small 1C clique, which hangs out at the skating rink.

In summary, the association structure among the girls in this school shows in every grade the middle-class, college-going, activities-oriented girls in control. Their interests are highly centered around social affairs. They maintain an interest in school activities (although their studying decreases) and in social activities. Among the seniors, these two emphases are pulled apart into two groups, with the more social of the two on top—the reverse of Marketville's sophomore and junior structure.

GIRLS IN GREEN JUNCTION: A "DEMOCRATIC" STRUCTURE

Green Junction is between Marketville and Elmtown in its social-class composition (less white-collar than Marketville, more so than Elmtown), and has about the same number of girls as Elmtown. It is far more like Elmtown than Marketville in the interconnectedness of its cliques (see Figures 7.2.4, and 7.6).

Only a few cliques and a few individuals are not connected in some way with a large complex of cliques and chains. Not all individuals are pictured in the sociogram—thirty-seven who were not involved in any mutual choices are left out—but even considering these girls, the interconnection of cliques and individuals is impressive. There are four large, connected complexes, each consisting of predominantly one grade—although the sophomore complex is more a half-and-half combination with seniors. Only two small cliques are unconnected to one of these large complexes.

The general "connectedness" of this system, in contrast to the others, conforms to the general impression of this school and community. The school newspaper appears once a week, not simply as a school paper, but as a page in the community newspaper. The adult community is highly identified with the school. (The parents had the highest response rate on the mail questionnaire of any school, despite the fact that its average income is second lowest of all the schools—second to St. John's—which would lead one to expect, on the basis of the lower response rate among lower-income families, a low response.)

There is not a divided set of hangouts, as in the other towns, one for the school-oriented crowd and another for the rough crowd. There are two hangouts, one a youth canteen, and the other a candy shop, but both are frequented by the same girls and boys. There are, to be sure, places where some go—particularly some of the senior girls—where others do not. The girls in the $4A_1$ group go sometimes on dates to taverns and cocktail lounges that will serve minors, while most of the other girls will not. Nevertheless, for all, the youth canteen and the candy shop serve as the central headquarters of social activity outside school. The

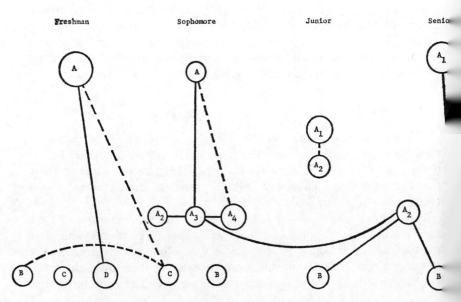

Figure 7.6—Status and connections among girls' cliques in Green Junction.

major differences between different groups in their social activity is not, as in the other schools, so much *where* they go as it is *how often* they go. Table 40 below shows the general characteristics of the cliques. The status structure is not so simple as in Marketville and Maple Grove, as has already been suggested by Figure 7.6, which shows the status and connections between the cliques. Although it is clear which clique is the top clique in every grade but the juniors, there are other cliques among the sophomores and seniors that are not without status as leaders.

Table 40—Characteristics of girls' cliques in Green Junction*

Clique	Size	Educ.	Occ.	Study hrs/day	Date No. wk	Smoke, drink	Be re-membered S–A–P	College plans Y–U–N	Grades
4A₁	12	0	3–8–1	0.9	1.0	.6	1–4–1	6–2–4	4.6
4A₂	7	.4	4–1–2	1.5	1.1	.1	2–4–1	6–1–0	7.2
4A₃	4	.5	3–1–0	1.6	1.0	.2	1–0–3	3–0–1	5.0
4B	7	0	1–3–2	0.5	2.1	.3	0–2–5	0–1–6	4.7
3A₁	9	.6	6–1–2	1.4	1.7	.3	3–3–3	5–1–3	5.6
3A₂	6	.3	1–4–0	1.2	1.5	.4	0–3–3	4–0–2	4.0
3B	6	0	1–3–2	1.6	.3	.2	0–3–3	1–2–3	5.0
2A₁	5	.3	2–2–0	1.6	1.2	0	0–2–4	4–1–0	4.6
2A₂	5	0	1–1–3	1.2	.5	.1	0–2–3	2–0–3	4.8
2A₃	5	.2	0–5–0	1.6	.8	0	0–1–4	2–2–1	4.4
2A₄	8	.1	4–2–1	1.4	.3	0	1–5–2	4–3–1	4.8
2B	5	0	1–0–4	1.6	.1	0	3–1–1	3–1–1	5.0
2C	5	0	1–1–3	0.9	.2	0	1–3–1	2–1–2	4.2
1A	15	.4	6–6–2	1.1	.3	0	1–2–12	10–1–3	4.3
1B	5	.4	2–2–0	1.1	0	0	1–0–3	2–2–1	3.2
1C	4	.3	3–1–0	1.5	.1	.1	1–2–1	1–2–1	4.0
1D	8	.6	6–0–2	1.6	.1	0	2–2–4	7–1–0	5.3

* Explanation of each column in the table is provided in a footnote to Table 37.

In the senior class, the 4A₁ clique is clearly in power. Comparing it with the 4A₂ clique in its backgrounds and orientations, there is an upset of status from that found in Marketville and Maple Grove, an upset similar to that which occurred among the Elmtown juniors and nearly occurred among the Elmtown seniors. The 4A₁ clique, from predominantly working-class backgrounds, contains a number of girls who date older boys who are either in the service or working. They are interested in a good time, are not primarily college-bound. They are involved to some extent in school activities, but not nearly so much as are the girls in 4A₂. Their grades are a low C+, compared to A— among the college-going 4A₂ girls.

How, then, did they gain their status? Primarily, according to reports of senior boys in interviews, through dating football stars when they were in lower grades. There are few activities in this school and no real clubs (it was the only school in which a question about school clubs prompted queries about what was meant), but the one status-gaining activity is football. Since girls cannot participate, the high-status girls are those chosen by the football players.

The same source of status exists for the leading sophomore clique of five girls, $2A_1$, in a somewhat different fashion. These girls are college-oriented, active around school, and conform to adult values. They are thus similar to the second senior clique, A_2. But their especially high status derives from the fact—again, according to interviews with senior boys—that some of the junior and senior athletes had dropped the "fast" girls in the $3A_1$, $3A_2$, and $4A_1$ cliques (girls who had ignored them in earlier years when older boys were available) and had begun dating some "very nice" sophomore girls. Whether such a pattern will repeat itself with these sophomore girls as they come to be seniors is problematical. Their grades suggest that it might. Nevertheless, at the time of the questionnaire, they were the one clique in this school having both very high status and not primarily oriented to a good time.

The junior leading crowd is split into two cliques of almost equal status, $3A_1$ and $3A_2$. The cliques are not fully separated, but are part of a large junior network, and are linked through an intermediary. They differ primarily in background, very little in orientation. The $3A_1$ clique, of mostly white-collar backgrounds, gets somewhat higher grades (B— compared to C for the $3A_2$ girls); but both are primarily oriented toward dates and partying. Their concern, like that of the $4A_1$ girls, is with social activities and a good time.

The freshman class exhibits a "status upset" similar to that among the seniors, between the 1A clique—mixed backgrounds, low grades, oriented to parties and a good time—and the 1D clique—white-collar, higher grades, high-studiers, college-oriented. The "good-time" clique has, in this case, all the status among the freshmen, while the more academically inclined 1D girls are quite outside the leading crowd. This is the clique that, by orientation, would be in a position of high status in Marketville and, by background, in a position of high status in Maple Grove. Here in Green Junction, however, it is the less scholastically oriented, working-class background girls who have status.

Many of the other cliques in this school consist of the quiet girls who "don't count." The 1B and 1C cliques, as well as 2B (a group of farm girls not much in the adolescent culture) and 2C (working-class girls with particularly low-status backgrounds but quiet and disciplined) and probably 3B are like this. Of the cliques with low status in school, 4B appears to be the only "fast" crowd, primarily interested in the pleasures of the adolescent culture. Yet, this should not obscure the strong emphasis among the leading junior and senior cliques on excitement, riding around, and a good time. There is no really "rough" crowd in Green Junction, as there is in Elmtown; but the leading cliques themselves among the juniors and seniors show rather free-wheeling patterns of leisure.

In sum, the structure of status and association among girls in this school may be seen as somewhere between that of Marketville and Maple Grove, on the one hand, and Elmtown, on the other. There is no fixed dominance of the white-collar middle-class background girls, as there is in Marketville and Maple Grove. The status system seems much more democratic, more dependent on the girl herself, than in those schools. Yet it is not dependent so much upon her scholastic or extracurricular accomplishments as it is upon her accomplishments with high-status boys —boys who have gained their status through football prowess. This is evidenced well by the top sophomore clique—middle-class girls, who in other schools would have gained their status through scholastic and extracurricular activities, but who gained it here through dating senior athletes.

The general orientation, then, of the leading cliques varies somewhat from grade to grade, but it is somewhat less concerned with propriety and adult standards, and more interested in a good time, than the comparable cliques of Marketville and Maple Grove—although it is no more socially oriented than the leading cliques in Maple Grove. At the same time, the elements of deviance and the traces of antischool activity to be found at all status levels among the cliques of Elmtown are absent here.

The only structural evidence of the relation between boys' and girls' status systems manifests itself in Green Junction. Earlier in the chapter, the bifurcation of the boys' leading crowd into a school-oriented clique $(4A_2)$ and a purely athletic non-school-oriented clique $(4A_1)$ was discussed. There is a corresponding division among the girls, and interviews with some of the seniors corroborated what one would suppose: the $4A_2$ boys date the $4A_2$ girls, and the $4A_1$ boys date the $4A_1$ girls—although several of the $4A_1$ girls date out-of-school boys.

SUMMARY OF GIRLS' STRUCTURES IN THE FOUR SCHOOLS

The purely structural differences between the associations in these four schools are great, as the discussion above has indicated. Some of these differences are compared more directly in Table 41.

This table shows Elmtown to have the largest number of cliques, the largest ratio of cliques to total girls, the largest proportion of girls involved in cliques, and the smallest average clique size. Marketville is at the opposite extreme in every one of these ways: it has the smallest

Table 41—Numbers and sizes of cliques among girls, relative to the size of student body in four schools

School	Total girls	Total cliques	No. of girls in cliques	Prop. of girls in cliques	Av. size of cliques*	No. cliques / total girls	No. of ties between cliques
Marketville	165	9	56	.30	6.4	.054	2
Elmtown	247	23	126	.51	5.7	.093	9
Maple Grove	204	14	89	.43	6.4	.069	3
Green Junction	258	17	106	.41	6.3	.066	12

* Girls in two cliques are counted twice in calculating the average size, so it is slightly higher than col. 3/col. 2, except in Green Junction, where there were no overlaps.

number of cliques, the smallest proportion of all its girls involved in cliques, and the cliques that it does have are largest in size. A marked similarity between Marketville and Maple Grove, on the one hand, and Elmtown and Green Junction on the other, is in the connectivity between cliques. There is little connectivity in Marketville and Maple Grove, much in Elmtown and Green Junction. It is this difference, more than any other, that makes the sociograms of the former two schools look alike, and those of the latter two schools look alike. Marketville and Maple Grove have autonomous, tightly knit cliques, with almost no connection between them, while Elmtown and Green Junction have a far more interconnected system. Looking further at the sociogram of Elmtown, we see that most of the interconnections are among the middle-class, school-oriented girls in the upper half of the sociogram, the girls who in Marketville and Maple Grove would be formed into larger, more cohesive, and separate cliques, in dominant positions in the school. In Green Junction, however, almost all cliques are part of a large network, and, in this highly "democratic" structure, the large networks are separated primarily along grade-in-school lines.

Patterns of Dominance, and Control by the Community

The structures of association examined in this chapter lead to some striking conclusions concerning the two fundamentally different patterns of dominance: the one exemplified by the girls' structures in Marketville and Maple Grove, and the other exemplified by the girls' structures in Elmtown and Green Junction. The boys' structures show a similar contrast, but one requiring a separate discussion because of its lesser dependence on parental background.

In Marketville and Maple Grove, there is a rather simple and straightforward pattern of control. A clique of girls largely from white-collar and better-educated families is the center of social activities, the center of school activities, and the center of adolescent attention. Of all the girls' cliques, these are the ones the teachers would most like to see in control of the student body, and the ones most encouraged by the adult community.[14] By popular consensus of the student body, they are the ones in control and the ones looked up to in these two schools. This concurrence of the student body with the adult community's choice appears to be due largely to two factors, one easily measured in this study, the other not. The easily measured factor is the social background of the student body. As Chapter IV showed, the more white-collar and high-educational backgrounds, the more likely the students are to have as a leading crowd a white-collar clique with a high-educational background. That is, the leading crowd must be in some fashion "in touch with" the student body as a whole, although not fully representative of it. The higher the proportion of white-collar, high-educational background students in the school, the more likely that the leading clique will be a predominantly white-collar one—which in these schools means one more oriented to adult goals, a college education, and to school activities and interests.[15] Yet these white-collar dominant cliques may not be particularly interested in learning. In Maple Grove, where their power is most absolute, they show little concern with academic success, and turn their attention to more social matters. As a result, they are no more scholastically oriented than are the more working-class leading cliques in Elmtown (although they are more oriented to school activities and to disciplined leisure).

The second factor influencing the emergence of a fully dominant clique with middle-class backgrounds and orientations is less tangible: the actions of the adult community, the school administration, and the teachers in the school. In the adult community, we can uncover some evidence from the parents' questionnaires. Table 42, showing the participation of different occupational groups in the P.-T.A., indicates the greater differential in participation between white-collar and working-class groups in Marketville and Maple Grove than in Elmtown and Green

---

14. There are, of course, individual students, such as the best scholars, whom the teachers would like to see more able to serve as examples to the student body. But except in the cases where these best scholars are in the leading cliques, they appear to be quite unorganized, and, as indicated earlier in the chapter for the boys, the teachers are not in favor of having these individualistic brilliant students as leaders.

15. This would not necessarily be the case in all schools, particularly those which are almost completely white-collar, such as Executive Heights. There, the choice is not between a white-collar, active-in-school clique and a working-class clique oriented to out-of-school pursuits. There are cliques with middle-class backgrounds but diverse orientations, so that the choice is not so predetermined. In fact, it may be the lack of a working-class, uninterested-in-school contingent, from which they must differentiate themselves, that opens the way to some of the middle-class delinquency that has occurred in homogeneous upper-middle-class schools. Matters related to this are discussed in detail in Chapter X.

Junction. In Marketville and Maple Grove, the difference is over 20 per cent; in Elmtown, it is only 10 per cent; and in Green Junction, only 3 per cent.

Table 42—Parental participation in P.-T.A. in four schools

Per cent of parents in P.-T.A.	Marketville	Elmtown	Maple Grove	Green Junction
White-collar	40	57	64	45
Blue-collar	18	47	43	42
Farmer	45	33	51	39
White-collar minus blue-collar	25	10	21	3

Thus, one factor affecting the emergence of a dominant, middle-class leading crowd with adult values is simply the control that the white-collar families maintain over the community and the school. The variation in control must stem partly from the various proportions of white-collar families in the communities, with the system of control among adults functioning in much the same way as it does among the adolescents themselves. In other words, the leaders of the adult community must be in touch with the rest of the community, so that the existence of more white-collar families in a community allows the emergence of even more white-collar dominance than usual. There are, however, variations that cannot be accounted for by the proportion of white-collar families in the community. A good example is Green Junction. Although there are more white-collar families here than in Elmtown, the participation patterns of the different occupational groups are closer together than in any of the other schools, including Elmtown. This corresponds to the patterns of association among their adolescent girls, who, as observed in the analysis of the association structure, were bound together in large, unbroken chains, more than in any other community.

Beyond the control of the school and the community by the white-collar segment, the patterns of dominance are affected by the teachers and the school administration, in ways of which we have only fragmentary knowledge. There is, however, some suggestive evidence for Elmtown, which will be examined in Chapter X.

Patterns of Dominance: Status Upsets as a Stable Pattern

In both Elmtown and Green Junction, there occurred "status upsets" in several grades, bringing into the top position cliques that were less middle-class, less oriented to school affairs, and less successful in schoolwork than another clique with somewhat less status. Yet in other grades in these same schools, the middle-class, school-oriented cliques were in control. Such a situation raises this question: why is there not a *complete* reversal in Elmtown and Green Junction of the dominance patterns found in Marketville and Maple Grove?

Of course, there are schools in which the adolescent status system brings into unchallenged ascendance cliques that are most deviant from school and adult goals. The pattern found in Elmtown and Green Junction, where the white-collar school-oriented cliques were sometimes successfully and sometimes unsuccessfully challenged, would seem to be only a kind of borderline case between the pure pro-school dominance of Marketville and Maple Grove, and its opposite, pure dominance by cliques oriented away from school. Yet this apparently "borderline" pattern is probably a rather frequent one. The school is an institution with various kinds of rewards which it can dispense and controls which it can institute. Insofar as it uses them, and manages not to create widespread rebellion, it can focus attention upon, and give prominence to, those whom it chooses. Such focusing of attention is, of course, subject to certain limitations.[16]

The school-oriented cliques, who conform to the standards and desires of teachers, are those whom the teachers and the administration reward. Similarly, the administration can, by skillful use of controls, make deviants the subject of ridicule or scorn—although the developing social maturity and autonomy of adolescents and the hedonistic values of adult society make this an increasingly more difficult task. Thus, so long as the administration and teachers are not faced by widespread rebellion, the cliques which they "sponsor" by the use of their rewards will gain some attention from the adolescents, and they will always be at least in contention for dominance of the system. It is probably no accident, then, that these seemingly unstable systems in Elmtown and Green Junction, with school-oriented and non–school-oriented groups both partly in positions of leadership, exist and are apparently maintained.[17]

---

16. The most important limitation is probably due to the school's participation in interscholastic competition, which gives extreme prominence to athletics and their accessory personnel, such as cheerleaders. The school's rewards are subject also to intense competition from without. The prestige that adult society accords to movie stars and to physical beauty, and the general attention of the adult society to symbols of pleasure, gives implicit encouragement to hedonistic values among adolescents.

17. The use of institutional rewards and controls for such purposes of course varies from school to school, depending upon the administrative philosophy, among other factors. Among the schools of this study, the one in which such controls were most directly and consciously used was St. John's, the Catholic boys' school. Rewards were given to the athletes and students in the form of special privileges, one

Boys' Systems and the Interruption by Athletics

The discussion of patterns of dominance has focused in general on the status system among girls, and has not dealt with that among boys. There is one extremely important added factor in the boys' systems, which divorces it far more from the status structure of the parental community. This is athletic achievement, which plays such an important role in the boys' status systems in all the schools of this study. Because of its dominant role in determining status, athletics makes less likely a challenge and status upset by a non–school-oriented group. For athletic achievement, unlike the dimensions by which a girl gains status, is a clear-cut objective achievement for the adolescent community as well as for self. Consequently, the status of the successful athlete is seen as far more legitimate than the status of the girl who is in a comparable position in the leading crowd, and who may be there by virtue of "knowing the right people." This greater legitimacy is evidenced by the fact that in response to the question, "Agree or disagree: 'there are a few who control things in this school and the rest of us are out in the cold,'" 43 per cent of the girls agreed in the fall, increasing to 48 per cent the next spring; while only 34 per cent of the boys agreed in the fall, and 32 per cent in the spring.

The reason athletics is important to the teen-agers is not intrinsic to the state of being a teen-ager, as the examples of schools 10 and 11 indicated (Figure 3.7, p. 79, Chapter III). In the status systems of these boys and girls, who come from a social background very much like that of the very athletic-conscious teen-agers in Executive Heights, athletics was far less important.

The importance of athletics in the status systems of high schools has a clear source. Teen-agers are highly identified with their respective schools and communities. This identification stems in part from the fact that, to them, the school and the community of adolescents are largely synonymous. They strive *as* a school in games against other schools, and thus develop common goals and a common identity. The

---

of which was being selected as messengers for the Brothers and the principal. These boys were clearly the leaders of the system, not only through their athletic and scholastic success, but because of the privileges and power such conformity to school goals reaped. Punishments were also swifter and less hesitant in this school, simply because there was not the problem, as there ordinarily is in public schools, of parents resisting the authority of the school over their children. The Brothers' religious status gives them an especially legitimate authority not held by public school teachers.

games and contests that exist are almost all athletic ones. Therefore, the heroes of the system, those who have status within it, are the boys who win for the school and for the community of adolescents, thus making all feel better about themselves. It is natural for this community to reward these boys by giving them status.

This general process has important implications for those concerned with modifying the system of secondary education. These implications will be discussed in some detail in Chapter X.

VIII Psychological Effects of
the Social System

THROUGHOUT THE PRECEDING CHAP-
ters, the focus has been on the social systems of adolescents as entities
in themselves: how the dominant values are related to the attributes of
the elite members, how these are related to the structures of association,
and the way all the elements are related to attributes of the community.
In addition, however, it is important to examine the *effects* of the systems
upon the adolescents themselves. To be sure, it is introspectively evident
to most persons that the adolescent social systems do have important
effects, but it is important nevertheless to indicate what some of these
effects are.

The present chapter will study two important "psychological" effects:
effects on the way adolescents feel about themselves, and effects on their
use of the mass media. These effects are taken as two indicators of the
psychological impact of these systems upon their members—not by any
means a measure of the total psychological impact, but an indication of
the kind of impact. Some psychologists, notably Erik Erickson, have
suggested that adolescence is the period during which a person's basic
identity—the image of himself that he carries through his adult life—
develops.[1] If this is so, then the succeeding pages indicate some of the
ways in which the adolescent system helps to shape that identity.

---

1. Erik H. Erickson, *Childhood and Society* (New York: W. W. Norton and
Co., 1950).

Effects upon Self-Evaluation

"If I could trade, I would be someone different from myself." The pathos inherent in this statement has peculiar relevance for a teen-ager. He cannot choose, as yet, the social situation or the activity that will make him feel at one with himself. He must see himself through the eyes of a world he did not make, the adolescent world of his community, into which the accident of residence has thrust him. If, in its eyes, he has done well, then he can be at peace with himself; if he is not accepted, recognized, looked up to, nor given status of any sort, he finds it hard to escape into another place in society where he can find recognition and respect. Instead, he turns inward; he must question his very self, asking whether it would not be better if he were someone quite different.

In the succeeding pages, those boys and girls deprived of status, recognition, and respect by their peers will be singled out, as well as those who are accorded positions of especially high status. For each group, a boy's or girl's tendency to "turn against himself" by wanting to be someone different from the person he is will be examined.

THE EFFECT OF HAVING FRIENDS

One element of acceptance or approval in an adolescent society is simply the number of friends one has. Does this have an effect on the way one sees himself—on the liking he has for himself as he is?

Figure 8.1 indicates that it does. Both boys and girls who are not chosen by others are more likely to want to be someone different. The relation is not great, but there is a general decrease in wanting to be someone different with an increase in the number of friends.

This impact of friends—or their lack—is quite different in different situations. Figure 8.2 shows that it is by far greatest for girls in the small schools. Among boys, the difference between small and large schools is less sharp, but here, too, it is greater for the small-school boys.

Why is this? In any of these small schools, almost the only adolescents available as potential friends are those in school. There are very few out-of-school teen-agers, and the towns are physically apart, so that a teen-ager's friends among others his own age must be found in his school. If no one in school names him as a friend, then he is without friends of his own age. In contrast, the large schools of this research are

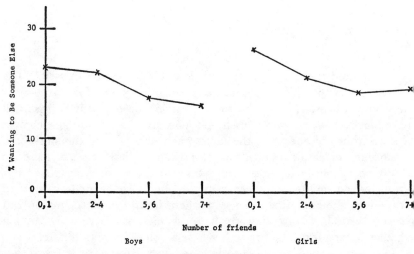

Figure 8.1—Relation between number of friendship choices received and wan ing to be someone else.

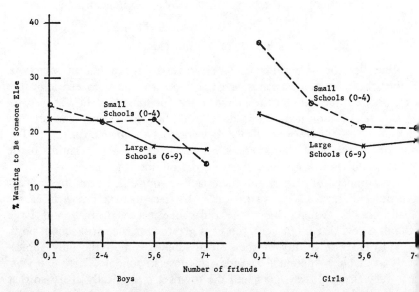

Figure 8.2—Relation between number of friendship choices received and wan ing to be someone else: large and small schools separately.

all part of larger communities, and not far from other high schools. A boy or girl who has no friends within the school may have friends outside it. He is less dependent upon the particular social system for psychological sustenance. Very likely, it is this that accounts for the more powerful impact of lack of friends in the small school than in the large school.

The small-school *girls* are those upon whom the impact of not having friends is greatest. This is consistent with all the results of the earlier chapters, which showed the greater importance for girls than for boys of the systems of cliques and crowds.

THE ELITES AND THEIR SELF-EVALUATIONS

Other dimensions of social recognition and status in these systems include membership in the various elites—being in the leading crowd, or being named as someone to be like or be friends with. The effects of these special positions of elite status within the system are shown in Figure 8.3 for boys and girls separately. The effect is apparent: the members of the elites are much less likely to want to be someone different than is the student body as a whole. Both the leading crowd and the exemplars feel better about themselves than does the ordinary boy or girl. The effect is greatest for the exemplars: their position reduces their tendency to want to be someone different by about *half*. One might, of course, expect that those whom others want to be like and want to be friends with would themselves be satisfied to be the person they are. But whether expected or not, the strong relationship shows the powerful effect of these systems upon the self-evaluations of people who have special positions in them.[2]

THE OUTSIDERS AND THEIR SELF-EVALUATIONS

What about the many boys and girls who are "outsiders" in these systems, yet have not fully reconciled themselves to being on the outside?

---

2. To be sure, another effect may help produce the relation: the general self-assurance associated with wanting to stay oneself may make one more likely to be elevated to one of these positions of elite status. However, the strongly ascriptive quality of the leading crowds among the girls in some schools means that the leading crowd is in considerable part independently determined by family background, and not by level of self-assurance. The girls in these more ascriptive leading crowds (in Marketville, Maple Grove, Midcity, and Executive Heights) are as low in their tendency to want to change as are the leading-crowd girls in the other schools (18.3 per cent for these schools, compared to 18.6 per cent for the other schools, for all those mentioned two or more times). This indicates that it is the fact of being in elite positions which increases one's self-confidence rather than the reverse.

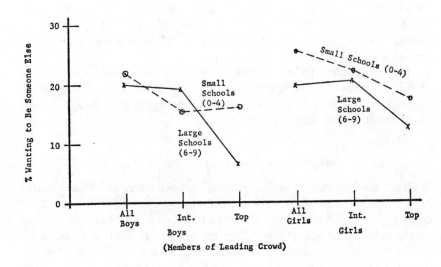

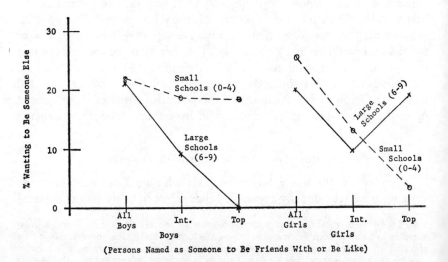

Figure 8.3—Relation between number of choices received on "elite" criteria and wanting to be someone else: large and small schools separately.

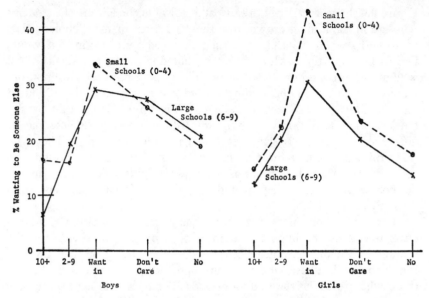

Figure 8.4—Relation between desire to be in leading crowd and wanting to be someone else, for large and small schools separately.

Such boys and girls cannot be singled out with perfect accuracy, but one question in the questionnaire does so reasonably well:

> I.49–50. Would you say you are part of the leading crowd?
> Yes
> No
> If no: Would you like to be part of the leading crowd?
> Yes
> No
> Don't care

Considering only those not named as being in the leading crowds, those who would like to be are, in effect, standing on the outside looking in.[3] They have not yet come to terms with their position in the society of adolescents. What impact has the system upon their self-evaluation?

3. Some students in each school say they are in the leading crowd, but are named by no one as being in. Their self-evaluations might be expected to be in some turmoil. At the same time, a girl may feel herself in the leading crowd (while others fail to see her there) for a special reason: she may not be "part of the crowd," but through a separate friendship with one of the girls in it, be included in its parties and other functions. One would expect such a girl not to have the negative self-conceptions that characterize the girl who is, and feels, truly excluded. The girls who report membership in the leading crowd but are not named are not included in the present examination.

Figure 8.4 shows this for both boys and girls. On the left are the students who are in the leading crowd, first those with ten or more choices, then those with two to nine choices; then those who are not in, but would like to be; next those who are not in, but don't care; and finally those who are not in and don't want to be. The girls or boys who are not, but would like to be, in the leading crowd are in the crucial position of tension. How is this tension resolved? The graph indicates that this tension often results in a turning inward, in wanting to be someone different. The effect is strongest for the small-school girls. They say, three times as often as the girls in the center of the leading crowd, and about two and one-half times as often as the girls who are not in but do not want in, that they would like to be someone different from themselves.

The implications of these facts for the internal equilibrium of adolescents would not be important if most boys or girls were either in the leading crowd or else outside and satisfied with being outside. But this is not so at all. Those who want in constitute more than a third of all those who are not in the leading crowd.[4] The ones who have settled the matter, and do not want in, are fewer in number than those who are not in but want in.

Thus, the adolescent culture has a great impact upon the self-evaluation of adolescents—especially upon those excluded from the positions they want. Regardless of what it takes to get into the leading crowd in a particular school, those who don't have what it takes, but who still aspire to be in, are powerfully affected.

THE OUTSIDERS WITHOUT FRIENDS

We would expect to find the most powerful effect of these social systems in making a person feel bad about himself among those who have *neither* status in the system as a whole, *nor* the social support of a set of friends. Those outside the leading crowd and bereft of friends as well should show the most negative self-evaluations. The combined effect of these two elements of social support is shown in Figure 8.5. The effect of these two variables together is powerful, again particularly for the girls in the small schools, all located in small towns, and isolated from other schools. Of the small-school girls who have fewer than three mentions as a friend and do not have the status of being in the leading

4. The proportion wanting in, of those who are not, is highest among the small-school girls and the large-school boys (40 per cent and 41 per cent compared to 34 per cent and 33 per cent for the small-school boys and large-school girls). This leads to a conjecture, reinforced by other data in the study, that in the small schools the girls are more dominant, while more boys have outside interests, and in the large ones, boys are more nearly in control.

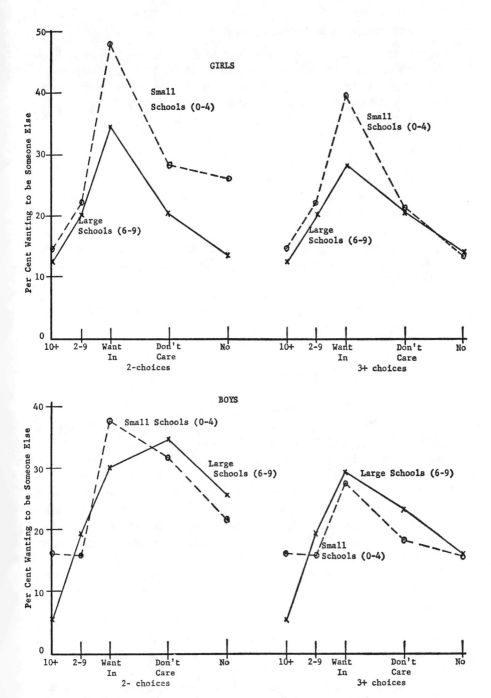

Figure 8.5—Relation between desire to be in leading crowd and wanting to be someone else among those with and without friends, for large and small schools separately.

crowd, 48 per cent say they would like to be someone different. Even the girls who say they do not want to be in the leading crowd have a high desire to change. Without friends, they have no alternative social support outside school, as do the girls in larger towns. But among the girls who *do* have friends, and among the boys, those who do not aspire to the leading crowd have their self-assurance restored. Among all groups except the large-school boys, they are no more likely to want to be someone else than are the boys and girls who are in the leading crowds in their schools.

These results point to a dilemma in secondary education. The students most involved in the school and most identified with it—those for whom school means most—are the ones upon whom exclusion from the leading crowd has its greatest impact. Those least involved in school, the ones who can take it or leave it, are least likely to be hurt by its social system. Thus, attempts to pull more and more of a teen-ager's interests toward school and the activities within it make him more vulnerable to the whims of its social system, less able to find internal peace through some alternative means.

REACTION TO NEGATIVE FEELINGS ABOUT SELF

Withdrawal from the System

A situation of internal disequilibrium such as that shown above is difficult to maintain. Rather than continuing to hold a negative image about himself, the adolescent will seek elsewhere, will focus his interests on out-of-school matters where he can feel good about himself.

It is important to remember that this feeling about himself is *not* a consequence of doing well or poorly in schoolwork; it is a consequence of being deprived of acceptance and status by his fellows. Preceding chapters have indicated that such acceptance and status depends far more on matters other than scholastic success. The psychological ill effects that a high school has upon a boy or girl who is "doing poorly" are not a result of doing poorly in studies but a result of doing poorly in the social system of the school.

In short, a person with any strength of ego will not sit still while his self-evaluation is being lowered by the social system of the school. He may attempt to gain status through those activities that give status. If this is not possible, either because status is ascribed to a predetermined group, or because he has no talents in status-bringing activities, he will take his psychological self and his energies elsewhere, leaving only a physical self in the school.

Two results suggest that such students *do* take their energies elsewhere. First, the proportion of those who are not in the leading crowd, but would like to be, decreases sharply over the four years—from 21.3 per cent of the student body for freshmen to 12.4 per cent for seniors among the boys, and from 24.5 to 11.0 per cent among the girls (data from spring questionnaire). It decreases sharply over the school year as well, from an average of 23.2 per cent in the fall, to 18.1 per cent in the spring for boys, and from an average of 25.1 to 18.8 per cent for girls. A few of these boys and girls have found their way into the leading crowds in their schools; but most have shifted away from school the interest and activity that they exhibited as eager freshmen, thereby keeping their egos from being too greatly damaged. A second change suggests the same thing: the proportion of students who want to trade and be someone different is greatest for freshmen and goes down over the four years: for girls, it begins at 24 per cent as freshmen and goes down to 15.5 per cent as seniors (fall). The boys go from 21.6 per cent as freshmen to 18.3 per cent as seniors.

Thus, the incoming freshman is particularly vulnerable and feels the hurt most: he wants most to be in the leading crowd, and if he is not in, his self-evaluation is lowest. As he remains in the system, equilibrating processes take place—some of them beneficial for the adolescent and for educational goals, others not. He will strive to achieve in activities that will gain him status and repair his self-evaluation. If these status-gaining activities are consistent with educational aims, then the social system is reinforcing these aims. If these activities are not consistent with educational aims—and, as we have seen, many are not—then the pressures of the system are not only hurting psychologically; they are pressing toward goals that will be of little help to him as an adult.

The boy or girl may try to find his status elsewhere, in deviant subgroups, in vicarious experiences in leisure, in turning his attention completely away from school. The girls, upon whom this system has most impact, most often list the vicarious pleasures of reading, listening to records, and watching television, as their favorite leisure pursuit (see Chapter II). Such leisure gratifications can serve as a substitute for the status a girl or boy lacks in the system—as an escape from a system that fails to give the social support so necessary to the turbulent period of life that is adolescence.

Rejection of the System

Perhaps the greatest indictment of a status system in which one's position is ascribed, in which one has no chance to gain status by achievement, is that it provides no avenues within the system by which a boy or girl can gain status, and rescue his self-evaluation. He must turn away from the system, either finding status within a deviant subgroup that rejects the system, or finding escape through vicarious activities, such as the mass media.

A system that reserves its rewards for those who did not work to earn them stifles the exertion of energy toward achievement in *any* dimension. Just as a system that reserves its rewards for athletic stars diverts energies into this one direction and away from all others, a system in which social status depends completely on family position stifles energies completely. If there is no possibility for mobility in the status system of the school, outsiders have nowhere to direct their energies, no way to regain a positive conception of themselves. One way out is to reject the insiders and develop a system of values of their own. Fortunately, in none of these schools is status completely ascribed. In all, an athletic star or a good-looking, well-dressed girl with a good personality stand a high chance of having friends and being looked up to, although in some, he (or particularly, she) may still find it hard to gain entrance into the leading crowd. It is likely that if these systems were highly ascriptive, deviant subgroups would develop in these schools on a large scale—subgroups with values bearing little resemblance to those of the school authorities or of the leading crowd. Athletics performs an extremely important function in schools—particularly those in stable, stratified communities—of maintaining a path for the outsiders to become insiders, undercutting the development of deviant subgroups.

Some of the effects of an ascriptive system may be seen in these schools, even though they all have large components of achievement in the status systems. The schools fall into two clusters in the degree to which family background is important for status: Marketville, Maple Grove, Midcity, and Executive Heights, where it is important; and the other schools, where it is not. The classification is the same for the leading crowds of boys and girls. Table 43 shows the degree to which these teen-agers feel outside, and the amount of rejection of the leading crowds in these two groups of schools. Two proportions are given in the table: First, there is the proportion of the total student body who see themselves outside of the leading crowd. This is greater, for both boys and girls, in the schools with more ascriptive status systems. Second is given the proportion who said they did not want to be in the leading crowd, based on all those who saw themselves outside of it. This proportion, too, is slightly higher in the more ascriptive systems. The relationship is quite weak, but it is evident and indicates that a lack of possibilities for achievement alienates the "outsiders" from the system.[5]

---

5. The responses upon which the "ascriptiveness" of the leading crowds is based are not given by the same persons as those who reject the leading crowd; the low frequency with which "coming from the right neighborhood" is mentioned in the

Table 43—Those who feel out of the leading crowd and those "outsiders" who reject the leading crowd, in systems that are more and less ascriptive*

	BOYS		GIRLS	
	More ascriptive (1, 3, 8, 9)	Less ascriptive (0, 2, 4, 6, 7)	More ascriptive (1, 3, 8, 9)	Less ascriptive (0, 2, 4, 6, 7)
Per cent who feel outside	65.9	60.4	70.5	65.2
Number of cases	(2,228)	(1,742)	(2,236)	(1,898)
Per cent of outsiders who do not want in	33.5	31.0	41.0	38.3
Number of cases	(1,469)	(1,051)	(1,576)	(1,239)

* St. Johns has been excluded from the less ascriptive group of schools for boys to make comparison possible with the girls. If included, the percentages would be 59.5 per cent (N = 2473) and 30.1 per cent (N = 1471), rather than 60.4 per cent and 31 per cent, leaving unchanged the relationship.

One point to be learned is that if high schools are to motivate all students effectively, they must provide avenues for status open to all. The correspondence in these schools between academically oriented status systems and those in which family background is important (e.g., Marketville and Midcity) suggests that these paths cannot be completely academic. Athletic achievement is the most important avenue that now functions to provide a path for mobility open to all boys, effectively helping to maintain a cohesive system. The adult community can blame its own lack of ingenuity for the absence of other paths more consistent with educational goals.

Self-Evaluations of Those Who Achieve

Besides the elite positions of exemplars and of leading crowds, there are other students with special recognition. They are students named as "best" in several dimensions: for boys, best athlete, best scholar, and most popular with girls; for girls, best dressed, best scholar, and most popular with boys. What is the effect of these various dimensions of achievement in making those named as "best" more satisfied to be themselves?

---

earlier question precludes this. Thus, the relationship here is more than mere consistency of response. The point is that the degree to which the leading crowd is "closed" to ambitious outsiders, indicated by answers to what it takes to get in the leading crowd, creates an alienation on the part of outsiders, most of whom did not even mention coming from the right neighborhoood as a criterion for membership.

The general result for all schools together has been shown in Chapter II (Figure 2.14, p. 55). It shows that people named in any one of these ways have a better feeling about themselves than those not named. But for both boys and girls, there are differences among the dimensions of achievement: those named as best scholars feel least good about themselves, both among the girls and among the boys. For the boys, it is the best athletes who have the most positive feeling about themselves; for the girls, it is those most popular with boys.

Chapter V showed the attention and status received by the scholars, athletes, and boys most popular with girls. The boy who was only an athlete won greatest recognition and respect from his fellows, in the sense of being named most often as a friend and on the elite criteria.[6] The boy popular with girls received second most attention, and the scholar received third most attention. The self-evaluations of these three types of "stars" correspond completely with the social rewards they receive: athlete first, ladies' man second, scholar third. In Chapter VI, only beauty (the girls seen as most popular with boys) and brains (the girls named as best scholars) were compared in the social rewards they received. Here, too, the feelings about self correspond to the social rewards: beauty was far ahead of brains. Thus, the status positions and the self-evaluations correspond fully, showing the dependence of a boy's or girl's attitude toward himself upon his status with his fellows.

SELF-EVALUATIONS OF THOSE WHO ACHIEVE IN VARIOUS STATUS SYSTEMS

The analyses in Chapters III, V, and VI showed the degree to which each type of achievement was rewarded by status and recognition from peers in the different schools. The differences in social rewards should result in differences in the self-evaluations of those who achieve. In the schools where athletic achievement brings most social rewards, the self-evaluations of the star athletes should not only be higher than those of the student body as a whole, but should be higher by a greater amount than in the schools where athletes receive fewer social rewards. Similarly with academic achievement: the scholar's self-evaluation should be highest in those schools where the social system rewards academic achievement most. So, too, with achievement in the competition for attention from the opposite sex: those named as "best" should be more self-assured in those schools where popularity, good looks, and social success is most important.

---

6. Excluding, of course, the athlete-scholar.

With respect to academic achievement, the schools were classified—in Chapter III—into three groups:

	High	Medium	Low
Boys:	Marketville	Elmtown	Farmdale
	St. John's	Maple Grove	Green Junction
	Midcity	Millburg	Newlawn
			Executive Heights
Girls:	Marketville	Newlawn	Farmdale
	Midcity	Executive Heights	Elmtown
			Maple Grove
			Green Junction
			Millburg

However, in the analysis of the rewards given to the scholar, in Chapter V, there were some slight inconsistencies: boys in Millburg, for example, gave more rewards to the scholars than did the St. John's boys. Because of these discrepancies and because of the fairly small number of cases involved in the analysis of those named as "best," the schools here will be presented in two groups, combining the high and medium groups.[7]

Table 44 shows the self-evaluations of boys and girls who were seen as best scholars in these two schools. Those who are "athlete-scholars" (among boys) and "best dressed plus scholars" (among girls) are excluded, to make the test a purer one; in later tables as well, the students whose achievement is in two areas will be excluded from the analysis.

Table 44—Negative self-evaluations of persons named only as best scholars, in schools where the rewards for academic success are high and in those where the rewards are lower

	BOYS		GIRLS	
	High (1, 2, 3, 5, 7, 8)	Low (0, 4, 6, 9)	High (1, 6, 8, 9)	Low (0, 2, 3, 4, 7)
Per cent wanting to be someone different	15.0	19.7	14.9	23.5
Number of cases	(133)	(101)	(114)	(91)

Among both boys and girls, the proportion wanting to be someone different is lower—that is, the self-evaluations are more positive—in the schools where academic achievement is rewarded by the culture than in the schools where it is not. For the girls, in fact, the self-evaluation of

---

7. Because the self-evaluations for the student body as a whole are, for all the groupings of schools in the analyses below, within a fraction of a per cent of one another, it is possible simply to look at the absolute level of self-evaluation of the different high-achieving groups in each set of schools, rather than the difference between them and the student bodies. (Among the students as a whole, 21 per cent of boys want to change, and 21 per cent of the girls.) This will not be possible in the subsequent analysis of leisure activities, which differ markedly in their incidence in different schools.

the scholars in schools where scholastic activities receive few social rewards is poorer than the *average* level in these schools. These results show clearly the effect of social rewards, or lack of them, upon the self-evaluation of a boy or girl seen as a scholar. In the schools where such activities receive social rewards from the adolescent culture, the best scholars do not want to be someone else; where the activities are not rewarded, they more often do.

For athletic achievement among the boys, schools can similarly be classed, on the basis of the analyses of Chapter III, into two groups: Green Junction, St. John's, Newlawn, Millburg, and Executive Heights, where the social rewards for athletic achievement are relatively high; and Farmdale, Marketville, Elmtown, Maple Grove, and Midcity, where they are lower. This oversimplifies the matter because, as Chapter V showed, there are structural differences as well in the degree to which athletes and scholars are rewarded as *separately* or as parts of an "all-around boy." Nevertheless, this classification roughly divides those schools where athletics is highly rewarded, and those where the social rewards are only moderate—although in all cases, there are far more rewards for the athlete than for the scholar. Table 45 shows the self-evaluation of the "best athletes" (excluding again the athlete-scholars) in these two groups of schools.

Table 45—Negative self-evaluations of boys named only as best athletes in schools where the rewards for athletic achievement are high and in those where the rewards are lower

	High (4, 5, 6, 7, 9)	Low (0, 1, 2, 3, 8)
Per cent wanting to be someone different	9.1	15.4
Number of cases	(132)	(91)

In the schools where athletics is highly rewarded, the star athletes less often want to be someone else than do their counterparts in schools where athletic success brings fewer rewards. Their general self-evaluation is more positive than that of the best students, in accordance with the generally greater social rewards they receive; but it is especially positive in those schools where athletes are especially rewarded.

For the effects of these status systems upon girls named as best dressed, the schools can be classified according to the proportion of girls who named "clothes" as an important attribute for being in the leading crowd. Although such a classification was not made in Chapter III, it can be done by inspecting Figure 3.2 (p. 71). Classing the schools into a set of five, where clothes are of more importance, and four where they are of less importance, we have Farmdale, Elmtown, Green Junction, New-lawn, and Millburg as the five where clothes are more important. These schools, incidentally, are those where the ascriptive criteria of family position are of little importance. Table 46 shows the self-evaluations of girls who were named as best dressed only (that is, not also named as best scholar) in these two groups of schools.

Table 46—Negative self-evaluations of girls named only as best dressed, in schools where the rewards for good clothes are high and in those where the rewards are lower

	High (0, 2, 4, 6, 7)	Low (1, 3, 8, 9)
Percent wanting to be someone different	14.8	21.8
Number of cases	(135)	(124)

In those schools where the best-dressed girl is rewarded less, her self-evaluation is no higher than those of the students as a whole. In the other schools, her self-evaluation is considerably higher than that of the average girl.

The boys named as most popular with girls and the girls named as most popular with boys constitute the final dimension of achievement measured in the study. For girls, the schools were classified according to the importance of popularity with boys, good looks, and cheerleaders. Those in which popularity with the opposite sex and good looks were important are Farmdale, Green Junction, Millburg, and Executive Heights. The schools were not classified this way for the boys, but by examining the proportion of times "good looks, popularity," etc. were mentioned as attributes for the leading crowd (see Figure 3.1, p. 70), they can be grouped into two groups of the five highest and the five lowest in this response. The five where it is most important are Elmtown, Maple Grove, Green Junction, Midcity, and Executive Heights.

Table 47 shows the self-evaluations of boys named only as most popular with girls (that is, not as athlete, nor as scholar) and girls named only as most popular with boys (not as best dressed, nor as scholar).

Table 47—Negative self-evaluations of persons named only as most popular with the opposite sex, in schools where the rewards for such popularity are high and in those where the rewards are lower

	BOYS		GIRLS	
	High (2, 3, 4, 8, 9)	Low (0, 1, 5, 6, 7)	High (0, 4, 7, 9)	Low (1, 2, 3, 6, 8)
Per cent wanting to be different	8.1	13.1	5.8	15.4
Number of cases	(74)	(61)	(55)	(60)

Again, in this comparison, it is in those systems that highly reward an activity—in this case, dating and activities with the opposite sex—where the persons who achieve in this activity feel best about themselves, and less often want to be someone different.

Altogether, then, the effects of these social systems on a boy's or girl's self-evaluation are extremely powerful. The analyses immediately above have all shown small effects, both because the differences in these systems are small and because they have dealt with the boy or the girl recognized as a high achiever in a given area. When we extrapolate these results to the student body as a whole, which includes many boys and girls who do not achieve in *any* recognized area, the effects of being in a system offering social rewards only to those who achieve in the few "right" activities are obvious. Such systems give only a few people a chance to feel good about themselves.

Effects on Uses of Leisure Time: The Role of Mass Media[8]

Aspirations to gain entrance to a crowd, and the negative self-evaluations that arise with exclusion, constitute one kind of response to the social strain that exists in these status systems. Another kind of response is to escape from the situation psychologically. One means of such escape can be the mass media; at least, various persons, from psychologists to students of popular culture, have attributed this function to the media, although there has been little systematic documentation that people use it in this way.[9]

To be sure, television, popular music, and movies can and do perform many other functions. Particularly for teen-agers, music and dancing provide a context within which they may more easily meet and enjoy the company of the opposite sex, and movies provide a place to be alone with a date. Watching television has less obvious social functions for a teen-ager, although many various kinds of gratification may stem from it. Consequently, most teen-agers, whether in a favored or unfavored position in the social system of their school, will attend to the mass media to some

---

8. This section of the analysis was carried out and written by John Johnstone, *op. cit.* It has been subject only to rewriting, and the form of the analysis differs slightly from that of the other sections of this chapter.

9. For a range of discussions of this sort, see various articles in *Mass Culture* (Glencoe: The Free Press, 1958) edited by Bernard Rosenberg and David M. White.

degree. It is the *amount* of such activities—how long a boy or girl stays glued to a television set—that is of concern in the analysis. The general hypothesis is that those who are in especially favored positions will not need to escape from the world in which they find themselves, and will turn to the world of mass media less often. Conversely, those in a particularly disadvantaged position will often use this way out of their unfavorable environment.

EFFECTS OF SYSTEMS WHICH REWARD ATHLETIC ACHIEVEMENT

Table 48 compares the media attended to by boys named as best athletes with those by boys who are not so named.[10] The effect of a social climate where athletic achievement is highly rewarded may be investigated by examining the differences between the media attention of "star athletes" and those of "others" in the various categories of schools. These differences are shown in the right hand column of Table 48, and the figures reveal consistently larger differences where the rewards for athletic achievement are greater. That is, the star athletes attend to the mass media much less often than the others in those schools where athletics is highly rewarded; they do not attend to it less in schools where athletics is less highly rewarded.[11]

The figures of Table 48 suggest that mass media uses are related to the status systems—and not just to personality differences beween athletes and non-athletes. There are differences between athletes and non-athletes, but these differences fail to persist in social environments where athletic ability is less highly rewarded. Thus, in the status system that rewards athletic achievement, the star athletes experience little or no "status frus-

---

10. In order to overcome the differences in size between the various schools, the average percentage for each cluster of schools was computed by averaging the *percentages* of high media-users in each school, rather than by adding the *numbers* of high users together and taking the percentage in this way. Thus, the 15.9 per cent in Table 48 is the average of the two percentages for "star athletes" in the two schools where athletics is most highly rewarded. This procedure weights each school equally, differing from the procedure used in other sections of this chapter, which weights each individual equally. Because each school is weighted equally here, the very small school, Farmdale, is omitted.

11. The absolute averages in mass media use must be disregarded; the *differences* between individuals of different types are relevant to the hypothesis. Many other factors, such as social-class composition and family rules about T.V. watching, affect the over-all level of media-attention in a school. These become partially controlled when the differences between two sets of individuals within the same school are examined. For this reason, this and subsequent sections of the analysis will measure the influence of a particular value system by comparing the difference between the individuals in the favored and unfavored positions vis-à-vis that particular system of values.

tration," and have far less reason to turn to the mass media than does the ordinary student.[12]

Table 48—Influence of value system rewarding athletics on mass media attention

	PER CENT WHO ARE HIGH USERS OF MASS MEDIA		Difference (others minus best athletes)
	Boys named as best athletes	Others	
Athletics of high importance			
Green Junction	13.6%	24.0%	
St. John's	18.2	26.8	
Percentage average	15.9	25.4	9.5
Athletics of medium importance			
Marketville	35.3	35.1	
Elmtown	30.0	26.3	
Newlawn	15.6	30.7	
Millburg	34.4	34.1	
Executive Heights	2.4	23.4	
Percentage average	23.5	29.9	6.4
Athletics of low importance			
Maple Grove	23.5	25.3	
Midcity	26.1	20.4	
Percentage average	24.8	22.9	−1.9
Number of cases			
Green Junction	(22)	(233)	
St. John's	(44)	(597)	
Marketville	(17)	(151)	
Elmtown	(20)	(209)	
Newlawn	(32)	(335)	
Millburg	(32)	(472)	
Executive Heights	(41)	(640)	
Maple Grove	(17)	(154)	
Midcity	(46)	(760)	

EFFECTS OF SYSTEMS WHICH REWARD SCHOLASTIC ACHIEVEMENT

Another status dimension in which these schools differ is that of academic achievement. In Table 49, the schools are separated according to the rewards given by the adolescent culture for such achievement.[13]

For the boys, the largest differences in mass media use between "scholars" and "others" occur in the schools where scholarship is most rewarded by the culture. In all sets of schools, the persons rewarded by the environment turn less to the mass media—and *least* in environ-

12. The over-all differences in mass media use between athletes and non-athlete would undoubtedly be greater in all schools except for the fact that many athlete are not highly academically oriented, and thus feel fewer constraints against usin; their free time in this way (see, for example, the more academically inclined group in Table 49).

13. The table separates the "high" group of the previous analyses into the hig and intermediate groups shown in Chapter III, for boys.

Table 49a—Influence of value system rewarding scholarship on mass media attention of boys

| | PER CENT WHO ARE FREQUENT USERS OF THE MASS MEDIA | | |
	Boys named as best scholars	Others	Difference (others minus best scholars)
Scholarship very important			
Midcity	13.5	21.2	
Marketville	20.0	36.0	
St. John's	16.1	26.7	
Percentage average	16.5	28.0	11.5
Scholarship of average importance			
Millburg	25.8	35.1	
Maple Grove	16.7	25.9	
Elmtown	37.5	26.1	
Percentage average	26.7	29.0	2.3
Scholarship of low importance			
Green Junction	13.6	24.3	
Newlawn	34.8	30.5	
Executive Heights	15.2	23.2	
Percentage average	21.2	26.0	4.8
Number of cases			
Midcity	(52)	(754)	
Marketville	(10)	(164)	
St. John's	(31)	(550)	
Millburg	(31)	(504)	
Maple Grove	(12)	(166)	
Elmtown	(16)	(218)	
Green Junction	(22)	(243)	
Newlawn	(23)	(367)	
Executive Heights	(46)	(656)	

ments that favor them most. Again, the inference is that the most rewarded persons less often need turn to the mass media as an escape from the real world. For the girls, the results, as shown in Table 49b, are inconclusive. The schools where scholarship is of intermediate importance show the greatest difference between scholars and others. Thus, it is questionable whether these effects do occur for girls on this dimension.

These effects may be seen rather sharply by examining three schools in which the boys' system and the girls' system reward scholarship quite differently. In Executive Heights and Newlawn, the girls' system rewards scholastic achievement more highly than does the boys' (see Chapter III). In these schools, the girl scholars are 13.7 and 11.1 per cent, respectively, less heavy users of the mass media than are the non-scholars; the boy scholars are only 8 per cent lower and 4.3 per cent higher, respectively, than the non-scholars. In Millburg, on the other hand, it is the boys' system that rewards scholarship more highly. Here, boy scholars are 9.3

Table 49b—Influence of value system rewarding scholarship on mass media attention of girls

	PER CENT WHO ARE FREQUENT USERS OF THE MASS MEDIA		
	Girls named as best scholars	Others	Difference (others minus best scholars)
Scholarship very important			
Midcity	13.9	29.2	
Marketville	33.3	35.6	
Percentage average	23.6	32.4	8.8
Scholarship of average importance			
Executive Heights	17.0	30.7	
Newlawn	25.9	37.0	
Percentage average	21.5	33.9	12.4
Scholarship of low importance			
Elmtown	31.8	37.8	
Maple Grove	10.0	23.3	
Green Junction	26.1	33.6	
Millburg	36.0	40.9	
Percentage average	26.0	33.9	7.9
Number of cases			
Midcity	(79)	(768)	
Marketville	(15)	(129)	
Executive Heights	(53)	(639)	
Newlawn	(54)	(343)	
Elmtown	(22)	(193)	
Maple Grove	(20)	(146)	
Green Junction	(23)	(205)	
Millburg	(75)	(594)	

per cent less often heavy users of the mass media than are the non-scholars; the girl scholars are only 4.9 per cent less often heavy users than are the non-scholars. In each of these three cases of a different value-system among boys and girls, the differences in mass media use support the hypothesis: heavy mass media use occurs when one is in a system where his achievements go unrewarded.

EFFECTS OF AN ASCRIBED STATUS SYSTEM

In the schools where the ascribed criteria of parental background are important, the teen-agers who do not have the "right" background are in a frustrating situation, unable to gain entry to the elite. Consequently, they should more often feel the need to escape via the mass media.

Television-viewing in general is known to be greater among lower social strata in society. Whether this is or is not due to the low social position, and the status frustration engendered by it, we cannot here determine. The point of the present analysis is that the particular status system of the adolescent community can intensify or diminish the tendency of lower social classes to watch more television. For example, while there are known differences between white-collar and working-class families in terms of the amount of television-viewing they do, the differences in their children's viewing will be greater where the working-class adolescents are most excluded from status in the adolescent community. The differences between these two groups, then, should fluctuate with social setting, becoming intensified where working-class teen-agers are prevented from gaining status in the community.

Table 50 separates schools into large and small schools, and within each size group, into those where family background is more important in the status system and those where it is less important. The students are divided into two groups according to family background: those whose fathers have had some college education, and those whose fathers have had no college.

Table 50a—Influence on boys' television-viewing of value systems where family background is important

Importance of family background in value system of school	PER CENT WHO VIEW TV 2 HOURS OR MORE A DAY		Difference
	Students with college-educated fathers	Students with non-college-educated fathers	
LARGE SCHOOLS			
High			
Midcity	37.4	51.8	
Executive Heights	25.1	47.5	
Percentage average	31.2	49.6	18.4
Low			
St. John's	55.4	63.9	
Newlawn	57.1	63.8	
Millburg	30.8	53.6	
Percentage average	47.8	60.4	12.6
SMALL SCHOOLS			
High			
Marketville	38.5	60.7	
Maple Grove	26.9	38.8	
Percentage average	32.7	49.8	17.1
Low			
Elmtown	53.6	55.5	
Green Junction	26.3	46.9	
Percentage average	40.0	51.2	11.2
NUMBER OF CASES			
Midcity	(203)	(689)	
Executive Heights	(530)	(360)	
St. John's	(56)	(574)	
Newlawn	(49)	(414)	
Millburg	(91)	(470)	
Marketville	(39)	(145)	
Maple Grove	(52)	(152)	
Elmtown	(41)	(200)	
Green Junction	(38)	(224)	

Table 50b—Influence on girls' television-viewing of value systems where family background is important

Importance of family background in value system of school	PER CENT WHO VIEW TV 2 HOURS OR MORE A DAY		
	Students with college-educated fathers	Students with non-college-educated fathers	Difference
LARGE SCHOOLS			
High			
Midcity	25.7	45.6	
Executive Heights	18.8	43.7	
Percentage average	22.2	44.6	22.4
Low			
Newlawn	47.0	62.9	
Millburg	38.0	43.5	
Percentage average	42.5	53.2	10.7
SMALL SCHOOLS			
High			
Marketville	27.0	50.0	
Maple Grove	27.0	47.3	
Percentage average	27.0	48.6	21.6
Low			
Elmtown	27.0	54.2	
Green Junction	30.0	42.8	
Percentage average	28.5	48.5	20.0
NUMBER OF CASES			
Midcity	(210)	(695)	
Executive Heights	(553)	(318)	
Newlawn	(51)	(418)	
Millburg	(108)	(586)	
Marketville	(37)	(114)	
Maple Grove	(63)	(131)	
Elmtown	(35)	(188)	
Green Junction	(40)	(203)	

The relevant figures in Tables 50a and b are the differences in television-viewing between students of different backgrounds, in the different kinds of value systems. The largest differences occur in schools where ascribed status is important. This relationship is quite evident in three of the four test cases, although it is not found among the girls in small schools. Among girls in large schools, however, the differences are more than twice as great in schools where ascribed status is important, than they are in schools where it is unimportant (22.4 to 10.7 per cent); and among boys, the differences in both large and small schools are about 50 per cent greater where ascribed status is important.

These relationships suggest the same kinds of effects that were found in the earlier cases dealing with athletics and scholarship. Deprivation of opportunities to gain status leads to higher mass media use.

On the basis of these findings, we would expect that the general level of television-viewing among students with a non-college background would be more frequent in schools where ascribed status is importan than in schools where it is unimportant. Upon examination of the differences in the vertical columns, however, this appears not to be the case. Television-viewing is more frequent among both groups of individuals in schools where ascribed status is unimportant; this is true in all of the four cases except the girls in the small schools. This suggests quite a different kind of cultural effect: there seems to be some sort of over-all variation associated with a middle-class community, which is not explained by the "status-frustration" hypothesis. Several factors may account for the generally lower television-viewing in a middle-class community, quite apart from parental education. Only one possibility will be mentioned here: the backgrounds of these students are in fact of higher social class than are those with similar father's education in the working-class communities. Those with non-college backgrounds in Newlawn are of considerably lower social background than their counterparts in Executive Heights; thus, they would be expected to view television more frequently—in accord with the general fact that families of lower social status watch television more often, regardless of community.[14]

This analysis of the use of mass media in adolescent status systems indicates the powerful effect of the adolescent culture upon the way a teen-ager spends his leisure time. The general result may be summed up succinctly: when he is in a system that fails to give him status and allow him a positive self-evaluation, the adolescent often escapes to a world where he need not have such a negative self-evaluation: the world of mass media.[15]

---

14. Other factors are discussed in detail in Johnstone, *op. cit.*

15. Johnstone, *op. cit.*, examines some of the further characteristics of mass media use in response to the adolescent's social situation, in particular, the type of popular singer he turns to, and the use of certain singers—such as Elvis Presley—as a reaction to the system that fails to accord him status.

IX Scholastic Effects of
the Social System

THE PRECEDING CHAPTER HAS EXAMINED
a few indicators of the psychological effects of adolescent social systems on their members. Important as these effects are, however, they are not the only important effects of a high-school experience. Schools are intended to do more than watch over their students' psyches.

Some of the most explicit goals of high schools are those having to do with matters of the mind: transmission of knowledge, development of mental skills, and inculcation of positive attitudes toward learning. Effects of the adolescent system on some of these matters are the concern of this chapter. As in the preceding chapter, the effects shown will be mere indications of broader effects of these social systems.

Effects upon the Image of Intellectual Activity

As Chapter IV indicated, the leading crowds of boys want more to be remembered as a star athelete, less as a brilliant student, than do the student bodies as a whole. Similarly, the leading crowds of girls were oriented away from thinking of themselves as a brilliant student, and were oriented toward, in some schools, the image of activities leader, and in others, the image of most popular. (See Figures 4.12, 4.13).

This means that the social elites of these high schools are less willing to see themselves as engaging in intellectual activity, and find the idea of being seen as "intellectuals" more repugnant, than do those who are outside the leading crowds. By extrapolation to. adulthood, these same social elites will be similarly oriented away from anything with a strong stamp of intellectual activity upon it. Such extrapolation is perhaps not too far-fetched, because this research includes not only small-town schools, part of whose leading crowds will remain in the town, and not only working-class schools, whose leading crowds will be a social elite only to their working-class constituency, but also urban middle-class schools—and, with Executive Heights, an upper-middle-class school that trains the children of some of the larger society's social elite. As was evident in Chapter IV (Figures 4.12 and 4.13, p. 135, 137), the leading crowds in this last school are even more oriented away from the "brilliant student" image than are the leading crowds of other schools, with less than 10 per cent of the boys 1 per cent of the girls in the leading crowd wanting to be remembered as a brilliant student.[1]

Even if this study included only leading crowds that would never become the social elite of the larger society, the matter would still be important. For they nevertheless come to be the elites of the towns and cities in which they remain, and thus become the "grassroots" leaders of attitudes toward intellectual activities.

Most of the post–high-school consequences of the leading crowd's wanting to be remembered as a brilliant student can only be conjectured, but from one outside source has come evidence of an important consequence. In a study of graduate students in American universities[2] a question was asked of each graduate student in the sample: "Were you a member of the leading crowd when you were in high school?" He could classify himself as a member of a leading crowd, as a member of another crowd but not a leading crowd, as a member of no crowd, or as an "out-

1. This almost complete absence of wanting to be remembered as a brilliant student is both more surprising and more disconcerting than in the other schools. For this leading crowd is about 50 per cent Jewish (56 per cent for boys, 62 per cent for girls, if only those with 10 or more choices are included; 41 per cent for boys, 49 per cent for girls if all with 2 or more choices are included); in view of the traditional Jewish cultural emphasis on education and learning, one would not expect this. These results strongly suggest the decay of this tradition, and its replacement by the values of the dominant Protestant social elite, among those Jews whose mobility brings them into this elite. It is very likely that the parents of these Jewish children, many of whom had lower-middle-class origins, themselves wanted to be thought of as a brilliant student when in school, rather than as star athletes or activities leaders, as their sons and daughters now do. See Chapter X, p. 293, for further discussion.

2. This study is being conducted by James A. Davis, at the National Opinion Research Center of the University of Chicago. I am grateful to NORC, to Professor Davis, and to Professor Jan Hajda, who carried out the analysis reported here, for permission to use these data.

sider." These students were also asked whether they regarded themselves as intellectuals. Table 51 below shows the proportion who considered themselves intellectuals as a function of the crowd they were in—or not in.

Table 51—Self-image as an intellectual among American graduate students, in relation to their social location in high school

	Members of leading crowd	Members of other crowd	Not members of any crowd, or outsider
Per cent who consider themselves definitely or in many ways an intellectual	43	48	49
Number of cases	(859)	(725)	(570)

The result is clear: even among the highly select group of high-school students who end up in graduate school studying for an advanced degree, those who were in the leading crowd in high school are slightly less likely to consider themselves intellectuals, although, by any definition, they are surely engaging in intellectual activity.

One might dismiss this result with the notion that anyone in a leading crowd, whatever the school's values, will less likely think of himself as an intellectual than someone on the outside. However, foreign students, who had attended high school in Europe or somewhere else outside this country, were included in this same graduate-student study.[3] Table 52 below shows their self-images as a function of whether or not they were in the leading crowd.

Table 52—Self-image as an intellectual among foreign graduate students in American universities, in relation to their social location in high school

	Members of leading crowd	Members of other crowd	Not members of any crowd, or outsider
Per cent who consider themselves definitely or in many ways an intellectual	63	42	59
Number of cases	(126)	(114)	(125)

Among students who had attended foreign high schools, there are two differences from the Americans: the average level of considering themselves intellectuals is higher; but most crucial to our analysis, those who were members of the leading crowd in their high school were slightly *more* likely to consider themselves intellectuals than those who

3. The analysis was done by a sociologist, Jan Hajda, who had himself attended a high school in Czechoslovakia. He was puzzled at the results of Table 51 when he found them, for, on the basis of his own high school experience, he had expected those from the leading crowds to more often think of themselves as intellectuals.

were not members of the leading crowd—exactly opposite to the result for graduates of American high schools.

To go back to the high-school level, are there any differences in the intellectual images—wanting to be remembered as a brilliant student— among those schools where the adolescent culture rewards such activity and those where it does not? Table 53 shows, for boys and girls, the proportions wanting to be remembered as a brilliant student among all students, and among those mentioned ten or more times as members of the leading crowd; in the schools where scholarship is more rewarded and in those where it is less rewarded.

Table 53—Per cent of boys and girls wanting to be remembered as a brilliant student, in schools where the rewards for academic achievement are higher and in those where these rewards are lower

BOYS	All boys	Those mentioned 10 times or more as members of leading crowd
"High schools"		
(1, 2, 3, 5, 7, 8)	35.1%	24.0%
Number of cases	(2,781)	(108)
"Low" schools		
(0, 4, 6, 9)	27.2	9.5
Number of cases	(1,578)	(74)
GIRLS	All girls	
"High" schools		
(1, 6, 8, 9)	24.6%	12.0%
Number of cases	(2,414)	(142)
"Low" schools		
(0, 2, 3, 4, 7)	34.6	19.7
Number of cases	(1,555)	(117)

The boys as a whole more often want to be remembered as brilliant students in "high" schools; and the boys in the leading crowds in these schools do also. Although, in both sets of schools, the members of the leading crowd less often want to be remembered as brilliant students than the school as a whole, this decrease is far less for the schools where there are more rewards for academic achievement.[4]

For the girls, the matter is somewhat different. In the schools where there are more social rewards for academic achievement, the level of wanting to be remembered as a brilliant student is *lower* in the total

---

4. The difference still exists, though it is attenuated, when Executive Heights, where so few in the leading crowd want to be remembered as brilliant students, is excluded. Excluding Executive Heights, the percentages are 29.7 and 15.8 for the student bodies, and leading crowd groups, respectively, in the "low" group of schools.

student bodies and among the members of the leading crowd than it is in the other schools. As will become evident shortly, this apparently derives from the fact that the "high" schools include three of the four most middle-class schools. As the analysis will show, the relation between boys and girls in a middle-class school operates to make the label of "brilliant student" something for a girl to shy away from, although lesser scholastic accomplishments may be desired. This is most evident in the most upper-middle-class school, Executive Heights, where not one of the 49 girls in the top leading crowd responded that she wanted to be remembered as a brilliant student.

IMPACT OF THE SYSTEM UPON SELF-IMAGE OF BOY SCHOLARS
AND GIRL SCHOLARS

To examine further the matter of "intellectualism," and the degree to which it is dampened or encouraged in these systems, another question may be asked: what about those named as best scholar? Do these systems "allow" a scholar to desire to be remembered as a brilliant student as much as they allow a star athlete to want to be remembered as an athletic star, or do they make him shy away from such an image of himself? And what about the self-image of the girl who is seen as best scholar, whom we have seen to be in such a disadvantaged social position in most of these cultures? How would she like to be remembered? Figures 9.1 and 9.2 show, for the boys and the girls, how the people who were considered as best scholars by others wanted to be remembered. The boys' chart, Figure 9.1, includes as well all students, those named as athlete-scholars, those named as athlete only, and those named as most popular with girls. The athletes and the scholars go very far toward 100 per cent in wanting to be athletic star or brilliant student respectively. But the athlete goes much nearer the 100 per cent point than does the scholar—presumably because the culture "allows" him to think of himself as an athletic star by giving very positive evaluations to this image, more so than to the image of brilliant student. This is reflected as well by the athlete-scholar, whose self-image is shifted in the athletic direction rather than the academic one. Given both achievements, so that he can think of himself in either way, he more often chooses to think of himself as an athletic star.

The picture is somewhat different for the girl scholars. They are "pulled" only about 14 per cent in the direction of the brilliant-student image, only up to 43 per cent (compared to 58 per cent for the boy scholars). (There were no "leaders in activities" identified by the questionnaire, so that there is no such comparison possible, as there was with athletes for the boys.) The girl who is named as best dressed and best scholar is no more likely to want to be remembered as best scholar than the average girl.

These results, then, show several things: first, the boy who is named as best scholar does not want to think of himself as a brilliant student nearly so much as the best athlete wants to think of himself as an athletic star. The culture has failed to encouarge such a self-image among those who are entitled to it by their achievement. The boy scholar, however, is far more likely to want to see himself as a scholar than is the girl scholar, who is presumably repelled by the culture's negative evaluation

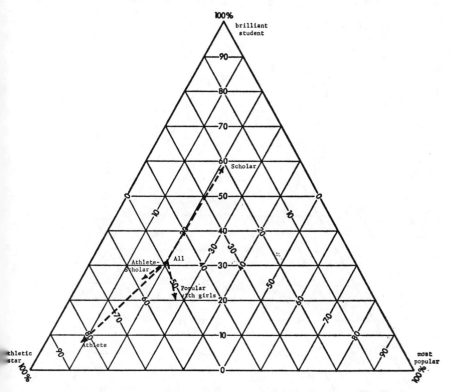

Figure 9.1—Relative choice of image of athletic star, brilliant student, and most popular, by all boys, and by boys named as athletes, scholars, and popular with girls.*

* Number of cases:

Scholar only	214
Athlete-scholar	50
Athlete only	192
Most popular	154

of this image. The lack of social rewards for the girl who is thought of as best scholar makes it understandable that these girls, good students though they might be, would not flock to this image in great numbers.

This different response on the part of girl scholar and boy scholar to their role in the school leads to the question: what happens over time? Are the girls discouraged from holding an image of themselves that is not rewarded and, therefore, move away from it? Do the high-school years move them away from a brilliant student image, or were they away to begin with?

The comparison between boys and girls, shown in Figure 9.3, is striking: boys and girls start very close to the same point, but then diverge, the

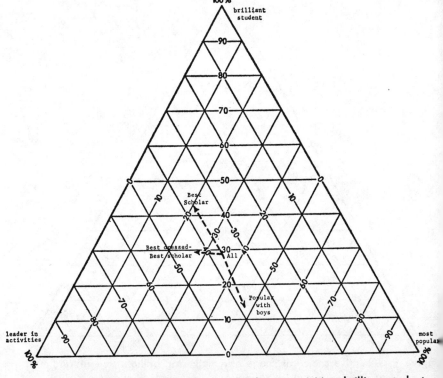

Figure 9.2—Relative choice of image of leader in activities, brilliant student, and most popular, by girls named as best scholar and most popular with boys.*

* Number of cases:
Student only   260
Best dressed student   89
Most popular   114

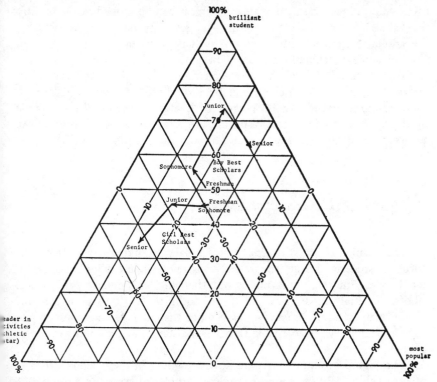

Figure 9.3—Relative choice of three images by boy and girl best scholars in each grade of school.*

* Number of cases:	Girls	Boys
Freshman	66	55
Sophomore	80	72
Junior	57	45
Senior	53	42

best girl students becoming *less* likely over the four years to want to be remembered for their scholastic achievements, and the best boy students becoming *more* likely to want to be remembered in this way.[5] This shows the differential impact of the culture upon girls who achieve highly scholastically, and boys who do so. It shows also the greater strain placed on girls, for they make considerably better grades, and they are more motivated to conform to parental and teacher's expectations. Yet they are under a constraint from the culture not to be "brilliant students."

This examination of budding intellectualism in the high schools—and,

5. There is a reversal in the senior year among boys; the small number of cases makes it difficult to know whether this is a general result.

as a cynic might put it, the way in which it can be nipped in the bud by the values of the adolescent culture—suggests the powerful impact that the adolescent culture can have on the larger society. People who can and do achieve scholastically are a nation's intellectual resource; if the social system within which their education takes place undercuts any desire to think of themselves, and be thought of, as intellectuals, then these resources stand a good chance of being wasted or ill-used. Some of the ways in which these resources are affected by the forces of the adolescent culture will be examined in the next section.

Boys' and Girls' Grades in School

The results above, showing girl scholars shrinking away from the "brilliant-student" image, suggests a constraint against a girl's appearing too bright. But this constraint is not the only one under which a girl labors. She is also constrained to "be a good girl," to "do well in school," to conform to adult demands—much more than a boy. One consequence of this has always been that girls work harder in school and get better grades.

The higher grades of girls are no less evident in these schools than in others. Table 54 below shows the average grades of boys and girls in each of these schools.

Table 54—Average grades of boys and girls in the ten schools of the study*

| | GRADES | | |
School	Boys	Girls	Difference
Farmdale	4.10†	4.71	.61
Marketville	3.65	4.58	.93
Elmtown	4.20	4.76	.56
Maple Grove	4.27	4.84	.57
Green Junction	3.96	4.38	.42
St. John's	3.66		
Newlawn	3.45	4.36	.91
Millburg	3.66	4.57	.91
Midcity	3.62	4.07	.45
Executive Heights	4.01	4.53	.52

* Average grades for each class were found; then these were averaged, weighting each class equally.
† A = 8, B = 6, C = 4, D = 2, F = 0.

The double constraints upon girls—to do well, but not to be brilliant —are evident in other ways as well. For many a girl, the solution to the dilemma of "good, but not aggressively brilliant" is an ingenious one: she gets good grades, but she is never extremely outstanding. She is neither better than the best boy student nor poorer than the worst. Her grades are "compressed" by the double constraints of conforming to the two norms. As a result, the grades of a girl are more nearly alike from course to course than those of a boy, and the within-girl variance in grades is less than for boys. If a girl has a B average, she has more B's and fewer A's and C's than does a boy with a B average.

Table 55 below shows the average variance among the various grades received by each girl, and the average variance for each boy's grades. In every school but Green Junction, the average girl's grades cluster together more closely than do those of the average boy. This suggests strongly that the girls are motivated to "do well" in everything, whether it is something at which they excel or not, while boys are less constrained by parents' demands and the demands of the adolescent culture to be "good" in those things they care less about. At the same time, the boys are free to excel in the things they do care about.

Table 55—The within-person variances of present grades for boys and girls in ten schools*

| | VARIANCE | | |
School	Boys	Girls	Difference
Farmdale	1.46	1.43	.03
Marketville	2.26	1.48	.78
Elmtown	2.19	1.94	.25
Maple Grove	2.02	1.65	.37
Green Junction	1.45	1.48	—.03
St. John's	2.65		
Newlawn	2.33	1.92	.41
Millburg	2.55	1.94	.61
Midcity	2.18	1.65	.55
Executive Heights	2.28	2.13	.15

* Variances were computed by calculating the variance of each student's grades, then averaging for each of the four classes in school. These averages were then averaged, with each class equally weighted. For those unfamiliar with the use of variances, this is the square of the standard deviation. One standard deviation from the mean in both directions will include about 70 per cent of the cases. Thus, to use the example of boys in Midcity, the variance is 2.18 and the standard deviation is 1.47. For a boy whose grade average was 4.0, about 70 per cent of his grades are within the range 4.00 ± 1.47, that is, from 2.53 to 5.47.

The results shown in Table 55 do not seem to relate to the value systems of the different schools. In general, the variances are larger in the larger schools than in the smaller ones. The average variance for girls in small schools is 1.60, compared to an average of 1.93 in the large schools; for boys, the small-school average is 1.88, compared to 2.33 for the four large schools, and 2.40 if St. John's is included. This suggests the possibility that low variances from course to course are partly a function of the greater consensus about a student that develops among teachers in the small schools. In the large schools, teachers will less often know a boy's or girl's reputation regarding schoolwork, and might therefore give a grade that is more independent of those given by other teachers. If this were so, the variance among a student's grades in different subjects should decrease from freshman to senior, as he is in school longer, and teachers know him better. But this is not so. The variance among each person's grades as a freshman was calculated, and this compared with the present variance from course to course, for the sophomores, juniors, and seniors. In all but two of the nineteen cases—ten schools for boys, nine for girls—the variance *increased* from year to year. Only for the girls of Market-ville and the boys of Green Junction is there an average decrease in variation. In all other school-sex groups, a boy's or girl's grades have become more and more heterogeneous through his high-school career. Thus, the teachers' consensus about a boy or girl seems not to be manifest in the grades.

Consistent with the generally lower variation in a girl's grades, the *increase* in variation of a girl's grades over the years of school is less than that of a boy's grades in most of the schools. A girl's grades are not only more tightly clustered, but the clustering is less likely to "loosen up" than is a boy's in the upper grades of high school. The girl apparently stays subject to constraints to be good but not aggressively brilliant, while a boy's grades in later years come more and more to be a function of his own variable interest.

I.Q.'s of Best Scholars among Boys and Girls

The lower variance among a girl's grades can be interpreted as a result of simply the one norm to "do well in school." By working at her capacity in all subjects, a girl would achieve roughly similar grades in all subjects, while a boy, working only in those which interest him, will have a wider range of grades. Girls would thus achieve higher average grades (as Table 54 showed that they do), along with a lower variance from one course to another. Is it simply that girls work harder in response to the pressures from parents and teachers, or do they respond also to the second constraint, the constraint not to be a "brain"?

The evidence suggests strongly that they are responding to this second pressure as well. In an earlier section, the tendency of girls named as best scholars to shy away from the image—or stigma, as it may sometimes be—of being a brilliant student indicates that they feel it best not to be seen as *too* bright. In other words, at the top levels of scholarship, the second norm, holding down effort, seems to operate. Further evidence in this direction is provided by looking at the I.Q.'s of best scholars. If there is a constraint against being too bright, then many of the girls who could be top scholars will be constrained not to work so hard. Those girls whom others see as "best scholars" in their grade will not be brightest. If, as suggested, there is less constraint upon a boy not to be aggressively bright, the boys named as best scholars should be, on the average, brighter than the girls so named.

This is in fact true, as Table 56 indicates. Even though the average I.Q. of boys is lower than that of girls, the average I.Q. of boys named as "best scholars" is *higher* than that of girls named as best scholars.[6] Furthermore, this result is consistent from school to school. The best boy scholars have higher absolute I.Q.'s than best girl scholars in every school but two; and in every school but Marketville is the relative I.Q. (measured in terms of standard deviations above the school-sex mean) higher for girls than boys. Throughout the analysis, Marketville has shown especially high rewards for girl scholars.

Table 56—Average I.Q.'s of best boy scholars and best girl scholars (named two or more times), compared with over-all sex means

	Boys	Girls	Boys minus girls
Best scholars	116.5 (N = 295)	114.0 (N = 348)	2.5
All students	101.3 (N = 3,688)	105.0 (N = 3,746)	−3.7
Scholars minus others	15.2	9.0	6.2

These results, together with the earlier ones showing the girls' grades to be better than boys', suggest the peculiar dilemma of the girl—she is pushed toward doing well in school by her allegiance to parents and teachers; but if she wants dates and popularity, she is constrained from working to her scholastic capacity. Consequently, many of the brightest girls manage to hide their intelligence, leaving somewhat less bright girls to be named as best scholars.

THE DIFFERENT ROLE OF GIRLS IN DIFFERENT SOCIAL CONTEXTS

It was evident in visiting the schools that a girl's role varies somewhat in different adolescent communities. One of the major differences seemed to be a class difference, as mentioned previously, in Chapter VI. In working class schools, there seemed a greater role-differentiation between boys and girls—boys more masculine, more aggressive, girls more feminine, more passive. Upper-middle class boys and girls seemed to be more *alike*.

6. The I.Q. tests differed from school to school, but since the number of boys and girls in each school was approximately equal, this difference has no effect on the result in Table 56. The I.Q. test used in each school is given in footnote 10 of this chapter.

One way this difference manifests itself is in dating behavior. In working class groups, girls tend to date boys *older* than themselves; in the modern middle class, where role-differentiation is at a minimum, boys date girls about the same age. This is best exemplified by a comparison of two extreme schools: Executive Heights and Newlawn, almost pure representatives of the upper middle class and working class respectively. Figure 9.4 shows the proportion of freshmen, sophomores, juniors, and seniors who reported that they date at least once a month, for boys and girls separately. The point of interest is the close correspondence between boys' and girls' dating in Executive Heights, and the sharp disparity in Newlawn. In Executive Heights, proportions of boys and girls who are dating each year are relatively close together; in Newlawn, they are

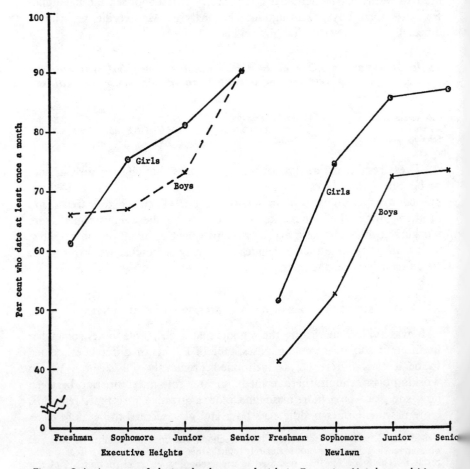

Figure 9.4—Amount of dating by boys and girls in Executive Heights and New-lawn, in each year of school.

widely separated each year, with the girls far ahead of the boys. The age discrepancy in Newlawn is not merely a second-generation carryover from Europe, for Millburg, whose residents have been in this country for several generations, shows about the same discrepancy (except among the freshmen, where the girls date less than the boys).

The age-discrepancy in dating, however, is only one manifestation of the role-differentiation of boys and girls in working class groups, and the lack of such differentiation in upper middle class. There are other manifestations more directly relevant to scholastic matters. One of these is the criteria boys use to evaluate girls. All girls were asked:

> I.149–54. Which of these items is most important in making a girl popular with the boys around here? That is, among the boys who really rate, which of these things count most? (Rank from 1 to 6.)
>
> Coming from the right family
> Leader in activities
> Clothes
> High grades, honor roll
> Being cheerleader
> Being in the leading crowd

The categories of this question are identical to those of an immediately preceding question, which asked about a girl's popularity with *other girls*. Responses to both questions were examined in Chapter II (Figure 2.12, p. 48). Our present concern is with the way in which girls feel that good grades affect popularity with boys, compared to the way they affect popularity with other girls. Do they see good grades as helping their popularity with boys *more* or *less* than it does their popularity with other girls?

The answer is *less*, in every school. In every school, the average rank of "high grades, honor roll" is considerably lower as an aid to a girl's popularity with boys than as an aid to her popularity with other girls. But the degree to which it is lower varies sharply from school to school, as Table 57 shows.

Table 57—Differences in rank of "high grades, honor roll" for a girl's popularity with other girls and her popularity with boys

School	Difference in rank
Farmdale	.38
Marketville	.87
Elmtown	.53
Maple Grove	.69
Green Junction	.53
Newlawn	.53
Millburg	.39
Midcity	.64
Executive Heights	.88

One might have expected this difference to be greatest in the predominantly working-class schools, where boys are presumably less interested in middle-class propriety and conformity. Yet exactly the reverse is true: the decrease is greatest in Executive Heights, then in Marketville, Maple Grove, and Midcity—all four of these the more middle-class, white-collar schools, with Executive Heights the most white-collar of all.

Why do the girls in the more middle-class schools feel that boys care nothing for their grades? The boys are themselves interested in grades, for many will need them for college entrance; one would suppose that they, far more than the boys from working-class backgrounds, would put a premium on a girl's scholastic achievement.

It seems, however, that matters work differently. In a working-class milieu, the greater role differentiation between the sexes affects the way boys evaluate girls. Schoolwork and good grades are a girl's achievement, something to make a boy look up to a girl, but not something for him to achieve himself. In contrast, academic success is not a girl's province in a middle-class milieu, but something with which a boy must be concerned as well. Conversely, a girl's grades are not something to make her more attractive to him as someone to date.

That this difference does exist is evident by an inspection of boys' and girls' grades, in Table 54, presented earlier. In three schools, the average girls' grades are at least .9 points higher than the average boys' grades, a difference far greater than in the other schools; these are Marketville, Newlawn, and Millburg. Two of the three—Newlawn and Millburg— have the smallest proportion of boys with white-collar backgrounds of any of the nine schools. At the other extreme, the three schools with the *least* difference between boys' and girls' grades are Green Junction, Midcity, and Executive Heights—and the latter two have the highest proportion of boys with white-collar backgrounds.

These comparisons suggest that there is a greater role differentiation in the working-class milieu with respect to academic work: girls outdistance boys further in these schools than in schools that are more nearly white-collar. However, this still does not imply that working-class boys give more status to a girl scholar than do middle-class boys. There is some evidence to indicate that among the white-collar, middle-class boys, the "activities girl"—the clubwoman of the high school—has preempted the place held by the outstanding girl scholar in the working-class schools. One question in particular in the questionnaire indicates this. Boys were asked, in the supplementary questionnaire:

I.s.30, 31. At the left, below, are some descriptions which we have taken from the yearbook of "M" high school, listing the activities in which . . . girls have taken part during the year in

high school. Can you guess what these girls were like? On the
line following each description put the number of the words that
would fit each girl from those listed at the right.

A. FHA; Yearbook editor; Octet;   1—a good example
Class Secretary; Prom Committee.   2—a square
                                        3—a scholar
                                        4—a grind or bookworm

B. National Honor Society; Spanish   5—an active leader
Club; Student Council; Dramatics   6—a joiner
Club.   7—prom queen
                                        8—beautiful but dumb
                                        9—popular with boys
                                      10—ambitious

Of these two hypothetical girls, the first is more active, the "clubwoman" of the school. The second is more nearly the student, less busily
active, conforming to the school's standards and being rewarded by
honors for her conformity.

Of the descriptive words at the right, 1, 5, 7, and 9 may be assumed
to have positive implications. We can then ask how many of these positive descriptions are given to each of these two hypothetical girls by
boys in the extreme schools—the working-class suburb, Newlawn, and
the well-to-do suburb, Executive Heights. In Newlawn, the sum of positive mentions, computed as a percentage of the total boys who answered
the question, was 68.9 per cent for the activities girl and 77 per cent for
the scholar. In Executive Heights, the activities girl received 85.2 per cent
positive mentions and the scholar only 75.7 per cent. The boys in Newlawn felt more positively about the scholar, while those in Executive
Heights felt more positively about the activities leader.

The same difference exists for the other schools. The four schools
that are most middle-class—the same schools in which the girls felt boys
most devalued good grades in judging a girl—have an average ratio of 1.03
positive mentions for the activities girl to the scholar. For the five more
nearly working-class schools, the ratio is 0.93.

It is true, then, that in the eyes of the boys in a white-collar school,
a girl's good grades are not as much of an asset as among the boys in
more nearly a working-class school. This result, out of accord with
initial expectations, suggests that as society becomes more and more
white-collar, the kind of image that girls will be striving for in school is
only obliquely related to academic achievement, and is more nearly that
of the activities girl, the teen-age replica of the adult clubwoman. That
this is more than mere speculation is indicated by the Executive Heights
girls' response to wanting to be remembered as a brilliant student (Figure
4.13, p. 137): they were by far *lowest* in the proportion choosing the

brilliant student image, by far highest in the proportion choosing the "leader in activities" image. Even the girls named as best scholars in this school were exceptionally low in wanting to be remembered as a brilliant student. Only 19 per cent of them—fewer than in any other school—wanted to be remembered as a brilliant student.

Thus, the lack of role differentiation in a white-collar milieu does more than pull up the average boy's grades. It draws the achievement-oriented girl away from scholastic achievement, toward achievement in "activities." In part, this is a shift from a rather passive role, conforming to adult demands, to a more active role as a "big wheel" in the activities of student life. This kind of girl responds less to the demands of parents, more to the demands of the adolescent community; she strives to be a leader in those activities the adolescent culture holds important rather than striving to achieve in what parents and teachers hold important.

Relation between Ability and Achievement in School

In every social context, certain activities are highly rewarded, while others are not. The activities that are rewarded are those for which there is strong competition—the activities in which everyone with some relevant ability will compete. In such activities, the persons who achieve most should be those with most potential ability. In contrast, in unrewarded activities, those who have most ability may not be motivated to compete; consequently, the persons who achieve most will be persons of lesser ability. Thus, in a high school where basketball is important, nearly every boy who might be a good basketball player will go out for the sport, and the resulting basketball stars will likely be those boys with most ability. If, in the same school, volleyball does not bring the same status to those who star in it, few boys will go out for the sport, and those who end up as members of the team will not necessarily be the boys with most potential ability.

Similarly with academic achievement: where such achievement brings few social rewards, those who are motivated to "go out" for scholarly achievement will be few. The high performers, those who receive good grades, will not be the boys whose ability is greatest, but will be a more mediocre few. The "intellectuals" of such a society, the best students, will not in fact be those with most intellectual ability. The latter, knowing where the social rewards lie, will be off in the directions that bring social rewards.

Based on these ideas, the original research design included the hypothesis that in those systems where academic achievement was rewarded by the adolescent culture, the correlation between I.Q. and grades in school would be higher. In carrying out the analysis, it became evident that this correlation (within a given class) changed over the course of the years in school—most often decreasing, but sometimes increasing. With such data on changes, it was possible to add a supplementary hypothesis: in those social systems where scholastic achievement is rewarded, the correlations either increase over time, or decrease less than in the other schools. The data that allow examination of these hypotheses are presented in Table 58.[7] For boys and girls separately, the correlation between I.Q. (ordinarily given in the eighth or ninth grade in all these school systems; in Elmtown, I.Q.'s were not available for the present freshmen) and average freshmen grades are given. The correlation is averaged over the four classes, but in each case using freshman grades of that class.[8] Along with the correlation is the average yearly increase or decrease in the correlation. This is based on changes in the correlation for a given class, that is, the correlation between I.Q. and present grades received, minus the correlation between I.Q. and freshmen grades. There were three such differences, one for each of the three upper grades, and an average yearly change was computed from these.

Table 58—Correlation within a class between freshman grades and I.Q., averaged over the four classes in schools; and the average yearly change in the correlation between grades and I.Q.

School	BOYS		GIRLS	
	Correlation	Change	Correlation	Change
Farmdale	.603	+.029	.607	—.131
Marketville	.591	+.097	.504	+.024
Elmtown	.516	+.007	.645	+.054
Maple Grove	.620	—.012	.579	—.017
Green Junction	.559	+.043	.583	—.029
St. John's	.404	—.046		
Newlawn	.615	—.053	.603	—.020
Millburg	.493	+.007	.446	+.080
Midcity	.611	—.026	.571	—.014
Executive Heights	.540	—.030	.682	—.112

Perhaps these data show some relationship to the variations in importance of scholastic achievement in the different schools. If they do, the relationship is an obscure or complex one. The schools where scholastic activity is more highly rewarded by the culture are not distinguishable

7. The I.Q. test given in each school is listed in footnote 10 to this chapter.

8. This correlation was generally lower for seniors than for freshmen, very likely due to (a) the fact that dropouts were eliminated from the computation for later grades, making the population more homogeneous in both grades and I.Q., and thus tending to lower the correlation; and (b) the grades and I.Q.'s were farther apart in time for seniors than for freshmen.

from those where it is not. There do not even appear *general* differences between boys and girls. In short, it appears that the original hypothesis is not at all validated.

Upon reflection, however, one might question the original hypothesis in that the reasoning on which it was based related only to those at the top, those with highest ability. Thus, at the intermediate and low levels of ability one would have no reason to expect a higher correlation in those climates that rewarded scholastic activity than in those that did not. The question is, are the *high* achievers the ones with the most ability?

To examine this, the I.Q.'s of all boys whose average grades were 7 or 8 (A or A–) were examined relative to the I.Q. of the student body as a whole.[9] The variations are quite great: in Marketville, the boys who made an A or A– average have I.Q.'s 1.53 standard deviations above the school average; in Farmdale, their I.Q.'s are only about a third this distance above the mean, .59.[10] Given this variation, the question may be asked: do these variations in ability of the high performers correspond to variations in the social rewards for, or constraints against, being a good student?

Figure 9.5 shows, for the boys, the relation between the social rewards for academic excellence—that is, the frequency with which "good grades" was mentioned as a criterion for being in the leading crowd—and the ability of the high performers, measured in terms of the number of standard deviations their average I.Q. exceeds that of the rest of the boys in the school.

For the boys, the relation is extremely strong. Only St. John's deviates. In this school, many boys have their most important associations

---

9. In each school but Maple Grove and Midcity, this constituted from 6 to 8 per cent of the student body. In order to provide a correct test of the hypothesis, it is necessary to have the same fraction of the student body in each case (since I.Q.'s of this group are being measured in terms of number of standard deviations above the student body). To adjust these groups, enough 6's were added—each being assigned the average I.Q. of the total group of 6's—to bring the proportion up to 6 per cent (from 3 per cent in Maple Grove and 4 per cent in Midcity).

10. Since the I.Q. tests differ from school to school, and since each school has its own mean I.Q. and its own variation around that mean, ability of the high performers is measured in terms of the number of standard deviations their average I.Q.'s are above the mean. In this way, it is possible to see where the high performers' ability lies, relative to the distribution of abilities in their school.

The I.Q. tests used in the different schools were as follows: in Farmdale, California Mental Maturity (taken seventh, eighth, or ninth grade); in Marketville, California Mental Maturity (taken eighth grade); in Elmtown, SRA Primary Mental Abilities (taken tenth grade); in Maple Grove, California Mental Maturity (taken ninth grade) Seniors took SRA PMA, which was tabulated as percentile, and they have been omitted from analysis reported above); in Green Junction, Otis (grades nine, ten; taken eighth grade) and Kuhlman Finch (grade eleven, twelve; taken eighth grade); in St. John's, Otis (taken ninth grade); in Newlawn, California Mental Maturity (taken eighth grade); in Millburg, California Mental Maturity (taken eighth grade); in Midcity, Otis (taken ninth or tenth grade); in Executive Heights, Otis (taken eighth grade).

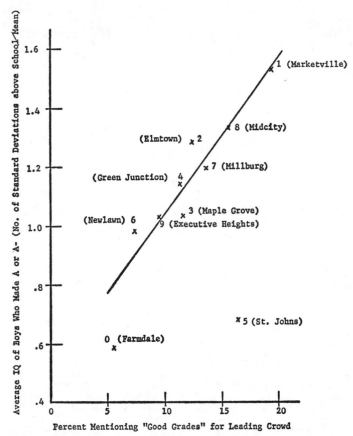

Figure 9.5—Relation between importance of good grades for membership in school's leading crowd and I.Q. level of those who made best grades in school, for boys.

outside, rather than within, the school, so that the student body constitutes far less of a social system, able to dispense social rewards and punishments, than in other schools.

Similarly for the girls, Figure 9.6 shows the I.Q. of high performers as a function of the proportion of girls saying that it takes "good grades" to get into the leading crowd.[11] Unfortunately, most of the schools are closely bunched in the degree to which good grades are important among the girls, so that there is too little variation among them to examine this

---

11. For the girls, only girls with a grade of 8 (that is, a straight A average) were included. Since girls get better grades than boys, this device is necessary in order to make the sizes of the "high performer" group roughly comparable for boys and for girls. Schools differed somewhat in the proportion of A's, constituting about 6 per cent of the students in the small schools, only about 3 per cent in Newlawn and

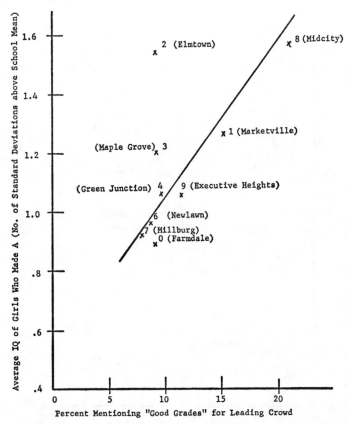

Figure 9.6—Relation between importance of good grades for membership in school's leading crowd and I.Q. level of those who made best grades in school, for girls.

effect as fully as would be desirable. Elmtown is the one school that, among the girls, deviates most from the general relationship.[12]

The effect of these value systems in letting academic ability express

Millburg, 1 per cent in Midcity, and 2 per cent in Executive Heights. In Midcity and Executive Heights, enough girls were added and assigned the average grade of the 7 (A—) group to bring the proportion to 3 per cent, comparable with the other large schools. The difference, however, between the large and small schools, remains. Newlawn is located, according to the leading-crowd question used for this graph, near the bottom, rather than in the upper group where it has been classified throughout the analysis. Because the proportion of girls getting A's is somewhat smaller than the proportion of boys getting A's and A—'s the relative I.Q.'s of the girls in Figure 9.6 cannot be directly compared with those of boys in Figure 9.5.

12. The I.Q.'s among the girls in Elmtown show a peculiar distribution. There were six girls whose I.Q. was listed in the office records as exactly 140, although no other girl in the school had an I.Q. listed above 130. Five of these six "140-I.Q." girls had a grade average of 8. Of the 18 other girls whose I.Q. was listed as 120 or above, the

itself in high achievement is evident among the girls as it is among the boys. It is important to realize that these effects are not merely due to the school facilities or its social composition. The two schools highest in the importance of scholastic achievement for both boys and girls are Marketville and Midcity, the first a small-town school of 350 students and the second a city school of 2,000 students. In both, there are fewer students with white-collar backgrounds than in Executive Heights, which is somewhere in the low middle in terms of the values its students place on academic achievement, but more than in Millburg or Green Junction, which are also somewhere in the low middle. The highest expenditure per student was $695 per year in Executive Heights, and the lowest was little more than half that, in Green Junction. These two schools are close together on the graphs of Figures 9.5 and 9.6.

These results are consistent with a recent (1956–57) extensive unpublished study through Connecticut using standard tests of achievement and ability, sponsored by the Connecticut Citizens for the Public Schools. The study found no correlation between per pupil expenditure in a school and the achievement of its 10th grade students relative to their ability. The effects shown in Figures 9.5 and 9.6 suggest why: that students with ability are led to achieve only when there are social rewards, primarily from their peers, for doing so.

As has been evident throughout this research, the variation among schools in the status of scholastic achievement is not nearly so striking as the fact that in all of them, academic achievement did not "count" for as much as did other activities in the school. Many other attributes were more important. In every school the boys named as best athletes and those named as most popular with girls were far more often mentioned as members of the leading crowd, and as someone to "be like" than were the boys named as best students. And the girls who were named as best dressed, and those named as most popular with boys, were in every school far more often mentioned as being in the leading crowd and as someone to be like, than were the girls named as best students.

The relative unimportance of academic achievement, together with the effects shown above, suggest that the adolescent subcultures in these schools exert a rather strong deterrent to academic achievement. In other words, in these adolescent societies, those who are seen as the "intellectuals," and who come to think of themselves in this way, are not really those of highest intelligence, but are only the ones who are willing to work hard at a relatively unrewarded activity.

---

grade average was far less: 5.9. It is hardly likely that this school contains 24 girls in the sophomore to senior classes with I.Q.'s of 120 or greater; the I.Q. test given undoubtedly overestimated the actual I.Q.'s in this school. The test used in this school is SRA Primary Mental Abilities, which has a top score of 140; six girls in the school had a raw score above this point and were given the top score.

The implications for American society as a whole are clear. Because high schools allow adolescent societies to divert energies into athletics, social activities, and the like, they recruit into adult intellectual activities many people with a rather mediocre level of ability, and fail to attract many with high levels of ability.

The actual loss of such persons with high potential to intellectual activities in society has been estimated in a study that shows the degree of loss with particular force. The table below is taken from that study.

Table 59—Estimated educational attainment of boys and girls with AGCT scores of 130 or higher*

	BOYS		GIRLS		BOTH SEXES	
	Annual no.	Per cent	Annual no.	Per cent	Annual no.	Per cent
In age group of 2,200,000	76,000	100	76,000	100	152,000	100
Finish high school	74,000	97	74,000	97	148,000	97
Enter college	48,000	63	32,000	42	80,000	53
Graduate from college	42,000	55	28,000	37	70,000	46
Receive Ph.D.	2,350	3.1	250	0.3	2,600	1.7

* From Dael Wolfle, America's Resources of Specialized Talent (New York: Harper and Brothers, 1954), p. 183.

Consequences of the Social Climate for Homework and College Attendance

Two factors that might at first seem highly dependent upon the social climate of the school are the amount of homework that a teen-ager does and his intentions about attending college. Yet both of these matters apparently have their primary sources elsewhere. The amount of homework done depends largely on two things: upon the amount of homework assigned by the teachers, and upon family background. College-going apparently depends more upon the aspiration a student's family has for him to attend college, and upon their interest in seeing him dependent upon them for four more years. However, the climate apparently has some effect—a peculiarly selective one—upon studying and upon college intentions.

Although father's education or occupation is only a rough indication of family constraints and desires for the child, it will be used here as a partial indicator of them. To be sure, in a community like Executive Heights, a boy or girl whose father has only a high-school diploma is likely to be of far higher status and have far greater aspirations for his child, than a father who has the same education but lives in Newlawn. Such differences should be kept in mind in interpreting the graphs below.

In Figures 9.7 and 9.8 the proportion of boys and of girls who spend

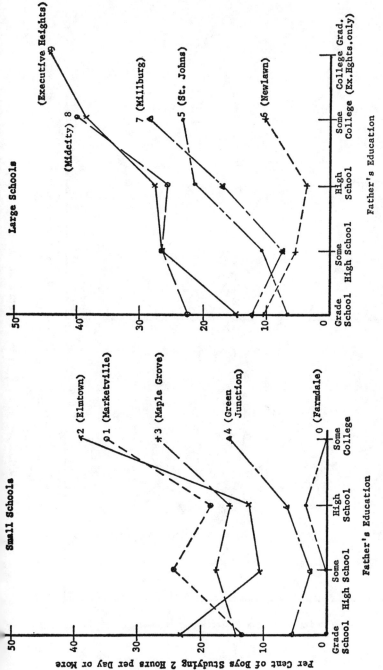

Figure 9.7—Relation between a boy's father's education and the time he spends studying at home, for each school.

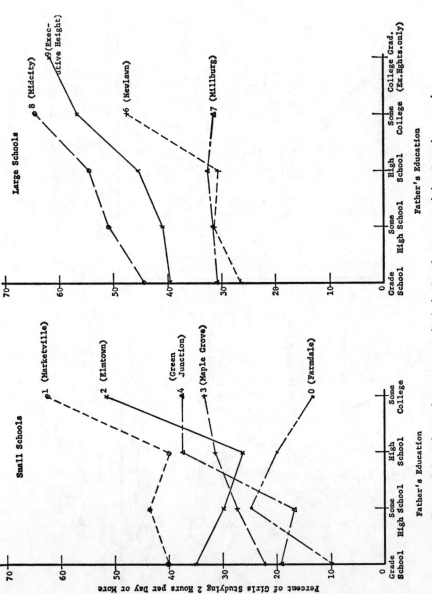

Figure 9.8—Relation between a girl's father's education and the time she spends

two hours or more per day on homework is given for four groups, classed according to father's education. Because the various educational groups are not large in some schools, some fluctuations are undoubtedly due to chance, so that no interpretation should be attempted for separate educational groups, but only for the school as a whole and for general trends.

There is some over-all increase in studying with increase in father's education—although not nearly so much as one might expect. Among the small schools the major deviations for the boys are Farmdale and Green Junction—two schools similar in two respects: little value attached to good grades, and much less homework is assigned than in the other schools. It is not possible to say which of these two factors is responsible for their difference from the other three small schools. A glance at the large schools, however, suggests that it is more nearly the teacher's assignments than the value system; for in St. John's and Millburg, where good grades are more important for status than in Executive Heights, studying is nevertheless lower. Executive Heights and Midcity, where most is expected of students by their teachers, are highest of the large schools.

It seems that the value system has an impact upon studying for all girls, and not only for those with high educational backgrounds (Figure 9.8). Girls in Marketville and Midcity, with the two most scholastically oriented value climates, are highest and about equal in studying for all educational groups. The value systems among the girls in these two schools differed sharply from the others. In general, it appears that the value climate has more effect upon girls' studying than upon boys'.

Figures 9.9 and 9.10 show the proportions of boys and girls in each school intending to go to college, by this same educational classification. The much higher correlation of father's education with college-going than with studying is striking. The students from higher educational backgrounds study slightly more than the others; but they plan far more to go to college than do the others.

Second, the proportion of Executive Heights girls and boys who say they are going to college is higher than in any of the other large schools —especially among the girls, although as Figures 9.8 showed, their studying was *less* in each educational group than among the girls in Midcity or Marketville. This apparently reflects parental expectations, and the fact that college going is the "thing to do" in this school. That is, the adolescent value system probably affects a boy's or girl's tendency to go to college in this school, *not* because the values emphasize scholastic achievement, but because they emphasize college-going.

Among the small-school girls, those in Elmtown are the only ones

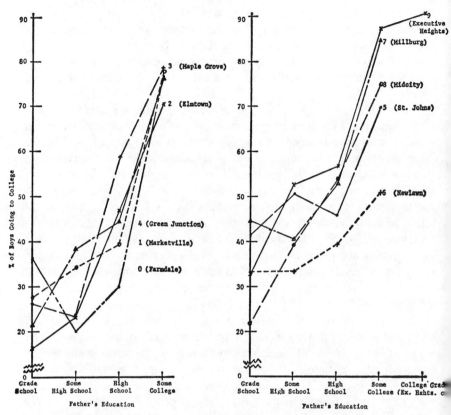

Figure 9.9—Relation between a boy's father's education and his intention to go to college, for each school.

who radically deviate, in every educational group, by their low college-going. One might be tempted to attribute this to the non-academic status system of the school, were it not for the fact that college-going in Farm-dale, Maple Grove, and Green Junction—where scholastic achievement is as unimportant as in Elmtown—is so much higher. It is more probable that this is, again, a value of the larger culture, as in Executive Heights but in reverse: that for a girl, going to college is not a highly valued matter in the community. This perspective is traditionally held to be a "working-class value"; but this community is not so working-class as Newlawn or Millburg, and little more so than Green Junction. Even when father's education is held constant, there is less college-going among the Elmtown girls than among the girls in those schools. In the white-collar occupational groups, the difference is 30 to 40 per cent compared to the other small schools—a difference that cannot be attributed to social class of parents. Thus, somewhat inexplicably, college-going is particularly low among Elmtown girls.

A final comparison of these graphs of college-going shows an interesting large school–small school difference. In the large schools, the college-going of *boys* is generally higher than in the small schools (when father's education is held constant). The reverse is true for the girls: college-going tends to be higher in the small schools (with the exception of Elmtown) than in the large ones, for each educational group. Furthermore, the boys in these small towns are less likely—at least according to intentions expressed—to go to college than are the girls in these communities from the same backgrounds. In the city and suburban schools, the boys are *more* likely to go than the girls from the same educational backgrounds.

These differences may be due to a different relationship of girls and

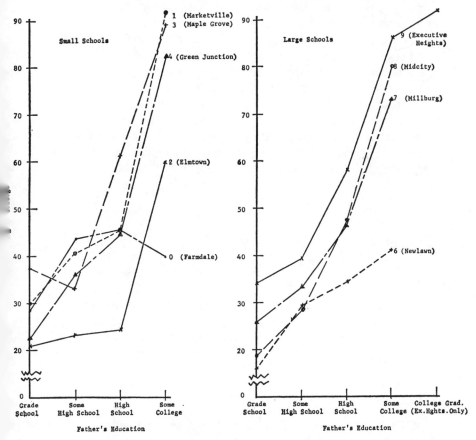

Figure 9.10—Relation between a girl's father's education and her intention to go to college, for each school.

SCHOLASTIC EFFECTS OF THE SOCIAL SYSTEM

boys to the community in large and small towns. In the small town, boys were far more likely than girls to say they would take a job in the same town rather than in a different one, if the jobs were equal (see Chapter IV, page 124). The girls far more often want to leave town. The dynamics of the process are unclear, but it is clear that girls want far more to leave town than do the boys. It is likely that many boys can follow into their father's occupation, business, or farm. In the city or suburb, following in parental footsteps is not so easy, since the father works away from home, often outside the community. Thus, the city or suburb has little to offer a boy unless he has formal training, and can get a job by virtue of training through bureaucratic channels. In contrast, the girls' "career chances," that is, their chances of making a good marriage, are more augmented by college for the small-town girl than for the city girl. For a small-town girl, college expands the range of boys from whom she can find a mate more than it does for the large-school girl, who already has a larger selection in her school and community.

These interpretations are only suggestive, for the evidence to test them is not available. The present evidence does suggest, however, that there are important differences in the relation of boys and girls to a small town, and that these differences vanish or reverse in the city.[13]

Altogether, the effects of the climates on college-going and studying seem less than one might a priori expect. When there *are* effects, they seem most pronounced for the girls—e.g., the high studying of Midcity and Marketville girls, the low college-going of Elmtown girls.

Consequences of Different Structures: The All-Around Boy vs. the Specialist

The different structures among elites have consequences for the ways in which boys will expend their energies. In a school where it is important to be *both* an athlete and a scholar, and perhaps a ladies' man as well, many boys will spread their energies over all these areas. In a school where it is important to be an athlete *or* a scholar, boys will tend to specialize. Some boys will concentrate on doing well scholastically, while others will concentrate on being good athletes.

---

13. The oppressive norms of a small town seem partly responsible for this result. Girls are more constrained by these norms, and if they stay in town are expected to become the upholders and transmitters of the norms. No such burden is imposed on the boys.

The different structures also have consequences on how the high achievers are perceived in the system. In a system that rewards the athlete-scholar, when a boy is thinking of someone to model himself after, he thinks of this all-around boy, leaving the specialist aside. In particular, when thinking of a good student to be like, his thoughts will quickly turn to the boy who is a "good all-around guy" as well—a boy who is not a grind, but who makes the football team and is popular with girls.

In the schools where athletics and scholastics are rewarded separately, they are seen as distinct activities. A good student who is regarded as a model is looked up to *because* he is a good student, not because this makes him a good all-around boy. If an athlete is looked up to as a model, it is *as* an athlete, not as an all-around boy who achieves in everything.

Is it better to create all-around boys or specialists? Is it better for the social system to push an athlete toward studying and a scholar toward athletics, or to push them further in their present directions? Is it better for the system to be pluralistic by giving rewards for various activities independently, or to be pluralistic in a more restricted sense, by giving rewards only for a certain combination of activities?

These questions cannot be answered here, but a few consequences of the two different systems may be examined. First, looking back to Chapter V, certain schools especially reward the "all-around boy." This is most pronounced in Executive Heights, but, among the large schools, Midcity and St. Johns show the same tendency. Millburg and Newlawn do not. Among the small schools, Maple Grove and Elmtown reward the all-around boy, as does Green Junction to a lesser degree. Marketville and Farmdale keep the two roles separate, and Marketville rewards them both highly.

CONSEQUENCES FOR GRADES OF TOP ATHLETES AND TOP SCHOLARS

One consequence of this structural difference is in the grades of the star athletes and star scholars. In a school where the two roles are rewarded only in combination, the star athletes will tend to work harder in school. Their grades should be higher than their counterparts in schools where the athlete is rewarded for athletic excellence alone.

Conversely, the boys seen as star scholars will not be extreme scholars. Both because the best students will have their energies diverted to other activities, such as athletics, and because the boys seen as best students will sometimes be good athletes who merely stand out somewhat in studies, the grades of "best students" will not be exceedingly high.

Where the roles are separate, and a boy receives no special rewards for being an all-around boy, the star athlete will not worry about good grades, and the star student will concentrate on them. And because scholastic success is a distinct arena of achievement, the boys named as best students will *be* the best students, not just athletes who do well in studies.

Table 60 below shows, for each of the small schools, the average grades of boys named seven times or more as best students and those named seven times or more as best athletes. The schools are grouped according to whether they offer rewards for the all-around boy or for the specialist. Grades are on an 8-point scale (8 = A, 6 = B, . . ., 0 = F).

Table 60—Average grades of top students (7 or more choices) and top athletes (7 or more choices) in the five small schools

	GRADES		
	Top scholars	Top athletes	Difference
Rewards for "all-around boy"			
Maple Grove	6.8	5.6	1.2
Elmtown	7.0	5.0	2.1
Green Junction	6.9	4.0	2.9
Rewards for "specialist"			
Marketville	7.4	3.2	4.2
Farmdale	7.5	3.0	4.5
Number of cases			
Maple Grove	(6)	(5)	
Elmtown	(6)	(7)	
Green Junction	(6)	(6)	
Marketville	(5)	(6)	
Farmdale	(2)	(1)	

Table 60 shows strikingly the effect of this structural difference: in Maple Grove, where there are a number of "all-around boys" and they are highly rewarded, the grade difference between the top students and top athletes is only 1.2 points—less than one letter grade. In Marketville, where the two roles are separately rewarded, and Farmdale, where neither is highly rewarded but there is no attention to the all-around boy, the grade difference is 4.2 and 4.5 respectively—more than *two* letter grades. The top scholars in these two schools make nearly straight A averages, and the top athletes C—; while in Maple Grove, the difference is between B+ and B—; in Elmtown, A— and B—; and in Green Junction, B+ and straight C.

The structural differences among these schools thus have a very powerful influence on the way top scholars and top athletes distribute their energies—whether they concentrate on their strengths or distribute their efforts.

The top scholars and athletes in the large schools are shown in Table

61. The top scholars and top athletes in the one school with greatest rewards for the all-around boy have the least grade difference. The school is Executive Heights, and the difference is between B+ and C+, one letter grade. At the opposite extreme is Millburg, the school where the all-around boy gets least rewards, beyond those of the pure athlete and pure scholar. The difference is between straight A and C−, more than two letter grades difference.

Table 61—Average grades of top students (7 or more choices) and top athletes (7 or more choices) in the five small schools

	GRADES		
	Top scholars	Top athletes	Difference
Rewards for "all-around boy"			
Executive Heights	6.8	4.8	2.0
Midcity	7.1	4.5	2.6
St. John's	7.6	4.1	3.5
Rewards for "specialist"			
Newlawn	7.4	4.3	3.1
Millburg	7.9	3.3	4.6
Number of cases			
Executive Heights	(17)	(17)	
Midcity	(11)	(20)	
St. John's	(11)	(20)	
Newlawn	(9)	(9)	
Millburg	(8)	(12)	

The other schools are in between. The only one where the grade difference seems inconsistent with the structure of rewards is St. John's. Here the grades of the two groups are rather far apart (A− and C), although, as Chapter V showed, there are rewards for the all-around boy. This is the only school among the ten in which the grades of the top athletes and scholars fail to reflect the structure of social rewards.

There are, then, definite consequences of the specialization of roles of athlete and student, or the pressure toward all-around achievement. In both small and large schools, grade differences of top athletes and top scholars correspond to the extra social rewards given to the athlete-scholar. Where there is little extra social encouragement of the athlete-scholar, the two roles diverge, with the athlete and scholar becoming "specialists." In schools like Maple Grove and Executive Heights, where there is much social encouragement of the combined roles, the boys seen as best students are not really such good students, while the athletes are less specialized as athletes and get better grades.

Such specialization, surprisingly enough, does not increase markedly as the size of the school increases. In the large schools, there is as much overlap of choice between the best scholars and best athletes as in the smaller ones, and the grades of top athletes and top scholars are no further apart in the large schools. The variation within each size group is far greater than the variation between groups. The two largest schools, for example, Executive Heights and Midcity, show *less* specialization among athletes and scholars than do the two smallest ones, Marketville and Farmdale.

CONSEQUENCES FOR THE STABILITY OF THE SYSTEM: MARKETVILLE AS AN EXAMPLE

The status system among the boys in Marketville is a particularly interesting one, because its structure is different from that of the other small schools. The status systems of Elmtown and Maple Grove encourage a combination of athlete and scholar in the same boy; the status system of Green Junction rewards only the athlete, regardless of his interest and capabilities in scholastic matters; the status system of Farmdale has few rewards for either athlete or scholar; but the status system of Marketville gives rewards to the athlete and the scholar, viewed as separate roles.

Here scholars and athletes are more nearly "specialists"—the first concentrating on doing well scholastically, and the second achieving little in scholastic matters. The best students think of themselves more as scholars in this school, and want to be remembered as a "brilliant student," more than is true in the other small schools. On the basis of both quantitative and qualitative evidence, it appears that the boys named as best scholars in Marketville had more interest in intellectual pursuits than their counterparts in the other small schools.

Yet there is some evidence for another consequence of this system of "separate but equal" roles for the student and athlete, a consequence for the value climate itself.

In Marketville, there is a great difference between the senior class and the other three in the importance of scholastic achievement for the status system. The seniors were almost the lowest of all the ten schools, while the other classes were at or near the top of the list (See Chapter III). No other school showed such a striking difference between classes. In another way as well, the boys in Marketville appeared to deviate from the general image of a scholastically oriented status system. Over the school year, the proportion choosing the image of brilliant student as the way to be remembered decreased greatly (over 6 per cent decrease, while no other school decreased more than 2 per cent). Thus, just as there was a great difference between classes in the value climate of Marketville boys, there was a great change over the period of the year.

What accounts for these peculiarities in a system that otherwise rewards scholastic achievement highly?

Marketville had a remarkably successful athletic season, both in basketball and in football. As small as this school is, two senior boys were offered athletic scholarships by state universities, one for his football prowess and the other for his basketball ability. In this senior class, no boys were really outstanding scholastically—in contrast to the junior class, where the boy most often named as best student was the center of the leading group, a boy with aspirations to study political science at Harvard.

In Marketville, the absence of an outstanding senior scholar and the presence of outstanding athletes seem to be responsible for the very great difference between the senior class and the others. Similarly, the extreme success in athletics may have been responsible for the changes in the value system that occurred over the year. It appears that this success in athletics "swamped" the value system of the school for 1957–58, and the presence of outstanding athletes in the senior class swamped the value system in that class.

How did athletics swamp the value system? Paradoxically, colleges had a hand in the matter—three respectable universities. One of the two star athletes in the senior class is a likable farm boy whose real interest was exhibited in an interview. When asked about his interests, he said, "I fight chickens." He and his older brother and father staged cockfights in the country. He had made the acquaintance of a racing man who offered him a job in Florida racing greyhounds. By springtime, matters had changed. When asked, "How long have you planned to go to college?" he replied, "Last semester—since I got this football recognition and track recognition, colleges became interested in me right away." They were colleges that most students in school might aspire to: the Universities of Indiana, Illinois, and Tennessee. Meanwhile, the brilliant junior boy, interested in studying political science and then law, was not being sought out by any college, and would doubtless need to ferret out information about college admission as best he could when time came for him to attend college.

Thus, not just the student body and the community, but colleges as well gave the laurels of success to the star athlete. Possibly as a result, the values of the school shifted sharply toward athletics.

It seems reasonable to assume that these radical shifts that occurred in Marketville were partially due to the structure of the status system, that is, the differentiation of roles between scholar and athlete. It seems likely that such a status system is in a balance far more delicate than one in which the roles of athlete and student are combined. Students differ from year to year; good athletes who are personally popular will turn up during some years, while other years will cast up good scholars with similarly likable personalities. If the good athletes are also induced to pass off as good scholars, and the good scholars induced to achieve in athletics, the value system cannot be radically altered by this varying supply from year to year, and by the variable success in athletics. If, however, as in Marketville, the roles are specialized, then it seems likely that the value system will fluctuate widely as the supply of scholars and athletes fluctuates from year to year.

In one sense, then, a value system that combines these two roles includes a "safety device" which the other does not. It will never become highly academically oriented, but neither will it become primarily focused on athletics. Which is the more desirable system from the point of view of these schools' aims is not easy to tell. Is dilution worse than swamping? Given the context in which these schools operate, they must decide this question, consciously or not. But the context, in which colleges play their part, as exemplified above, forces the alternatives upon them.

This instability should of course be less and less with increase in the size of the school, for the supply of boys is large enough not to be affected so much by chance factors. It is in the small schools where this structural difference in the status system may be expected to have its greatest impact.

X Sources of the Adolescent
Value Systems

THE PRECEDING CHAPTERS HAVE EX-
amined the nature of the adolescent social systems in these high schools
and have noted some of their effects on the lives of the boys and girls
who find themselves in these systems. The casual observer's reaction
might be: "So what? Is this not the way matters have always been, will
always be, and must be, among adolescents?" The present chapter is
intended as a partial answer to such a question. To be sure, the variations
in value systems among different schools indicates that these values are
not fixed and unmovable; it is important to learn what accounts for these
variations. Even if the variations did not exist, however, it would be important to ask why these systems are in general as we found them: for
example, why do athletics dominate the scene so often? Why is popularity with boys so important in the girls' status system?

Thus, the aim of this chapter will be to examine a few of the elements
that give these adolescent social systems their particular values. Some of
these elements differ from school to school, and thus account for differences in the climates. Others are alike in all of these schools, thus account-
ing for the over-all similarities in values. But even many of these general
elements are subject to *change*, and may be altered by changes in the
structure of high-school education.

Population Composition of the Community

The cumulative impact of the previous analysis suggests a curious and complex effect of the population composition of a school and community. In particular:

a) Chapter III showed that "family background," as an element in the status system, was important in only the most middle-class schools: Executive Heights, Midcity, Maple Grove, and Marketville. In the more working-class schools, whether in small town, city, or suburb, it was seldom mentioned as a criterion for membership in the leading crowd.

b) Chapter IV showed two tendencies in the background characteristics of elites in the schools. First, there was a general tendency, stronger for girls than for boys, favoring students from higher educational backgrounds. Thus, in general, the elites contained more sons and daughters from the higher-status segments of the community.[1] Beyond this, however, there was a tendency for the elites to be like the student body in their characteristics. In the elites of the more working-class schools, the middle-class bias was either reduced or vanished altogether. Consequently the backgrounds *and* the interests come to be closer to the rest of the school, more infused with out-of-school concerns. For example, in Farmdale, Elmtown, and Newlawn, where the boys as a whole were most interested in cars, the elites themselves were not only more interested in cars than were the elites in other schools, but their interest in cars most closely approached that of their respective student bodies.

c) Chapter VII showed that there were "status upsets" in some grades in the leading cliques in Elmtown and Green Junction, but no such upsets in Marketville and Maple Grove. Girls whose interests veered away from school gained control of the system in some grades of the former schools, both of them schools in which the student bodies had lower educational backgrounds than those in Marketville and Maple Grove.

---

1. It is important to note that such a tendency need not be caused by ascriptive criteria for membership in the leading crowd. Although such ascriptive criteria are important in some schools, the kinds of attributes a higher-status family gives its child are important as well: interest in school activities and in scholastic achievement; skills in these same directions; obedience to the formal demands of the school; good clothes; social skills ranging from manners to dancing, and so forth. Perhaps one of the most important of these attributes is the ability to defer gratifications, to make short-term sacrifices in view of long-term gains. See the paper by Schneider and Lysgaard, *op. cit.*, which discusses this pattern among middle-class children.

d) The school at the high-status end of the population continuum, Executive Heights, has shown throughout a system giving little status to academic achievement. This status system exists in the face of great *individual* concern of students with college admission and the grades necessary for admission. The leading crowds were not unconcerned with school and not anti-school; to the contrary, they were very much involved in the various things surrounding the classroom—activities and organizations, athletics, and, above all, social activities in and around school. But the leading crowd of boys did not contain the top scholars more often than did the leading crowds in working-class schools, such as Newlawn and Millburg; the leading crowd of girls was not much more hospitable to the top scholars.

These four results together suggest two quite different effects of population composition. Suppose the schools to be divided into three groups, according to their proportion with middle- or upper-middle-class backgrounds, or the proportion with high educational backgrounds. There appear to be three distinct segments of this continuum, in terms of the functioning of the status system. At the low end is a segment within which lie Farmdale, Elmtown, Green Junction, St. John's, Newlawn, and Millburg. In the middle is a segment represented by Marketville, Maple Grove, and Midcity. At the high end is a third segment, represented here only by Executive Heights, but a segment toward which more and more high schools are drifting, as educational and income levels increase in this country.

SCHOOLS AT THE LOW END

At the low end of the continuum, the prevalence of working-class backgrounds and out-of-school interests in the whole student body tend to generate elites with similar backgrounds and orientations. Elites in a fluid social structure, such as high schools represent, must have some attributes in common with their followers, for they are elites only by virtue of nomination by, or at least acquiescence of, the followers. Thus, they must exemplify those interests most important to their followers.

The elites of a student body may be interested in scholarship only so long as the student body contains enough *others* interested in scholarship that social support can develop for this interest. When the student body contains a high proportion of those uninterested in scholarship—because their parents lack interest in education or because there are bad relations between students and teachers—then the elites must also be this way, or lose their positions of leadership. Elites can sometimes lead their popular support in directions they choose, but often they must themselves be led by it if they are to remain its leaders.[2] Such observations about leadership and followers have often been made; that they are in fact true for high schools is shown by the evidence mentioned in (b) and (c) above.

When a school's population is predominantly uninterested in school, there are at least two ways for a school-oriented elite to lead the school:

1) If there is a very special organization of activities in school, and skill on the part of teachers to transform the interests of a large part of the student body from out-of-school matters to in-school matters, a school-oriented elite may survive. For boys, interschool athletics, although it has its own added consequences in shaping the values of the culture, creates an elite whose interests are within the school, and undercuts the bid of anti-school groups for leadership of the system. There is nothing comparable to this for girls. If girls were not far more school-oriented and obedient than boys to begin with, the lack of activities comparable to athletics might have unfortunate consequences for schools with a population base such as Farmdale, Elmtown, Green Junction, Newlawn, St. John's, and Millburg.

2) Dominance from the white-collar segment of the adult community will insure an unchallenged school-oriented elite. Although such dominance has its ill consequences in creating a system that stifles rather than stimulates energies of those who are excluded, it is effective in insuring that the dominant elite in school will be oriented to school and its activities. Probably an important change in Elmtown between 1941, when it was studied by Hollingshead, and 1957–58, when this study took place, is the reduction in external dominance and dictation from the parental community.[3] This has created a system wherein the chances for leadership are more independent of parental background than they once were (as Hollingshead implicitly encouraged throughout his research); but it has brought other problems with it, as the data of the present study indicate.

SCHOOLS IN THE MIDDLE

Perhaps the task of the school administration is simplest when the population falls into the middle region, as does that of Marketville,

---

2. See Merei, *op. cit.*, for an excellent example of this.
3. See Hollingshead, *Elmtown's Youth*. Another important change has been the increase in high-school attendance among working-class boys and girls. Without a change in the population base of the adult community, this has created a change in the population composition of the *school*, shifting it much further in a working-class direction, perhaps from the middle segment of the population continuum to the low segment.

Maple Grove, and Midcity. Here the "natural leaders" are also those who do best in school. There is a large enough middle-class population base in school to support such leaders. The situation does not necessarily mean that the leading crowd will hold high achievement in school as a positive value: in Maple Grove, the leading crowd's values and major interests are far more social than in Marketville, which falls into the same population region. It is the *opportunity* for the leading crowd to use such criteria to differentiate it from the others that is created, not the *necessity* to do so. That is, the leading crowd in this region has a number of attributes that differentiate it from the rest of the students: they are brighter; better trained in early years; better dressed; more skilled in the organizational qualities required for extracurricular activities; and more skilled in social graces, such as dancing, how to behave toward the opposite sex, self-assurance with others their age and with adults. Any one or several of these attributes can become the dominant feature that the leading crowd uses to distinguish itself. In Maple Grove, it seems to be primarily social matters, then extracurricular activities; in Midcity and Marketville, the leading crowd combines these social attributes with a greater importance attached to good grades.[4] Other factors, such as the teachers in the school, help determine which of these attributes become the ones that the leading crowd "uses" and is proud of. The major point, however, about schools in this middle population region is that the "natural leaders" combine in themselves social and intellectual skills that set them off from other students with less advantaged backgrounds.

SCHOOLS AT THE HIGH END

In the third population region, the large *majority* of the population is school-oriented. Social skills, participation in school activities, and the ability to make good grades are widely distributed throughout the school population. Since the elite, by definition, can be only a small segment of the student body, a question arises in such a school that never comes up where these skills are concentrated in a minority: *which* of these groups—the socially adept, the activities leaders, or the scholars—is to be the leading crowd? All are oriented to school and even to further educa-

---

4. One informant, who recently graduated from Springfield High School, in Springfield, Illinois, reports that the leading clique of girls was so strongly concerned about maintaining their grade average that they coached members whose grade in a course threatened to fall below B. This clique was highly exclusive and based on family background, but its values included excelling in grades. Thus, as in Midcity and Marketville, the leading crowd had its origins in family position, but maintained its dominance partly through high grades.

tion after school, but some specialize in social activities, others specialize in extracurricular activities, and still others specialize in academic pursuits. This is illustrated well by the data of Table 35 (p. 171), which shows the overlap between "beauty" and "brains" in each school. Of the large schools, the overlap is far lowest in Executive Heights—less than half its value in the other large schools. In contrast, in a school like Midcity, with a middle-class minority, popularity with boys and good grades are more nearly located in the same girls.

Schools like Executive Heights are typical of the third population region. As more and more of the population in this country becomes well educated and oriented to sending their children to college, more and more schools will be in this region. In such a school, *which* of these interested, eager students is going to capture the attention of their fellows, and direct the energies of the student body?

Given the fact that intellectual activities, in contrast to organizational or social or athletic ones, are primarily *individual*, it seems unlikely that the "intellectuals" can become the primary focus of attention. Highly individual activities offer little opportunity to capture the attention of the school. Debate is an exception, for it incorporates the notion of interscholastic competition. The debate team in Midcity was a center of the leading crowd and, at the same time, a center of intellectual interests. There is, as it happens, no debate in Executive Heights.

There are, then, distinctive problems concerning the nature and interests of the leading crowd in school—and hence the pull exerted by the adolescent status system—in each of these three different population regions. Since the third is becoming more prevalent in society, and since it presents especially difficult problems, their solution becomes particularly important.

This discussion of the dependence of the status system upon the population composition is most relevant to the girls' status system. For boys, the extremely powerful impact of interschool athletics overcomes, to some degree, the importance of the population differences. Athletes come from all strata of the population. The status systems of the boys are more alike from school to school, and less dependent upon the social composition of the school, than are those of the girls. The similar importance of athletics in all the schools was evident in Chapter III and elsewhere. Another piece of evidence was seen in Chapter V, in the overlap between athlete and scholar. In contrast to the separation of "beauty" and "brains" among girls in Executive Heights, there is as much overlap between Executive Heights' athletes and scholars as in the other large schools.

Deterioration of Student-Teacher Relations and Its Effects

Relations between students and teachers have important effects on the status system, as well as effects beyond high school. Elmtown illustrates a situation that is undoubtedly a frequent one in allowing the emergence of generally anti-school groups as serious contenders for adolescent leadership. In interviews with girls in this school, it appeared that there was a general lack of sympathy between teachers and adolescents, and between the general adult community and the adolescents. For example, the school board had just abolished the traditional senior trip, taken at the end of the senior year, a custom followed not only by this school but by a number of other small-town schools in the area. This action was retaliation for escapades of the previous year's seniors on their trip. As a second example, there was, at the time of one group interview, a current dispute over a class play, which had been cut and rearranged by the faculty sponsor to the irritation of the girls being interviewed. During the interview, the way in which the deterioration of relations undercut the school-oriented crowd was quite evident: whenever a girl from the non–school-oriented group would discuss the teachers negatively, the school-oriented girls were silent or gave assent; whenever a positive point was mentioned by one of the latter girls, it went unsupported and was often successfully challenged by the non–school-oriented group. Thus, the ground was cut from under the school-oriented girls, and their bid for popular control of the student body was left with little effective support from the teachers.

The deterioration of relations is evident in answers to a question asked students about the teachers and one asked teachers about the students. Teachers were asked:

> T.44. In which of the following areas would you say there are problems of discipline with the students in this school? (Check items that are problems.)
>
> 1. Stealing (small items of little value)
> 2. Stealing of serious nature (money, cars)
> 3. Destruction of school property
> 4. Sex offenses
> 5. Impertinence and discourtesy to teachers
> 6. Fighting
> 7. Truancy
> 8. Physical violence against teachers

9. Using profane or obscene language
0. Using narcotics
x. Drinking intoxicants

Answers to this question can be seen partly as accurate responses on the teachers' part and, thus, a measure of the amount of "problem" activities on the part of the student; but they can also be seen as a measure of the teachers' discord with, and alienation from, the students.

Students were asked:

I.142. Which of the items below fit most of the *teachers* here at school? (Check as many as apply.)

5. Friendly
6. Too strict
7. Too easy with schoolwork
8. Understand problems of teen-agers
9. Not interested in teen-agers
0. Willing to help out in activities

One of these items, "not interested in teen-agers," is a general negative response concerning the teachers. Thus, the number of responses to this item should indicate, from the students' side, their discord with, and alienation from, the teachers. Table 62 shows the responses to these two questions in all schools together, and in Elmtown.

Table 62—Responses of students to negative item about teachers, and of teachers to negative items about students

	All schools	Elmtown
Per cent of students saying teachers are "not interested in teen-agers"	12.4 (N = 8,888)	16.0 (N = 512)
Average number of negative items mentioned by teachers	2.7 (N = 389)	3.4 (N = 25)

For the students and for the teachers, the negative responses are higher in Elmtown than in the other schools. It seems very likely that the deteriorated relations undermined, in the way indicated in some of the examples above, the possibility of unchallenged dominance by the school-oriented cliques of girls. This undermining of the school-oriented cliques, together with their precarious position as a minority of the population, helped give the status system its focus on out-of-school activities.

There is a further consequence of the poor relations between students and teachers in Elmtown, which has implications far beyond the value climate of the school itself. In both fall and spring, all girls were asked whether they would most like to be an actress or artist, a nurse, a model, or a schoolteacher, assuming that they could be any of these (question I.68).

The proportion checking "schoolteacher" among all schools together and among the girls of Elmtown are shown below in Table 63. In the fall, Elmtown's girls were second lowest in the proportion who wanted to be a schoolteacher—lowest were the girls of Farmdale, who increased between fall and spring, rather than decreasing, as did those of Elmtown. In the spring, they were not only lowest of nine schools, their number had decreased by 8 girls out of 59, the largest percentage drop that occurred in any of the schools.

Table 63—Girls checking "schoolteacher" in fall and spring, in all schools and in Elmtown

	Fall	Spring
All schools		
Per cent	20.6	20.6
Number	(4,057)	(3,922)
Elmtown		
Per cent	15.8	12.8
Number	(242)	(242)

It is not possible to say with assurance that the deterioration of relations shown in Table 62 caused the initially low choice of school-teacher, or the drop over the school year. Yet the circumstantial evidence is certainly great. The implications, of course, are far more general than the implications for Elmtown alone. They suggest that adolescents' desires to go into teaching are strongly affected by their experiences in school, and by the relations that exist between them and their teachers. A girl coming into a school with aims of being a schoolteacher may find her interest dampening if there is a less-than-pleasant state of relations between her friends and her teachers.

Traditional Constraint, Modern Liberation, and Early Social Maturity

The degree to which an adolescent is kept a child or given the free-doms of an adult differs among schools and among the students within a school. It has traditionally been assumed that parental constraints are greater and continue over a longer period of time in middle-class families than in working-class families. One of the important advantages that a middle-class girl in Farmdale, Marketville, Elmtown, Maple Grove, or Green Junction has over a working-class girl is the control her parents exercise over her dating—not allowing her to date so young or with such freedom from scrutiny as the average girl from a working-class family.

Yet the greater attention of the modern upper-middle-class parent to his child may be accompanied by other tendencies that free the child sooner from parental control. One evidence of this is provided by responses to the question asking whether or not they would join a particular club in school if their parents did not approve of the group (I.134). For simplicity, only the girls' responses to this question will be examined. The boys' are similar, although the effects discussed below are less pronounced.

One's expectation is that a middle-class girl would obey her parents, staying away from the disapproved club more than would the girl from a working-class background. As it turns out, this is true in the small schools. Precisely the opposite is true in the large schools (Figure 10.1). The contrast between the small and large schools is striking. In the small-town schools, the daughters of better-educated parents are *less* likely to join the club than are the girls from lower educational backgrounds. In the large schools, the girls from better-educated backgrounds are *more* likely to join.

This question serves as a good indicator of the degree to which a girl is "released" from her family's demands, into the adolescent culture. As such, it suggests that the usual notion of stronger and longer parental

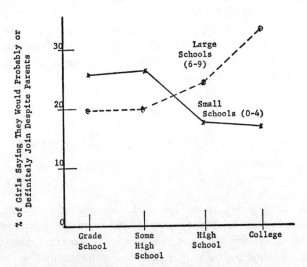

Figure 10.1—Relation between willingness of girls to join a club in school despite parents' disapproval, and father's education, for large and small schools separately.

constraints from middle-class families is true only in the small towns, and not in the city or suburb, where the style of life of middle-class families is very different from that of their counterparts in a small town. Further evidence that this is so is provided by the separate communities (Figure 10.2). (The small ones are grouped into those that are more middle-class —Marketville and Maple Grove—and those that are less so—Farmdale, Elmtown, and Green Junction.) For each of the schools, there is the opposite tendency in the small-town schools and in the city and suburban ones: in the small-town, the daughters of well-educated families are less likely to go against parents' demands than are the girls from lower educational backgrounds; in the large schools, the *reverse* is true. But there is an important added confirmation from this graph of the separate schools: in the small-town schools, the entire level of disregarding parental demands is lower in the more white-collar schools—Marketville and Maple Grove—for girls from *all* social backgrounds. In the large schools, the level of disregarding parents' demands is by far highest in Executive Heights; it is lowest in Millburg.

As a result of the family and community effects, the Executive Heights daughters of well-educated fathers are higher than any other group in their decision to join the club in the face of parental protest. *Nearest* them in this regard are the daughters of poorly educated fathers in the most working-class small towns; *furthest* from them are the daughters of well-educated fathers in the most white-collar small towns of Marketville

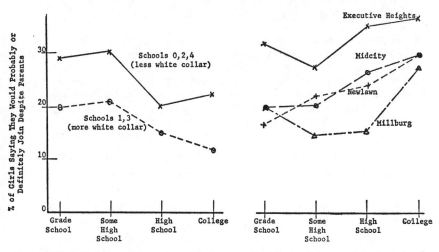

Figure 10.2—Relation between willingness of girls to join a club in school despite parents' disapproval, and father's education, for specific schools.

and Maple Grove. Thus, the daughters of "traditional middle-class" parents in small towns and the daughters of "modern middle-class" parents in Executive Heights are at opposite poles: the former least likely to join a club against parents' wishes, the latter most likely to do so.

What is responsible for this strange reversal in the cities and suburbs, and what are the implications of it? There is one phenomenon among upper-middle-class parents, apparently related to this—the extreme concern of these parents with the child's social maturity. Attempts are made, within school and without, to give the child self-assurance and social skills. It is useful to repeat part of an excerpt from the school newspaper of Executive Heights:

SOPHOMORES, this is your chance to learn how to dance. The first day of sophomore dancing is Nov. 14, and it will begin at 8:30 A.M. in the Boys' Gym. . . .
    NO ONE is required to take dancing but it is highly recommended for both boys and girls. . . .

Similarly, in the very academically oriented university high school that was added to the study, No. 10, the pre-freshmen (seventh-graders) have formal dancing instruction in the school. One of the members of the staff reports that one of the problems in the school is that of handling boys and girls whose self-assurance and social maturity are great, but whose sense of responsibility is only that of an ordinary teen-ager.

Reports from some parents in Executive Heights give a similar sense of a community in which some parents are concerned with giving their children "all the advantages":

The outstanding negative characteristic particularly noticeable in the school is the definite "class" division created by those students who are given too many material advantages, such as cars, clothes, and money. The students whose parents cannot afford or who do not believe in such extravagances are ostracized from certain groups or clubs. Snobbishness is definitely noticeable. The creation and maintenance of tightly formed "cliques" formulated in grammar school and maintained through the high-school years prevents many students being asked to join various clubs or being invited to various social activities.

It is as if the parents, whose children must compete with many others of the same educational and intellectual background, want to make certain that their child can compete socially, on equal terms, without material disadvantages, and without shyness or clumsiness of gesture and speech. The small-town middle-class parents have no such worry, for their children's educational and social background has set them apart from the others, and they have grown up in the town. In other words, by the very virtue of his background and status in the community, a middle-class child already has a recognized position in the community and will very probably be in the leading crowd in school. This is not true where the community is large, contains a large number of middle-class children, and has a high rate of migration. There, the question of a girl's being on the inside or outside is more dependent on her observable material advantages and social adeptness, a matter about which her parents can do something.

The implications of this difference between the two sets of schools, and the two sets of social situations, are great, because in both sets of schools, the norms are set by, and the leading crowd is composed of, girls with higher educational backgrounds. In the small schools, these are the girls most subject to parental constraint; in the large schools, they are the girls who have been most fully brought to social maturity by their parents. For example, the small-school girls named as exemplars checked the item "stirring up excitement" as something important in their crowd *less* often than other girls, while their counterparts in the large schools checked this item *more* often than did other girls in school (see Chapter IV).

One consequence of the increasing social liberation of adolescents is the increasing inability of parents to enforce norms—about hours at night, conditions of dating, etc.—constraining their teen-agers' behavior. In a few homogeneous middle-class communities, there have recently been "public opinion polls" among parents and adolescents to establish such norms. The adult community, unable to develop such norms informally as a community, must resort to this artificial technique to rescue its authority.[5]

The ultimate consequence, then, of this shift from traditional middle-class constraint to modern middle-class concern with social skills and self-assurance is a greater and greater tendency for the adolescent community to disregard adult dictates, to consider itself no longer subject to demands of parents and teachers, and to pay less and less attention to the prescribed scholastic "exercises." It is, of course, not inevitable that early social maturity lead to disinterest in learning, but so long as the learning is purely exercises prescribed by adults—something adolescents must passively accept and cannot respond to actively—the adolescent culture, as a young semi-adult community, will probably turn away from interest in learning.

Another example of the disdain of a passive learner's role, the interest in positive responsible activity on the part of modern middle-class adolescents, was provided by girls' responses to the question regarding how they wished to be remembered. In Chapter IV, the responses of girls in each

---

5. Part of the breakdown of such norms is due to the high mobility in and out of the community, which undercuts the development of a real adult community.

school to this question were shown (see Figure 4.13, p. 137). In Executive Heights, the proportion of girls choosing "brilliant student" was far below that in any other school; the proportion responding "leader in activities" was far above that in any other school. One can only assume that these modern upper-middle-class girls have discarded the passive role of "brilliant student," in favor of a more active, positive role as a cheerleader—the activity that seems to have highest status among girls in this school—or leader in another activity. At the other extreme is the predominantly working-class school of Millburg, where the proportion of girls responding "brilliant student" is highest. These girls are not yet so grown up, not yet so eager for activity and responsibility as are their fellow-adolescents in middle-class suburbia.

Even more strikingly, the impatience of the adolescent community with the imposed role of passive learner is shown by the responses of the leading crowds of girls to the same question. Chapter IV (Figure 4.13, p. 137) shows that in every school, the leading crowd of girls pulls *away* from the "brilliant-student" image. In Executive Heights, the rejection of this role by the leaders is most complete: only 1 per cent of the leading crowd say they would most like to be remembered as a brilliant student.

In short, the most modern adolescents in our modern society are most impatient with the passive dependency that the school imposes upon them in its educational activities. They have been liberated by parents and by the worldliness that today's mass media bring, and are no longer pleased by the congratulations that follow good report cards. Their parents have liberated them, and the liberation is more social than intellectual. The areas on which this liberated adolescent society focuses are those areas in which it has responsibility and authority to act: the social games of dating and parties, athletic contests for the boys, yearbook, newspaper, and drama groups for the girls.

Such a shift in the social maturity of adolescents need not wreak havoc with education, although it will likely do so if the structure of secondary education remains as it presently is. If intellectual activities remain passive exercises, while the excitement of *doing, exploring, creating,* and *meeting a challenge* is left to the athletic field, the yearbook office, and the back seat of a car, then interest in academic directions will certainly decline. But if the bright scholar is no longer merely a grind working for good grades, but becomes the captain in brilliant moves of strategy or discovery (as he is in the adult world), then his image will again become an attractive one.

Imaginative activity on the part of adult society, modifying the whole educational structure, is necessary to create such a change. For an example of such imagination, consider the recent action of the mayor of Haifa, Israel: he appropriated approximately $250,000, not to be used to establish teen-age centers or to help teen-agers by combating juvenile delinquency, but for the high-school students to use responsibly *themselves* for civic improvements. In effect, he said to them: here's money to use as you see fit—let's see what you can do with it.[6]

Newcomers, Conformity to Community Values, and Materialism

Jews have been in Executive Heights for a long time. Nevertheless, there has been a great influx of Jews from the city to this suburb since World War II. No accurate estimates are available, but a considerable proportion of the Jews in this community have come in the postwar migration and are relative newcomers to the community. This migration has brought the number of Jews in the school not far from that of the Protestant plurality.

One might suppose, knowing the importance of education in the Jewish cultural tradition, that such a migration would shift the adolescent culture in a direction more oriented to learning. Has this been true? To help answer the question, one might ask: in what areas do the Jews, a large part of them newcomers, overachieve, relative to the Protestants and Catholics? Figures 10.3 and 10.4 (pp. 294 and 295) show the Protestant-Catholic-Jewish composition of the school as a whole, and at the end of arrows, the composition of the leading crowd and of each "achievement group"—best athletes, best scholars, ladies' men; for girls, best dressed, best scholars, and most popular with boys.

For the boys, it is somewhat as the cultural stereotype would suggest: Jewish boys underachieve as athletes, overachieve as scholars. But they overachieve even more as members of the leading crowd, and nearly as much as ladies' men. The girls' chart, Figure 10.4, shows a very different pattern: the Jewish girls overachieve slightly as scholars, but less than in any of the other areas of achievement. They overachieve most as members of the leading crowd and as best dressed, and their overachievement with the opposite sex is somewhere between these two and the best scholar. In other words, these girls overachieve, not at the

---

6. The general problem of motivation induced by the structure of activities in a high school is discussed in James S. Coleman, "Academic Achievement and the Structure of Competition," *Harvard Educational Review*, 29, 1959, pp. 330–351.

activity most consistent with their cultural tradition, but at the activities most consistent with the pre-existing values of the community, that is, in areas important in this new cultural situation.

The attributes that are "important" in the new cultural situation do not derive wholly from the existing values in the community. They derive in part from the fact of newness itself. A newcomer must *exhibit* his attributes, or they are not known. When his contact with the established members of the community is superficial—as the contacts are between the recently immigrant Jews and older Jews and Protestants in Executive Heights—these attributes must be evident on superficial contact. They must literally be *worn*. One parent wrote the following:

There is one thing concerning the future of our community about which I am greatly perturbed. I am not prejudiced against any race of people and have brought my children up in the same way. Many of our dearest and most

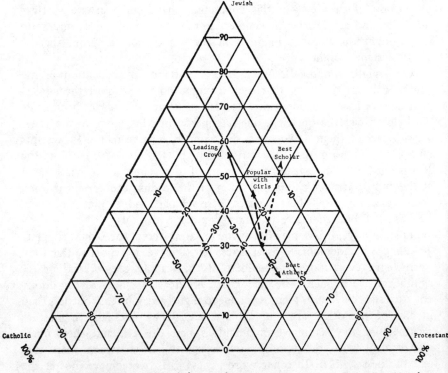

Figure 10.3—Representation of three religious groups among Executive Heights boys as a whole and among athletes, scholars, ladies men, and members of leading crowd.

admired friends are Jewish. However, many of us have noticed that with the increased influx of the Jewish people to our community, there seems to be prevalent among them a type which even the other Jews in our town find hard to accept. Not only are they (the newcomers) more brazen in many ways but their children seem to be frighteningly materialistic in their attitudes and beliefs. Morals, too, are what I would call "loose," but what their parents indulgently call "progressive." My daughter has gone to Sunday School all her life, but suddenly the things she has learned to be important are "old-fashioned" and "corny." Perhaps I seem unduly alarmed, but there is undoubtedly a trend being set by these newcomers which I cannot accept as a good thing. . . . I have digressed, but the materialistic influence of some of these children is worrying many a parent.

The newcomer's materialism is not identical with the existing community values, but it is related to them. Economic success, and the material results thereof, is and has always been the basis of this community's distinctiveness. The newcomers accept this, but since their

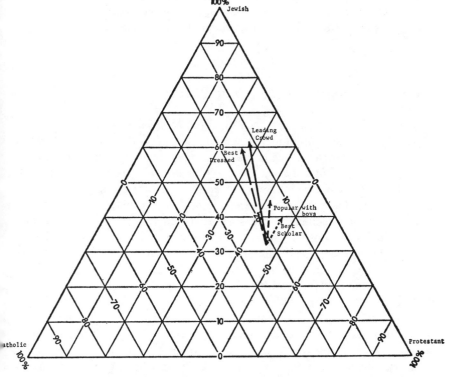

Figure 10.4—Representation of three religious groups among Executive Heights girls as a whole and among best dressed, scholars, most popular with boys, and members of leading crowd.

community position is not established, their economic success must *show*. It has always been thus with newcomers, and where economic success is the dominant value, the newcomers will be especially materialistic, will be the *nouveau riche*.

The implications of this for our increasingly mobile society are quite general ones. The modern upper-middle-class suburb is composed of extremely mobile people, moving in and out at a rapid rate. As a consequence, these communities are filled with people whose position is not secure, who must show their success. Consequently, mobility alone raises the level of materialism, of ostentation, in such communities—not as a temporary matter, but as a continuing state. If the mobility in a community is 20 per cent per year, this means that each year a high proportion of the population will be concerned with establishing itself, with *showing* its symbols of status. This is perhaps most true in the adolescent community, for it is a true community, while many adults maintain their associations outside. Thus, a new girl in school feels a *need* for a cashmere sweater, not merely to keep up with the others, but to establish her position, to help break into the tightly knit community of her peers.

Visibility of Stars and the Status System

Visibility is an important element in any status system. A boy may be famous or notorious, but unless he is *either* famous or notorious, that is, unless he is *visible*, he cannot serve as a model after whom others can pattern their behavior. Two elements are involved in such modeling: one is the visibility of the potential model; the other, the positive or negative value attached to the area in which the model is achieving. Thus, whatever positive values a boy or girl might attach to being a scholar, he cannot model himself after a good scholar in school if the good scholars are not easily visible. In a small school, visibility is a relatively unimportant problem, since everyone knows everyone else. But as a school becomes five hundred, a thousand, two thousand, three thousand in size, the problem of visibility may be a crucial one. One indicator of such visibility is the degree of consensus which exists within a system concerning the "stars" in a given activity. Such consensus indicates the degree to which people agree about who the stars are, quite apart from the values attached to the activity.

In three activities, each boy was asked to name the "best" in his grade: the best athlete, the best scholar, and the boy that girls go for most. If everyone names the same boy as best athlete, there is perfect consensus about who the best athlete is; if many boys are named, there is little consensus.

A measure was calculated for each school, and for each of the three activities, showing the equivalent number of independent choices which would have given the concentration or consensus that actually occurred. (By independent choices is meant that each person chooses independently from among his classmates, all of whom have exactly the same probability of being chosen.)[7] If there were perfect consensus, this number would be 1.0; if there was no consensus at all, it would equal the average number of boys in each grade of school.

The consensus in each school for athletes, scholars, and ladies' men can give some indication of the degree to which each kind of star is "visible"—and of particular importance, it can indicate how this visibility of athletes, scholars, and ladies' men changes with size of school.

Figure 10.5 shows the effective number of independent choices in

-----

7. Let there be N choices made to n people. Individual i will receive N_i choices, or p_i $(= N_i/N)$ of the total. If there is some hypothetical number, N^*, of choices distributed independently over n objects with N_i^* for each object, then the expected

value of the variance of N_i^* [variance $= N^* \sum\limits_{i=1}^{n} \dfrac{(p_i - \frac{1}{n})^2}{1/n}$] is the expected value

of χ^2 with n–1 degrees of freedom. Since E $(\chi^2_{n-1}) \approx n-2$, then one can set up the following equation, with N^* as the unknown:

$$N^* \sum \frac{(p_i - \frac{1}{n})^2}{1/n} = n-2$$

This simplifies to $N^* = \dfrac{n-2}{n \sum p_i^2 - 1}$. The proportion of each choice which is inde-

pendent is given by $\dfrac{N^*}{N}$, which will vary between zero and 1.0. The measure used here is this number times the average class size in the school, to give the effective number of independent choices in each grade (acting as if every person in the grade made one choice). The higher the measure (which can range up to the class size), the greater the uncertainty about who is "best." It is convenient to think of the construction of the measure as equating the *actual* variance in p_i to that variance which would have been expected if a hypothetical number, N^*, choices had been independently distributed over n objects. The measure used is then N^* divided by N (the actual number of choices made), times the average class size. This measure is mathematically closely related to the measure of uncertainty used in information theory.

The measure used in Table 16, Chapter IV, is a slight modification of this: $\dfrac{100\,N^*}{N}$. The average class size in Farmdale is ⅛ the total size, rather than ¼, since the students were actually in two schools when the questionnaires were administered. The average class size in Midcity is ⅓ the total size, for it is a 3-year high school.

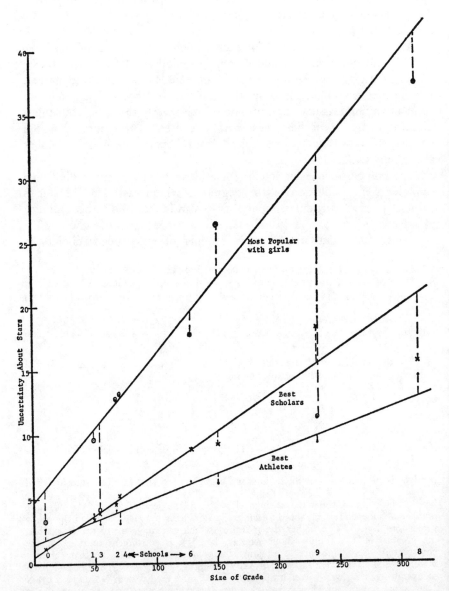

Figure 10.5—Relation between uncertainty about stars and size of school, among boys.

each school, with the schools located along the X-axis by size of grade. In almost every school, the uncertainty about the best athlete is least, and uncertainty about the best ladies' man is greatest,[8] with the scholar between. This indicates the high visibility of athletics, and the low visibility of social success with girls, carried on largely outside the school.

For each of the three kinds of stars, there is an increase in independence of choice (a decrease in consensus as to who the stars are) with increase in school size. This is to be expected; in a grade that includes 200 boys, there is likely to be less agreement on who the best athlete or best scholar is than in a grade of 40 boys. But, as Figure 10.5 shows, this increase in uncertainty about the best boy in the grade varies sharply for the three criteria of achievement. The uncertainty about who is the best athlete increases only slightly as the size of grade goes up. Uncertainty about the best ladies' man increases most sharply; and uncertainty about the best scholar is in between these.

This graph indicates, then, that the relative visibility of the athlete is higher in the large schools—boys agree upon who the best athlete is, and he can thus serve as a model for those who hold him in high esteem. The scholar can be less a model as school size increases, because there is more uncertainty about who the best scholar is. The increase in uncertainty for the ladies' man indicates that for boys, this area of achievement breaks up into several arenas as the school size increases, while the school itself keeps sports and studies in a single arena.

It is worthwhile to note that the two schools in which uncertainty about the best ladies' man is sharply lower than the line in the graph are Maple Grove and Executive Heights. These are the two schools which earlier chapters have shown to be highly focused on social affairs—and the two schools with a highest component of well-to-do upper-middle-class families. The concern with social matters in these schools is once again evidenced by these data.

The pattern for the girls is somewhat different. Figure 10.6 shows this pattern, for the three areas of achievement examined earlier: best dressed, best scholar, and most popular with boys (the counterpart of the ladies' man). First, in all three areas, there is less regularity in the increase in uncertainty than there was for the boys. This curious "scattering" for the girls' status systems accords with a similar result to be discussed in a later section of the chapter.

There is a general tendency for the most uncertainty to be about

8. St. John's, the boys' parochial school, is not included on the graph. Its minimal social system, and particularly the absence of girls in the school, cause it to show a quite different pattern. Its measures of independence were 13.20 (best athlete); 7.50 (best scholar); and 53.80 (ladies' man).

the best dressed (in six of the nine schools, this has the highest uncertainty). There is no clear-cut difference between the uncertainty about the best scholar and the most popular with boys. However, in contrast to the boy who is a ladies' man, uncertainty about the girl who is most popular with boys increases *least* with size of grade. The relative visibility of the girl who is most popular with boys increases as the school size increases (e.g., it is more uncertain in three of the four small schools, less uncertain in three of four large schools than is the best scholar).

Thus in contrast to the boys, the girl who does best with the opposite sex retains her visibility as size of school increases. These graphs suggest, as has earlier analysis (e.g., Figure 2.14) that her role in the status system parallels the role of the athlete for boys.

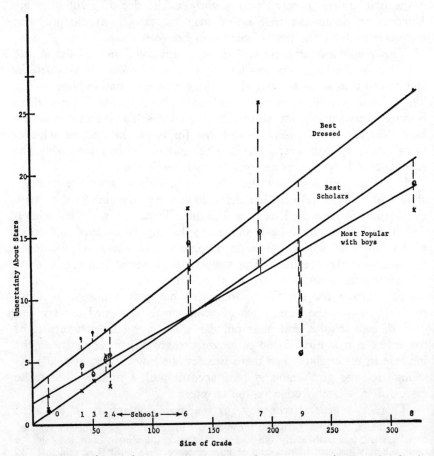

Figure 10.6—Relation between uncertainty about stars and size of school, among girls.

It is important, of course, not to equate the *visibility* of a potential arena of achievement in a school with its attractiveness. Knowing who the best performers are makes it possible to use them as a model; but it does not mean they are highly valued. In Green Junction, for example, Figure 10.6 shows that the girls really know who the best scholars among them are; but this school is one in which the girls particularly look down on these scholars.

The point is merely that the very structure of activities in school provides an arena of performance for the athlete (and for the popular girl) which keeps his visibility high, regardless of school size. Thus he *can* become someone to serve as a model for others. This is not a result of the nature of athletics as opposed to scholastic activity. It is a result of the way these activities are carried out in school—of the degree to which the school allows a spotlight to shine on the high performers, primarily through the existence of interscholastic games in athletics, and their absence in academic activities.

Visibility of Athletes and Scholars over Four Years of School

The relative visibility of athletes and scholars over the four years of school affects the flow of energy into these two areas of achievement. If the image of the athletic star permeates most to the freshmen and sophomore levels, then the athletic star's importance is further strengthened. Not only does he stand out among those in his grade, who know both him and the scholar; his is the image that carries furthest, influencing those on the fringes.

Everyone acquainted with American high schools today knows that the athletic star's image does permeate furthest. it is ordinarily the only image that overcomes the bounds of the school itself, for his achievements are known throughout the community. Few persons outside school know the best students. Consequently, the incoming freshman is in a peculiar position. The boys who "stand out" most among the upperclassmen are the athletes; they are the only models he has to emulate in his early and impressionable weeks in high school.

But what about his *fellow-freshmen* who achieve? Within his own grade, what achievements become most quickly visible to the incoming freshman? How soon does a boy learn who is the best scholar and who is the best athlete in his class? The fall questionnaire was administered only a few weeks after school started, so that the incoming freshmen were new to the system, having come from different grade schools, and were just in the process of "shaking down" into some sort of status order.

Figure 10.7 shows for large and small schools separately the frequency with which the freshmen, sophomores, juniors, and seniors were able to name a "best" athlete or a "best" scholar in their grade. In both large and small schools, the visibility of the scholar starts out much lower than that of the athlete. It rises more rapidly, finally becoming about equal at the senior year. Thus, to the incoming freshmen, the image of the star athlete—not only the junior or senior star on the varsity team, but also the star athlete in his own grade—is considerably more visible, and thus more available as someone to emulate, than is the scholar. It is only toward the end of his high-school career that the scholar is as well known, as available as a model. Although figures for each school are not

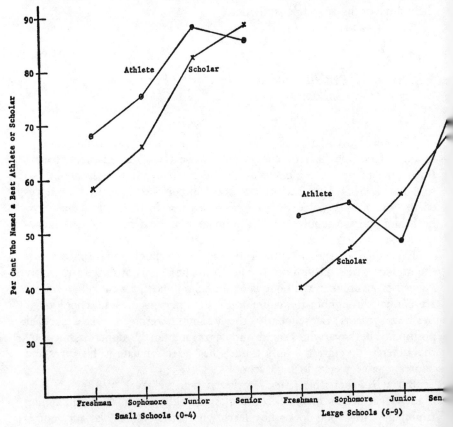

Figure 10.7—The per cent of boys who named a best athlete or best scholar in their grade, in large and small schools.

shown separately, the results are as indicated above in all schools, working-class and upper-middle-class, small-town and city. In each of these schools, the teachers and administration are not able to make the best scholar as visible as the best athlete. Only time and experience make him known.

These results might seem to imply that the popularity of the scholar as a "model" would approach the star athlete's popularity over the four years of school. As his image became more visible, then more students would want to model themselves after him.

Is this true? It may be tested indirectly by seeing just how many boys would like to be remembered as a brilliant student, compared with those who would like to be remembered as a star athlete, among freshmen, sophomores, juniors, and seniors. By examining what they say in the fall and in the spring, we see eight points in a student's progression through high school.

Figure 10.8, showing for all schools together the changes from fall to spring and from year to year, suggests that rather complex changes occur through school. First of all, the brilliant-student image is never as attractive as that of the star athlete. The 50 per cent point is never reached.

Looking at changes, the short-dash line connects the four grades in the

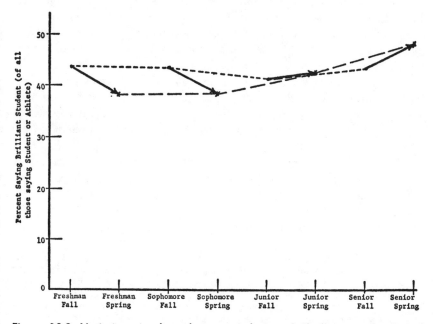

Figure 10.8—Variations in the relative popularity of "brilliant student" and "athletic star" image over eight points in a high school career.

fall. It shows almost no variation over the four years, with only a slight drop in the junior year in the brilliant student's popularity.[9] The spring questionnaire responses show a very different pattern. They are *below* the fall responses for freshmen and sophomores, but they show a climb from year to year.

Combining the two patterns gives no straight trend at all, but something quite different. There appear to be two processes, working in opposite directions. With regard to freshmen, over the period of the school year there is a *decrease* in the relative attr   .ness of the brilliant-student image. The experience of school for ι.ι. freshman appears to diminish the desire to be seen as a brilliant student. Over the summer, the image of the brilliant student reasserts itself, only to drop again over the sophomore year. Then, through the summer between sophomore and junior years, the brilliant student image jumps back up to its original position.

Throughout the junior and especially the senior years, the process of decline during the school year does not occur. It is as if there were another counteracting process, which raises the image of the brilliant student. Perhaps, in these last two years, boys begin to anticipate the end of athletics, to anticipate leaving this special world with its peculiar values and its special emphasis on athletics.

Thus, far more than a change in relative visibility is occurring here. The school year seems to provide, for freshmen and sophomores, an *intensification* of the elements that make a brilliant student a less attractive image than a star athlete. Then, late in a boy's high-school career, the culture of the high school begins to lose its grip on him as he anticipates post–high-school life. In talking to high-school seniors, one feels that they are looking back on high-school days with a kind of longing, while simultaneously wondering how they could have been so deeply embedded, so much in "another world," as are the present lower-classmen.

These results present a rude awakening for those who believe that high school constitutes an influence toward making the image of the brilliant student attractive. Whatever the effects of the curriculum, they are overbalanced, for freshmen and sophomores, by the effects of sports and the adolescent culture's focus on athletic events. Only during sum-

---

9. Considering the four grades to be random samples from the same universe, the standard deviation around any one of these points is less than .001, since the smallest sample size is 487. According to such reasoning, the slight drop in the junior year, being .025 in size, is statistically significant. The peculiarly interdependent behavior of the members of each class means that to some degree, it "acts together," thus making the effective sample size not this large, and the statistical significance of the result more questionable. Even so, the difference between sophomores and juniors may reflect a slight decline that occurs from sophomore to junior year.

mer, when school is closed, does the image of the brilliant student regain the position it had when the eager freshman entered high school.[10]

Since we are accustomed to thinking of schools as educational institutions, these results appear paradoxical. Consider, however, the earlier analyses: When these students are asked, as individuals, how they would like to be remembered, the ratio of saying athletic star to brilliant student is about 60:40, as Figure 10.8 shows. But in Chapter V, it was evident that the pure athlete received more than twice as many social rewards from his peers, in the form of membership in the various elites, as did the pure scholar. As someone to be friends with or to be like, the ratio was almost 3:1; as a member of the leading crowd, it was more than 2:1. Thus, the social rewards a boy receives from his peers pull further toward athletic achievement than is consistent with the 60:40 ratio of individual responses. The operation of these unequal social rewards, over the period of the school year, pulls down the impressionable freshman's or sophomore's desire to be seen as a brilliant student, and raises his desire to be seen as a star athlete. During the summer, when he may working, camping, or on vacation trips, and when there are no high-school sports events, his desires to be seen as a brilliant student reappear.

The average boy, as an individual, appears to be more oriented to scholarship than is the social system of the high school. The norms of the system constitute more than an aggregate of individual attitudes; they actually pull these attitudes away from scholarship. The implication is striking: the adolescents themselves are not to be held accountable for the norms of their adolescent cultures. As individuals, they are less oriented away from scholarship than they are as a social system.

The norms of the system are created in large part by the activities to which it is subject. And it is the adult community that fixes the activities of the adolescent community. It does so by fixing the activities of the *school*—for example, by using high-school sports as community entertainment, and as contests between communities—and by restricting adolescent activities outside of school. The adolescent has little or no possibility of responsibility today; adults have shut him out of the job market—have told him, in effect, to go off to school and not bother them. Seldom are adolescents allowed any sort of responsibility in modern society. If the adult community regularly created responsibilities for adolescents, then

---

10. A survey conducted in three Baltimore schools shows the same result.
The inferences about changes over the summer are based on comparisons of freshmen with sophomores, not on changes of the same freshmen from spring to fall. Each student was followed only through the school year, not into the next year. The inferences may be drawn rather confidently, however, since the sample size for freshmen and sophomores were each over one thousand. Granting even the interdependence due to each grade being a somewhat separate social system, differences of the size found (over 5 per cent) could hardly have arisen by chance.

the status system of the adolescent culture would hardly be what it presently is. As things now stand, however, it is the adult community, in its role, not as parents, but as community members and designers of school policy, who must be held to account for the values of the adolescent culture.

Interscholastic Athletics and the Structure of Activities in a School

Looking again at Figures 4.12 and 4.13, which show the proportions of boys and girls in each school choosing the various images of brilliant student, athletic star (for boys), leader in activities (for girls), and most popular, a curious difference emerges. The proportions of boys choosing each of the three images are very nearly the same in each school. And in every school, the leading crowd "pulls" in similar directions—and at least partly in the direction of the star-athlete image. For the girls, however, the same schools are much more dispersed, and the leading crowds "pull" in varying directions, far less uniformly than they do for the boys. Why such a difference in diversity?

The question may best be answered indirectly. The questionnaire was administered in two other schools besides those in the research, primarily to discover why academic achievement was of so little importance among the adolescents in Executive Heights. The Executive Heights parents were professionals and business executives (over twice as many were going to college as in any of the other schools), and yet academic excellence counted for little in their status system. The two added schools largely "held constant" parental background, for they were private, co-educational day schools whose students came from upper-middle-class backgrounds quite similar to those of Executive Heights. One (No. 10) was in the city, the other (No. 11), in a suburban setting almost identical to that of Executive Heights. These schools will be used here to help discover why, in regard to desired images, the schools were clustered for the boys, and more diverse for the girls.

When we look at the responses of adolescents in these two schools to the question of how they would like to be remembered, the picture becomes even more puzzling than before, as Figures 10.9 and 10.10 indicate. For the *boys*, these two schools are extremely far from the cluster of the other schools. Thus, although it was with the boys that the other schools clustered so tightly, these two deviate sharply from the cluster; for the girls, where the schools were already dispersed, these two are not distinguishable. Furthermore, the leading crowds of boys in these schools do not "pull" in an athletic direction as do those in almost all the other schools. To be sure, they pull away from the brilliant-student image, but the pull is primarily toward a social image. For the girls, the leading crowds pull in different directions, and are rather indistinguishable from the other schools.

The answer to both these puzzles—that is, first the great cluster for the boys and, now with these two new schools, the greater deviation—seems to lie in one fact: interscholastic athletics for the boys. The nine public schools are all engaged in interscholastic leagues, which themselves are knit together in state tournaments. The other school of the first ten, St. John's (No. 5), is in a parochial league, which is just as hotly contested as the public leagues, and is also knit together with them in tournaments.

Schools 10 and 11 are athletically in a world apart from this. Although boys in both schools may go out for sports, the private-school league

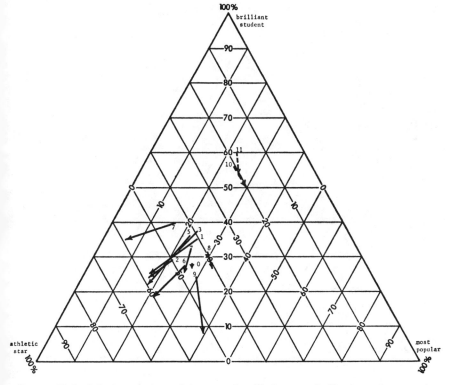

Figure 10.9—Relative choice of image of athletic star, brilliant student, and most popular, by boys in each school and leading crowd of boys in each school (two private schools, 10 and 11, included).

is almost nonexistent. It is composed of scattered schools, none of whom feel in real competition with, or are even much aware of, the others.

There is nothing comparable for the girls to interscholastic athletics for the boys. There are school "activities" of one sort or another, in which most girls participate, but there are no interscholastic games involving these activities. The absence of such games, and the leagues that knit all schools together into a system of competition, means that the status system in each school can "wander" freely from the others, depending on factors peculiar to the school. In athletics, however, each school, and each community surrounding the school, cannot hold its head up if it continues to lose games. It *must* devote roughly the same attention to athletics as do the schools surrounding it, for athletic games are the only kind of games in which it engages other schools and, by representation, other communities.

These games are almost the only means a school has of generating

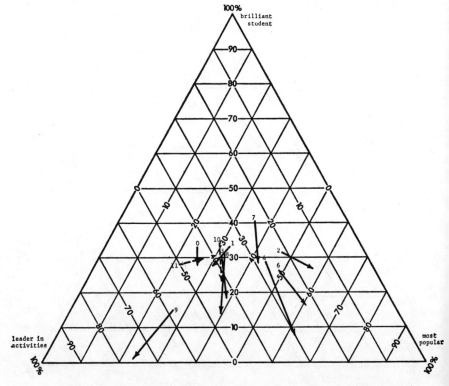

Figure 10.10—Relative choice of image of leader in activities, brilliant student, and most popular, by girls in each school and leading crowd of girls in each school (two private schools, 10 and 11, included).

internal cohesion and identification, for they constitute the only activity in which the school participates *as* a school. (This is indicated well by the fact that some students in school 10 have been concerned by the "lack of school spirit" in their school.) It is a consequence of this that the athlete gains so much status in these schools. He is doing something for the *school* and the *community* in leading his team to victory, for it is a school victory.

The outstanding student, by contrast, has few ways—if any—to bring glory to his school. His victories are purely personal ones, often at the expense of his classmates, who are forced to work harder to keep up with him. Small wonder that his accomplishments gain little reward, and are often met by such ridicule as "curve raiser" or "grind," terms of disapprobation having no analogues in athletics.

The effects of this different structure of activities on the status of a scholar and that of an athlete is probably far greater than the evidence in this book indicates. It was quite clear in discussions with adolescents that they sharply differentiated the student whose good grades were a result of high intelligence plus average effort, and the "grind," whose good grades were a result of average intelligence plus high effort. The latter student was looked down on in all schools, even school 10, the university laboratory school. Note, however, that such expenditure of effort is not scorned but respected in athletics. The boy who overcomes natural obstacles to win a place on the team, and to help bring victory to his school, is accorded respect and prestige, while the natural athlete who fails to try his best is scorned.

Thus the boy who goes all-out scholastically is scorned and rebuked for working too hard; the athlete who *fails* to go all-out is scorned and rebuked for not giving his all. Why this difference? The answer, as suggested above, lies in the structure of activities. The scholar's efforts can bring glory to no one but himself, and serve only to make work more difficult for the others. But the athlete's achievements occur as part of a collective effort. He is working for his school, not merely for himself, and his extra efforts bring acclaim from his classmates, while loafing brings rebukes—all a consequence of the structure of activities in a school, which allocates interscholastic games to athletics, and allocates interpersonal competition (in the form of grades) to academic work.

The distinction an adolescent in these systems makes between a brilliant student and one who is merely studious cannot be determined from the data of this research. However, another recent research shows this extremely well. Abraham Tannenbaum examined differentially the attitudes of students toward others who are *brilliant* vs. average; *studious* vs. non-studious, and *athletes* vs. non-athletes. His study covered "615 juniors in a large New York City comprehensive high school located in a predominantly Jewish middle-class neighborhood." The technique was as follows:

Written descriptions of stereotyped fictitious students were prepared. Every imaginary character was portrayed in three sentences, each exposing one of two contrasting attributes. The first sentence alluded to the student's ability (Brilliant or Average), the second to his scholastic effort (Studious or Non-studious), and the third to his sportsmindedness (Athletic or Non-athletic). The three dichotomized characteristics appeared in every possible combination, producing descriptions of eight stimulus characters in all. Beneath each description there appeared a trait list empirically developed from the free reactions of 200 teen-agers to the typical "brilliant student" and "athlete." The subjects then indicated for every trait whether or not it typified each of the eight stimulus characters. Obtained thereby was a rating of each character based on the relative frequency with which desirable and undesirable traits were ascribed to him.[11]

On the basis of these traits ascribed to each imaginary student, Tannenbaum calculated a mean acceptibility rating. The eight imaginary characters were ranked as follows in terms of their acceptability:

1. Brilliant Non-studious Athlete
2. Average Non-studious Athlete
3. Average Studious Athlete
4. Brilliant Studious Athlete
5. Brilliant Non-Studious Non-athlete
6. Average Non-studious Non-athlete
7. Average Studious Non-athlete
8. Brilliant Studious Non-athlete

The results are striking. The four top characters are athletes; studious characters occupy positions as low as possible consistent with the dominance of athletics at the top. That is, being an athlete is important enough so that a studious athlete (3 or 4) is higher than a non-studious non-athlete (5 or 6). Within the four athletes in the top ranks, and within the four non-athletes in the bottom ranks, the studious students sink to the bottom. Brilliance is scattered over all ranks: the top-ranked character is the brilliant non-studious athlete, and the bottom one the brilliant studious non-athlete. In these data, brilliance hurts a boy's status only if he is studious as well.

These data show clearly the effects of the structure of activities on the status system, and as a consequence, on the allocation of energies in scholastic directions. School forces a scholar to choose between being *selfish* by studying hard, and being *unselfish* by working for the glory of the school in its interscholastic games.

11. Abraham J. Tannenbaum, "Adolescents' Attitudes Toward Academic Brilliance," Ph.D. Dissertation, New York University, 1960. The statements quoted above are taken from a mimeographed Summary of this study.

XI Adolescence and Secondary Education in Modern Society

the character of the adolescent society in ten high schools. These schools do not represent the whole United States, but they cover a wide range of living conditions—from farm to city to suburb; from working class to executive class. Most important, it includes segments of American society likely to be representative of the future, especially in the affluent suburb of Executive Heights.

The results of this research are disturbing to one concerned with the ability of an open society to raise its children today and in the future. This was once a task largely carried out within the family or in local places of work, a task with which the larger society had little need to concern itself. But the rationalization of society more and more inhibits the "natural" processes, by separating the adolescent off into institutions of his own, and insulating him from adults' work and adults' perspective. The adolescent remains in these institutions, treated as a child, for a longer and longer period, while he gains social sophistication earlier and earlier. If there was one most striking difference between the adolescents of Marketville or Farmdale and those of Executive Heights, it was the greater social sophistication of the latter. They were more nearly teen-agers, less children; their own peers were of more importance to them, and their parents of less importance. Yet most of them would be forced to remain in school, as children, longer than their small-town counterparts.

As our society moves more and more away from the era of farm and small town, the family has less chance to train its adolescents—not only in their occupation, but in all areas of life. It was once true that the major interaction between a father and son were in the father's activities —helping with his work, or in jobs around the house. In these activities, the boy learned adult work and adult responsibilities. Now the major interactions must be in the *son's* activities—Little League baseball, Boy Scouts, and play activities of various sorts. The father's participation brings him into the son's world; but the son gets no chance to move into the father's world. (Every teacher knows the distinction between the teacher who becomes popular with students by coming down to their level, and the teacher who gains his popularity—or at least respect— by bringing them up to his level. The first type of teacher has lost his potential for influence, for he has tacitly agreed to become like them, rather than the reverse.)

The adolescent lives more and more in a society of his own, he finds the family a less and less satisfying psychological home.[1] As a consequence, the home has less and less ability to mold him.

One strategy to solve this problem is to bring the adolescents back into the home; to reduce the pervasiveness of the adolescent society, and return to a state in which each boy and girl responds principally to parents' demands. This strategy should be seriously considered, for if successful, it would make a society's task of educating its adolescents far simpler. But it is well to recognize the kind of effort it would require. For example, families must reduce their mobility, both geographic and social. Such mobility rips a child from the community which provides, along with his family, a psychological home. A move from one neighborhood to another insures that the adolescent will not know personally any adults other than his parents, adults to whom he might turn for advice and aid.

If such a strengthening of the home and weakening of the adolescent community is to occur, families must exert many other efforts as well as that of staying in one place. Parents in modern middle class suburbia must forego the social patterns to which they have become accustomed. Their social engagements must cease being the evening parties and cocktail parties which include adults alone; they must have association with other families *as families,* including all members of the family. A few recent developments, such as boating and similar leisure pursuits, facilitate

---

1. One important reason for the latter has been the radical shift in family structure. A family of husband, wife, and children, geographically mobile, has no existence for a child apart from its particular members. In contrast, the three-generation stable family of the past was a unit with an existence over and above its particular members. If one member died or left, the family went on. It had continuity through generations, and a physical location. Now, if husband or wife is gone, the family is truly disrupted for the child.

this, but most developments, such as the removal of man's work to a bureaucracy which is physically far from the family, and the increasing removal of the woman from the home into the labor market, discourage such family association. Family institutions and "occasions" must be consciously developed, so that the life within the family has a richness and attractiveness to the adolescent. Further, the family must reinstitute more authoritarian control, keeping the implements of adult pleasures out of its children's hands: cars, expensive dress, commercial entertainment. If this is not done, the economic affluence of the adolescent, whether gained through family money or his own after-school job, gives him independence from the family, and the ability to carry out activities autonomously with his peers.

The family must be prepared, if it is to regenerate itself to take over the adolescent, to deal with his early social sophistication. Mass media, and an ever-increasing range of personal experiences, gives an adolescent social sophistication at an early age, making him unfit for the obedient role of the child in the family.

It should also not be overlooked that, even if such a strategy were extremely successful, it would have serious disadvantages: a child's success in society would depend more on his parents' position in it than is presently true. If his parents were criminals, he would learn their habits, their attitudes, their techniques, just as surely as he would if his parents were law-abiding citizens. Equality of opportunity, which becomes ever greater with the weakening of family power, would hardly be possible.

Thus the strategy of strengthening the family to draw the adolescent back into it faces serious problems, as well as some questions about its desirability. It is a strategy which an individual family may carry out successfully, and one toward which the exhortations of ministers, family counselors, and social psychiatrists can be devoted. It seems particularly unpromising, however, as a solution for the society itself, in designing its educational system, and its programs for adolescents.

The other possible strategy is just the reverse of this: to take the adolescent society as given, and then *use* it to further the ends of adolescent education. Rather than bringing the father back to play with his son, this strategy would recognize that society has changed, and attempt to improve those institutions designed to educate the adolescent toward adulthood. In order to do this, one must know how adolescent societies function, and beyond that, how their directions may be changed. The first of these tasks has been the aim of this book. It is the second to which a few comments will be directed now.

The two major effects of the adolescent social system to which these remarks will be directed are upon the amount and direction of *energy* or *effort* that it induces in its members; and its *psychological effects* upon them. (These two effects correspond roughly to the areas examined in chapters IX and VIII respectively.) The means through which the adolescent society has these effects is primarily the rewards and punishments it dispenses among its members. These rewards and punishments include popularity, respect, acceptance into a crowd, praise, awe, support and aid, on the one hand, or isolation, ridicule, exclusion from a crowd, disdain, discouragement, disrespect. As in the larger society, these rewards and punishments, coming from others who are important to a person, exert a powerful influence on his subsequent efforts, and can have a powerful effect upon his psychological equanimity.

These rewards and punishments dispensed by the adolescent society to its members are largely incorporated in the status system. The adolescent society has little material rewards to dispense, so that its system of rewards is reflected almost directly in the distribution of status. This is the reason for our focus on the status system among adolescents throughout this book—because this status system shows the pattern of rewards and punishments dispensed by the adolescent society.

Several attributes of a status system have been examined here, all of them important to our inquiry:

a) the *content* of those activities which are rewarded and those which are punished. This content varied somewhat from one school to another, but in all cases athletics was extremely important for the boys, and social success with boys was extremely important for girls. Scholastic success received differing amounts of rewards, and sometimes punishments, in the different schools.

b) the degree of *ascriptiveness* of a system: whether status was awarded because of who a person *is*, or because of what he *does*. The schools differ sharply in the importance of family background for the status system, with family background generally being more important in schools which have a high component of upper-middle-class children. In such systems, where social acceptance depends upon a person's fixed attributes rather than what he *does*, there are many people whose efforts are dampened completely, since these efforts can gain them nothing.

c) the *range* of activities rewarded. In some schools, such as Green Junction, a single activity (e.g., football) completely dominates the status system. In others, like Marketville, a boy can be *either* a scholar or an athlete, and receive the rewards of his peers. In still other schools, like Maple Grove and Executive Heights, the range of rewarded activities is just as narrow as in Green Junction, but the rewarded "activity" includes a combination of elements: a boy must be an athlete *and* a reasonably good student *and* have social sophistication *and* have enough money to dress well and meet social expenses. The system is no more pluralistic than that of Green Junction in the activities it rewards; it is the special combination called the "all-around boy" that is rewarded.[2]

How then can the status systems among adolescents be changed? There have been many clues throughout the preceding chapters, and it will be the intent of the succeeding sections to examine the implications of these clues.

The Opportunity for Responsible Action

One of the most important recent changes in adolescents has been their increasing social sophistication. They are no longer content to sit and be taught. It is Executive Heights, not Farmdale, where the "brilliant student" image is most shunned by girls; it is Executive Heights where the boys are uninterested in the quiet, conforming, studious girl, obedient to teachers' and parents' demands. Modern adolescents are not content with a passive role. They exhibit this discontent by their involvement in positive activities, activities which they can call their *own*: athletics, school newspapers, drama clubs, social affairs and dates. But classroom activities are hardly of this sort. They are prescribed "exercises," "assignments," "tests," to be done and handed in at a teacher's command.[3] They require not creativity but conformity, not originality and devotion, but attention and obedience. Because they are exercises prescribed for all, they do not allow the opportunity for passionate devotion, such as some teen-agers show to popular music, cars, or athletics. Compare again, for example, the diversity among students in time spent watching television with their homogeneity in time spent on homework, as shown in Figure 2.1. Television apparently "captures" some adolescents and pulls them further and further, while homework captures no one, but remains compressed toward an average level. Jacques Barzun, discussing the school-work carried out by students, notes this lack of passionate devotion:

No, it is at best industry, a virtue not to be despised, but lacking the essential element of work, which is passion. It is passion in work and for work that

2. There are numerous important variations in status systems which remain unexamined. For example, there has been no examination of the question of whether all students in school award status on the same bases, or whether these bases differ from group to group. Is the school broken down into relatively separate status systems, or does it have a single, all-encompassing one?

3. I do not mean to suggest that all schoolwork is of this sort. Some teachers are able to devise projects involving positive, responsible, creative action of the sort I suggest below. However, these are sporadic cases, dependent on the special abilities of a teacher. The problem is to build a structure of education in which the ordinary teacher can easily develop such activity.

gives it its dramatic quality, that makes the outcome a possession of the worker, that becomes habit-forming and indeed obsessional. Of all the deprivations that modern life imposes on intellectual man, the abandonment of work is the cruellest, for all other occupations kill time and drain the spirit, whereas work fills both, and in the doing satisfies at once love and aggression. That is the sense in which work is "fun," with an irresistible appeal to man's love of difficulty conquered.[4]

Barzun writes of college students, where the problem exists as it does in high schools. In college as well as in high school, the opportunity for passionate devotion to scholarly work is nearly absent. The structure of education puts both a floor and a ceiling upon scholarly effort, and prevents scholarship from truly competing for an adolescent's energy.[5]

In part, the floor and the ceiling are established by the prescribed "assignments"; in part by the norms of the adolescent community against excessive effort. Not only do these "exercises" seldom provide the opportunity for passionate devotion by a boy or girl; when they do so, his efforts are purely individual, and contribute nothing to the adolescent community as a whole. Instead, they make matters more difficult for others, who must work harder to keep up with this "curve-raiser." The norms of the adolescent community, damping down such excessive effort, are merely a response to this situation.

Another consequence of the passive, reactive role into which adolescents are cast is its encouragement of irresponsibility. If a group is given no authority to make decisions and take action on its own, the leaders need show no responsibility to the larger institution. Lack of authority carries with it lack of responsibility; demands for obedience generate disobedience as well. But when a person or group carries the authority for his own action, he carries responsibility for it. In politics, splinter parties which are never in power often show little responsibility to the political system; a party in power cannot show such irresponsibility. In an industrial plant, a group of workers that has no voice in decisions affecting it is purely irresponsible; a stable union with a role in decision-making is responsible. An adolescent society is no different from these.

In the history of education in America, this fact is exemplified well. One of the major avenues for positive action, for passionate devotion to a task in high schools and colleges, is in athletic contests. However, colleges and high schools did not always have such contests. Their introduction had a great impact upon discipline problems in school. As one pair of authors notes, "The early history of American colleges, before the advent of organized sports, is full of student violence, directed

---

4. Jacques Barzun, *The House of Intellect* (New York: Harpers, 1959), p. 125.
5. For a discussion of education and the competition for energy, see James S. Coleman, "The Competition for Adolescent Energies," *Phi Delta Kappan,* 1961.

at each other, at the faculty, the institution, and the townies."[6] Organized athletics provided an avenue for positive action of the student body as a unit, and this action carried its own discipline with it. It is likely that without organized athletics, some of the high schools in this research would show violence and rebellion of the sort described above. In other schools, there are enough different extracurricular avenues to capture this energy. But in none of the schools is this possibility for positive, responsible action built into the purely scholarly activities—except in isolated examples, like debate teams.

The present research, and more particularly this chapter, cannot lay out a concrete plan for a structure of education which answers this problem. The above paragraphs state the problem, and the comments below indicate possible means of partial solution.

Competition

Competition in schools has always had an ambiguous position. It has always been explicitly utilized as a motivating device in scholastic activities through the use of grades. It has at times been utilized in other ways, such as spelling bees, debates, and other contests. Yet some educational theory, particularly that of recent years, has emphasized the psychological ill effects which competition, and the resultant invidious comparison, can bring about. Thus the movement in education in the 1930's, 40's, and 50's has been away from scholastic competition, toward a minimization of differences in achievement. At the same time, the attempt to do away with grades has never met with success, and even in the recent anti-competition climate of public education, the use of I.Q. tests has come to be greater than ever.[7]

The attempt to do away with competition as a motivating device in schools is based on three important misconceptions, as follows:

---

6. Burton R. Clark and Martin Trow, "Determinants of College Student Subculture," in *The Study of College Peer Groups*, Theodore Newcomb, ed., 1961. See also Richard Hofstadter, "Part One: The Development of Higher Education in America," in R. Hofstadter and C. Hardy, *The Development and Scope of Higher Education in the United States* (New York: Columbia University Press, 1952).

7. It can probably be easily shown that I.Q. and achievement tests in school serve primarily two purposes, and have increased in use as these two purposes have become more important: as classification devices, for allocating students to classes grouped by achievement level, and as protective devices, to give the teacher an objective standard to justify to parents the poor performance of a child. For example, Executive Heights, in which these needs are greatest, administered a multitude of standardized tests to parents; Farmdale, where these needs are least great, administered almost none.

a. There is a failure to recognize that the fundamental competition among children, adults, or anyone, is a competition for respect and recognition from others around them. In different systems, different achievements will bring this respect and recognition. The removal of scholastic achievement as a basis of comparison does not *lessen* the amount of competition among adolescents; it only *shifts* the arena from academic matters to non-academic ones. There is nothing so awesome as the competition between two girls for the attention of a boy; there is nothing so cruel as the world of a girl who's been rejected by a crowd she aspires to. Thus the psychological ill effects of competition are fully as present in a school where there are no grades and no possible comparison of scholastic achievement, as in a school where such criteria are in full view. There are no fewer psychological effects of competition in Green Junction than in Marketville, no fewer in Executive Heights than in Midcity. It is only the *bases* of competition which are different.

b. Learning never takes place without a challenge, that is, a discrepancy between a desired state and one's existing state. A "satisfied" person does not learn, as the similarity of this word to the concept of "satiation" in learning theory suggests. The remarkable strides of young children derive in large part from the wide discrepancy between their present state and an ability to cope with the social world.

Competition is a major means by which such a challenge occurs. Competition against nature, against other persons, against other groups constitute attempts to overcome obstacles. If such competition is removed and no other challenge is substituted, then learning will not take place at all. Because of this, most attempts to do away with competition in schools through a removal of grades have failed, because no substitute challenge was provided. There has been much talk of substituting co-operation for competition, with little recognition that cooperation is not a substitute for competition as a motivating device. It is a tribute to the inconsistency of American ideology that Americans can extol "free competition" as the only device for generating economic enterprise, and at the same time deplore the existence of competition in the classroom, attempting to replace it by communal cooperative efforts.

c. In pointing to the psychological ill effects of the invidious comparisons produced by differential achievement, there is usually a failure to realize that these invidious comparisons are not due to competition itself, but to the *structure* of competition. A person is psychologically hurt when he fails *relative to those around him.* Thus when he fails relative to his friends, when they progress and he stays behind, his psychological equilibrium must be upset. Or when he succeeds while his friends fail, the relation between him and his friends is eroded. Interpersonal competition, and the resulting distinctions it creates between potential friends, undercuts bonds between people.[8]

However, such erosion of interpersonal ties stems not from competition, but from the *interpersonal* structure of scholastic competition. When a boy or girl is competing, not merely for himself, but as a representative of others who surround him, then they support his efforts, acclaim his successes, console his failures. His psychological environment is supportive rather than antagonistic, is at one with his efforts rather than opposed to them. It matters little that there are others, members of other social communities, who oppose him and would discourage his efforts, for those who are important to him give support to his efforts.

Another element in the structure of competition also shapes its psychological consequences. This is the source of the reward. If the win or loss depends upon subjective judgment of a "judge," then there can be maneuvering for position, claims of unfairness, attempts to gain favor of the judge, conformity to the judge's (i.e., teacher's) wishes rather than an all-out attack on the problem, and numerous other degrading activities. Yet when the win or loss stems truly from the activity at hand, as in a footrace, a game of football, or a game of chess, no such subjective judgment occurs. Thus the degrading activities so familiar in the classroom (where teacher is judge and student is competitor for a grade) are absent in other competitions where the race itself decides the winner.

In sum, then, the criticism of scholastic competition in education has been misplaced on several counts. And while this criticism developed, competition of the kind whose effects are most deleterious continued unabated in schools, both in the scholastic arena and in the social arena. It has continued in the scholastic arena simply because educators have

---

8. This is evidenced in numerous arenas of life. Two examples of research illustrate this well. In the American Army during World War II, the morale of different army units was studied. It was found that Military Police noncommissioned officers had greater satisfaction with the promotion system than did Air Force noncommissioned officers, although their rate of promotion was less. Further investigation indicated that the faster rate of promotion created invidious comparisons among the Air Force officers, and left them dissatisfied. Where almost no one was promoted, in the Military Police, then everyone was doing as well as those around him, and there was satisfaction with the system. See S. A. Stouffer, et al., *The American Soldier*, Vol. 1 (Princeton: Princeton University Press, 1949), pp. 250–254.

A study of the system of ranks and levels among sales clerks in department stores shows the proliferation of minute gradations, each level with its own title. The study shows how these gradations and frequent tiny promotions undercut the development of strong communal relations among the clerks, and reduce the possibility of collective bargaining or union formation. See Carl Dreyfuss, "Prestige Grading: A Mechanism of Control," in R. K. Merton et al., *Reader in Bureaucracy* (Glencoe: Free Press, 1952), pp. 258–264.

found no alternative to it as an energizing device—just as economic systems, including those in Communist countries, have found no substitute for it. The proposals below do not attempt to do away with scholastic competition, but even to increase it in some areas (thus draining off the abscess of purely social competition, with its ill effects). The proposals are aimed at the *structure* within which competition takes place.

Interscholastic Competition, and the Channeling of Effort

One approach is made obvious by the dominant role of interscholastic athletics in the schools studied here. It is evident in the chapters above that it is the interscholastic structure of athletic competition that directs so much energy toward athletics. It is evident also that part of the reason for less ascriptiveness in the boys' status system is the lack of anything for girls comparable to interscholastic athletics.

Similarly, it is possible to substitute interscholastic (and intramural) competition in scholastic matters for the interpersonal competition for grades which presently exists. Such a substitution would require a revision of the notion that each student's achievement must be continually evaluated or "graded" in every subject. It would instead make such evaluations infrequent or absent, and subsidiary to contests and games, both within the school (between subgroups) and between schools.

Such a change from interpersonal to intergroup competition would also make it necessary to create, with considerable inventiveness, the vehicles for competition: intellectual games, problems, group and individual science projects, and other activities. Yet there are some examples which show that it can be done: debate teams, music contests, drama contests, science fairs (though science fairs as now conducted lack one crucial element, for they are ordinarily competitions between individuals, and not competitions between schools, thus lacking the group reinforcement which would go along with "winning for the school"). There are, in one place and another, math tournaments, speaking contests, and other examples of interscholastic competition.

In other places, one can find the bases from which to develop new kinds of scholastic competition. For example, Rand Corporation sociologists have developed "political gaming," in which teams represent policymakers in various countries. An international situation is set up, the policy-making teams respond to it and to one another's moves (under the supervision of referees), and a game is pursued in earnest. It is not too difficult to see how this, and modifications of it to include legislative politics, union-management bargaining, and other such situations, could be brought to the high school level and used in interscholastic competition. (Rand reports that an experiment in political gaming at MIT induced such interest among the student players and spectators that for weeks afterwards they avidly followed international news events, to see how their moves corresponded with actual policies as they developed.)

As another example, business executives are now being trained in a few companies by "management games," in which hypothetical situations are set up requiring teams of executives to make decisions and take the consequences. Electronic computers provide the hypothetical situation, and teams of executives "play games" in which each team is a firm in competition with the other. With effort and ingenuity, such games could be adapted to training in high school, not only in business economics, but in other areas.

A similar example is a political game recently devised at Johns Hopkins University in conjunction with the 1960 election. A sample of voters was interviewed to determine their attitudes toward various issues. Then processes by which these attitudes could affect vote intentions were programmed on an electronic computer. A class was divided into two sets of campaign strategists (a "Nixon team" and a "Kennedy team") and each team made campaign decisions in an attempt to influence the electorate. These decisions were fed into the computer, which gave back preliminary vote intentions. New decisions were made, and their consequences assessed. After a fixed number of decisions, the campaign was ended, and the candidate with most votes was the winner. In one use of this game, the class learned far more about election processes than in previous courses using ordinary techniques. In part, they taught each other, through their meetings and discussions of strategy. In part they were taught by the results of their previous decisions, as manifested in the effect on the electorate.

There are many examples in high schools which show something about the effects interscholastic competitions might have. When I was attending a small-town school in Ohio, a slight, unprepossessing senior boy placed among the first ten in a state-wide physics competition. From that day, the senior boy—and physics as well—enjoyed a prestige and a prominence neither would have otherwise had. Rather than ridicule or indifference, his efforts were treated with respect and encouragement —for he was bringing glory to the school.

It is true that many of the examples and experiments mentioned above have had far less effect in bringing informal social rewards, encouragement, and respect to participants than the present analysis would suggest. The reason is clear, however: such social rewards from the student body as a whole are only forthcoming in response to something the individual or team has done for *them*, such as bringing glory to the school by winning over another school. If the activity, whether it be debate or math competition or basketball, receives no publicity, no recognition in the newspapers and by the community generally, then its winning will have brought little glory to the school, and will bring little encouragement to the participants. If it does receive recognition, it will encourage not only the participants, but those on the sidelines as well. In many high schools, boys not on the basketball team shoot baskets at noontime; every football team has its "Monday-morning quarterbacks"; a chess game has its kibitzers. In such ways, the energies of even the non-participants turn toward the game activity.

Sporadic and infrequent cases of interscholastic competition in non-athletic activities, with no attention to promotional activity, have little effect. However, if there were systematically organized games, tournaments, and meets in all activities ranging from mathematics and English through home economics and industrial arts to basketball and football, and if promotional skills were used, the resulting public interest and student interest in these activities would undoubtedly increase sharply. Suppose such a set of activities culminated in a "scholastic fair," which like a state fair included the most diverse exhibits, projects, competitions, and tournaments, not between individuals, but between *schools*. I suspect that the impact upon student motivation would be remarkably great—an impact due to the fact that the informal social rewards from community and fellow-students would reinforce rather than conflict with achievement.

These are simply examples of what might be done to change the structure of rewards in high schools—to shift from interpersonal competition, with its conflict-producing effects, to intergroup competition, in which group rewards reinforce achievement. More important than these examples, however, is the general principle—that motivations may be sharply altered by altering the structure of rewards, and more particularly that among adolescents, it is crucial to use the informal group rewards to reinforce the aims of education rather than to impede them.

Contests, Games, and the Absence of Judges

Even when games and contests are interpersonal, rather than interscholastic, they constitute an important difference from the present structure of competition in the classroom. For another deleterious consequence of competition as it exists in the classroom is the prevalence of subjective judgment to decide a student's success. Teachers are forced, by the system which exists, to be judges as well as teachers. Much of the rebellion and the conformity, the alienation and the subservience of students can be traced to this role of the teacher. A system which eliminates these judgments would restore the role of teacher *as* teacher, remove from the teacher the onus of sorting and grading students, and allow a boy or girl to see far more clearly the relation between his work and his resulting success. This is the virtue of contests and games which provide their own criterion of success. In the games decribed above, the outcome of the game provides the success or failure; no intermediate judgment of a teacher is necessary. To be sure, it is difficult to devise such games in certain areas (e.g., creative writing); but it is not impossible. And even in such areas, the existence of contests (such as debates) makes more explicit the criteria of success, so that attempts to influence the teacher (or judge) can have far less effect.

In general, games and contests, with their explicit (and usually intrinsic) criteria of success remove the ill effects of a teacher's subjective judgment. No longer do the rewards go to the quiet little girl in the front row who makes no trouble for the teacher and is always ready with the "right" answer; the rewards are directly linked to achievement.

Two recent researches are relevant in illustrating the difference between these two kinds of competition. John Holland has studied creativity of National Merit Scholarship winners. He found that among the winners, there was no correlation between scores on tests of creativity and grades received in school. On the other hand, there was a correlation between creativity scores and success in various contests of skill during high school; winning music, speech, art, writing, or science contests, writing something which was published, etc. Those students who had *won* in some such contests of skill were not generally students with the highest grades, but were students with a high potential for creativity. Further, the creative students showed such personal traits as independence, intellectuality, low sociability, while those with high grades showed perseverance, sociability, responsibility, and were rated high on "citizenship" by teachers.[9]

In another study, Getzels and Jackson compared two groups of students: those high in scores on creativity tests, but not especially high in scores on I.Q. tests; and those high in I.Q., but not especially high in scores on creativity tests. Although the two groups were nearly identical in their performance on standardized achievement tests, they differed sharply in other respects: the highly creative were far less interested in conforming to the teacher's demands, were far more imaginative, more

9. John L. Holland, "Creative and Academic Performance among Talented Adolescents," submitted for publication to *Journal of Educational Psychology.*

given to humor, more wide-ranging in their interests. The personal traits they preferred for themselves were negatively correlated with those they felt teachers preferred, while the personal traits preferred by the high I.Q. students were highly correlated with those they felt teachers preferred. Correspondingly, the teachers in fact preferred the high I.Q. students to the highly creative ones.[10]

The results of these two studies suggest that the teacher's role as judge tends to inhibit creativity, and to systematically underselect creativity. This could hardly be otherwise, for teachers must also be disciplinarians, and their judgments must reward conformity as well as achievement. Creativity can be troublesome to a teacher confronted with classroom discipline. When the outcome is intrinsic to the competition, however, the pure achievement, unadulterated with conformity, is rewarded. At the same time, the contest provides its own discipline for the highly creative, who must organize their energies to succeed, and cannot get by with uncoordinated flashes of brilliance or with mere verbal adroitness.

Games have also a peculiar motivating quality, quite apart from the above considerations. This perhaps derives from the close connection they provide between action and outcome. A player sees the consequence of his moves, and is immediately able to test them against a criterion: the moves of the opponent. An economist has this to say about games and motivation:

Most human motives tend on scrutiny to assimilate themselves to the game spirit. It is little matter, if any, what we set ourselves to do; it is imperative to have some objective in view, and we seize upon and set up for ourselves objectives more or less at random—getting an education, acquiring skill at some art, making money, or what-not. But once having set ourselves to achieve some goal it becomes an absolute value, weaving itself into and absorbing life itself. It is just as in a game where the concrete objective—capturing our opponents' pieces, carrying a ball across a mark, or whatever it may be—is a matter of accident, but to achieve it is for the moment the end and aim of being.[11]

Unfortunately, the game spirit induced by the present structure of competition in high schools is often a game between students and teachers, the students devising strategies (individual and collective) to reduce the effort necessary for a grade, and the teacher devising strategies to increase this effort.

10. J. W. Getzels and P. W. Jackson, "The Study of Giftedness: A Multidimensional Approach," in *The Gifted Student*, Cooperative Research Monograph No. 2, U.S. Department of Health, Education, and Welfare (Washington: United States Government Printing Office, 1960), pp. 1–18.

11. Frank H. Knight, *Risk, Uncertainty and Profit* (Boston: Houghton Mifflin, 1948), p. 53.

Competition among Schools for Students

Competition as a motivating device may be used in other ways as well. Almost all high schools in almost all cities serve a single district, and all the students in that district attend that school. Because of this, the school is never induced to attract "customers" by competing in the marketplace of students. There is no such marketplace. As a consequence, a principal's rewards are all for holding the school together, for keeping it running without upsetting the equilibrium, except in special cases when outside forces press for addition or modification of courses. There is no mechanism built into the system itself for change and improvement.

The effect of competition on such a state of affairs can be illustrated by the recent history of certain colleges in the United States. Before World War II, the admissions policies of Harvard, Yale, and Princeton Colleges were heavily weighted toward wealth and position. These were schools for the sons of the business elite in the East, most of whom had attended private preparatory schools. They were too expensive for other boys, and an old graduate's son was given special preference. Since the war, however, a sharp change has occurred in the student composition in these colleges. This occurred first at Harvard, with the introduction of broad scholarship funds, and has occurred more recently at the other colleges. The composition of these student bodies has moved sharply in the direction of public-school scholarship boys.

The consequence of this change has been a sharp shift in the social climate of these colleges. They were once dominated by the "gentleman's C," and all that went with it. Today there are still adherents of this standard, but they are in a minority. The climate of these colleges has shifted from one approximating that which exists today in Executive Heights High School to a climate in which scholastic achievement is a valued accomplishment.[12] The change has been largely wrought by the change in admissions policies. The schools are now competing for talented boys, not merely accepting their old grads' sons.

This example serves to show how the climate of certain colleges has changed as a result of competition for students. A similar change is occurring in colleges throughout the country, colleges which once attracted only a local audience, but are now competing for a national

---

12. However, because the structure of competition is interpersonal, the student's psychological environment is not supportive, but antagonistic. The atmosphere is one of intense and sometimes bitter interpersonal competition for grades.

one. This competition is fraught with more uncertainties about admission, both for the colleges and the applicants. But for those colleges which are entering the national market, this competition has sharp effects on their social climates.[13]

To be sure, competition *per se* does not bring these effects; the content upon which the competition is based is important as well. But so long as that content includes a large academic component (and in high schools this is partially assured by the increasingly important goal of college admission), then it will shift the social climate of the school in an academic direction.

Such competition is not unknown among high schools, though it is infrequent. There are now, and have been in the past, schools in large cities which accepted only students who qualified by an examination: Townsend Harris and others in New York, Walnut Hills in Cincinnati. But the examples are few, and usually limited to a single school in a city. If all high schools in a city were forced to compete for students, then we might expect surprising changes.[14]

The major point is that school administrators have been deprived of the competitive market as a mechanism for sharpening and improving their products. The structure of schools today militates against change, for every school administrator sees his job as keeping the system in some kind of equilibrium, and keeps a protection against elements which might "rock the boat." If the community desires continual change and improvement in its schools, it must build in a mechanism for such change.[15]

Competition for Salary by Teachers

Teachers have characteristically been paid according to seniority. However, there has been some use, and wide discussion, of merit pay increases. Yet the problems which such a salary scale introduces are great,

---

13. For a discussion of the changes in some schools, see L. Bloomgarden, "Our Changing Elite Colleges," *Commentary*, February, 1960, *29*, pp. 150–154.

14. David Riesman has proposed the formation of public boarding schools for other effects which the free selection of a school might bring about: the chance for a student to find others who shared his interests, and focus his energies. See his *Constraint and Variety in American Education*, Introduction to Anchor Edition (Garden City: Doubleday, 1957).

15. The example of competition among colleges shows that a perfect mechanism for such change in colleges is a national scholarship policy, in which the scholarships are *not* allocated to specific colleges, but for which the colleges must compete. A slight variant of this has already occurred with the National Merit Scholarships, for some colleges have begun to seek out near-winners with scholarship offers.

for the evaluation of a teacher is difficult. The principal's evaluation of teachers is based on subjective and debatable criteria even more than is the teachers' allocation of grades. Merit pay raises in such a situation of ambiguous criteria of merit provide a perfect context for charges of favoritism and unfairness. Furthermore, teachers are hardly known outside their own school, so there is no market mechanism to give them bargaining power and to provide a measure of their value. For one type of teacher in the school, however, merit is far easier to assess, and there does exist a market mechanism for adjusting his value. This is the athletic coach (and in places where debate or music contests are prominent in schools, the debate or music coach as well). The existence of interscholastic competition allows his abilities to be known outside his own school, and the success of his teams provides the criterion. To be sure, there is more to a good coach than providing winning teams; but the coach, like the athlete, has the possibility of becoming known outside the school, and having his talents appraised, while the teacher, as the student, remains in seclusion, his abilities and deficiencies hidden by the walls of the classroom. It is no coincidence that coaches' pay in many schools is so much higher than that of teachers. The structure of activities makes the coach able to bargain for his salary, while the teacher, caught inside the classroom, must wait for his pay increase until national attention becomes focused on the plight of the schoolteacher.

Special Tasks of Education in Modern Society

Let us go back some time, to an earlier way of life. A child at one time had little more to learn than to cope with his physical environment. He needed to learn to draw back when he touched a hot substance; to watch out for moving objects. He needed no school to learn these things, other than the school of hard knocks. Neither did he need a school to learn how to survive, for he learned at the hand of his father to hunt or to till the soil. But when men came to depend on others at far distances, a boy needed to learn to read and write; and when money came into existence, he needed to learn to count and calculate. He needed to know these things simply in order to survive in this new environment, for the environment involved relations-at-a-distance, and the skills for such relations were not learned by first-hand experience. Thus schools became necessary to inculcate these skills: the three R's of reading, 'riting, and 'rithmetic.

But this change in society to relations-at-a-distance has been succeeded by another, equally important in its implications for education. It might well be termed relations-with-large-institutions. No longer are a man's essential relations mostly with other men; they are often with large institutions or organizations: big government, big manufacturers, big employers, big unions, mass entertainment, and mass persuasion through advertising. Credit financing has become the basis of economic activity, for the consumer as well as the businessman.

Yet a boy or girl has no experience, either in his daily life or in his school classes, with this impersonal world of large institutions. Growing up as a young adult, he has no way of extrapolating his past (which involves only relations with other *people*) into the future, where he is tiny compared to the large entities which surround him. He often does not even know of those agencies designed to help him out of trouble, or to give him advice. So what can he do, except learn by bitter experience?

The recent development of games of strategy using electronic computers provides an answer to this question. Games can be devised in which a boy or girl would face decisions like those he will face in later life, and then feel the consequences of these decisions as they develop. A computer game is possible which is simply the reverse of the management game discussed earlier. The computer would make the many demands upon a consumer's budget, and the student would make decisions as a hypothetical householder. After a hypothetical twenty-year period, the unwary consumer at age 40 would find himself with a new car but a double mortgage on his house and no money to send his children to college.

Games of this type, a game of "careers," in which a boy or girl must weave his or her way through the occupational structure, political games, legislative games, collective bargaining games, and others would provide the adolescent with practice in dealing with those large institutions which make up his environment as an adult. Such games would not be difficult to devise; they would be little more than existing parlor games like Monopoly, Careers, and others, made immensely more realistic and detailed.

The general idea, then, is this: a boy or girl growing up never has a chance to "practice" with many of the difficult problems which will face him as an adult, because these are not interpersonal problems. They are problems involving a more impersonal and more powerful environment—the large institutions with which he must cope if he is to survive in this complex society. Computer games can be used in schools as they have already been used in management training, to provide this practice—to condition him to the world he will face.

A Concluding Note

When problems in education convulsively come to the attention of the public and the government, the responses are simple and direct. If only teachers are paid more, if only school buildings are better, if only laboratory equipment is better, the schools will be all right. But it simply is not so. Besides the examples in this research, there are many others: the survey mentioned earlier of 10th graders in all Connecticut schools showed no relation between achievement and per-pupil expenditure, when intelligence was held constant; a study of the productivity of scientists among American colleges showed that the schools with highest productivity were not the high-cost colleges, but others which had some intangible quality, though they spent less money in educating students.[16]

Like the *nouveau riche*, a newly rich society looks to the simple solutions which can be purchased with money. But neither the status problems of the *nouveau riche* nor the educational problems of a newly rich society can be so easily solved. The solutions are more costly in effort and in reorganization, though sometimes less costly in dollars. To put the matter briefly, if secondary education is to be successful, it must successfully compete with cars and sports and social activities for the adolescents' attention, in an open market. The adolescent is no longer a child, but will spend his energy in the ways he sees fit. It is up to the adult society to so structure secondary education that it captures this energy.

16. See R. H. Knapp and H. B. Goodrich, *Origins of American Scientists* (Chicago: University of Chicago Press, 1952).

Appendix

The appendix includes the research proposal on which this study was based, followed by questionnaires used at various stages of the research.

Research Proposal

An application to the Commissioner of Education, U.S. Department of Health, Education, and Welfare, for Funds to Support a Research Project under the Provisions of Public Law 531, 2d Session, 83d Congress, Submitted by University of Chicago, Chicago 37, Ill., on November 7, 1956.

1. Title: A Study of Social Climate in High Schools

2. The Problem of the Research, and Its Significance for Education

Adolescent social climates have their own norms and values—ones which may differ radically from those governing adult society. As a consequence, adolescents immersed in these social climates of their own making—as most young people in our society are—find themselves in status systems which may affect their whole future in a quite capricious manner. In one school, only athletic prowess counts among boys, and "popularity" among girls. In another, a variety of activities may bring status. The stroke of chance which sends a boy to the one school or to the other may modify his whole future—for if my hypotheses are borne out, then these adolescent status systems affect the very motivations and perceptions of the persons immersed within them.

The problem of the research is twofold: first to understand the nature of these social climates and their specific consequences on students within them, and second to learn something about why one kind of climate exists in one school, while a totally different kind exists in another.

The significance of this research for education is evident. At a crucial choice point in life, the peer-group social climate can help mold the adolescent into a responsible adult and guide him toward a fruitful career, or it can in contrast direct him to a misfitting occupation and leave him ill-equipped and poorly-motivated for further education.

Yet little is known about these adolescent climates and status systems. Their consequences are only dimly seen, and their sources are the subject of speculation. This research is intended to help fill the void, making it possible to first learn which adolescent status systems are most conducive to attainment of particular educational goals, and then to learn how one might modify the existing systems in this direction. As it is now, the controls which govern many adolescents' lives are those of their peer group. This research is intended to find out some of the less obvious effects of these controls, and to learn how the controls may themselves be harnessed so that their effects on adolescents' lives may be beneficial ones.

3. The Principal Objectives of the Project

The broad goals of the project are, as stated above, twofold: to inquire into the nature and consequences of adolescent social climates for the persons within them, and to learn what factors in the school and community tend to generate one or another adolescent climate. The research is better adapted to the study of consequences than the study of sources of these climates; hence the emphasis of the project will be on the former.

The specific hypotheses listed below refer to consequences of two kinds of variation in adolescent climates: First, there is the variation between those climates which are "monolithic," giving status and approval for a single activity alone (whether it be football, grades, social graces, or something else) in contrast to "pluralistic" climates, which offer equal prestige for a wide range of activities. Secondly, some adolescent climates emphasize values which strongly conflict with school values; others emphasize values largely consistent with those of the school. The effect of this conflict or consistency is the subject of several of the hypotheses below.

The major hypotheses concerning the effects of the monolithic-pluralistic dimension are these:[1]

Effects on:

a. Self-evaluation	It is hypothesized that a monolithic struc-
b. Leisure activities	ture creates low self-evaluations among all
c. Delinquent activities	those persons except those few at the top,
d. Authoritarianism	and that three responses to such a perceived
	social location are to turn to passive escapist
	leisure activities (movies, TV, reading fic-
	tion); to achieve notoriety and some sort
	of status by delinquent activities, and to be-
	have in a typically authoritarian way, show-
	ing excessive deference to those above,
	scapegoating those below.

e. Career plans and aspirations: It is hypothesized that the range of adolescents' post-high school plans is far wider in a pluralistic status system than in a monolithic one, where in a sense the group has stamped as acceptable only a narrow range of pursuits. The group will motivate its members only toward those pursuits it holds in esteem. As a corollary to this, in the monolithic system it will be only the social isolates who chose deviant careers, while in the pluralistic system it will as often be the leaders.

The major hypotheses about the effects of the value-conflict value-consistency dimension are:[2]

a. *Career orientations:* It is hypothesized that in the value-conflict situation, the choice of a career will be highly influenced by the student's reaction to an interpersonal cleavage (i.e., the cleavage between teachers and peers), while in the value-consistency situation, career choices can depend more upon the nature of the career itself.

---

1. As mentioned earlier, the status systems were found to be far more complex than this, and in fact there was far less variation along this dimension than had been hoped. The major structural differences in the status systems found were differences between some schools in which status was given to a boy for accomplishment in *several* areas simultaneously, the "all-around boy," and others in which status was given for the same activities, but separately, so that different boys tended to specialize in different areas, some in athletics, others in scholastic efforts. These structural differences are examined in Chapter 7, and their consequences are discussed in Chapters 9 and 10. Of the five dependent variables for which hypotheses are listed here (a to e), the effects of the status systems on two are explored in detail in Chapter 8—self-evaluation and leisure activities. Suggestive evidence concerning (c), delinquent activities, is presented in Chapter 7, though the incidence of delinquent activities in these schools was not high enough to allow full investigation. It was not possible to adequately treat (d), authoritarianism, and (e), career plans, because of the above-noted lack of variation among the schools in the monolithic-pluralistic dimension. The effect of a different aspect of the climate upon certain kinds of career plans is examined in Chapter 10 in connection with Elmtown.

2. Of the hypotheses listed in this section, (a), career orientations, is examined, though not at length, in connection with Elmtown in Chapter 10; (b) is examined in Chapter 9; (c) has been examined, but results were inconclusive except in one case, in Elmtown, where effects were found on attitudes toward education; this is reported in Chapter 10.

b. *Ability and achievement:* Where student values are in conflict with those of teachers, it is hypothesized that students with high intelligence will often be found among the leaders of the rebellion, excelling in activities valued by peers rather than those valued by teachers. This would leave only mediocre students to make good grades. Thus the correlation between intelligence and scholastic achievement should be lower in such a situation than in the situation in which peer and teacher values coincide.

c. *Residual attitudes toward community and toward education:* It is hypothesized that as a result of the value-conflict between students and school, a student's selection of teachers' standards and rejection of his peer-group standards is often tantamount to rejection of the community as a whole. If the hypothesis is true, this may mean some communities unintentionally force out of the community those very young persons they would like most to keep. Conversely, it should follow that in the conflict situation, those who accept the peer-group standards and reject the school standards have little respect for the school or for education when they become adults.

Obviously, these hypotheses are far too simple, for such status systems among adolescents are exceedingly complex. To cite only one example, it is likely that an adolescent status system which conflicts with that of the school often arises in reaction to a set of monolithic rewards laid down by the teachers. In short, what will be studied is a complex system whose interdependent parts must be carefully ferreted out. Isolated hypotheses like those above oversimplify matters; a more appropriate scientific model is that of the physiologist studying the circulatory system of the body to learn how certain abnormalities in the system affect metabolism.

As stated earlier, this research will study not only the consequences of these status systems, but their sources as well. Teachers' values, the size and facilities of the school, and the school's relation to the community all contribute in some fashion to the adolescent climate; the question of concern is just *how* do they contribute.[3]

4. The Plan of the Research

a. SCOPE OF THE PROJECT, AND RELATED LITERATURE

The project is designed to examine the above problem in a small geographically clustered sample of schools, approximately ten in number. Thus its immediate descriptive results are limited to these schools and those like them; yet the level of generality of the analytical results is

---

3. These sources are examined at various points in the report, but particularly in the early part of Chapter 4, in the latter part of Chapter 7, and in Chapter 10.

intended to be broad enough to apply to adolescent climates throughout this country. Obviously, to explore in full the variations in social climates would require a much larger study than this one, and in this sense the study is a pilot study for much more extensive coverage of the total range of social climates.

No research of which I am aware focuses explicitly on the problem outlined above. However, there is a wealth of tangential and contributory literature. Some of the most relevant items are:

i. Ferenc Merei, "Group Leadership and Institutionalization" (*Human Relations*, 1949). Merei examines what happens when children who have exhibited leadership and dominance traits are introduced into groups which have developed their own "culture," that is, their own games and activities. The outstanding result is that although the new member often becomes the leader, he leads the group in those activities which the culture dictates, rather than imposing his own upon it. This research suggests that adolescent leaders, perhaps just as much as followers, may be molded by the dominant values of the adolescent culture: they excel, but the group values tell them what to excel in.[4]

ii. A. B. Hollingshead, *Elmtown's Youth*. Hollingshead examines in a community study the ways in which the status system within the school can parallel parental positions in the community's status structure, and the effects of such a parallelism upon the success of educational aims.[5]

iii. Hallworth, H. J., "Sociometric Relationships Among Grammar School Boys and Girls Between the Ages of Eleven and Sixteen Years," *Sociometry*, 1953. This British study shows the formation and disintegration of groups over time, and relates these to the values of the groups and the values of the school as a whole.

iv. Theodore Newcomb's study of Bennington girls reported in his *Social Psychology* and elsewhere. This study examines the responses of girls at Bennington College to a situation in which the value system current in the school was at wide variance with parental values.

b. KINDS AND AMOUNT OF DATA TO BE USED, INCLUDING SAMPLING PLANS

i. Selection of schools: Approximately ten schools will be selected. Systematic variation in size and in urban-suburban-rural location will be

---

4. Chapter 10 discusses, though not in great detail, the way in which this same process seems to have occurred in school 9, where Jewish adolescents, with a cultural background which strongly emphasizes education, have come to excel, but in those activities which the culture of this well-to-do suburb held: primarily social activities.

5. "Elmtown," the school which Hollingshead studied, is one of the schools in the present research.

attempted, but with enough preliminary observation of the schools to insure that they encompass the desired variations in adolescent status systems. Present intentions are to carry out the research either in Kansas City and surrounding area, or in Chicago and surrounding area. These tentative plans are made on the basis of convenience to the investigation, and the likelihood of cooperation of the school systems involved. Preliminary inquiries both at Chicago and at Kansas City indicate that there will be full cooperation of the Kansas City school system, and probably full cooperation at Chicago.[6]

ii. Data to be collected: Questionnaires administered to all students in the selected schools at two (or possibly three) time periods and interviews with all teachers will constitute the primary data for the analysis.[7] This will be supplemented by school records for each student, census data on the neighborhood or area served by the school, and interviews with a small sample of parents.[8] The questionnaire data will include sociometric questions and semi-projective items, as well as the usual kinds of attitude and background items of various sorts. The teachers' interview will use more nearly standard interview items, with the primary aim of assessing the standards set for the students by the teachers and the school as a whole.

C. DATA COLLECTION

In the spring of this school year, field teams of two to four persons each (depending upon the size of the school) will spend two or more weeks at each school administering questionnaires in classrooms, interviewing teachers, and copying school records. In the fall of 1957, the field team will again administer questionnaires to the same students. Between these periods, interviews will be obtained with a sample of parents from each school. Preliminary to all this, observations and pretesting of the questionnaire and interview schedules will be carried out.[9]

---

6. The research was carried out on schools in the Chicago area, though no public schools in Chicago were included. In the end, the Chicago school system, which is not known for its sympathy to research, was not cooperative. The schools included in the research, and the means by which they were selected, are discussed in the Introduction.

7. Data from teachers was obtained by means of questionnaires rather than interviews.

8. Instead of interviews with a sample of parents, mail questionnaires, approximately 70% of which were returned, were sent to all parents.

9. The administration dates were set back a half-year, to allow for pretesting in each of the ten schools. Pretests of the questionnaire and interviews with students were carried out in spring of 1957. In September, 1958, field teams spent one day at each school, administering questionnaires. This was repeated with a new questionnaire in May 1958.

d. RESEARCH TECHNIQUES

As mentioned above, survey interview and questionnaire methods will be used, incorporating sociometric and semi-projective methods. The second set of questionnaires will allow the use of panel techniques, in which changes of the same students over a period of time can be examined.

e. METHODS OF DATA ANALYSIS

The data will be processed by IBM methods, and a statistical analysis will be carried out. However, the analysis will be somewhat more complex than the usual statistical analysis in which individuals alone are the units of analysis; here the analysis must proceed at the level of the school and the level of subgroups within the school, as well as at the level of the individual. The analysis can perhaps best be characterized as a statistical analysis of social structure, using field data.

f. TIME SCHEDULE

Design and pretesting: December 1956–March 1957
First data collection: April, May, 1957
Coding, further data collection: June–August, 1957
Second data collection: September, October, 1957
Second coding: November–December, 1957
Analysis and writing: January, 1958–December, 1958
Final report completed: December 31, 1958[10]

---

10. This time schedule, compared with the date at which the report was completed (September 1, 1959), suggests the usual over-optimism of the researchers. However, the analysis has been extended beyond that which was originally intended, and an extended interruption due to illness also contributed to the change in completion date.

I. Fall students' questionnaire: Boys' version

STUDY OF HIGH SCHOOL SOCIAL CLIMATES

conducted by

The University of Chicago

under a grant from

The United States Office of Education

Attitude Questionnaire

e .... Age .... Grade ....

· questionnaire is part of a study being carried out in ten selected high schools, to learn about the interests and
·udes of high school students in various kinds of high school situations., We think you will find the questions
·w interesting to answer. Try to go through the questionnaire quickly, without spending too much time on any
·le question. Answer the questions in order, without skipping.

· free to answer exactly the way you feel, for no one in this school will ever see the answers. When finished, hand
questionnaire to the research worker from the University of Chicago, who will take them directly to the Uni-
·ity for statistical tabulation.

·ember: This is an attitude questionnaire, and not a test. There are no right or wrong answers. Most of the
·tions can be answered by a check in a box (like this: ☑), or by numbers on short line (like this: .3..). Specific
·uctions are given where needed. Disregard the small numbers on the left of the boxes; they are only to aid in
·lating your answers in the office. If you come to a problem, raise your hand, and the research worker who has
·n you the questionnaire will come to your desk and answer your questions.

(You may start immediately)

·-9. What program are you taking in school?

¹ ☐ not yet decided
² ☐ vocational
³ ☐ commercial
⁴ ☐ general
⁵ ☐ college preparatory
⁶ ☐ other (What?..)

·0. What subjects do you like best in school?

(Check only the ones you like best)

¹ ☐ science courses (physics, biology, etc.)
² ☐ mathematics courses (geometry, etc.)
³ ☐ social science (civics, history, etc.)
⁴ ☐ English (including speech)
⁵ ☐ shop or vocational courses
⁶ ☐ physical education
⁷ ☐ foreign languages
⁸ ☐ music
⁹ ☐ art
⁰ ☐ other (What?.............................. ....)

1. Did you go out for football this fall?

¹ ☐ yes
² ☐ no

2. Are you going out for basketball this year?

³ ☐ yes
⁴ ☐ no
⁵ ☐ undecided

3. If school were not compulsory, and it were completely up to you, would you ...

¹ ☐ stay in school until graduation
² ☐ leave school before graduating
³ ☐ don't know

14. If you had your choice of going to another school
the size of this one, or to a smaller school, or to
a larger one, which would you choose?

⁷ ☐ this size
⁸ ☐ smaller
⁹ ☐ larger

15. Thinking back to the 7th and 8th grades, did you
enjoy them more than you are enjoying high
school, or are you enjoying high school more?

⁷ ☐ 7th and 8th more
⁸ ☐ high school more
⁹ ☐ both same

16. What would you most like to get from high
school?

....

....

....

17. How much time, on the average, do you spend
doing homework outside school?

¹ ☐ none, or almost none
² ☐ less than ½ hour a day
³ ☐ about ½ hour a day
⁴ ☐ about 1 hour a day
⁵ ☐ about 1½ hours a day
⁶ ☐ about 2 hours a day
⁷ ☐ 3 or more hours a day

18. Suppose you had an extra hour in school and
could either take some course of your own choosing, or use it for athletics or some other activity,
or use it for study hall. How would you use it?

(Check one)

¹ ☐ course
² ☐ athletics
³ ☐ club or activity
⁴ ☐ study hall, to study
⁵ ☐ study hall, to do something else

19. About how many evenings a week do you spend out with other fellows?
(Circle the number of evenings)

0   1   2   3   4   5   6   7

20. About how many evenings a week do you spend at home?
(Circle the number of evenings)

0   1   2   3   4   5   6   7

21. How many records have you bought in the last month?
(Circle the number of records bought)

0   1   2   3   4   5   6   7   8   9 or more

22. Do you have a favorite record right now?

¹ ☐ yes
² ☐ no

If yes; what is it?..................................

23. Who is your favorite recording artist?

....

24. Among the following singers, which one do you like best?

¹ ☐ Pat Boone
² ☐ Perry Como
³ ☐ Elvis Presley
⁴ ☐ Tommy Sands
⁵ ☐ Harry Belafonte
⁶ ☐ Frank Sinatra

25. What kind of music do you enjoy most?

¹ ☐ rock and roll
² ☐ calypso
³ ☐ other popular music
⁴ ☐ jazz
⁵ ☐ classical
⁶ ☐ country and western

26. How often do you go to the movies?

⁵ ☐ never, or almost never
⁶ ☐ about once a month or less
⁷ ☐ about once every two or three weeks
⁸ ☐ about once a week
⁹ ☐ about twice a week
⁰ ☐ more than twice a week

27. With whom do you go *most often?*

⁶ ☐ by myself
⁷ ☐ with a date
⁸ ☐ with other fellows
⁹ ☐ with a group of boys and girls
⁰ ☐ with members of my family

28. About how much time, on the average, do you spend watching TV on a weekday?

⁴ ☐ none, or almost none
⁵ ☐ about ½ hour a day
⁶ ☐ about 1 hour a day
⁷ ☐ about 1½ hours a day
⁸ ☐ about 2 hours a day
⁹ ☐ about 3 hours a day
⁰ ☐ 4 or more hours a day

29-32. Different people strive for different thin[gs]. Here are some things that you have proba[bly] thought about. Among the things you strive [for] during your high school days, just how import[ant] is each of these?
(Rank from 1 to 4)

......pleasing my parents.
......learning as much as possible in schoo[l]
..... living up to my religious ideals.
......being accepted and liked by other stude[nts]

33-36. Now rank the following four items in term[s of] their importance for you:
(Rank from 1 to 4)

..... groups and activities outside school
......activities associated with school
......having a good time
......a good reputation

37. Below is a list of items on which some par[ents] have rules for their teen-age children, w[hile] others don't. Check each item that your par[ents] have definite rules for.

¹ ☐ time for being in at night on weekends
² ☐ amount of dating
³ ☐ against going steady
⁴ ☐ time spent watching TV
⁵ ☐ time spent on home work
⁶ ☐ against going around with certain boy[s]
⁷ ☐ against going out with certain girls
⁸ ☐ eating dinner with the family
⁹ ☐ no rules for any of the above items

38. What fellows here in school do you go aro[und] with most often? *(Give both first and last nam[e])*

....
... .
....
....
....

38a. What do you and the fellows you go around here at school have most in common—wha[t are] the things you do together?

....
....
....
....

38b. Among the popular places around here, w[hich] is the one you go to together most often?

... .

39. What fellows from school do you go around most often *when you're out with the girls*—at a party or double dates?

....
....
....

—2—

Among the crowd you go around with, which of the things below are important to do in order to be popular in the group?

(Check as many as apply)

1 ☐ be a good dancer
2 ☐ have sharp clothes
3 ☐ have a good reputation
4 ☐ stirring up a little excitement
5 ☐ have money
6 ☐ smoking
7 ☐ being up on cars
8 ☐ know what's going on in the world of popular singers and movie stars

. Among the crowd you go around with, what are the styles or things that are popular right now —that is, in your group?

Description of style

Clothing ....

Haircuts ....

Cars and accessories...................................

Anything else?..

. Of all the *boys in your grade,* which boy . . .

is the best athlete?...................................

is the best student?.................................

do girls go for most?..............................

would you most like to be friends with?...............................

3. Do you date?

3 ☐ no
4 ☐ yes, about once a month
5 ☐ yes, once every 2 or 3 weeks
6 ☐ yes, about once a week
7 ☐ yes, about twice a week
8 ☐ yes, about three or four times a week
9 ☐ yes, more than four times a week

If yes: Do you go steady with one girl?

1 ☐ yes

2 ☐ no

If yes: What is her name?..................................

About how long have you been going steady with her?

3 ☐ less than a month
4 ☐ 1-3 months
5 ☐ 4-6 months
6 ☐ 6 months-1 year
7 ☐ 1 year-2 years
8 ☐ more than 2 years

f no: Who are the girls you date most often?

....

....

44. What girl in school would you most *like* to date?

....

45. Thinking of *all the boys in this school,* who would you most want to *be* like?

....

46. Suppose the circle below represented the activities that go on here at school. How far out from the center of things are you?

(Place a check where you think you are)

47. Now, in the circle below, place a check where you would *like* to be.

48. What does it take to get in with the leading crowd in this school?

....
....
....
....
....

49-50. Would you say you are a part of the leading crowd?

1 ☐ yes
2 ☐ no

If no: Would you like to be part of the leading crowd?

3 ☐ yes
4 ☐ no
5 ☐ don't care

51. If a fellow came here to school and wanted to get in with the leading crowd, what fellows should he get to be friends with?

....
....
....
....

—3—

52. Are you...
   7 ☐ an only child
   8 ☐ the oldest child in your family
   9 ☐ the youngest child in your family
   0 ☐ between the oldest and the youngest

53. Where were you born?
   7 ☐ in this town or county
   8 ☐ outside this county but in Illinois
   9 ☐ outside Illinois but in the U. S.
   0 ☐ outside the U. S.

53a. When were you born? ....19.... .
   Month   Day

54. Where was your father born?
   6 ☐ in this town or county
   7 ☐ outside this county but in Illinois
   8 ☐ outside Illinois but in the U. S.
   9 ☐ outside the U. S.
   0 ☐ don't know

55. Where was your mother born?
   6 ☐ in this town or county
   7 ☐ outside this county but in Illinois
   8 ☐ outside Illinois but in the U. S.
   9 ☐ outside the U. S.
   0 ☐ don't know

56. How much formal education did your father have?
   3 ☐ some grade school
   4 ☐ finished grade school
   5 ☐ some high school
   6 ☐ finished high school
   7 ☐ some college
   8 ☐ finished college
   9 ☐ attended graduate school or professional school after college
   0 ☐ don't know

57. How much formal education did your mother have?
   3 ☐ some grade school
   4 ☐ finished grade school
   5 ☐ some high school
   6 ☐ finished high school
   7 ☐ some college
   8 ☐ finished college
   9 ☐ attended graduate school or professional school after college
   0 ☐ don't know

58. What is your father's occupation? What does he do? Be as specific as you can. (If he is dead, say what his occupation was.)

....

59. In what place, business, or organization does he work?

....

60. Does your mother have a job outside the home?
   4 ☐ yes, full-time
   5 ☐ yes, part-time
   6 ☐ no

61. Are your parents living?
   7 ☐ both living
   8 ☐ only mother living
   9 ☐ only father living
   0 ☐ neither living

62. Are your parents divorced or separated?
   1 ☐ yes
   2 ☐ no

63. Do you live with ...
   3 ☐ mother and father
   4 ☐ mother and stepfather
   5 ☐ father and stepmother
   6 ☐ mother
   7 ☐ other (Write in:.......................................

64. What is your religion?
   1 ☐ Protestant
   2 ☐ Catholic
   3 ☐ Jewish

65. How often do you attend church?
   4 ☐ every week
   5 ☐ 1 to 3 times a month
   6 ☐ less than once a month
   7 ☐ never

66. Do you earn any money by working outside the home? (Not counting summer work.)
   1 ☐ yes
   2 ☐ no

   If yes: how many hours a week do you work?..

   What do you do?..

67. Do you get any money from your parents?
   3 ☐ no
   4 ☐ I get money when I need some
   5 ☐ I get a regular allowance.
      (How much per week?...........................

68. If you could be any of these things you wanted which would you most want to be?
   (Check one)
   7 ☐ jet pilot
   8 ☐ nationally famous athlete
   9 ☐ missionary
   0 ☐ atomic scientist

69-73. Rank the following five occupations in terms of their desirability.
   (Rank from 1 to 5)
   ......writer or journalist
   .....scientist
   .....business executive
   ......medical doctor
   .....chemical engineer

74-77. Now rank the following four occupations terms of their desirability.
   (Rank from 1 to 4)
   ......sales manager for a large business
   ......trained machinist
   ......proprietor of a small store
   ......owner-operator of a printing shop

78. If you had a chance for two similar jobs, one this town, and one in another town the same s but in another state, which would you take?
   1 ☐ the job in this town
   2 ☐ the job in another town

If one of the jobs were in this town and the other in a larger city, which would you take?

- ³ ☐ the job in this town
- ⁴ ☐ the job in a larger city

Thinking realistically, do you think you will probably live in this town when you are out of school and have a job?

- ⁵ ☐ definitely yes
- ⁶ ☐ probably yes
- ⁷ ☐ don't know
- ⁸ ☐ probably no
- ⁹ ☐ definitely no

What kind of work do you plan to go into when you finish your schooling?

....

What do you plan to do about military service

- ⁶ ☐ enlist after high school
- ⁷ ☐ wait until drafted
- ⁸ ☐ go after college
- ⁹ ☐ get a deferment for reasons other than college
- ⁰ ☐ don't know

. Rank the five items below in terms of their importance to you on a job.
Rank from 1 to 5)

......the security of steady work

......the opportunity for a rapid rise

· ...·..the enjoyment of the work itself

......friendly people to work with

·......a high income

What is your favorite way of spending your leisure time?

....
....
....
....

When a new clothing style comes out, how soon do you change to the new style?

- ¹ ☐ I'm usually one of the first in my group to change.
- ² ☐ I change about the same time that most other people in my group change.
- ³ ☐ I usually don't change until most of my friends have changed.
- ⁴ ☐ I don't follow the change at all.
- ⁵ ☐ Clothing styles don't matter to me.

Suppose you had money to buy a new sport jacket for a special dance. How would you decide what style or fashion to look for?

- ⁶ ☐ I'd ask a friend my own age for advice.
- ⁷ ☐ I'd ask a friend a little older than I am for advice.
- ⁸ ☐ I'd ask one of the members of my family for advice.
- ⁹ ☐ I'd find out what is in style from a magazine.
- ⁰ ☐ I wouldn't consult anyone or anything.

111. What boy around here would be best able to keep you informed about what the latest style is?

....

112. If you had a hundred dollars, and you were completely free to do with it whatever you wanted, what would you do with it?

- ¹ ☐ spend it all
- ² ☐ spend most of it
- ³ ☐ save most of it
- ⁴ ☐ save it all

113. If you were going to college, and money were no problem, would you rather go away to college or to a college where you could live at home?

- ⁵ ☐ away to college
- ⁶ ☐ live at home

114. If you were going to a college, and had to choose between going to a good small college and a large college or university, which would you choose?

- ⁷ ☐ small college
- ⁸ ☐ large college or university

115. Are you planning to go to college atfer high school?

- ⁹ ☐ yes
- ⁰ ☐ undecided
- ˣ ☐ no

IF NO: SKIP TO QUESTION 127 AT TOP OF NEXT PAGE.

116. What college or colleges are you considering? (In order of preference.)

....
....

117-20. Looking forward to your years in college, how important do you think each of the following will be to you?
(Rank from 1 to 4)

......the stimulation of new ideas

......preparation for making a living

......campus activities and social life

......new friends who share my interests

121. What will you study in college?

- ¹ ☐ undecided
- ² ☐ a liberal arts program
- ³ ☐ a science program
- ⁴ ☐ a business program
- ⁵ ☐ engineering
- ⁶ ☐ agriculture
- ⁷ ☐ pre-medicine, pre-dentistry, pre-law
- ⁸ ☐ education

122. If you have already decided on a specific field within one of the above categories, what is it?

....

123-6. Rank the following colleges in terms of your preference, if you had to choose among them.
(Rank from 1 to 4)

......University of Illinois

......Princeton, Yale, Harvard

......M.I.T., Cal. Inst. of Technology

......Knox, Oberlin, or Carleton College

-5-

127. Check the category which comes closest to your feeling about yourself:
- 7 ☐ I don't like myself the way I am; I'd like to change completely.
- 8 ☐ There are many things I'd like to change, but not completely.
- 9 ☐ I'd like to stay very much the same; there is very little I would change.

128. A situation like this might face anyone sooner or later. Suppose your parents planned a special trip to New York to celebrate their wedding anniversary, and they wanted to take the whole family along. But then it happens that this year your basketball team gets to the state tournament. The state finals are the very weekend that your family is going to New York. Your parents can't change their plans, and they leave it up to you: to go with them or to go to the tournament. Which do you think you would do?
- 5 ☐ go with parents
- 6 ☐ go to tournament

129. Suppose you had a chance to go out with either a cheerleader, or a girl who is the best student in class, or the best looking girl in class. Which one would you rather go out with?
- 7 ☐ cheerleader
- 8 ☐ best student
- 9 ☐ best looking

130. A lot of times people make plans and then find that the plans cut into something else. Suppose your family had planned a trip to the West for a vacation in the summer. If you go along with them, it means you can't go camping with your friends, as you've been planning to do. What do you think you would do?
- 7 ☐ go West with parents
- 8 ☐ go camping with friends

131. If you could be remembered here at school for one of the three things below, which one would you want it to be?
- 4 ☐ brilliant student
- 5 ☐ athletic star
- 6 ☐ most popular

132. When you read about sports, which of these three do you prefer to read about?
- 7 ☐ a local athletic team
- 8 ☐ a college professional team in Chicago or elsewhere in Illinois
- 9 ☐ college or professional teams throughout the country

133. Suppose school was dismissed an hour early one day for a pep rally down at the athletic field, and the principal urged everyone to go to the rally, although it wasn't compulsory. On the way some of your friends asked you to go riding instead of to the pep rally. What do you think you would do?
- 1 ☐ definitely go to the rally
- 2 ☐ probably go to the rally
- 3 ☐ probably go with friends
- 4 ☐ definitely go with friends

134. Let's say that you had always wanted to be to a particular club in school, and then fir you were asked to join. But then you found that your parents didn't approve of the gr Do you think you would . . .
- 7 ☐ definitely join anyway
- 8 ☐ probably join
- 9 ☐ probably not join
- 0 ☐ definitely not join

135. What if your parents approved, but the tea you like most disapproved of the group. W you . . .
- 1 ☐ definitely join anyway
- 2 ☐ probably join
- 3 ☐ probably not join
- 4 ☐ definitely not join

136. But what if your parents and teachers appr of the group, but by joining the club you w break with your closest friend, who wasn't a to join. Would you . . .
- 7 ☐ definitely join anyway
- 8 ☐ probably join
- 9 ☐ probably not join
- 0 ☐ definitely not join

137. Which one of these things would be harde you to take—your parents' disapproval, teacher's disapproval, or breaking with friend?
- 7 ☐ parents' disapproval
- 8 ☐ teacher's disapproval
- 9 ☐ breaking with friend

138. Just suppose you *were* chosen to join the which you most wanted to be in here at sc

What club would it be?.............................

Do you already belong to this club?
- 5 ☐ yes
- 6 ☐ no

139. Do you belong to any clubs or groups outsi school, such as a neighborhood club, scouts church young people's group?
- 7 ☐ yes
- 8 ☐ no

If yes: what are the names of the groups?

....

....

....

140. Which of the items below fit most of the here at school?
(Check as many as apply)
- 1 ☐ friendly
- 2 ☐ catty
- 3 ☐ hard to get to know
- 4 ☐ mad about clothes
- 5 ☐ active around school
- 6 ☐ boy-crazy
- 7 ☐ studious
- 8 ☐ out for a good time
- 9 ☐ snobbish to girls outside their group

141. Which of the items below fit most of the *boys* here at school?
(Check as many as apply)
¹ ☐ friendly
² ☐ disinterested in school
³ ☐ hard to get to know
⁴ ☐ crazy about cars
⁵ ☐ active around school
⁶ ☐ girl-crazy
⁷ ☐ studious
⁸ ☐ out for a good time
⁹ ☐ sports-minded

142. Which of the items below fit most of the *teachers* here at school?
(Check as many as apply)
⁵ ☐ friendly
⁶ ☐ too strict
⁷ ☐ too easy with schoolwork
⁸ ☐ understand problems of teen-agers
⁹ ☐ not interested in teen-agers
⁰ ☐ willing to help out in activities

143-8. Among the items below, what does it take to get to be important and looked up to by the *other fellows* here at school?
(Rank from 1 to 6)
......coming from the right family
......leader in activities
......having a nice car
......high grades, honor roll
......being an athletic star
......being in the leading crowd

149-54. Which of these items is most important in making a fellow *popular with the girls* around here? That is, among the girls who *really rate,* which of these things count most?
(Rank from 1 to 6)
......coming from the right family
......leader in activities
......having a nice car
......high grades, honor roll
......being an athletic star
......being in the leading crowd

155-62. Do you agree or disagree that...
Agree Disagree
¹ ☐   ² ☐   The real qualities of a person come out in the group.
³ ☐   ⁴ ☐   If I could trade, I would be someone different from myself.
⁵ ☐   ⁶ ☐   I enjoy social gatherings just to be with people.
⁷ ☐   ⁸ ☐   I am often not able to keep up with the rest.
¹ ☐   ² ☐   There are a few who control things in this school, and the rest of us are out in the cold.
³ ☐   ⁴ ☐   I am not doing so well at school.
⁵ ☐   ⁶ ☐   If a fellow wants to be part of the leading crowd around here, he sometimes has to go against his principles.
⁷ ☐   ⁸ ☐   I often find myself day-dreaming.

163-66. Rank the following in terms of their attractiveness for you, if you could be any of these ...
(Rank from 1 to 4)
......an executive in a large national corporation.
......a respected leader in civic and political affairs in your community.
......a statesman in the affairs of the nation.
......a successful businessman in your community.

167. Do you smoke?
¹ ☐ yes, regularly
² ☐ yes, occasionally
³ ☐ no

168. Do you drink beer?
⁴ ☐ yes, regularly
⁵ ☐ yes, occasionally
⁶ ☐ no

169. Do you drink liquor?
⁷ ☐ yes, regularly
⁸ ☐ yes, occasionally
⁹ ☐ no

170. If you had to register in the next election, how would you register?
⁴ ☐ Republican
⁵ ☐ Democrat
⁶ ☐ Independent

171. If independent, which party do you think you would prefer most often?
⁷ ☐ Republican
⁸ ☐ Democratic
⁹ ☐ don't know

172a. What make and year is your parents' car or cars?)
Make(s) ....
Year(s) ....

172b. Do you have a car of your own?
¹ ☐ yes
² ☐ no
If yes: What make and year is it?
Make........................... Year...............

173. From the list below, check the things you have done to it.
³ ☐ nothing
⁴ ☐ duals or Hollywood muffler
⁵ ☐ modified engine
⁶ ☐ customized outside

174. If you could spend some money on making a car like you wanted it, would you modify the engine or customize the outside?
⁷ ☐ modify engine
⁸ ☐ customize outside
⁹ ☐ neither

175. What boy among the fellows here at school knows most about cars?
....

EN YOU ARE FINISHED PLEASE HAND YOUR QUESTIONNAIRE TO THE RESEARCH WORKER WHO WILL GIVE YOU A SHEET WITH SUPPLEMENTARY QUESTIONS.

Fall

STUDY OF HIGH SCHOOL SOCIAL CLIMATES—*Supplementary Questionnaire*

Name..

1-4. Put down the first thing that comes to your mind when you read the following words or phrases:
   a. rock and roll:...
   b. studying: ....
   c. intellectuals: ....
   d. hotrods: ....

5. If you could get a brand new car, what one would you want among the three listed below?
   ¹ ☐ Ford
   ² ☐ Chevrolet
   ³ ☐ Plymouth

6. Which one would you choose from the list below?
   ⁴ ☐ De Soto
   ⁵ ☐ Edsel
   ⁶ ☐ Dodge
   ⁷ ☐ Mercury
   ⁸ ☐ Buick
   ⁹ ☐ Oldsmobile
   ⁰ ☐ Volkswagon

7. Can you use your parents' car?
   ⁷ ☐ yes, when I want it
   ⁸ ☐ yes, but only for special occasions
   ⁹ ☐ parents don't have a car right now
   ⁰ ☐ no

8-10. Complete the following sentences by checking *one* ending for each sentence.
   a. A person who is alone is........
   ¹ ☐ bored or unhappy
   ² ☐ lonely
   ³ ☐ afraid
   ⁴ ☐ better off
   ⁵ ☐ relaxed, thinking, or reading
   ⁶ ☐ happy
   b. When you have to decide between yourself and the group . . .
   ⁷ ☐ I always go along with the group
   ⁸ ☐ I usually go along with the group
   ⁹ ☐ I usually decide for myself
   ⁰ ☐ I always decide for myself
   c. The years in high school have been . . .
   ⁶ ☐ full of fun and excitement
   ⁷ ☐ interesting and hard work
   ⁸ ☐ fairly pleasant
   ⁹ ☐ fairly dull
   ⁰ ☐ unhappy

11-14. Complete the following sentences:
   a. More than anything else, I'd like to...........
   ....
   b. The best thing that could happen to me this year at school would be ....
   ....
   c. The most important thing in life is...........
   ....
   d. I worry most about......... ....
   ....

15-18. Put down the first thing that comes to your mind when you think about the following universities:
   a. Purdue ....
   b. Iowa ....
   c. Cornell ....
   d. U. of Chicago.................................

19. Pick any one of the four universities given above and put down in some detail your impression of that school:
   ....
   ....
   ....
   ....
   ....

20. Check any of the following drinks that are served in your home:
   ⁴ ☐ martinis
   ⁵ ☐ beer
   ⁶ ☐ highballs
   ⁷ ☐ whiskey
   ⁸ ☐ table wine
   ⁹ ☐ other alcoholic beverages
   ⁰ ☐ none of these

21. What are your favorite TV programs? (List many or as few as you like, in order of your preference.)
   ....
   ....

22. Do you read any magazines regularly or fairly regularly?
   ⁵ ☐ yes
   ⁶ ☐ no
   If yes; which ones?.....................................
   ....

23. When you buy new clothes, where do you usually buy them?
   ⁷ ☐ a local store; which one?....................
   ⁸ ☐ a store in downtown Chicago: which one
   ....
   ⁹ ☐ a store in another town.

24. How much do you spend on clothes per month on the average?
   ⁵ ☐ less than $5
   ⁶ ☐ between $5 and $10
   ⁷ ☐ between $10 and $15
   ⁸ ☐ between $15 and $25
   ⁹ ☐ between $25 and $35
   ⁰ ☐ $35 or more

25. In some schools, there seems to be one group that more or less runs things among the students. What about here? Is there one group that seems to be always in the middle of things, or are there several groups like that?

⁷ ☐ one
⁸ ☐ two
⁹ ☐ more than two

Who are the leading people in this group or groups? (Give first and last names.)

(first group)   (second group)

....
....
....
....

(third group)   (fourth group)

....
....
....

1. At the left, below, are some descriptions which we have taken from the yearbook of "M ...." high school, listing the activities in which three boys have taken part during their year in high school. Can you guess what these boys were like? On the line following each description put the number of the words which would fit each boy from those listed at the right.

National Honor Society; Math. Club;
Debating Society; Tennis.   ....

Football; Basketball; "M" Club;
Homecoming Committee.   ....

Newspaper staff; Band;
Student Council; Swimming   ....

1—a good example
2—a square
3—a scholar
4—a grind or bookworm
5—an active leader
6—a joiner
7—an all-round athlete
8—all brawn and no brains
9—popular with girls
10—an all-American boy

Now do the same thing for the following three girls:

Cheerleader; Pep Club;
G.A.A.; Chorus.   ....

F.H.A.; Yearbook editor; Octet;
Class Secretary; Prom Committee.   ....

National Honor Society; Spanish Club;
Student Council; Dramatics Club.   ....

1—a good example
2—a square
3—a scholar
4—a grind or bookworm
5—an active leader
6—a joiner
7—prom queen
8—beautiful but dumb
9—popular with boys
10—ambitious

2. In the first questionnaire you were asked quite a few questions about what it takes to be popular here. Now would you put down in *your own words* what you feel are the really important things that make a person popular here. In other words, what is it that makes this high school tick? *Use the remaining space below.*

II. Spring students' questionnaire

STUDY OF HIGH SCHOOL SOCIAL CLIMATES

Conducted by

THE UNIVERSITY OF CHICAGO

under a Grant from

THE UNITED STATES OFFICE OF EDUCATION

GIRLS' ATTITUDE QUESTIONNAIRE

Name.. Age......................

This questionnaire is something like the one you took last fall. There are no right and wrong answers—we want to I the attitudes and interests of teen-agers. Try to get through the questionnaire quickly but without skipping.

Answer exactly the way you feel, for no one in this school will ever see the answers. When finished, hand the questionn to the research worker from the University of Chicago, who will take them directly to the University.

Most of the questions can be answered by a check in a box (like this: ☑) or by numbers on short line (like this: Disregard the small numbers on the left of the boxes. They are only to aid in tabulating your answers in the office.

If you come to a problem, raise your hand, and the research worker will come to your desk and answer your question.

(You may start immediately)

6. What school did you attend in 8th grade?

....

7. Thinking back to the 7th and 8th grades, did you enjoy them more than you are enjoying high school, or are you enjoying high school more?
   - 7☐ 7th and 8th more
   - 8☐ high school more
   - 9☐ both same

8. If you had your choice of going to another school the size of this one, or to a smaller school, or to a larger one, which would you choose?
   - 7☐ this size
   - 8☐ smaller
   - 9☐ larger

9. If school were not compulsory, and it were completely up to you, would you . . .
   - 1☐ stay in school until graduation?
   - 2☐ leave school before graduating?
   - 3☐ don't know

List any clubs or activities in school in which you are *presently a member.* If you are an officer in any, list the office you hold in each.

Club or Activity	Office
....	....
....	....
....	....
....	....
....	....

10. Since you've been in high school have you won any honors or awards?
    - 1☐ yes
    - 2☐ no

    If "yes," which ones?...

What one honor or achievement would you most *like* to win in high school?

....

11. Is it easier for a girl to get to be important well-known among the students in this scho making friends with a very popular girl o dating a very popular boy?
    - 1☐ making friends with a popular girl
    - 2☐ dating a popular boy

12. Roughly, what proportion of home baske games did you attend this year?
    - 1☐ less than half of home games
    - 2☐ about half of home games
    - 3☐ more than half of home games
    - 4☐ all the home games

13. Do you remember your basketball team's wo record during regular season play this year?
    - 7☐ yes: ....games won; ....games lost
    - 8☐ no, I don't remember

14. What subjects do you like best in school?
    (Check only the ones you like best)
    - 1☐ science courses (physics, biology; etc.)
    - 2☐ mathematics courses (geometry, etc.)
    - 3☐ social science (civics, history, etc.)
    - 4☐ English (including speech)
    - 5☐ home economics courses
    - 6☐ physical education
    - 7☐ foreign languages
    - 8☐ music
    - 9☐ art
    - 0☐ other (What?.......................

15. Of all the subjects you've studied here at s are there any you would like to follow up in life, just for pleasure?
    - 1☐ yes
    - 2☐ no

    If "yes," which ones?.................................

—1—

How much time, on the average, do you spend doing homework outside school?

1☐ none, or almost none
2☐ less than ½ hour a day
3☐ about ½ hour a day
4☐ about 1 hour a day
5☐ about 1½ hours a day
6☐ about 2 hours a day
7☐ 3 or more hours a day

Suppose you had an extra hour in school and could either take some course of your own choosing, or use it for athletics or some other activity, or use it for study hall. How would you use it? (Check one)

1☐ course
2☐ athletics
3☐ club or activity
4☐ study hall, to study
5☐ study hall, to do something else

4. Different people strive for different things. Here are some things that you have probably thought about. Among the things you strive for during your high school days, just how important is each of these?
Rank from 1 to 4: 1 for the highest in importance to you, 2 for the second highest, 3 for the third highest, and 4 for the lowest.)

___pleasing my parents
___learning as much as possible in school
___living up to my religious ideals
___being accepted and liked by other students

5. Now rank the following four items in terms of their importance for you:
Rank from 1 to 4; 1 is highest, 4 is lowest)

___groups and activities outside school
___activities associated with school
___having a good time
___a good reputation

How many records have you bought in the last month? (Circle the number of records bought)

0 1 2 3 4 5 6 7 8 9 or more

Who is your favorite recording artist?

_____

Among the following singers, which one do you like best?
(Check one)

☐ Pat Boone
☐ Perry Como
☐ Elvis Presley
☐ Tommy Sands
☐ Harry Belafonte
☐ Frank Sinatra

What kind of music do you enjoy most? (Check one)

☐ rock and roll
☐ calypso
☐ other popular music
☐ jazz
☐ classical
☐ country and western

30. Do you belong to any fan clubs?
4☐ yes
5☐ no, but I used to belong to one
6☐ no, I have never belonged to one

31. How well do you know how to dance?
7☐ very well
8☐ fairly well
9☐ not very well
0☐ not at all

32. About how many evenings a week do you spend out with other girls?
(Circle the number of evenings)

0   1   2   3   4   5   6   7

33. About how many evenings a week do you spend at home?
(Circle the number of evenings)

0   1   2   3   4   5   6   7

34. Of the girls you go around with most often, are most of them . . .
6☐ in this school?
7☐ in another school?
8☐ graduated from high school?
9☐ dropped out of school?

What girls here in school do you go around with most often? (Give both first and last names.)

_____
_____
_____
_____
_____

35. Among the crowd you go around with, which of the things below are important to do in order to be popular in the group?
(Check as many as apply)

1☐ be a good dancer
-2☐ have sharp clothes
3☐ have a good reputation
4☐ stirring up a little excitement
5☐ have money
6☐ smoking
7☐ know how to dress properly
8☐ know what's going on in the world of popular singers and movie stars

36. Most of my friends think TV is . . .
(Check one only)

1☐ fun
2☐ boring

Of all the girls in your grade, which girl . . .

is the best dressed?_____
is the best student?_____
do boys go for most?_____
would you most like
to be friends with?_____

—2—

37. Do you date?
3☐ no
4☐ yes, about once a month
5☐ yes, about once every two or three weeks
6☐ yes, about once a week
7☐ yes, about twice a week
8☐ yes, about three or four times a week
9☐ yes, more than four times a week

38. Do you go steady with one boy?
1☐ yes: What is his name?..
2☐ no: Who are the boys you date most often?

....

....

39. Is the boy (or boys) you mentioned above ...
5☐ in this school?
6☐ in another high school?
7☐ graduated, and not in school?
8☐ graduated, and in college?
9☐ dropped out of school?

What boy *in school* would you most like to date?

....

Thinking of all the girls in this school, who would
you most want to be like?

....

Of all the *teachers* you've had here at school, which
teacher do you like best?

....

40. Would you say you are a part of the leading crowd?
1☐ yes
2☐ no

41. If no: Would you like to be part of the leading crowd?
3☐ yes
4☐ no
5☐ don't care

If a girl came here to school and wanted to get in
with the leading crowd, what girls should she get to
be friends with?

....

....

....

....

42. Suppose you had a chance to go out with either a
star athlete, or a boy who is the best student in
class, or the best looking boy in class. Which one
would you rather go out with?
7☐ star athlete
8☐ best student
9☐ best looking

43. If you could be remembered here at school for one
of the three things below, which one would you
want it to be?
4☐ brilliant student
5☐ leader in activities
6☐ most popular

44. Which do you think is most important in school?
1☐ for the teachers to be fair in their judgment
of you
2☐ for the other students to be fair in their judgment of you

45–50. For each of the kinds of people at the left, p
from the list on the right the first word that occ
to you when you think of the person at the left
(*Write in the number of the word on the line at the left*)

......teacher

......father

......scientist

......congressman

......musician

......mother

3. dull
4. inspiring
5. odd
6. challenging
7. you can have it
8. good example
9. frightening
0. interesting

51. If you could be any of these things you want
which would you most want to be? (*Check one*)
7☐ actress or artist
8☐ nurse
9☐ model
0☐ school teacher

52–56. Rank the following five occupations in term
their desirability for a man.
(*Rank from 1 to 5; 1 is highest, 5 lowest*)

......writer or journalist

......scientist

......business executive

......medical doctor

......chemical engineer

57–60. Now rank the following four occupations
terms of their desirability. (*Rank from 1 to 4*)

......secretary to a business executive

......journalist

......interior decorator

......airline hostess

61. If you had a chance for two similar jobs, on
this town, and one in another town the same
but in another state, which would you take?
1☐ the job in this town
2☐ the job in another town

62. If one of the jobs were in this town and the o
in a larger city, which would you take?
3☐ the job in this town
4☐ the job in a larger city

63. Thinking realistically, do you think you
probably live in this town when you are ou
school?
5☐ definitely yes
6☐ probably yes
7☐ don't know
8☐ probably no
9☐ definitely no

64. Here are three different jobs. If you had
choice, which would you pick? (*Check one*)

1☐ a job which pays a moderate income but w
you were sure of keeping
2☐ a job which pays a good income but which
have a 50-50 chance of losing
3☐ a job which pays an extremely good incom
you make the grade, but in which you
almost everything if you don't make it

—3—

Do you say prayers before you go to bed at night?

6☐ yes, every night
7☐ yes, usually
8☐ yes, sometimes
9☐ no, never

What is your religion?

1☐ Protestant
2☐ Catholic
3☐ Jewish

How often do you attend church?

4☐ every week
5☐ 1 to 3 times a month
6☐ less than once a month
7☐ never

hat church do you go to?

....

Do you earn any money by working outside the home? (Not counting summer work.)

1☐ yes
2☐ no

If "yes": how many hours a week do you work?........

What do you do?..

If you had to register in the next election, how would you register?

4☐ Republican
5☐ Democrat
6☐ Independent

If independent, which party do you think you would prefer most often?

7☐ Republican
8☐ Democratic
9☐ don't know

Can you use your parents' car?

6☐ yes, when I want it
7☐ yes, but only for dates
8☐ parents have no car
9☐ no

Do you have a car of your own?

1☐ yes
2☐ no

If "yes": What make and year is it?

Make.............................. Year............................

How much do you spend on clothes per month, on the average?

5☐ less than $5
6☐ between $5 and $10
7☐ between $10 and $15
8☐ between $15 and $25
9☐ between $25 and $35
0☐ $35 or more

at girl around here would be best able to keep you rmed about what the latest style is?

....

In the last year, have you ever cut school?

7☐ yes
8☐ no

75. Do you smoke?

1☐ yes, regularly
2☐ yes, occasionally
3☐ no

76. Do you drink beer?

4☐ yes, regularly
5☐ yes, occasionally
6☐ no

77. Do you drink liquor?

7☐ yes, regularly
8☐ yes, occasionally
9☐ no

78. Do you agree or disagree that . . .

Agree Disagree

1☐ 2☐ The real qualities of a person come out in the group.
3☐ 4☐ If I could trade, I would be someone different from myself.
5☐ 6☐ I enjoy social gatherings just to be with people.
7☐ 8☐ I am often not able to keep up with the rest.

79. 1☐ 2☐ There are a few who control things in this school, and the rest of us are out in the cold.
3☐ 4☐ I am not doing so well at school.
5☐ 6☐ If a fellow wants to be part of the leading crowd around here, he sometimes has to go against his principles.
7☐ 8☐ I often find myself day-dreaming.

106. Check the category which comes closest to your feeling about yourself: (*Check one*)

7☐ I don't like myself the way I am; I'd like to change completely.
8☐ There are many things I'd like to change, but not completely.
9☐ I'd like to stay very much the same; there is very little I would change.

107. A person who is alone is . . . (*Check one*)

1☐ bored or unhappy
2☐ lonely
3☐ afraid
4☐ better off
5☐ relaxed, thinking, or reading
6☐ happy

108. I think TV is . . .

1☐ fun
2☐ boring

109. For each of these situations, check whether you think you would "go along with it" or "try to get out of it."

Go along Try to get
with it out of it

1☐ 2☐ The school is sponsoring a big picnic.
3☐ 4☐ Your family is planning a get-together.
5☐ 6☐ You are asked to help decorate the school gym for a big dance.
7☐ 8☐ Your parents want you to go with them to a movie.

110. Ann was doing well in biology class, because she had a hobby of collecting and identifying insects. One day her biology teacher asked Ann if she would act as the assistant in the class. Ann didn't know whether this was an honor to be proud of or whether she would be the "teacher's pet." How would you feel—that it would be something to be proud of, or wouldn't it matter?

1☐ something to be proud of
2☐ something I wouldn't care for
3☐ I'd have mixed feelings

111. Now suppose you decided to agree to be the assistant in biology. What would your friends think when they found out about it?

6☐ they would envy me and look up to me
7☐ they would kid me about it, but would still envy me
8☐ they would look down on me
9☐ they wouldn't care one way or the other

112. If something like this happened to you, would it be something that would make your parents proud of you, or wouldn't they care?

5☐ both would be very proud of me
6☐ they might feel a little proud
7☐ mother would be proud, father wouldn't care
8☐ father would be proud, mother wouldn't care
9☐ they wouldn't care

113. What if a different situation occurred—you were chosen as a cheerleader, much to your surprise. Would that make your parents proud of you, or wouldn't they care?

5☐ both would be very proud of me
6☐ they might feel a little proud
7☐ mother would be proud, father wouldn't care
8☐ father would be proud, mother wouldn't care
9☐ they wouldn't care

114. Sue had always liked to sew and had even begun to design her own clothes. This meant that the home ec teacher singled Sue out as her special assistant for a fashion show. She didn't know what to do, since she had no use for girls who hung around the teacher. If you were in Sue's place what would you do?

1☐ I would agree to be assistant
2☐ I wouldn't agree to be assistant
3☐ I am not sure

115. If you did become the assistant in the sewing class, would your friends look up to you for it, or would they look down on you?

6☐ they would envy me and look up to me
7☐ they would kid me about it, but would still envy me
8☐ they would look down on me
9☐ they wouldn't care one way or the other

116. Let's say that you had always wanted to belong to a particular club in school, and then finally you were asked to join. But then you found out that your parents didn't approve of the group. Do you think you would . . .

7☐ definitely join anyway
8☐ probably join
9☐ probably not join
0☐ definitely not join

117. What if your parents approved of the group, b by joining the club you would break with yo closest friend, who wasn't asked to join. Wou you . . .

7☐ definitely join anyway
8☐ probably join
9☐ probably not join
0☐ definitely not join

118-123. For each of the colleges at the left, pick fr the list on the right the first word that occurs you when you think of that college.
(Write in the number of the word on the line at the left.)

......University of Illinois
......Vassar
......Stanford
......Carlton
......Illinois State Normal
......Notre Dame

0. don't know it
1. athletic teams
2. expensive
3. lots of fun
4. religious
5. nice location
6. snobbish
7. intellectual
8. hard to get throu
9. free-thinking

124. If you were going to college, and money were problem, would you rather go away to college o a college where you could live at home?

5☐ away to college
6☐ live at home

125. If you were going to a college, and had to cho between going to a good small college and a la college or university, which would you choo

7☐ small college
8☐ large college or university

126. Are you planning to go to college after high sch

9☐ yes
0☐ undecided
x☐ no

IF "YES" OR "UNDECIDED," GO ON WITH QUESTIONS BELOW. IF "NO," SKIP TO QUESTI 146.

127. What will you study in college?

1☐ undecided
2☐ a liberal arts program
3☐ a science program
4☐ a business program
5☐ nursing
6☐ home economics
7☐ pre-medicine, pre-dentistry, pre-law
8☐ education

128. If you have already decided on a specific field w in one of the above categories, what is it?

In thinking about a college to attend, what coll have you ever considered as possibilities for yours
(List all colleges that you've considered)

----

129. How many of the catalogues of these colleges h you seen?

6☐ none
7☐ less than half
8☐ half or more
9☐ all

—5—

. How many of the campuses of these colleges have you visited?

6☐ none
7☐ less than half
8☐ half or more
9☐ all

w, considering all the colleges in the country, if could completely have your way, what would be r ideal college? (*Name only one*)

....

at are the things that make this college an eal" school to you?

....
....
....

. In thinking about college, which of the persons listed below have you talked to about it?
(*Check those with whom you have talked about college*)

1☐ parents
2☐ friends here in school
3☐ friends or acquaintances attending college
4☐ social studies teacher
5☐ mathematics or science teacher
6☐ English teacher
7☐ athletic coach
8☐ guidance counselor
9☐ another teacher
0☐ college representative

For each of the items below, check which ones you and your parents *agree* about, which ones you *disagree* about, and which ones you *haven't discussed* with your parents.

Agree	Don't Agree	Haven't Discussed	
1☐	2☐	3☐	What course of study you should take
4☐	5☐	6☐	Which college you should go to
1☐	2☐	3☐	Whether you should live away from home
4☐	5☐	6☐	How your college education will be paid for

Considering living costs, tuition, and fees, about how much do you expect your first year in college to cost, including the amount covered by any scholarships?

1☐ don't know
2☐ under $500
3☐ $500–$999
4☐ $1,000–$1,499
5☐ $1,500–$1,999
6☐ $2,000–$2,499
7☐ $2,500+

. About what percentage of your college education do you expect that your family or relatives will pay for?

5☐ none
6☐ 25%
7☐ 50%
8☐ 75%
9☐ 100%

. About what percentage do you expect to pay from summer earning and part-time jobs?

5☐ none
6☐ 25%
7☐ 50%
8☐ 75%
9☐ 100%

ANSWER QUESTIONS BELOW IF YOU ARE A SENIOR PLANNING TO GO TO COLLEGE NEXT FALL. NON-SENIORS SKIP TO QUESTION 144.

What colleges have you applied to for admission? List the colleges on the lines to the left, *in the order of your preference.*

1.......................... 4..........................
2.......................... 5..........................
3.......................... 6..........................

Write in the names of the ones to which you've been admitted and the ones at which you've been rejected, in the appropriate space.

Admitted..........................
Rejected..........................

Write in the names of the ones to which you've applied for scholarships (if any) and the ones from which you've received a scholarship offer.

Applied for a scholarship..........................
Received scholarship..........................

137. Did you take the College Entrance Board Exams?

5☐ yes
6☐ no

138. Do you definitely know yet which college you will attend?

7☐ yes Which one?..........................
8☐ no

139. If "yes," how does this school compare to the others you were considering, in each of the following ways?

Better	About Equal	Worse	Don't know	
1☐	2☐	3☐	4☐	offering the course of study you want
5☐	6☐	7☐	8☐	general reputation of the school
140. 1☐	2☐	3☐	4☐	location and campus
5☐	6☐	7☐	8☐	athletic teams
141. 1☐	2☐	3☐	4☐	campus activities and social life

142. What were the most important considerations you had in mind when you were deciding which school to attend? (*Check all the things that were important for you*)

1☐ tuition costs and living expenses
2☐ closeness to home
3☐ the high educational standards
4☐ course of study offered
5☐ chances of a scholarship
6☐ the religious character of the school
7☐ your chances of getting admitted
8☐ people you know who went to those schools

143. During the time when you're actually going to school, about how much time, if any, do you expect to work per week at a paying job?

7☐ none
8☐ less than 20 hours per week
9☐ 20 hours or more per week

SKIP TO QUESTION 151 ON THE NEXT PAGE.

— 6 —

EVERYONE ANSWER THE QUESTIONS BELOW.

NON-SENIORS WHO ARE PLANNING TO GO TO COLLEGE OR ARE UNDECIDED, ANSWER QUESTIONS 144 AND 145.

144. Now, regardless of where you would ideally like to go, do you have an idea what college you will probably attend?
1☐ yes, definitely } Which one? ....
2☐ yes, probably }
3☐ no

145. What were the most important considerations for you in thinking about which college to attend? *(Check all the things that were most important for you)*
1☐ tuition costs and living expenses
2☐ closeness to home
3☐ high educational standards
4☐ course of study offered
5☐ chances of a scholarship
6☐ the religious character of the school
7☐ your chances of getting admitted
8☐ people you know who went to those schools

SKIP TO QUESTION 151 IN THE NEXT COLUMN.

IF YOU ARE *NOT* PLANNING TO GO TO COLLEGE AT ALL, ANSWER QUESTIONS BELOW.

146. Check the most important reasons why you are not going to college. *(Check as many as apply)*
1☐ I never considered going to college.
2☐ I couldn't afford it.
3☐ Most of my friends aren't going to college.
4☐ My grades aren't high enough.
5☐ I don't need a college education.
6☐ My parents haven't encouraged me.
7☐ I don't need a college education.
8☐ The school wouldn't give me a good recommendation.

147. Suppose you were to decide that you'd like to go to college. How would your family react to this?
7☐ They would feel happy and encourage me.
8☐ They would think I was doing the wrong thing and would discourage me.
9☐ They wouldn't care much one way or the other.

148. What do you plan to do after you're out of high school?
1☐ help at home
2☐ marry right away and not work
3☐ marry right away and also get a job
4☐ get a job
5☐ go to business school or other school
6☐ undecided

149. If you will get a job, will it be at a place where you've been working while you're in school, or somewhere else?
1☐ same place I've been working
2☐ somewhere else
3☐ don't know for sure

150. Do you know yet (or have an idea) what your job will be?
7☐ yes, definitely } What?...................................
8☐ yes, probably }
9☐ no

151-157. For each of the situations listed on the left, pick the one item from the list on the right that comes closest to what you think you would feel like doing. Write the number of the activity you chose on the line: you may use the same number more than once if you like.

.....When I'm bored ...
.....When I finish my homework on a weeknight ...
.....I've had a bad day at school ...
.....I've had an argument with my best friend...
.....I've had an argument with one of my parents ...
.....Our basketball team has just won an important game ...
.....Our basketball team has just lost an important game ...

1. go down to the drugstore
2. watch television
3. ride around with friends
4. stay home and read
5. go over to friend's house
6. raid the icebox
7. listen to the radio by myself
8. listen to records with friends
9. go to a movie

158. How often do you go to the movies? *(Check one)*
5☐ never, or almost never
6☐ about once a month or less
7☐ about once every two or three weeks
8☐ about once a week
9☐ about twice a week
0☐ more than twice a week

159. With whom do you go *most often*? *(Check one)*
6☐ by myself
7☐ with a date
8☐ with other girls
9☐ with a group of boys and girls
0☐ with members of my family

160. About how much time, on the average, do you spend watching TV on a weekday?
4☐ none, or almost none
5☐ about ½ hour a day
6☐ about 1 hour a day
7☐ about 1½ hours a day
8☐ about 2 hours a day
9☐ about 3 hours a day
0☐ 4 or more hours a day

161. With whom do you watch most often? *(Check one)*
6☐ by myself
7☐ with a date
8☐ with other girls
9☐ with a group of boys and girls
0☐ with members of my family

162. Which of the following kinds of television programs do you enjoy watching? *(Check all those you enjoy watching)*
1☐ variety shows (like Ed Sullivan)
2☐ popular music shows; popular singers
3☐ comedy shows
4☐ plays or other drama
5☐ detective, police, or mystery shows
6☐ westerns
7☐ quiz shows
8☐ sports broadcasts
9☐ movies

Turn to Page

3-166. Rank the following four activities in the order that you best like doing them.
(*Rank from 1 to 4; 1 is highest, 4 is lowest.*)

......watching TV

......going to movies

......listening to the radio or to records with friends

......listening to the radio or to records by yourself

. Putting these four activities together, how much of your *spare time* do you spend on them? Put a check on the line where you think you fall.

None of my spare time				All of my spare time

. Of just the time that you spend with your friends, how much of it do you spend doing any of the things listed above? Place a check somewhere along the line.

None of it				All of it

, Which of the items below fit *most of the girls* here at school? (*Check as many as apply*)

1☐ friendly
2☐ catty
3☐ hard to get to know
4☐ mad about clothes
5☐ active around school
6☐ boy-crazy
7☐ studious
8☐ out for a good time
9☐ snobbish to girls outside their group

, Which of the items below fit *most of the boys* here at school? (*Check as many as apply*)

1☐ friendly
2☐ disinterested in school
3☐ hard to get to know
4☐ crazy about cars
5☐ active around school
6☐ girl-crazy
7☐ studious
8☐ out for a good time
9☐ sports-minded

171. Which of the items below fit most of the *teachers* here at school? (*Check as many as apply*)

5☐ friendly
6☐ too strict
7☐ too easy with schoolwork
8☐ understand problems of teen-agers
9☐ not interested in teen-agers
0☐ willing to help out in activities

172. If you had a hundred dollars, and you were completely free to do with it whatever you wanted, what would you do with it? (*Check one*)

1☐ spend it all
2☐ spend most of it
3☐ save most of it
4☐ save it all

173. If you could get a brand-new car, what one would you want among those listed below? (*Check one*)

4☐ De Soto
5☐ Edsel
6☐ Dodge
7☐ Mercury
8☐ Buick
9☐ Oldsmobile
0☐ Volkswagen

174. Suppose the circle below represented the activities that go on here at school. How far out from the center of things are you? (The center of the circle represents the center of things in school.)
(*Place a check where you think you are*)

175. Now, in the circle below, place a check where you would *like* to be.

WHEN YOU ARE FINISHED PLEASE HAND YOUR QUESTIONNAIRE TO THE RESEARCH WORKER, WHO WILL GIVE YOU A SHEET WITH SUPPLEMENTARY QUESTIONS.

— 8 —

STUDY OF HIGH SCHOOL SOCIAL CLIMATES

conducted by

The University of Chicago

under a grant from

The United States Office of Education

Parents' Questionnaire

Most of the questions can be answered by a check in a box (like this: ☑, or by numbers on short lines (like this: **3**.. Specific instructions are given where needed. Disregard the small numbers to the left of the boxes; they are only aid in tabulating your answers in the office. If you want to elaborate on any question, use the blank space on page

Certain questions are slightly different for parents of a boy in high school and for parents of a girl in high school. you have no girls in high school, then do not answer the part of a question marked "Girls". If you have no boys high school, then do not answer the part of a question marked "Boys".

1. What did you like best about school when you were a teen-ager?

(Check one)

1 ☐ courses in school
2 ☐ athletics
3 ☐ clubs and activities
4 ☐ friends you went around with
5 ☐ don't remember

2. What did you hope to become when you left school or started work?

....

3. Thinking back to your own school days, what is the one thing that you would most want to change if you could live them over again?

....
....
....
....

4. How do you feel about the progress your child is making in his or her studies in high school?

(Check one)

1 ☐ very satisfied
2 ☐ fairly satisfied
3 ☐ not very satisfied
4 ☐ very unsatisfied

5. How do you feel your child is getting along in other activities in high school?

(Check one)

1 ☐ very satisfied
2 ☐ fairly satisfied
3 ☐ not very satisfied
4 ☐ very unsatisfied

6. How do you feel about the friends that your child has made in high school?

(Check one)

7 ☐ very satisfied
8 ☐ fairly satisfied
9 ☐ not very satisfied
0 ☐ very unsatisfied

7. What would you like most to see your child get from high school?

....
....
....
....

8. Would you rather see your son or daughter concentrate on . . .

(Check one)

7 ☐ studies in school
8 ☐ other things in school
9 ☐ things outside school

9. If you saw that your teen-ager was doing badly in high school, how far would you go in straightening out his or her difficulties? Indicate the *most extreme* action you would be willing or able to take.

(Check one)

5 ☐ nothing
6 ☐ help him at home
7 ☐ talk with his teachers
8 ☐ arrange special instruction outside school
9 ☐ send him to a private school
0 ☐ move to another town or school district

Which of the categories below do you think come closest to fitting the majority of teachers in this school?

(Check as many as apply)

⁵ ☐ friendly
⁶ ☐ too strict
⁷ ☐ too easy with school work
⁸ ☐ understand problems of teen-agers
⁹ ☐ not interested in teen-agers
⁰ ☐ willing to help out in activities

14. Among the things teen-agers strive for during their high school days, just how important do you think each of these should be?

(Rank from 1 to 4)

......pleasing their parents
......learing as much as possible in school
......living up to religious ideals
......being accepted and liked by other students

18. Now rank the following four items according to how important you think each of them should be for a teen-ager.

(Rank from 1 to 4)

......groups and activities outside school
......activities associated with school
......having a good time
......a good reputation

14. If your son or daughter could be outstanding in high school in one of the three things listed below, which one would you want it to be?

(If you have a son in high school check below)

⁴ ☐ brilliant student
⁵ ☐ athletic star
⁶ ☐ most popular

(If you have a daughter in high school check below)

⁴ ☐ brilliant student
⁵ ☐ leader in activities
⁶ ☐ most popular

20. Do you agree or disagree that . . .

Agree Disagree

¹ ☐ · ² ☐ There are a few students who control things in the high school my child is in, and the rest are out in the cold.
³ ☐ ⁴ ☐ If the leaders in this town favor something, you can be pretty sure it's all right.
⁵ ☐ ⁶ ☐ If a teen-ager wants to be a part of the leading crowd in high school, he sometimes has to go against his principles.
¹ ☐ ² ☐ The real qualities of a person come out in the clutch.
³ ☐ ⁴ ☐ In this community, there are a few who run things, and the rest of the people are left out.
⁵ ☐ ⁶ ☐ Fluoridation of the water system of a town is a good thing.

21. Among the crowd that your son or daughter goes around with, what are the things which are important to do in order to be popular in the group?

(Check as many as apply)

¹ ☐ be a good dancer
² ☐ have sharp clothes
³ ☐ have a good reputation
⁴ ☐ stirring up a little excitement
⁵ ☐ have money
⁶ ☐ smoking
⁷ ☐ know how to dress properly
⁸ ☐ know what's going on in the world of popular singers and movie stars
⁹ ☐ being up on cars

22. Are there any of these things that you wish they *wouldn't* emphasize so much? If so, please circle below the numbers referring to those items.

1 2 3 4 5 6 7 8 9

23. Check below the rules which you make for your teen-age children.

¹ ☐ time for being in at night on weekends
² ☐ amount of dating
³ ☐ against going steady
⁴ ☐ time spent watching TV
⁵ ☐ time spent on homework
⁶ ☐ against going around with certain boys
⁷ ☐ against going out with certain girls
⁸ ☐ eating dinner with the family
⁹ ☐ no rules for any of the above items

24-25. Of the five items below, what is the single most important thing you would like to see your child accomplish in his or her life?

Check one	Check one	
Boy	*Girl*	
⁶ ☐	⁶ ☐	A healthy, financially secure, family life.
⁷ ☐	⁷ ☐	Be outstanding in his chosen field of work.
⁸ ☐	⁸ ☐	Be a respected citizen in his community.
⁹ ☐	⁹ ☐	Do what gives him the most personal satisfaction.
⁰ ☐	⁰ ☐	Reach a higher social standing. ·

26-30. Rank the following five occupations in terms of their desirability for a man.

(Rank from 1 to 5)

......writer or journalist
......scientist
......business executive
......medical doctor
......chemical engineer

31-34. Now rank the following four occupations in terms of their desirability for a man.

(Rank from 1 to 4)

......sales manager for a large business
......trained machinist
......proprietor of a small store
......owner-operator of a printing shop

35-38. Now rank the following four occupations in terms of their desirability for a *woman*.

(Rank from 1 to 4)

......secretary for a business executive

......journalist

......interior decorator

......airline hostess

39. If it were completely up to you, what kind of work would you like to see your son go into?

....

....

40. If it were completely up to you, would you prefer your son or daughter to . . .

¹ ☐ stay in school until graduation
² ☐ leave school before graduating
³ ☐ don't know

41. If your son or daughter had a chance for two similar jobs, one in this town, and one in another town the same size, but in another state, which would you advise him to take?

¹ ☐ job in this town
² ☐ job in another town˙

42. If one of the jobs were in this town and the other one in a larger city, which would you advise him or her to take?

³ ☐ job in this town
⁴ ☐ job in the larger city

43. Thinking realistically, do you think he or she will live in this town when he is out of school and has a job?

⁵ ☐ definitely yes
⁶ ☐ probably yes
⁷ ☐ don't know
⁸ ☐ probably no
⁹ ☐ definitely no

44. If you have a boy in high school, what would you like him to do about service?

⁶ ☐ enlist after college
⁷ ☐ wait until drafted
⁸ ☐ go after college
⁹ ☐ get a deferment for reasons other than college
⁰ ☐ don't know

45. Do you want your son or daughter to go to college after high school?

⁹ ☐ yes
⁰ ☐ undecided
˟ ☐ no

IF NO: SKIP TO QUESTION 65, THAT IS, IF YOU DO NOT WANT YOUR SON OR DAUGH-TER TO GO TO COLLEGE, SKIP TO THE TOP OF THE NEXT PAGE (PAGE 4).

46-47. If money were no problem, would you rath that he or she went away to college, or go to college where he could live at home?

Check one	Check one	
Boy	*Girl*	
⁵ ☐	⁵ ☐	away to college
⁶ ☐	⁶ ☐	live at home

48-49. If he had a choice between going to a go small college and a good large college or u versity, which would you prefer him to go t

Boy	*Girl*	
⁷ ☐	⁷ ☐	small college
⁸ ☐	⁸ ☐	large college or university

50-51. What college would you like to see him or h go to?

Boy ....

Girl ....

52-59. Rank the following groups of colleges in ter of your preference for your son or daughter, you had to choose between them.

(Rank from 1 to 4 if you have a boy in high school)

......University of Illinois

......Yale, Harvard, Princeton

......M.I.T., Cal. Inst. of Technology

......Oberlin, Knox, or Carleton College

(Rank from 1 to 4 if you have a girl in high school)

......University of Illinois

......Wellesley, Vassar, or Smith

......Oberlin, Knox, or Carleton College

......DeKalb Teachers College or Illinois State Normal U.

60-63. There are many things that young people get from college. How important do you th each of the following *should be* for your son daughter in college?

(Rank from 1 to 4)

......the stimulation of new ideas

......preparation for making a living

......campus activities and social life

......new friends who share his interests

64. What would you like to see your son or daugh study in college?

(Check one)

¹ ☐ undecided
² ☐ a liberal arts program
³ ☐ a science program
⁴ ☐ a business program
⁵ ☐ nursing
⁶ ☐ home economics
⁷ ☐ pre-medicine, pre-dentistry, pre-law
⁸ ☐ education
⁹ ☐ engineering
⁰ ☐ agriculture

Does any adult in your family belong to any community organizations, like clubs, lodges, veterans', sports, or church groups?

(Check as many as apply)

¹ ☐ fraternal organizations (Elks, etc.)
² ☐ veterans' organizations (American Legion, V.F.W., etc.)
³ ☐ civic or service clubs (Rotary, Chamber of Commerce, etc.)
⁴ ☐ religious social groups (Knights of Columbus, etc.)
⁵ ☐ hobby or sports groups
⁶ ☐ youth organizations (YMCA, Scouts, etc.)
⁷ ☐ P.T.A.
⁸ ☐ country club (what one?................................)
⁹ ☐ labor union
⁰ ☐ other (what ones?......................................)

How well do people in your community cooperate and work together?

⁷ ☐ work together very well
⁸ ☐ work together fairly well
⁹ ☐ usually don't work together
⁰ ☐ never work together

How close do you feel to this community?

⁷ ☐ I feel that I belong here and that this is my home community.
⁸ ☐ I feel quite close to this community but do not consider it to be my home.
⁹ ☐ I do not feel very close to this community.
⁰ ☐ I feel like a complete stranger in this community.

Suppose the circle below represented the activities that go on here in this community. How far out from the center of these activities are you?

(Place a check where you think you are)

How would you describe the facilities for and the programs of recreation for young people in your community?

⁶ ☐ very good
⁷ ☐ good
⁸ ☐ fair
⁹ ☐ poor
⁰ ☐ don't know

3. Rank the following in terms of their attractiveness for you, if you could be any of these . . .

(Rank from 1 to 4)

......an executive in a large national corporation
......a respected leader in civic and political affairs in your community
......a statesman in the affairs of the nation
......a successful businessman in your community

74-78. Rank the five items below in terms of their importance to you in a job.

(Rank from 1 to 5)

......the security of steady work
......the opportunity for a rapid rise
......the enjoyment of the work itself
.....friendly people to work with
......a high income

101. If you could get a brand new car, which one would you want among the three listed below?

⁴ ☐ De Soto
⁵ ☐ Edsel
⁶ ☐ Dodge
⁷ ☐ Mercury
⁸ ☐ Buick
⁹ ☐ Oldsmobile
● ☐ Volkswagen

102-3. About how much time on the average do you spend watching TV on a weekday?

Husband	Wife	
⁴ ☐	⁴ ☐	none, or almost none
⁵ ☐	⁵ ☐	about ½ an hour a day
⁶ ☐	⁶ ☐	about 1 hour a day
⁷ ☐	⁷ ☐	about 1½ hours a day
⁸ ☐	⁸ ☐	about 2 hours a day
⁹ ☐	⁹ ☐	about 3 hours a day
⁰ ☐	⁰ ☐	4 or more hours a day

104. If you had just won some money on a quiz show and you were completely free to do with it whatever you wanted, what would you do with it?

¹ ☐ spend it all
² ☐ spend most of it
³ ☐ save most of it
⁴ ☐ save it all

105-6. How many years have you been married?........

107-8. Where did you go to high school (or grade school if you did not attend high school)?

Husband	Wife	
⁶ ☐	⁶ ☐	this high school
⁷ ☐	⁷ ☐	another school in this county
⁸ ☐	⁸ ☐	another school not in this county but in Illinois
⁹ ☐	⁹ ☐	a school outside Illinois but in the U. S.
⁰ ☐	⁰ ☐	a school outside the U. S.

ANSWER THE TWO QUESTIONS BELOW ONLY IF YOU WISH

109. Check the group into which your family's total income falls.

⁴ ☐ under $2000
⁵ ☐ between $2000 and $4000
⁶ ☐ between $4000 and $6000
⁷ ☐ between $6000 and $8000
⁸ ☐ between $8000 and $10,000
⁹ ☐ between $10,000 and $15,000
⁰ ☐ $15,000 and over

110. What is your political party affiliation in national politics?

⁷ ☐ Republican
⁸ ☐ Democratic
⁹ ☐ Independent

111. Do you live in a . . .
  5 ☐ one family house
  6 ☐ apartment or flat

112. Do you own the house in which you live?
  7 ☐ yes
  8 ☐ no

113. What is the occupation of the head of the family? What does he do? Be as specific as you can.

....

114. In what place, or business, or organization does he work?

....

115-118. How many children do you have . . .
  . . . altogether?   . . . in high school?
  ..... .boys   ....boys
  ....girls   ....girls

119. This questionnaire was completed by . . .
  7 ☐ father
  8 ☐ mother
  9 ☐ both together

120-1. Besides the things you have mentioned abo
  is there anything about this town or this sch
  that has a particularly important effect on the
  velopment of teen-agers, including your ow

  Mention either positive or negative things. (
  the rest of this page for extended comments.)

STUDY OF HIGH SCHOOL SOCIAL CLIMATES
conducted by
The University of Chicago
under a grant from
The United States Office of Education

Teachers' Questionnaire

st of the questions can be answered by a check in a box (like this: ☑, or by numbers on short lines (like this: .*3*.).
ecific instructions are given where needed. Disregard the small numbers to the left of the boxes; they are only to aid
tabulating your answers in the office. If you would like to elaborate on any question, use the blank space on page 5.

5. Which of the categories below comes closest to the attitude of most of the students toward the teachers in this school?

(Check one)

    1 ☐ They feel close to the teachers; will confide in them; and feel that the teachers understand them.

    2 ☐ They feel that the teachers are trying to help them, but don't really understand their problems.

    3 ☐ They feel that the teachers are fairly indifferent to their problems.

    4 ☐ They are distrustful of the teachers, and suspicious of the teachers' intentions.

6-9. Thinking only of the following four things, just how important do you think they should be for a teen-ager?

(Rank the items from 1 to 4)

    ......pleasing their parents

    ......learning as much as possible in school

    ......living up to religious ideals

    ......being accepted and liked by other students

10. Some schools seem to have one group of students that more or less dominates student life around the school. What about this school? Is there one group that seems to be always in the middle of things or are there several groups like that?

    7 ☐ one
    8 ☐ two
    9 ☐ more than **two**

11. Who are the leading students in this group or groups?

(first group)	(second group)
....	....
....	....
....	....
....	....

(third group)	(fourth group)
....	....
....	....
....	....
....	....

12. What does it take for a student to become part of the leading crowd in this school?

....

....

....

....

13. What is the best way to describe the *different* groups of students in this school according to the interests and behavior which characterize each group?

....

....

....

....

....

—1—

14. What is the best way to describe the group of students in this school which offers the greatest *problems* for a teacher or for the school?

....

....

....

(use page 5 if more space is necessary)

15. Which of the three things below do you think the majority of boys here at school would like most to be?

⁴ ☐ brilliant student
⁵ ☐ athletic star
⁶ ☐ most popular

16. Which of the three things below do you think the majority of girls here at school would like most to be?

⁴ ☐ brilliant student
⁵ ☐ leader in activities
⁶ ☐ most popular

17-18. If you could see any of three boys elected president of the senior class, which would you rather it would be?

⁷ ☐ brilliant student
⁸ ☐ athletic star
⁹ ☐ leader in extra-curricular activities

Why? ....

....

....

19-24. Among the items below, what ones are most important in giving a boy prestige or making him looked up to by *other boys* here at school?

(Rank from 1 to 6)

......coming from the right family

......leader in activities

......having a nice car

......high grades, honor roll

......being an athletic star

......being in the leading crowd

25-30. Now, among the items below, what ones are most important in giving a girl prestige or making her looked up to by *other girls* here at school?

(Rank from 1 to 6)

......coming from the right family

......leader in activities

...:.clothes

......high grades, honor roll

......being a cheerleader

......being in the leading crowd

31. Suppose one of your students had a chance two similar jobs; one was in this town, and o in another town the same size but in anoth state. Which do you think you would advise h to take?

¹ ☐ the job in this town
² ☐ the job in another town

32. If one of the jobs were in this town, and other in a larger city, which would you adv him to take?

³ ☐ the job in this town
⁴ ☐ the job in the larger city

33. If he were going to college, and had the cho between going to a good small college an good large college or university, which would advise?

⁷ ☐ small college
⁸ ☐ large college or university

34-37. If you had a student who could go to college he chose, which would you like to see h select from the groups below?

(Rank from 1 to 4)

......University of Illinois

......Princeton, Yale, or Harvard

......M.I.T. or Cal. Tech.

......Knox, Oberlin, or Carleton

38-41. There are many things young people can from college. How important do you think each the following *should be* for a student in his coll experience?

(Rank from 1 to 4)

......the stimulation of new ideas

.....preparation for making a living

......campus activities and social life

......new friends who share his interests

42-43. Do you agree or disagree that . . .

Agree Disagree

¹ ☐   ² ☐ There are a few students who c trol things among the stud body in this school, and the are out in the cold.

⁵ ☐   ⁶ ☐ If a student wants to be part the leading crowd around here sometimes has to go against principles.

44. In which of the following areas would you there are problems of discipline with the stude in this school?

(Check items which are problems)

¹ ☐ stealing (small items of little value)
² ☐ stealing of serious nature (money, cars)
³ ☐ destruction of school property
⁴ ☐ sex offenses
⁵ ☐ impertinence and discourtesy to teache
⁶ ☐ fighting
⁷ ☐ truancy
⁸ ☐ physical violence against teachers
⁹ ☐ using profane or obscene language
⁰ ☐ using narcotics
ˣ ☐ drinking intoxicants

—2—

Which of the categories below do you think come closest to fitting the majority of teachers in this school?

(Check as many as apply)

5 ☐ friendly with students
6 ☐ too strict
7 ☐ too easy with schoolwork
8 ☐ understand problems of teen-agers
9 ☐ not interested in teen-agers
0 ☐ willing to help out in activities

What seating arrangement do you use in your classes?

7 ☐ I assign them desks which they keep throughout the semester.
8 ☐ They choose their desks at the start of the semester, and keep them for the semester.
9 ☐ They choose the desks they like each day.

What is the average number of clock hours per week that you devote to your job? Include all time spent on activities which are required or definitely expected of you as part of your job whether you do the work at school, at home, or elsewhere.

1 ☐ under 30
2 ☐ 30-34
3 ☐ 35-39
4 ☐ 40-44
5 ☐ 45-49
6 ☐ 50-54
7 ☐ 55-59
8 ☐ 60-64
9 ☐ 65 or more

2. Would you rank the following five occupations in terms of their desirability?

(Rank from 1 to 5)

......writer or journalist
......scientist
......business executive
......medical doctor
......chemical engineer

If "high school teacher" were ranked along with these according to its desirability, which rank would you assign to it?

(Circle the appropriate number)

1   2   3   4   5   6

7. Now rank the following four occupations in terms of their desirability.

(Rank from 1 to 4)

......sales manager for a large business

......trained machinist

......proprietor of a small store

......owner-operator of a printing shop

If "high school teacher" were ranked along with these according to its desirability, which rank would you assign to it?

(Circle the appropriate number)

1   2   3   4   5

59-62. Now rank the following four occupations in terms of their desirability *for a woman.*

(Rank from 1 to 4)

......secretary to a business executive
......journalist
......interior decorator
......airline hostess

63. If "high school teacher" were ranked along with these according to its desirability, which rank would you assign to it?

(Circle the appropriate number)

1   2   3   4   5

64. How close do you feel to the community in which you teach?

7 ☐ I feel that I belong here and that this is my home community.
8 ☐ I feel quite close to this community but do not consider it to be my home.
9 ☐ I do not feel very close to this community.
0 ☐ I feel like a complete stranger in this community.

65. Do you belong to any community organizations, like clubs, lodges, veterans', sports, or church groups?

1 ☐ fraternal organizations (Elks, etc.)
2 ☐ veterans' organizations (American Legion, V.F.W., etc.)
3 ☐ civic or service clubs (Rotary, Chamber of Commerce, etc.)
4 ☐ religious social groups (Knights of Columbus, etc.)
5 ☐ hobby or sports groups
6 ☐ youth organizations (YMCA, Scouts, etc.)
7 ☐ N.E.A.
8 ☐ country club (What one?..........................)
9 ☐ American Federation of Teachers
0 ☐ other (What ones?.................................)

66. How well do people in your community cooperate and work together?

7 ☐ work together very well
8 ☐ work together fairly well
9 ☐ usually don't work together
0 ☐ never work together

67. If you had it to do over again, would you enter teaching?

7 ☐ definitely yes
8 ☐ probably yes
9 ☐ probably no
0 ☐ definitely no

68. If you had it to do over again, would you . . .

5 ☐ rather teach at this high school
6 ☐ rather teach at another high school

69. If you were to teach in a different high school, would you prefer to teach in a .

7 ☐ high school in a smaller town
8 ☐ high school in a town about this size
9 ☐ high school in a large city

70. Counting the present year, what is the number of years of full-time teaching experience you have had in the school system where you are now teaching?

¹ ☐ 1-2 years
² ☐ 3-4 years
³ ☐ 5-9 years
⁴ ☐ 10-14 years
⁵ ☐ 15-19 years
⁶ ☐ 20-24 years
⁷ ☐ 25-34 years
⁸ ☐ 35-44 years
⁹ ☐ 45 or more years

71. Where did you go to high school?

⁶ ☐ this high school
⁷ ☐ another high school in this county
⁸ ☐ another high school not in this county but in Illinois
⁹ ☐ a high school outside Illinois

72. In what type of institution did you take the larger part of your years of college education?

⁵ ☐ public (tax supported) university or land-grant college
⁶ ☐ public teachers college or normal school
⁷ ☐ other public college
⁸ ☐ nonpublic (privately supported) university
⁹ ☐ nonpublic teachers college or normal school
⁰ ☐ other nonpublic college

73. What is the highest college degree you hold? If you hold a degree not listed, check the one that is most nearly equivalent to the one you hold. Do not report honorary degrees.

⁶ ☐ no degree
⁷ ☐ a degree based on less than four years' work
⁸ ☐ bachelor's degree
⁹ ☐ master's degree
⁰ ☐ doctor's degree

74. If you have at least a bachelor's degree, is it in . .

⁷ ☐ education
⁸ ☐ liberal arts (What major?.....................
⁹ ☐ science (What major?...... ....

75. How much formal education did your father have?

³ ☐ some grade school
⁴ ☐ finished grade school
⁵ ☐ some high school
⁶ ☐ finished high school
⁷ ☐ some college
⁸ ☐ finished college
⁹ ☐ M.A., Ph.D., or professional degree
⁰ ☐ don't know

76. What is your age?

¹ ☐ under 21 years
² ☐ 21-25 years
³ ☐ 26-30 years
⁴ ☐ 31-35 years
⁵ ☐ 36-40 years
⁶ ☐ 41-45 years
⁷ ☐ 46-55 years
⁸ ☐ 56-65 years
⁹ ☐ 66 or over

77. Marital status:

⁷ ☐ single, never married
⁸ ☐ married
⁹ ☐ widower
⁰ ☐ divorced or legally separated

78. Sex:

⁵ ☐ male
⁶ ☐ female

79-80. As you know, this a study of the values of the student body and the various groups within it as they affect a boy's or a girl's path through high school and beyond. The categorical questions above provide only a crude way of learning this. We would appreciate any further comments you might have about the school or its students which are relevant to our purpose. You may use the remaining space in the questionnaire, or, if necessary, an added sheet.

Name..

Address...

Index

Ability, 260
Academic orientation (*see* Grades)
Achievement, 39, 126, 260
Active leaders (*see* Elites)
Active roles, 280
Activities, 3, 12, 281
  among elites, 135
  as basis of evaluation, 50
  extracurricular activities, 192
  importance of for popularity, 72
  importance of for status, 164
  leaders in, 28, 29, 43
  leisure time, 12, 76, 187, 236
  orientation to, 142
Administration, 282
Age-segregation, 3
Air Force, 319
All-around boy, 272, 315
American Army, 319
Amish, 1, 9
Ascriptive status systems, 83, 92, 230, 240
  See also Family background.
Association, structures of, 173
  among small-school boys, 186
  among small-school girls, 196
Athletes, 186, 244, 273, 293, 296
  best athlete, 231
  like to be remembered as, 28, 134
  like to date, 30
  popularity of, 43
  social rewards for, 146
Athlete-Scholars, 146, 248
Athletics, 12, 19, 230, 237, 281, 315
  among elites, 130
  as organizer of freshman cliques, 193
  importance of for leading crowd, 90
  importance of for popularity, 72
  importance of for status, 143
Authoritarian control in family, 313
Automobiles, 4, 8, 12, 23, 129, 187, 188, 280, 315
  among elites, 128
  as basis of attractiveness, 50
  importance of for leading crowd, 41
  importance of for popularity, 43, 72

Background, family (*see* Family)
Baltimore, 16, 32, 97, 113, 120, 126, 129
Barzun, Jacques, 315, 316
Beauty (*see* Physical attractiveness)
Beer, 188, 190
Belafonte, Harry, 23
Best student (*see* Scholar)
Bloomgarden, L., 326
Boating, 312
Boone, Pat, 23, 205
Boy Scouts, 312
Brilliant student (*see* Scholar)
Bureau of Applied Social Research, viii

California, 56
California Mental Maturity I.Q. Test, 262
Cars (*see* Automobiles)
Catholics, 24, 67, 84, 112, 199, 200, 202, 217, 293
Channeling of effort, 320
Cheerleader, importance of for popularity, 72, 91, 292
  like to date, 30
Chicago, 6, 23
Chorus, 208

Cincinnati, 326
Clark, Burton R., 317
Classes, 102, 229, 256, 261, 276, 301
  different value climates in, 74
Classical music, 22
Cliques, 76, 121, 129, 183
  cross-cutting grades, 194
  importance of for popularity, 91
Clothes (*see* Dress)
Clubs, 15
  See also Activities.
Cocktail parties, 312
Coeducation, 51
Cohen, Albert, 3, 174
Coleman, James S., 183, 316
College intentions, 114, 198, 269
Colleges, 316
Columbia University, viii
Communist countries, 320
Community control, 213
Community values, conformity to, 293
Como, Perry, 23
Competition, 143, 317
  for salary by teachers, 326
  for students, 325
  psychological effects of, 318
  structure of, 318
Conformity, 323
Connecticut, 268, 329
Consensus, in choices of elites, 99, 296
Contagion effect, 19
Cooperation, 318
Courtship, 121
Czechoslovakia, 246

Dancing, 13, 200, 236
  importance of for popularity, 91
Dating, 172, 187, 198, 202, 256, 315
  double-dating, 200
Davis, James, 29, 245
Davis, Kingsley, 174
Day, Charles W., 19
Debate, 284, 317, 320
Deferred gratification, 280
Delinquency, 5, 15
  of middle class, 215
Dickson, Lenore, 173
Division of labor, 15
Divorce, 123
Dominance patterns, 214
Double standard in dating, 122
Drama clubs, 315
Drama contests, 320
Dress, as basis of evaluation, 50
  best dressed, self-conception of, 54, 231, 293
  importance of for leading crowd, 37
  importance of for popularity, 72, 90
  See also Physical attractiveness.
Dreyfuss, Carl, 319
Drinking, 16, 38, 187, 189, 198, 202, 205
Ducktail haircuts, 188

East European, 24
Eastern High School, 32, 97, 113, 120, 126
Economic barriers, 9
Economic specialization, 2
Education, philosophy of, 9, 147
  of father, 76, 103
  practice, 11
  theory of, 11, 317
  See also Social position of family.

THE ADOLESCENT

The Adolescent Society